"Systems Leadership is an approach that is applicable to any systems who organise work around people – I utilise it frequently to understand my work in healthcare. This book will offer a practical guide, equipping leaders with tangible actions to navigate their systems with ease."

**Doctor Julie Highfield**, *Cardiff and Vale UHB – Psychology*

"*The Work of Management* is a practical guide for leaders of all organizations to increase the effectiveness of their operations. From task assignment to team leadership, *The Work of Management* offers concrete steps that leaders can take to make their teams more productive. The authors' focus on the day-to-day actions that leaders can take is based on Systems Leadership Theory, but provides specific steps that must be taken to implement that theory. I highly recommend this book for any leader who is looking to significantly improve the performance of their organization."

**John Fielder**, *President, Southern California Edison, retired*

"Leading complex modern organisations requires a purposeful movement towards a desired culture of positivity. The theory, tools and models of Systems Leadership Theory gives contemporary leaders an invaluable insight into creating such a positive culture, particular one that underpins the technical work of organisations. Most importantly, Systems Leadership Theory provides the methodology to achieve this technical work whilst also focussing on the social processes that create positivity that is truly productive – this in particular is its greatest impact."

**Noel Rawlins**, *Executive Principal, Upper Coomera State College, Department of Education*

"It makes leadership so much easier, that it almost feels like cheating."

**Fred Stanford**, *former CEO of Torex Gold*

"As a leader in education, Systems Leadership is the methodology I apply to lead my organisation. The application of Systems Leadership enables me to lead with clarity, to achieve our desired culture. By enabling others to exercise their talents, the application of Systems Leadership tools in my work is a multiplier to improve lives. I proudly apply Systems Leadership tools in other aspects of life too, including my small business which raises funds for Australian charities. Systems Leadership helps me direct my energy and ideas to enable others to flourish. It's life-changing."

**Mark Allen**, *Principal, Malanda State School, Chair, Systems Leadership Association*

"Being introduced to Systems Leadership has had a profound and positive effect on my work as a leader in education. Nothing else I have learned in the last 45 years has been as useful as the concepts, models and tools of Systems Leadership. This latest book finds a place on the top of the 'go to pile' on my desk because it provides a detailed understanding of its practical application in the day-to-day work of managers. It's invaluable, the nexus of good theory and good practice."

**Clive Dixon**, *International Consultant in education, previously Regional Director of Education Far North Queensland*

"This is the stuff that really works!"

**Jim Kelly**, *Senior Vice President Transmission and Distribution, Southern California Edison, retired*

"*The 'Work of Management'* has used 3 words to define what leaders have been trying to figure out for thousands of years. Leadership is not simply about a Vision, and Management is not simply about organising things to get work done. Understanding how to bring all the moving parts together, while inspiring every individual to give of their best is not something that happens very often and it can be lost in a day. Ian, Catie and Karl bring their insights and experience into a conversation on how aspiring leaders can think through and be deliberate in creating an extraordinary workplace for ordinary people that just want to make a difference."

**Mark Cutifani**, *Chairman, Vale Base Metals and former CEO for Anglo American*

# The Work of Management

*The Work of Management* demonstrates how the concepts, models and tools of Systems Leadership can be applied, enabling you to become a more effective manager by improving your own work to create a more positive and effective organisation.

Positive organisations, where people come together to achieve a productive and personally satisfying purpose, and which provide the basis for a good society, do not occur by chance. They are created by the work of leaders and members who are dependent upon the way the organisation is designed and operates – its structure and systems. While the theory is explained, this book primarily presents the practical aspects – the specific values, methods and tools – that can be used to improve work and the work performance of direct reports. Building on the bestselling book *Systems Leadership*, this book provides leaders with a manual for the application of concepts as well as an introduction to Systems Leadership Theory, a method that has been used successfully by businesses from large multinational firms and banks, to SMEs, public agencies and NGOs. It provides a predictive capability, allowing a leader to predict what will work well and what is likely to fail, according to the context. It gives the benefit of foresight as decisions must be made.

Designed as a leader's manual for the application of the concepts around Systems Leadership, this book is for people who want to improve their own, and their organisation's, work practices and performance.

**Ian Macdonald** is Founder and Director of Macdonald Associates, an international organisational consultancy. He is a Director of BIOSS International Ltd. He is also an honorary fellow at Brunel University and teaches at Surrey Business School and works with NHS Wales and the Welsh government.

**Catherine Burke** was Associate Professor of Public Administration, University of Southern California. Her research focuses on organisation and systems design, management theory and leadership. She has been a consultant to Southern California Edison, the cities of Los Angeles and Pasadena, the Congressional Office of Technology Assessment, businesses and non-profit organisations. Her publications include *Innovation and Public Policy* and articles in various academic journals. She was a Director at Commonwealth Aluminum.

**Karl Stewart** trained as a mining engineer but spent most of his working life in leadership positions. He spent four years as an internal managerial consultant developing the theory and good practices to strengthen the leadership of people in organisations and the systems which underpin them. He demonstrated the effectiveness of these ideas implementing them as Managing Director of Comalco Smelting.

# The Work of Management

## A Leader's Guide to Applying Systems Leadership

Ian Macdonald,
Catherine Burke
and Karl Stewart

LONDON AND NEW YORK

First published 2025
by Routledge
4 Park Square, Milton Park, Abingdon, Oxon, OX14 4RN

and by Routledge
605 Third Avenue, New York, NY 10158

*Routledge is an imprint of the Taylor & Francis Group, an informa business*



*British Library Cataloguing-in-Publication Data*
A catalogue record for this book is available from the British Library

*Library of Congress Cataloging-in-Publication Data*
Names: Macdonald, Ian, 1950 October 23– author. | Burke, Catherine G., 1939– author. | Stewart, Karl, author.
Title: The work of management: a leader's guide to applying systems leadership / Ian Macdonald, Catherine Burke and Karl Stewart.
Description: Abingdon, Oxon; New York, NY: Routledge, 2024. | Includes bibliographical references and index.
Identifiers: LCCN 2024018428 (print) | LCCN 2024018429 (ebook) | ISBN 9781032604381 (hardback) | ISBN 9781032604374 (paperback) | ISBN 9781003459118 (ebook)
Subjects: LCSH: Management. | Organizational sociology. | Organizational effectiveness. | Leadership.
Classification: LCC HD58.7 .M3218 2024 (print) | LCC HD58.7 (ebook) | DDC 302.3/5—dc23/eng/20240430
LC record available at https://lccn.loc.gov/2024018428
LC ebook record available at https://lccn.loc.gov/2024018429

ISBN: 978-1-032-60438-1 (hbk)
ISBN: 978-1-032-60437-4 (pbk)
ISBN: 978-1-003-45911-8 (ebk)

DOI: 10.4324/9781003459118

Typeset in Sabon
by codeMantra

# Contents

# Acknowledgements

This book reflects the work and contributions of researchers who preceded us and those who are carrying out the work today. We owe much to our colleagues, executives and employees in the many organisations who have used these ideas, our students, family members and many others who have made invaluable contributions to our thinking and our writing.

Dr. Elliott Jaques and Wilfred (later Lord) Brown began a concerted effort to bring the discipline of science to the practice of management. They developed explicit theories with hypotheses (predictions) to test their validity. Brown was the Managing Director of Glacier Metals who collaborated with Jaques in developing the ideas and putting them into practice (see books by Jaques, Brown and Gray in the Bibliography). Our work draws on their early work. especially the concepts of work, levels of work and organisational structure. We have, in the light of our experiences, modified their ideas but their work was seminal to our efforts.

Later Jaques founded and was the first Director of the Brunel Institute for Organisational and Social Studies (BIOSS) at Brunel University near London. Macdonald began his career working with Jaques at BIOSS. Dr. Gillian Stamp became Director of BIOSS following Dr. Jaques, and has done research on human capability and development that has informed our thinking. Other important research was conducted at Brunel by David Billis, R.O. Gibson, John Isaacs, Richard Joss, Lucy Lofting, B.M. O'Connor, Ralph Rowbottom, Stephen Cang and many others. A selection of their publications is listed in the Bibliography. This was a very creative time involving many staff at BIOSS contributing to what came to be called Stratified Systems Theory.

Sir Roderick Carnegie, chairman and Chief Executive Officer (CEO) of CRA Ltd. of Australia (now Rio Tinto), began introducing many of these ideas into the company. Along with Jack Brady of CRA Ltd., he led the implementation of these structural ideas in their organisation and provided major intellectual and material support as the work progressed.

One of the authors, Karl Stewart, had the privilege of working for Sir Roderick and Jack Brady, first as an internal group consultant to CRA and later as Managing Director of Comalco Smelting. While at Comalco, he had the opportunity to extend the concepts and apply them in practice. It was during this time that many of the theories and models in this book were conceived, developed and implemented.

As group consultant, Stewart was given the task of developing a plan to restructure Hamersley Iron (HI) Pty, a large mining complex in Western Australia. He was also to devise a set of theories that would allow the development of systems to underpin the restructuring. These systems were then to be used in other CRA business units. Members of the Hamersley Iron Organisation Development (OD) teams made significant contributions to this work.

Terry Palmer took over from Stewart to lead the third and fourth HI OD teams. Later he became Managing Director of Hamersley Iron and then CEO of Comalco, Ltd. He was a long-time friend and colleague who made major contributions to the work of the authors. Before his untimely death he put these ideas into practice and provided clear evidence of their usefulness in helping a manager to predict behaviour and deliver outcomes. Ian Macdonald worked with Stewart and Palmer at CRA where they created the "values model," theories of leadership, behaviour, systems and symbols and the ideas concerning teams and teamwork.

Burke began working with Stewart and Macdonald in 1984 and contributed to the development of these ideas in the United States. She has been able to test these ideas in an academic setting over many years and to encourage her students to carry on further research. She also worked as a consultant to Southern California Edison, a large electric utility. She is particularly grateful to John Fielder who was a general manager when she began her work and late in his career became President of the company. He had the courage and foresight to adopt many of these ideas, bringing them into his organisation. He was especially instrumental in demonstrating by application the value of the theories in a rapidly changing high-technology environment of computing and communications.

The original, and crucial, support at SCE came through the efforts of Dr. Dan Smith, Manager of Quality and Training in the Information Services Department who brought Burke in as a consultant. They enjoyed a close collaboration for nearly ten years. Other managers at SCE who worked on OD in other parts of the corporation also made important contributions especially Jim Kelly, Sr. VP

Transmission and Distribution, and Robert Ramirez who made significant contributions in several departments of the company.

Don McIntyre, City Manager of Pasadena, CA, demonstrated how these ideas could improve the structure, systems and leadership in a public organisation.

Brigadier General Roderick Macdonald of the British Army (and brother to Ian) spent a year on a Defence Fellowship with Burke at the University of Southern California studying leadership processes (Macdonald, R, 1991). While still in the army, he spent significant parts of his leave time working with his brother and Stewart to develop the values model and theories of leadership. Brigadier Macdonald was able to bring the personal experience of combat leadership as a test of the concepts of leadership. Since leaving the British Army he has moved to the United States, where he continues to work with us and to apply the theories in a wide range of settings.

In the 1980s and 1990s Ian Macdonald formed an international association of consultants, Macdonald Associates Consultancy Ltd. (maconsultancy.com), which is active to this day. All the consultants have contributed to our work. These include the Rev. David Dadswell, Dr. Richard Joss, Tony Dunlop, Phillip Bartlett, Tony Tiplady, Clive Dixon and the late Rev. Michael Evers and Rev Philip Biggs. We are grateful to Fred Stanford who contributed many practical ideas as he successfully formed a new company using the ideas in this book. Mark Cutifani has extensively used and contributed to these ideas in leadership roles in Canada, South Africa and most recently as CEO of Anglo American. As he has said, "Don't read this book if you don't have the courage and perseverance to lead change."

This work has now developed and expanded through the formation of the Systems Leadership Development Association (based in Australia); the work is further tested and refined through this association. In addition, Ian has rejoined BIOSS, another international consultancy (see bioss.com).

David Sadler as both Managing Director and Associate has developed and implemented these ideas particularly regarding safety where his work and advice has without doubt saved many lives. We are fortunate that David was willing to be the primary author of the Safety chapter in this book.

Steve Burke was Chief Operating Officer at a large electrical construction firm. His experience in that field has added another dimension to our work. He has also worked as a consultant with Dr. Burke for many years. He has made significant contributions to our thinking and especially to the systems of performance management. He was also an informal editor who helped clarify the ideas in this book.

Over the years, managers and scholars in Argentina, Australia, Canada, Denmark, Russia, Singapore, South Africa, Sweden and the United States as well as the United Kingdom contributed to the development of both theory and practice. We are deeply indebted to all these people, many of whom we have worked with closely up to the present time. The late Dr. Neils Busch-Jensen, Les Cupper, Kathy Gould, the late Colonel (and Dr.) Larry Ingraham, Dr. Harry Levinson, Geoff McGill, David Brewer, Dr. Carlos Rigby, and Mark Woffenden. There are many other managers and theorists that have contributed, perhaps more than they realise.

In addition, we are indebted to the managers and employees of the organisations we have been associated with. The organisations include mines, smelters, city governments, voluntary organisations, churches, indigenous communities, housing associations, colleges, schools, banks, health authorities, the US and British Armies, rolling mills, computing organisations, utilities, an internet service provider, an airline and even a manufacturer of vitamins. They used and commented upon earlier versions of this book. They also gave their time to test, argue, criticise, develop and anguish over the application of the theories in practice. Without their perseverance, this work would not have been possible.

There are many doctoral students who contributed by testing these ideas through their dissertation research with Dr. Burke. Drs. Wilsey Bishop, David Boals, Loren Goldman, Donald Gould, Edward Pape and Mu Dan Ping have used these theories to study nursing, public libraries, police agencies, university libraries and cross-cultural relationships.

We are also indebted to those in the Far North Queensland Region of Education. This work, which was published as a separate book in 2020, has tested and refined the ideas in the education of young Australians especially Aboriginal and Torres Straits Islander students. Special mention goes to Tony Tiplady who has worked tirelessly with these ideas across many organisations since the 1980s and provided friendship and support as well as ideas. Clive Dixon introduced the ideas and tested them throughout the entire region.

We thank them all. This book represents their thinking as well as our own, though their interpretations and thinking may differ from ours. We hope we have not abused their ideas, and we accept full accountability for any errors, misinterpretations and omissions.

We also thank Rebecca Marsh, our editor, and her assistant Lauren Whelan who were patient, kind and have undoubtedly improved the quality of the final product. Anandan B was the Production Manager who put the book into print. We are very grateful for his ability to help us get through this process. Finally, we thank our families for their continuing support even when we were preoccupied and unavailable to give them the attention they deserved.

# Introduction

## Purpose

The purpose of this book is to demonstrate how the concepts, models and tools of Systems Leadership can be applied, enabling our readers to become more effective managers by improving their own work to create a more positive and effective organisation.

## Context

In today's industrial and post-industrial societies, the ability to organise and manage the functions of productive enterprises over time has allowed a significant proportion of the world's population to live decent lives as individuals and societies. It is largely through organisations, whether businesses, governments or non-governmental organisations (NGOs), that we influence and shape our present and our future. In these societies, the majority of us are employed in such organisations, and the quality of our lives is dependent upon the quality of work we carry out in organisations, which in turn depends, most importantly, on their leadership.

This book focuses on the leadership of organisations, i.e., the work of managers. Their work is to create positive organisations where people come together to achieve a productive and personally satisfying purpose. Human survival has always depended upon our ability to form and sustain social organisations. At the same time, people have a deep personal need to be creative and to belong as individuals. By creating positive organisations these needs can be fulfilled simultaneously and can provide the basis for a good society.

Positive organisations do not occur by chance. They are created by the work of leaders and members who are dependent upon the way the organisation is designed and operates – its structure and systems. These, of course, must be designed and operated based upon a sound understanding of the general principles of human behaviour. We cannot over-estimate how the quality of our

DOI: 10.4324/9781003459118-1

organisations, and the decisions made by their leaders, impacts us as individuals, our families, our communities and the planet.

In this book, we use Systems Leadership Theory (SLT) as the underlying basis to provide a coherent and integrated theory of organisational behaviour, which is presented in the second edition of *Systems Leadership: Creating Positive Organisations*. It is based on over 50 years of research and its application across many types of organisations and cultures worldwide. It focuses on the social processes of organisational leadership, while recognising how these impact the technical and commercial aspects of organisations. When applied, it allows leaders to improve the working lives of people and hence the effectiveness of their organisation. It provides a predictive capability allowing a leader to predict what will work well and what is likely to fail, according to the context. It gives the benefit of foresight (Macdonald, Burke and Stewart, 2018).

This has proven to be highly successful in businesses, government agencies and NGOs in a variety of countries and cultures. Whether or not you work in an organisation that decides to implement this approach, individual managers can use significant elements within their own area of authority to improve their own and their direct reports' work performance. This book is written to help you improve your leadership performance in order to improve your own part of the organisation and its work practices.

Understanding the universal shared values, mythologies and culture can help you improve your understanding of the various behaviours and reactions of your workers, peers and managers. The role relationships model as well as most of the essential people systems can be applied to improve your own managerial work and the work performance of your direct reports. To do this we have provided more detailed information on how to apply the ideas in everyday practice.

This book reflects our experiences in teaching Systems Leadership concepts and practices to managers at different organisational levels as well as to graduate students interested in public, business or NGOs as a career. The book expands upon the work presented in the second edition of *Systems Leadership* yet stands on its own as an informative text on the current best practices of organisational leadership as we and others have observed, learned and evaluated them. We see this book as a leader's manual for the application of concepts rather than the details of articulating the concepts that make up much of *Systems Leadership: Creating Positive Organisations*.

**Box I.1**

We cannot improve the language of any science without at the same time improving the science itself; neither can we, on the other hand, improve a science, without improving the language or nomenclature which belongs to it. However certain the facts of any science may be, and however just the ideas we may have formed of these facts, we can only communicate false impressions to others, while we want words by which these may be properly expressed.

Lavoisier, 1789 in Bolles, 1997:380

## Clarity in Purpose, Language, Relationships and Authority

Clarity is stressed in SLT and is an essential element in a positive organisation. It is also essential in the development of knowledge in any field of endeavour. This was expressed by the scientist Antoine-Laurent de Lavoisier who developed the language of chemistry in the late 18th century. It was only after his publication of a standard vocabulary that the science of chemistry began its rapid development. His statement of the importance of language to the development of knowledge applies as much today as in his own time.

Like chemistry before Lavoisier, the language of organisational theory and management, for the most part, has little clarity or precision. To study, with discipline, any subject involving social processes, such as management, we must recognise two types of meaning – *scientific* where an entity or term has an agreed-upon meaning so that we can determine whether an entity is one of *those* or not. The second type is largely in the general conversational domain, where in our daily lives we use words and assume an overlap in understanding without worrying too much whether we mean precisely the same thing.

Of course, we have a general understanding of terms such as manager, leader, authority, power, team or organisation, but there are often significant differences of meaning among the people using the words. That has limited the development of clear concepts in the field of organisation behaviour, leadership and management. We need more precise terms if we are to improve the science as Lavoisier stated.

**Box I.2**

To demonstrate this problem to many classes of sceptical master's students, Burke asked them to write a brief definition of manager during the first class meeting. They then shared their definitions with the entire class. As predicted, there was some overlap in meaning, but the differences were significant. They agreed that if they tried to identify the managers in a given organisation, they would not be able to agree.

To advance our knowledge of leadership and organisations, we and others worked to provide clear and precise terms where an entity or term has an agreed-upon meaning which allows the development of useful theories. Like physics, chemistry or engineering, we need concepts as clear as mass, DNA, acceleration or tensile strength, which have agreed-upon meanings within their scientific fields.

Unlike other scientific and technical bodies of knowledge, we are at the disadvantage of not having clear and shared language and consequently shared meaning. This is unfortunate because cultures are dependent upon shared language and meaning.

To solve this problem, SLT provides a precise language for developing, discussing, thinking and working with propositions about organisations and management. While the words used in SLT have a common social meaning, which is unavoidable, we have defined them carefully for our purpose so that those who use them can have shared definitions and meanings (see Glossary).

This does not mean other definitions are wrong, they are simply not useful for our purpose – to create positive organisations – because they lack precision. If you choose to use different words and definitions, that is your prerogative, but be sure they are as clear and well-defined as the language of SLT.

## Overview of Book's Contents

This book is presented in four parts. **Part 1** provides basic concepts and tools of Systems Leadership. Chapter 1 begins with Purpose, which is at the heart of the tools of Systems Leadership whether one is clarifying the overall organisational purpose, developing a system or assigning a task. Chapter 2 outlines the fundamentals of work including the definitions of terms, and the models and methods as well as presents the domains of work – social, technical and commercial. Systems Leadership does not ignore the technical

### Box I.3 On Managers and Leaders

There is considerable confusion in the literature regarding the concepts manager and leader. Often, leader is used as a positive term implying vision and charisma, while "manager" is used in a slightly denigrating way indicating someone who is concerned only with efficiency, not with effectiveness. Often managers are depicted as managing inanimate resources not people, or negatively associated with pure administration.

We agree with Drucker (1999:9) that "management is the specific and distinguishing organ of any and all organizations." We define a manager as a person who is "*accountable for his or her own work and the work performance of his/her direct reports over time.*" Using this definition, all managers are leaders of people; they have no choice. Their only choice is whether to be a good or bad leader (see Chapter 10). In this we again agree with Drucker, "one does not 'manage' people. The task is to lead people. And the goal is to make productive the specific strengths and knowledge of each individual" (1999:21, 22).

and commercial domains, but its focus is on the social and how the social impacts on the technical and commercial.

Chapter 3 provides ways of formulating and assigning tasks which have been tested by managers around the world with great success. It will give you something you can use immediately to improve your own leadership practices. This leads directly into Chapter 4, which discusses something you are aware of, that different people have different capabilities to carry out a particular task or the entire work of a role. This chapter clarifies the specific elements of capability to help you recognise and analyse why some people succeed in performing a task and others do not. This information helps not only in task assignment, but also in evaluating work performance, mentoring, selecting for roles, promotion and career development. It also explains why most organisations have too many organisational levels and how to get the levels of work right.

**Part 2** deals with the structures best suited to foster positive organisations because they match the varying capabilities of humans as discussed in Chapter 4. Chapter 5 defines eight levels of work we have found in organisations of varying sizes from small, medium, large to extremely large such as the US military. Chapter 6 demonstrates how a variety of organisational structures can be effective in an employment hierarchy depending upon the work itself and the context in which it must be carried out. It also explains three essential business functions – operations, service and support – which are necessary if an organisation is to thrive over time.

Chapter 7 discusses organisational roles – their work and authorities. It illustrates how there is high-level work in many organisations which is not managerial work, and how the use of job titles can keep this distinction clear. Chapter 8 discusses a tested method of developing role relationships within the organisation and a way for sorting out problems between individuals, working groups and differing units in the organisation.

**Part 3** further develops the work of leadership. Chapter 9 articulates the universal shared values held by all human beings and why they are universal. It clarifies why we often believe "our" values are different from "their" values, because of the stories we tell, our mythologies and the behaviours we assume to demonstrate those values, which do differ. We also define what we mean by a culture and how it is formed among people with shared mythologies. Chapter 10 discusses the difficult process of creating a new culture using behaviour, systems and symbols. Very often we see and hear people expressing a need for "culture change" but with little shared understanding of what is a culture, or practical advice about how to change it.

Chapter 11 expands on systems and the importance of their equalisation and differentiation. We also provide a matrix to discriminate between productive and counterproductive systems, both of which may be authorised by the leadership of the organisation, and how unauthorised systems develop. Chapter 12 makes clear the importance of safety systems if we are to have positive organisations and systems and behaviour which can improve outcomes. Chapter 13 provides insights into how Systems Leadership can improve social processes in a virtual world where considerable work is carried out through systems such as *Teams* and *Zoom*.

**Part 4** focuses on essential people systems that are the primary tools of managers in organisations using SLT. Chapter 14 shows why a good role description (created by a manager and his or her manager, not HR) is essential both for the individual and for the selection process. Chapter 15 clarifies the important distinction between the idea of Performance as Output and the concept of Work Performance. Chapter 16 discusses the "muddle" that has been created that makes honest performance evaluation and salary setting difficult and unpleasant. Chapter 17 provides more details on the types of task assignments and provides tools for providing task feedback and review. Chapter 18 articulates a way to improve performance planning and review. Chapter 19 takes on the often difficult and dreaded task of Performance Evaluation. Chapter 20 provides a tested method of Salary Administration that is closely linked to performance evaluation. Chapter 21 examines career development and succession planning. Chapter 22 provides ideas on how to deal with discipline along with a Fair Treatment system.

Last there is a Conclusion where we discuss the benefits of foresight.

Although we present a great deal of material that suggests ways of designing and operating organisations based on our own and the experience of others who have used these ideas in a variety of organisations, ultimately the final decision to use or not use what we present is yours. When these theories and tools are used well, we have found organisations can make better predictions and are able to change faster, thus gaining considerable competitive advantage.

Nonetheless, theories and systems can only provide the necessary conditions for success; the sufficient conditions must be provided by human judgement – your human judgement. We wish you the best in this endeavour and hope our ideas and experiences ease your path.

# Part I

# The Basics – Purpose and Work

Here we introduce and emphasise the importance of purpose and how it leads to an analysis of the work that is required to achieve a purpose. We carefully define work and the domains of work as well as introducing the basics of task assignment processes in order to be clear about the context, purpose, and work to be done including quantity and quality of ouput, resources to carry out the work and the targeted time to completion.

DOI: 10.4324/9781003459118-2

# 1 The Importance of Purpose

## Introduction

Developing a clear purpose is the most important piece of work to do when creating an organisation that is successful and lasts through time. One highly successful business CEO said "there is no point in having a strategy if you don't have a clear and concise purpose." This is not a trivial issue.

While many organisations have mission and vision statements as well as values statements, they may vary considerably in terms of how specific they are and whether they can be observed or measured. While such statements can be displayed, and people can often relate to their sentiments, there is often no direct connection between what was written and the work people are expected to do. The generality of the statements does not provide an obvious way to measure the success or failure of outcomes. Indeed, if such statements are vague or simplistic slogans they can actually be counterproductive.

Purpose is a fundamental concept of Systems Leadership Theory because it makes clear what is to be achieved by the entire organisation. This helps to identify what work must be done to achieve the purpose. The same process can lead to clarity about the purpose of various organisational units that link to the overall purpose. Clarity of purpose will improve organisational systems, clarify the work of individual roles, task assignments, and even the purpose of organisational meetings, and communications. Doing so provides people with a clear understanding of what they are expected to achieve, the work they must do to achieve it and how outcomes can be measured.

The importance of a clear and specific purpose has been shown by organisations which have such a purpose. For example, Merck pharmaceutical company has had the same purpose for several generations.

> Merck is in the business of preserving and improving human life.
> (Collins & Porras, 1994)

DOI: 10.4324/9781003459118-3

> The specific words have been modified over the years, but the fundamental purpose has not changed.
>
> We try never to forget that medicine is for the people. It is not for the profits.
>
> (George Merck, founder)
>
> We are workers in industry who are genuinely inspired by the ideals of advancement of medical science, and of service to humanity.
>
> (George Merck II, 1935)
>
> Above all, let's remember that our business success means victory against disease and help to humankind.
>
> (CEO P. Roy Vagelos, 1991)
>
> We use the power of leading-edge science to save and improve lives around the world.
>
> (Merck website, 2022)[1]

The strength of this purpose was demonstrated in 1947 shortly after World War II. Merck brought streptomycin to Japan to eliminate tuberculosis which was devastating their society. Merck made no money by doing that, but as Vagelos said, "it's no accident that Merck is the largest American pharmaceutical company in Japan today. The long-term consequences of [such actions] are not always clear, but somehow I think they always pay off."[2]

Based on their research, Collins and Porras write that successful companies live by what they term a core ideology:

> Purpose: The organization's fundamental reasons for existence beyond just making money – a perpetual guiding star on the horizon not to be confused with specific goals or business strategies.
>
> Core Values: The organization's essential and enduring tenets – a small set of general guiding principles; not to be confused with specific cultural or operating practices; not to be compromised for financial gain or short-term expediency.[3]

## Developing a Clear and Specific Purpose

To gain clarity of purpose, we have found it is useful to start with a simple statement of purpose that is the primary objective of the overall organisation. Such a statement of purpose, whether for the organisation, a division, a role or a task needs to be stated in a single sentence without an "and."[4] To do this requires discipline that often leads to an interesting and usually very productive discussion concerning why the organisation exists and what it is trying to achieve.

Of course, most organisations of any size have many objectives, activities and outcomes. What we are arguing is that unless you have a clear and overriding purpose that is easily understood by people within the organisation and outside, the work can be fragmented, disconnected and even contradictory. Once a clear organisational purpose has been agreed upon, it can then cascade throughout the organisation as each organisation unit will have a purpose that links to the overall purpose. Every role and task assignment should have a purpose that is connected to the overall purpose of the organisation.

The point of the purpose statement is to provide coherency to all those activities in order to realise the intention of the organisation. If the purpose statement is clear, it also indicates what measures are relevant to show whether that purpose is being achieved. It also becomes the benchmark for judging work activity to be productive or counterproductive. It allows us to see whether any activity is contributing to the achievement of that purpose or not. If it is not, it should be seriously considered for elimination.

Once a purpose is articulated, that is not the end of the matter. It is important to review this purpose, perhaps annually in the first years, to see if it is still relevant. As with Merck, once an organisation has exactly the right purpose, changing some of the wording (but not the purpose itself) may make sense as conditions change. Unfortunately, we have seen a number of organisations where activities continue, long after the purpose has changed. They are assumed to be necessary when in fact they have become counterproductive. If someone asks, "why are we doing this?" the classic answer is, "We've *always* done it this way."

### Box 1.1 True Story: Unnamed to Protect the Guilty

One of our associates was asked to help improve the productivity in an oil refinery. He was working with a group of engineers when he noticed that five of them stopped doing their regular work and spent a week producing an enormous technical report. "What is the purpose of the report?" "It provides information on the functioning of technology X." "Who uses the report?" "We don't know, but our secretary sends it to this department." Our associate was curious as to who used it and for what. He went to the department named, but no one there remembered ever seeing such a report. Finally, he asked the departmental secretary, "Have you ever seen this report?" "Oh yes. It comes in every month, but I just throw it away. No one is interested in it."

After more investigation, it turned out that the technology used in the past had been replaced several years earlier. The report was not needed with the new technology. No one had ever told the people putting all the time and effort into the report that no one needed it anymore. Interestingly, we've told this story many times and few people have doubted this could really have happened. An argument for clarity of purpose and for work to be regularly checked for relevance.

## Purpose in Many Types of Organisations

Although the examples used so far are businesses, clarity of purpose is essential in not-for-profit organisations, public agencies, schools, hospitals, police departments. It may seem that some of these organisations are essentially the same, but as has been demonstrated in a project to improve the schools in Far North Queensland, a school is not just a school.[5] Each school is affected by the context in which it operates, and this greatly influences what it needs and what it can achieve. The statement that a school exists to educate children is too general and cannot guide behaviour unless the verb educate is unpacked in the context of the individual school.

NGOs, such as Save the Children and Doctors without Borders, can work in the same areas with the same people, but their purposes and the measures of success are quite different. Such organisations may appear to have similar or even the same purpose, but differing contexts, countries of origin and cultural differences often means that if the "real" purpose is agreed upon, they have significant differences.

Interestingly, smaller organisations, such as neighbourhood councils, a Homeowners Association, a tennis or swim club with a Board voted in by members, often find that discussions of purpose are deemed irrelevant by some members. "We know what our purpose is," without discussing how each member sees the purpose (rarely are these ideas of purpose exactly the same). We have found that such assumptions can be unhelpful. When examined we have discovered that people can have quite different ideas as to the core purpose. Without a clear purpose it is hard to agree on the work to be done, who is to do it or whether or not the outcomes can be measured or agreed upon. There is often little agreement regarding what the role of a Board member is. Many such Boards, however, have by-laws where the role of the Board is defined, and Board members duties are outlined.

This frequently leads to destructive arguments and intimidation of some Board members into voting against the best interests of the council and the larger community. With the purpose left to the discretion of each individual member, it becomes irrelevant and leads to the exercise of power by the most aggressive or dominant members. There appears to be a "rule" that in such organisations, there will always be at least one toxic member who is against what anyone proposes, especially if it comes from a woman or minority. There is another alleged "rule" that says if that person leaves the Board, he or she will rapidly be replaced by another apparently toxic member. These are not in fact rules but the consequences of having no shared, explicit purpose.

Public agencies confront a different situation and often find it more difficult to articulate a clear purpose, as the politicians who oversee them do not agree among themselves what the purpose of a particular agency is or should be. In a large federal government such as the United States, individual Departments may have multiple purposes specified in law, such as Homeland Security or the Department of Defense. Both may have what appears to be a similar purpose, protecting the United States from those who would do it harm, but as with the schools, the context and direction from Congress or the President makes all the difference in what they are expected to do. Thus, clarity of overall purpose may be difficult to agree upon. Often the best that can be done is to make clear the purpose of each individual part of the organisation – the purpose of the Secret Service as compared to the Customs and Border Protection; the Marine Corps compared to the Air Force.

So, finally, who should decide what the purpose is? While we recommend that in determining purpose a number of people and/or groups should be consulted, in many cases both inside and outside the organisation, consultation is not the same as decision-making. It needs to be clear who has the authority to decide. We would expect the leader of the organisation to put forward a statement of purpose based on the consultations, but the decision would typically be that of the governing board or the political authorities.

As stated, articulating a concise purpose is not easy; however, there is little point moving on to strategies, plans, targets and objectives unless this work has been done.

A clear and agreed-upon purpose directly leads to two questions which are the essence of Systems Leadership Theory. They can be summarised as asking and helping to answer these fundamental but simple questions:

1. What is the work to be done to achieve the purpose?
2. Whose work is it?

First, however, we need to define work as we use the term in Systems Leadership.

## Notes

1 https://www.merck.com/company-overview/?utm_source=cpc&utm_medium=Google&utm_campaign=Merck_Brand&utm_content=Biopharmaceutical_Company&utm_term=Brand&gclid=EAIaIQobChMImdGt7tiL_AIVojWtBh33aQNBEAAYASAAEgKye_D_BwE retrieved 12/21/2022

2 Collins and Porras, 1994:47

3 Collins and Porras, 1994:73. Although this book is 30 years old, it still carries important ideas for organisations today. It also explains why General Electric was so valued and respected with its clear purpose, originally stated by Thomas Edison, and how things went terribly wrong when the purpose was changed.
See David Gelles, *The Man Who Broke Capitalism: How Jack Welch Gutted the Heartland and Crushed the Soul of Corporate America – and How to Undo His Legacy.* New York: Simon and Schuster, 2022. This book reports on what went wrong when the purpose was changed to ever increasing profits on a quarterly basis.

4 This appears to contradict the use of "and" in the Merck statement of purpose. We have found, however, that the discipline of articulating a purpose without an "and" is most effective. There are few "and" purposes which are so tightly integrated as those in the Merck statements.

5 Macdonald, Dixon and Tiplady, *Improving Schools Using Systems Leadership: Turning Intention into Reality.* Milton Park, Abingdon, Oxon, England: Routledge, 2020.

# 2 Work and the Domains of Work

## Work Defined

If we are to determine what work needs to be done to achieve the purpose, and whose work is it, we need a common definition of work. In social conversations we use the word work, which has many different meanings that generally overlap, but not perfectly. The *Oxford English Dictionary* refers to work as expenditure of effort, striving, exertion of force in overcoming resistance, tasks to be undertaken, achievement, employment, earning money and to have influence or effect – to mention only a few. We have defined work for use in the scientific sense where we can all agree if a particular action is work or not.

> **Box 2.1 Definition of Work**
>
> Turning Intention into Reality

Work is the process by which an idea developed by a person is made visible in the external world and open to recognition. While this undoubtedly requires effort it is not simply the expenditure of effort. Our definition is closely related to Jaques' definition,

> The term work refers to activity, to behaviour, to that human activity in which people exercise discretion, make decisions and act so as to transform the external physical and social world in accord with some predetermined goal in order to fulfill some need.
>
> (Jaques, 1976:101)

In short, turning intention into reality. As Macdonald (1990) wrote, "The whole process allows the person to identify themselves as an active agent in the world." Sigmund Freud (1930, 2010) stressed the importance of work when he stated, "no other technique attaches

DOI: 10.4324/9781003459118-4

the individual so firmly to reality as laying emphasis on work; for work at least gives a secure place in a portion of reality."

Like these and other authors, we regard work and recognition of it as essential to mental health and well-being; it is a fundamental part of our identity. This contrasts with views of work as labour or toil. For example, Dahrendorf's (1985)'s description of "work in the simple everyday sense of the word, has never been regarded as a particularly agreeable dimension of life." Marx in *Das Kapital* (1992/1867) even argues that freedom begins where work ends: "instead of working, people are free to fish or write poetry as they please" (an understandable view given the miserable working conditions of the 19th century).

Fortunately, conditions in most of our organisations today are significantly better. Those that have a clear statement of purpose that explains the intention allow us to consider how the purpose can be achieved. If we start with a clear purpose, we can then ask, "What do we have to do to achieve it?" We then must answer two simple questions.

1 What is the work that must be done to achieve the purpose?
2 Whose work is it?

In our personal lives, we set the purpose and then decide on the work to be done to achieve it. Our purpose is to remodel the living room, so we set the tasks from painting the walls to buying the furniture. Only you and perhaps your family decide if the work achieves the desired transformation you intended.

When one has a job in an organisation, however, there is a qualitatively different experience in realising someone else's intention rather than realising one's own. This is why it is so important for a leader to engage with team members so that the entire team genuinely shares the purpose (intention) and therefore can identify with the transformation and gain recognition for their contribution to the result.

To put it very simply, if we are:

(i) Prevented from realising our intentions or
(ii) Not recognised for our contribution to the process and result then we arenot only alienated from our work, but our identity too suffers.

Macdonald used this understanding to explain both violence, often initiated by inmates, in institutions and attention seeking in general. It is better to gain personal recognition even punishment for a (destructive) act than to have one's work ignored and treated with indifference; the attention and recognition we receive may well be negative, but at least we know we exist. Work is essential to our well-being; it is potentially a creative expression of ourselves when recognition is given accurately and appropriately (see Chapter 17 and other chapters in Part 4).

This definition, "turning intention into reality," clearly extends beyond the realm of employment work. It encompasses many activities that we do not normally recognise as work. For example, a child building a sandcastle at the beach is usually thought of as playing. Nonetheless, the child has a clear purpose – the castle he or she envisions – and is working very hard, applying intense concentration, and may experience immense frustration when the tide comes in or joyful success when the castle stands as he or she envisioned. These processes continue throughout our lives if we are to enjoy a positive identity. Just because it is self-chosen and fun does not mean it is not work as we define it. The same is true of a man building a sailing boat for his friends and family to use. He has a clear intention and is working to achieve it.

All work whether paid or not is an activity directed towards achieving a purpose (or goal) which can be specified in advance. This activity will always be bounded by constraints or limits as shown in Figure 2.1. The work is to create a pathway within limits to achieve the goal. Note that it is the creation of the pathway where there is discretion in deciding how to achieve the purpose (goal).

### Box 2.2 Being Paid Does Not Define Work

Burke's husband, Bill, built and raced cars on the dry lakes of Southern California and at the Bonneville Salt Flats in Utah. He loved both creating new types of cars and driving very fast. He was an early member of the 200 mph Club at Bonneville.

In both places it was hot, sometimes windy and at the lakes very dusty and dirty. On a particularly hot and dusty day she asked him, "How much would someone have to pay you to do what you are doing now?" "There's not enough money in the world." This said as he happily sweated, covered in dirt, dust and grease sliding on his back under the car to replace a faulty transmission under time pressure with the clear intention to get the new transmission ready to run another time trial. A hobby is also work.

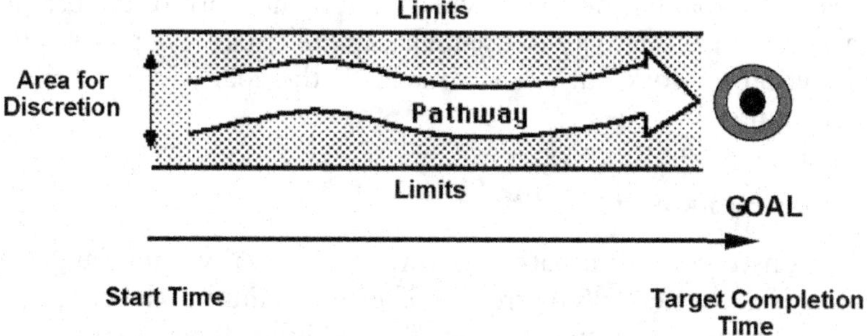


*Figure 2.1* Work

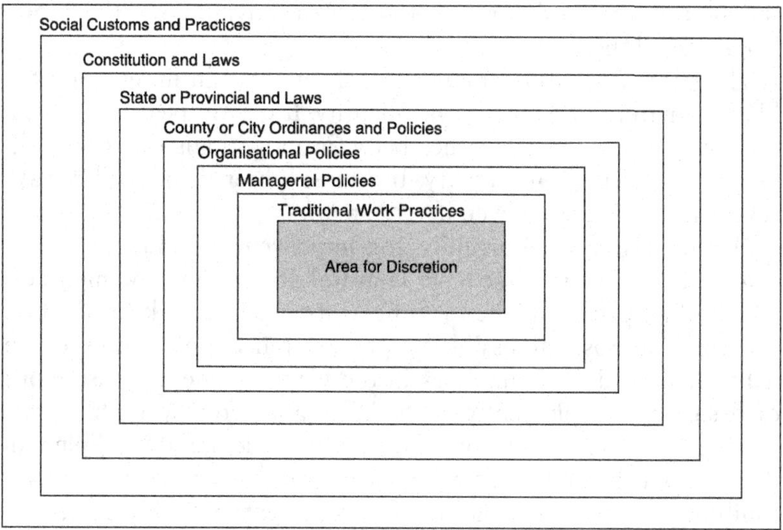


*Figure 2.2* Limits or Constraints on Work Activities

The limits can be variously described in terms of the social customs and practices, laws of society in the case of self-generated work. In employment work there is an additional constraint from policies of the company, the specific authority of the role and, more particularly, the resources available – materials, money, people and so on. These must be discussed and agreed upon in the task assignment process in Chapter 3 (Figure 2.2).

Further, the goal is set in a time context. It is never open ended; there is always a maximum completion time, which if not achieved means the goal has not been achieved. It is the work of the person carrying out the activity to use their capability (see Chapter 4) and discretion to work out a way to achieve the goal within all these constraints.

## Human Work and Identity

The construction of a pathway towards the goal within the given limits is at the person's discretion. The person must make decisions and choices, overcoming obstacles while staying within the constraints. It is this discretion to make decisions that is essentially human. No two people will ever construct the exact same pathway or method. The same person will rarely, if ever, construct the same pathway twice even if the goal is similar and the constraints remain the same, if for no other reason than taking advantage of the knowledge gained the prior time.

The pathway is thus unique to each of us as an individual; it is like a signature and part of our identity. It may appear to a casual observer to be the same either between individuals or as an individual "repeating" an activity, but close observation will always reveal some difference even if very small.

Herein lies the opportunity for improvement. Human beings given the freedom to do so have a natural drive to improve methods. Think of an occasion when you have attempted a task for the first time; it is almost impossible to prevent reflection on how to do it better next time. Sometimes in the way that we organise work or design and implement systems in organisations, we inhibit this process or actively try to prevent it. Nonetheless, most people will think about improvement even if they cannot act on those ideas. Inhibiting a person's ideas for improvement not only frustrates the individual, it also destroys an opportunity to advance the organisation's goals.

If we consider work to be a constructive and productive process, which contributes to individual well-being, then it is important that the person carrying out the work identify with the purpose or goal. This is not to say that the person would carry out this work whether employed or not, but rather the person should see the goal as a worthwhile objective that he or she actively wants to achieve.

The person should also understand the nature of and reason for the constraints. It is not good enough merely to be informed of them and instructed to achieve the goal. If the person is not aware of the purpose or why the constraints are there, it may lead to dangerous or illegal behaviour as the person sees no rationale for a constraint and therefore breaches it while trying to reach the goal. We can find this situation in extreme form in forced labour camps and less extreme in poorly led organisations that use the rationale, "Just do as I say," a statement that effectively treats a person as an object rather than a human with a will and an opinion.

## Importance of Recognition of Work

The affirmation of our contribution to the process and outcome, especially when positive, recognises that we exist and that the output of our thinking has genuine worth; it encourages us to use and develop our capabilities. This is why recognition of work is so important. It is very significant for the leader to accurately recognise the different contributions of team members.

In all probability, each of us has had the experience of our work being wrongly attributed to or even claimed by others. We have also had the experience of our work being ignored. These are very demoralising experiences, causing disappointment, anger, resentment and often a feeling of "why bother?"

We use the term recognition because it is a neutral term and does not presuppose a successful outcome (unlike reward). It is important to understand the failure of a process to produce the desired result, which needs to be recognised in order to improve in future performance. This type of recognition does not necessarily imply blame as the person may have done everything she or he was able to, and this needs to be recognised. Without proper recognition there can be very little learning.

## The Domains of Work

Work is essentially about the *how* – how to construct a method or path to achieve a desired result. While work may differ in complexity (see Chapter 5), it has a common feature of requiring human judgement and decision-making. Such work is also connected to the purpose of the organisation in that an organisation is a way of trying to bring intention into reality. To create an organisation, people have to agree on what sort of organisation is most likely to realise that intention. Then they must decide how work is to be categorised, distributed and what authority people have – to spend money, use resources, direct others or be directed in order to achieve the purpose (intention) of the organisation.

We have found it is helpful to distinguish between three different domains of work – Social, Technical and Commercial

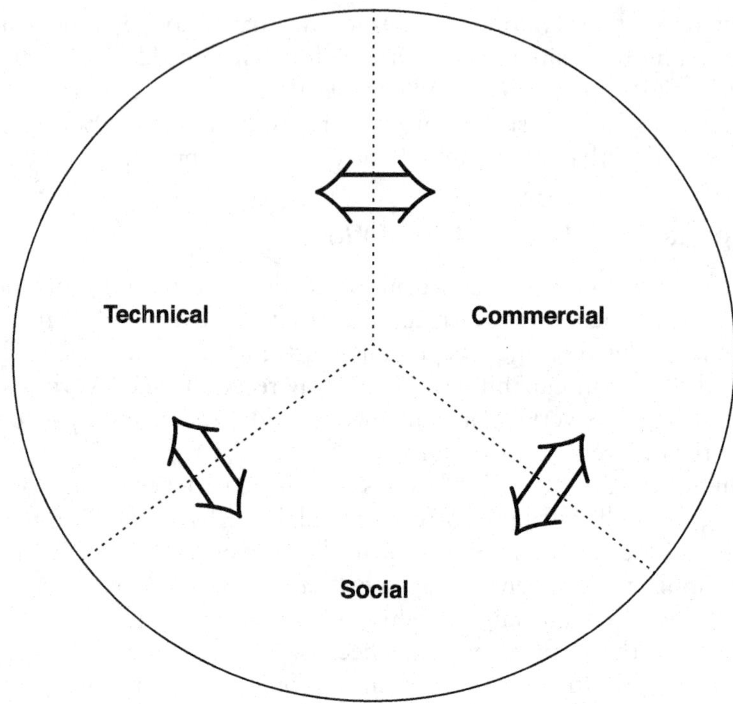


*Figure 2.3* The Domains of Work

(see Figure 2.3). No organisation can function unless all these three domains are operating effectively. It is not a matter of determining which is more important but rather to understand the work that needs to be done in each domain and how it interacts with the other two interdependent domains. Understanding this interdependency is of critical importance. Between them they cover all the work of an organisation. They can be used to help think about how the organisation is structured and roles are created and systems designed.

The **Technical** domain includes all the specialist activity. Traditionally, it has been associated with the core purpose of an organisation. For example, in a business it is producing a product or service, in a school it is educating, in a hospital it is curing and caring, in a civil engineering company it includes designing, engineering and constructing. It includes the specialised processes involved in manufacturing, mining, transporting, indeed all the verbs that describe the particular nature of the organisation. It includes the required technical expertise that is needed to source, produce, sell and deliver whatever constitutes the business or purpose of the organisation.

This could be products or services, tangible (manufacturing) or intangible (insurance). It requires knowledge, skill and training.

The **Commercial** domain includes an understanding and management of all costs, revenues, margins, capital and generally value for money. It includes all the systems associated with assets, cash flow, net present value, budgets, taxation, financial auditing, and accounting, everything required to ensure that the organisation continues to be financially viable over time. This requires sound and accurate knowledge of what constitutes cost and revenue as well as sources and use of capital. This domain also includes an understanding of markets and hence price, competitors and contracts with suppliers and customers. It requires expertise in all aspects of finance including loans and interest. It requires sound expertise and knowledge in terms of bookkeeping, accountancy and banking. Governments require much the same knowledge plus an understanding of the politics regarding authorisations, budgets, deficits and issuance of bonds. Non-governmental organisations (NGOs) and voluntary associations have costs, revenues and the need to raise money via their Boards, members, foundations and government grants. Most of them also have strict reporting requirements to maintain their tax-exempt status and to assure donors they are carrying out their purpose effectively.

The **Social** (or People) domain is concerned with all the ways in which people work together to achieve the purpose of the business including the structure. This includes all the *people systems* – recruitment, selection, appraisal, review, promotion, discipline – as well as all the systems that go to answer *the three questions everyone has at work*.

- What am I meant to do?
- How am I doing?
- What is my future?

It includes Role Descriptions, Task Assignment, Succession Planning, and Career Development. It includes the daily social processes: how people interact, the quality of leadership and team members' behaviour and generally how people communicate directly and symbolically. It includes all the daily work scheduling systems such as meetings and working hours.

We have yet to find an organisation that thrived over time unless it was effective in ALL three domains. Some were better in one domain or another, but neglect of one domain ultimately led to problems, and sometimes failure meaning bankruptcy or takeover by a stronger organisation.

There was a time from about 1940 through the early 1980s, which has been referred to as "The Golden Age of Capitalism," when the Technical domain was the main focus because the purpose of the organisation was usually found in the Technical domain. The products or services provided are produced in the Technical domain. Organisations also realised that without the Commercial domain to ensure that the organisation remained solvent or the Social domain to provide decent working conditions, the organisation would fail, if not in the short term, certainly in the longer term.

The purpose of most organisations was to develop and produce great products and services – a strong focus on the technical domain. The Commercial domain was also perceived as important and its expertise recognised. Perhaps because they are the dominant domains, Technical and Commercial domains have a precise and clear language to describe the work and identify the requirements of any job. Whether an engineer, teacher or someone to stack shelves, we know what we need to fill a role. The same is true of a CPA or loan specialist in the Commercial domain. In both areas we are familiar with and understand the education and skills required.

In the Social domain, however, there has been much less clarity. Even the need for clarity is often underestimated, or even denied. The Social is denigrated as subjective or "soft," while the Technical and Commercial are objective or "hard." Part of the reason for the misunderstanding of the Social domain is because we develop ideas regarding the social from childhood. We learn to read our parents and their moods; we learn how to get along in school and on the playground. We even see social behaviour on television and social media. Most of us believe we have a good understanding of the social domain even though our ideas may or may not be clear and others may have quite different views and definition of terms, yet we assume we are all in agreement, until something happens and we are not.

This assumption about the existing knowledge of the Social is reflected in many MBA and Mental Processing Ability (MPA) programmes which are supposed to be preparing technical people for managerial roles. Their emphasis is largely on the Commercial – economics, accounting, policy/data analysis. Yet it is widely recognised that the organisations fail without excellent leadership and adequate systems to support those who are doing the work of the organisation.

We argue that it is just as important to be clear as to what we mean in the Social domain as it is to be clear about what we mean in the Technical and Commercial domains. Misunderstandings about such basic terms as manager and supervisor or leadership and culture lead to confusion and mistakes. It is hard to change a culture if you don't agree on what an organisational culture is. Lack of a precise language, which leads to a lack of clarity around expectations and meaning in the Social domain, is in our view a major cause of distress, inefficiency, ineffectiveness and poor-quality working relationships.

That is why the material in this book and the content of Systems Leadership Theory is all about the Social domain and how, by being clear about what we mean and expect in that domain, we can significantly enhance the quality of work in the organisation and improve the chances of achieving the purpose of the organisation. We also improve the quality of life for the people who work in the organisation.

## Use of the STC Model

We, and people we have worked with, have found this model has utility in several ways.

### First, as an Analytical Tool

We can examine an organisation in terms of its relative strengths and weaknesses in each of these domains. We can look at an organisation to see the balance of the three domains. Is the content clear and connected to the purpose? Is it balanced appropriately? Are certain aspects over- or underappreciated? We can also examine a part of the organisation or even an individual role asking the same or similar questions.

Examining the three domains and their relative strengths and weaknesses can provide important information about what is needed to have a more balanced use of all three. It can also provide useful information to improve the structure and systems of the organisation. In using it as an analytic tool we must not jump to conclusions as to which domains need addressing. It may be one, two or all three.

It is easy and quite common to see the Technical as the only worthwhile work and so to denigrate the other domains when all are essential. It is a little like arguing which is most important – the heart, lungs or liver? For example, a manager might see a problem with production as Commercial. "We can't produce enough because we need to buy new equipment." In fact, the lack of production may be poor maintenance perhaps due to the lack of skilled, technical expertise to keep the current equipment running. It may be a Social issue. Perhaps the leadership is poor or roles are poorly defined or there is poor training leading to bad use of equipment. Similarly, problems of safety may again appear Technical or Commercial when in fact the root cause is Social – poor organisation, systems and leadership.

### Second, as an Explanatory Tool

On Wall Street and in universities, concerned individuals have wondered what went wrong at General Electric (GE), once perceived as a giant of industry? How did a company known for the safety and quality of its airplanes, like Boeing, certify a plane with known defects that led to two major crashes and the deaths of 346 people in Africa and Indonesia?

The simple answer is that the purpose of each of these organisations changed from focus on the Technical domain to produce excellent goods and services to the Commercial domain to improve profits and, most importantly, the share price of each. At the same time, both companies diminished the importance of the social domain, breaking decades of good labour and community relations.

#### Box 2.3 GE from Balanced STC to Commercial Dominance

It all began in 1981 when Jack Welch became CEO of GE. He became the most famous and most influential CEO in the late 20th century by focusing on share price to produce value for investors, including the top executives of GE. This appeared to be wildly successful as GE's market capitalisation went from $14 billion in 1981 to $600 billion in 2000.

> The changes he unleashed at GE transformed the company founded by Thomas Edison from an admired industrial behemoth known for innovation, quality engineering and laudable business practices into sprawling multinational conglomerate that paid little regard to its employees [Social domain] and was addicted to short term profits [commercial domain].
>
> (Gelles, 2022:3)

Jeff Immelt, who followed Welch as CEO, had the misfortune of starting the job on September 10, 2001. On September 11, he stated, "My second day as Chairman, a plane I leased, flying with engines I had built, crashed into a building I insure and it was covered by a network I own" (Gelles, 2022:114). Despite all that GE kept going and its capitalisation was up to $500 billion in 2005,[1] but the problems were mounting. During the Great Recession of 2009, GE needed the government to insure as much as $139 billion in debt for its lending facility, GE Capital.[2] It also got a $3 billion investment from Warren Buffet who also helped by adding to the idea that GE would survive.[3]

GE Capital, which at one time produced as much as 60% of GE profits, had to be sold in April 2015, and as of this writing GE is worth about $98 billion, and has been removed from the Dow Index; it is about to be divided into three separate companies. Focusing on one domain led to disaster.

Because GE seemed wildly successful in terms of market capitalisation, many other companies started hiring GE executives to bring the Welch magic to their organisations. The organisations that put these ideas into practice had, perhaps without being aware of it, shifted their purpose from the Technical domain – innovating and producing excellent products and services – to the Commercial domain where the primary purpose was to raise the price of their stock to provide value for investors. For many of these companies, it has been a long-term disaster as it has been at GE.

When organisations lose track of their fundamental purpose – the reason they exist – to produce goods and services, the evidence from the last 40 years indicates that in the short term the organisation can make a lot of money, but in the longer term it will fail. Viewing workers as costs, not assets, failure to innovate and produce new products, and buying and selling companies to improve profits leads to long-term destruction.

Boeing is still doing well financially, despite its problems, but it has lost much of its reputation for safety and quality. Despite

### Box 2.4 Boeing Following the GE Way

Boeing Corporation's technical expertise in aeronautics and its strong well-trained workforce were legendary for decades. Over that time Boeing produced major innovations in military and commercial airplanes. It had a clear statement of purpose focused largely on the Technical domain. It was founded in 1916 by William E. Boeing who declared its purpose:

To be on the leading edge of aeronautics; being pioneers
Tackling huge challenges and risks

Product safety and quality
Integrity and ethical business
To "eat, breathe, and sleep the world of aeronautics"[4]

They were also well-balanced with the Social domain where relations with employees were excellent – as one worker said after the changes described below, "people were treated as people, not numbers" (Gelles, 2022:90). Boeing decided to bring in former GE executives who made the Commercial domain dominant as had Welch. The Technical domain was so critical to Boeing that it continued to function, although at a diminished capability that was not immediately apparent. Both the Technical and Social domains, which had long been a strength of Boeing, were seriously damaged when the executives decided to outsource more work to contractors, and they announced they would be eliminating 53,000 jobs. As one former Boeing engineer and union leader said, the company's "safety culture" was replaced with "a culture of financial bullshit, a culture of groupthink" (Gelles, 2022:89).

A new CEO (from GE), Jim McNerney, slashed wages and did away with the company pension plan. As the first GE CEO said in 2004,

> When people say I changed the culture of Boeing, that was the intent, so it's run like a business rather than a great engineering firm. It is a great engineering firm, but people invest in a company because they want to make money.
>
> (Gelles, 2022:90)

In recent years, Boeing's great reputation for high-quality and safe aircraft was seriously diminished when the development of the new 787 Dreamliner was projected to take four to six years with a cost of $6 to $10 billion dollars. Outsourcing gave Boeing less control over quality and delivery time of components and ultimately of the Dreamliner itself. The result was a cascading series of delays and glitches such that the new plane took nine years and $32 billion to complete.

Even more damaging was the decision to modify the existing 737 airplane to create the 737 Max rather than designing a whole new aircraft. The whole world learned of the problems that were created as 346 people were killed in crashes in Indonesia and Africa. A single sensor caused a software system to force the planes to crash. After two years of investigations the planes are now flying as Boeing put in two sensors to prevent the problem from recurring. Soon, however, they will have to provide triple redundancy as the European Union Aviation Safety Agency (EASA) has demanded they provide three sensors. When the Technical domain was dominant, Boeing planes had up to quadruple redundancy on the most critical systems. There was a reason for the pilot's slogan, "If it's not Boeing, I'm not going."

Although Boeing's share price is down considerably from its peak, it is still a valuable company, even if its reputation for safety and quality are diminished. We will see how they operate in the future – to increase share price at the expense of technical quality or to increase share price by restoring the technical and social domains with their commitment to quality and safety.

having only one real competitor, we can predict it is likely, unless they return to their original purpose, and focus on building innovative, safe and quality airplanes (Technical domain), they will no longer be the leader in aeronautical innovation, and their profits will suffer. They could also return to their excellent systems in the Social domain, and balance all three domains, including the commercial. Time will tell if they are willing and able do this.

#### Third, as a Problem-Solving Tool

Any problem in the organisation can be looked at through these domains. After deciding on purpose, the next question of what is the work we must do to achieve purpose. A good place to start is by asking what is the work that must be done in each domain? The domains provide a tool for analysing what must be done in each area. Often the focus is on the technical, because that is where the purpose is produced. Clarifying what financial work must be carried out now and in the future is also essential. The social domain is the one that is often least considered since we "know" all about that. Take care, the social can make or break an organisation if not properly thought through.

Another example if we are considering a capital project, an acquisition, a significant restructure, we can categorise issues in terms of these three domains. What are the Technical, Commercial and Social critical issues we need to address if the work is to be successful?

While it has been standard practice to examine the commercial (financial) aspects in an acquisition, in recent decades, environmental issues have become just as important as they can be hugely costly and with legal consequences far into the future. We would recommend that social issues also be very seriously analysed in any acquisition. Are the cultures compatible or not, and what must be done if they are not compatible? One example is the issues between pilots of differing airlines who have different procedures that are very important to them. Following the merger of two companies, getting the pilots from each organisation to work together was a significant issue. While the problem appears to be technical, in our opinion it was largely social (Sotham, 2016).

## Conclusion

We find that many organisations are more conscious of how important it is to understand and manage the Technical and Commercial aspects with discipline and rigour based on sound principles and theory. There is less awareness that the Social or people aspect should be subject to similar rigour. We have developed Systems Leadership Theory to help redress the balance, not because the Social processes are the most important but because they are equally as important: successful and positive organisations need all three to be in balance.

But there is still more to consider when we think about work. How are tasks formulated and assigned to ensure work is carried out correctly and the assignments respect human capabilities and dignity?

## Notes

1 New York Times Archive, Nov 12, 2008. https://archive.nytimes.com/dealbook.nytimes.com/2008/11/12/fdic-to-back-139-billion-in-ge-capital-debt/
2 Ibid.
3 Business Insider. https://www.businessinsider.com/the-rise-and-fall-of-general-electric-2019-8#2001–2017-troubled-times-6 retrieved March 9, 2023
4 Business Insider. https://www.businessinsider.com/the-rise-and-fall-of-general-electric-2019-8#2001–2017-troubled-times-6 retrieved March 9, 2023

# 3 The Importance of Task Clarity

## Introduction

In Chapter 2 work was defined as turning intention into reality. This involves the exercise of discretion – making decisions and acting on them within prescribed limits in order to achieve a goal. In organisations the intention is first articulated in the purpose statement and passed down through organisational sub-units until it gets to a manager who must articulate the purpose of an assignment to direct reports in order for them to carry out that assignment.

Task assignment, properly understood, is a subtle and complex process – one which requires considerable practice to master. This chapter introduces the basic processes of task formulation and assignment using direct assignment as the example. There are other kinds of assignments as well as task feedback and task review explained in Chapter 17. All of these are necessary if you are to be effective in assigning tasks to your team members. Many readers have started to use this process even before completing the book. They report considerable success, but if you do this, it is essential to read Chapter 17 if you want to apply these ideas with your own team.

Of course, reading or exercises in the classroom can only provide an introduction; your skill will depend on your own on-the-job practice. Initially it may seem more difficult than it appears when you read about it. Over time, however, most managers find it makes them more successful communicators and it becomes second nature.

This chapter introduces the basic concepts of good task assignment. Proper task assignment increases the likelihood that task doers:

- Have a clear understanding of the task they are to do
- Have had an opportunity to contribute and comment on the task assigned
- Are able to commit themselves to doing it
- Are best placed to accept their manager's judgement of their performance as fair

DOI: 10.4324/9781003459118-5

Despite endless articles and books on "delegation," many managers have considerable difficulty with the task assignment process. Rather than using the term "delegation," we have found the terms task, task formulation and task assignment make clear what is to be done. This can then lead to a fairer Task Review (see Chapter 17).

**Task:** A statement of intention articulated as an assignment to carry out work with a statement of boundary limits as known or provided in the task assignment process.

**Task Formulation:** Determining the output of a task, estimating the required resources and the time for completion and deciding which dimensions to specify and which one to scope. Taking into account the context and purpose as well as assessing the complexity of the pathway that will have to be created by the person executing the task. Task formulation is a more complex endeavour than carrying the work of the task.

**Task Assignment:** A statement of intention to carry out work within limits set by law, organisational policy, work practices as well as the specific Context, Purpose, Quantity and Quality of Output expected, the Resources available and the Time by which the objective is to be reached (CPQ/QRT).

**Preparation:** Before reading further, create a task assignment for one of your team members as you have done it in the past. Or write a task assignment as it has been given to you by your manager.

## Task Formulation

Task formulation is a process whereby the manager evaluates the situation, determines what is to be done, why it is to be done, by when it should be done, the resources available to perform the task and the limits within which it must be accomplished. Managers may also seek guidance from the task doers as to some of these elements of task formulation as will be shown further on.

All tasks which are to be assigned to another person begin in the mind, often of the manager, but also from team members who may suggest ideas and certainly make contributions. If what is intended is to result in productive work done by the task doer, a clear task assignment must be formulated by the manager – the Context, Purpose, and components of the task – Output Quality and Quantity, Resources, Time to completion, the deadline (CPQ/QRT).

Limits set by social practices, law, organisational policies must also be clear though often unstated unless a person is new to the role and might not be aware of them, or one or another limit is especially important regarding this task.

## Stating Purpose/Setting Context

**Purpose:** Why the task is to be done. What is to be achieved by accomplishing this task? Best stated in a single sentence without an "and."

**Context:** The situation in which the task will likely be performed. Background, relationship to other tasks, any unusual factors to be taken into account. Context refers to the environment in which the work will take place.

Often the environment is taken for granted and assumed to be much as it has been in the past. Where the environment is changing quickly, considerable effort is necessary to plan for a range of potential environments. You may have had the experience of being assigned a task and had your manager say, "You will need to be a bit careful with Fred for a few days. His daughter is quite ill, and he is sometimes distracted." This is a manager assigning a task to be performed in an environment that is different from what the task doer has been accustomed to.

Setting the context involves answering questions about the circumstances in which the task is to be performed, the background as to how the task needs to be done and may connect with other work. Is there an ongoing problem or an emergency? Other key points:

- Why the task is important.
- How it fits into the process, relates to other tasks.
- Who is doing related tasks.

There is one aspect of clear context provision that is often overlooked in task assignment. That is the articulated requirement for the task doer to refer back to the manager if the context being experienced during the performance of the task differs substantially from that predicted by the manager when the task was assigned. Without a clear articulation of the expected context, the team members do not have a sound reference for the assessment of change.

Good managers, if they suspect that the context may change unexpectedly, will tell the task doer, "If you see the emergence of this type of change in context, I want you to stop your work and get back to me immediately." Even if they are not expecting change in context, a good manager will ensure that all of his or her team members know that in the event of a substantial context change, they have to cease work and report back.

The reasoning for this requirement is because every statement of context for the performance of a task articulated by a manager is a prediction about future events. The exercise of discretion by the task doer (his or her work) is to complete the task as assigned within the context predicted.

The context is generated by the often confusing environment in which we live and work. Sometimes it will serve up a context that greatly assists in the performance of the task (not often, given Murphy's law), and sometimes the chaos will serve up a context in which the task is much more difficult (higher complexity; much greater resource requirement) or in fact its achievement may be counterproductive to the purpose of the manager.

To cope with these inevitable, but usually rare occurrences, it is essential that task doers have a very sound understanding of the expected context and an equally sound understanding that it is their work to desist and get back to their manager quickly with a description of the actual context.

Too often we see examples of good people continuing to complete the assigned task in the face of a markedly changed context, and being caught up in an unfolding disaster that takes lives or damages people severely. One of the very substantial changes for the better in industrial safe work practice over recent decades has been the spread of the dictum and the practice of "If you are unsure, STOP and seek advice."

Many organisations have gone to considerable lengths to educate their employees about their individual authority to stop all work if they believe a practice has or is about to become unsafe and to seek advice.

### Purpose

The most vital element in the task assignment process is the statement of the purpose you hope will be achieved by the accomplishment of the task. Why do you want the task performed? Too often the purpose is assumed or ignored when telling someone to "do this." This is particularly true at the lower levels of the organisation where employees may be treated more as objects (machines) rather than as human beings. We recommend that the purpose should be stated in a single sentence without an "and." This drives clarity and prevents the task doer from having to try to determine among a range of options, second-guessing the manager.

Knowing the purpose of the task and its context will enable the task doer to exercise discretion more effectively. A task doer with high capability may, perhaps, develop an innovative solution – achieving task results that are better, faster or less costly than the manager had envisioned. It will allow the task doer to recognise if the context changes and make it more likely that the unforeseen change will be overcome. Most importantly, knowledge of context and purpose will allow the task doer to come back to the manager quickly to advise him or her of the proposed innovation or unforeseen change in context or if the task does not appear to be achieving its intended purpose. In this way errors, injury, damage or waste may be avoided. Such abilities are essential in an environment which is changing and are essential where the rate of change and the volatility of change are increasing.

Knowledge of context and purpose has other benefits as well.

#### Box 3.1

There is an old story about two medieval stone masons, one bent and drained from a day's work, one singing. When asked what they had been doing, the first said, "I have been lifting heavy stones all day." The second, "I have been building a cathedral."

### Task Assignment

While there are a several different kinds of task assignments as discussed further on, there is a basic model that underlies all of them. After providing Context and Purpose, the manager must be clear about the desired Output, described in terms of Quality and

Quantity, Resources available and Time to Completion. To do this effectively, one of the components of the task must be left open (or scoped), while the other three must be specified.

**Specified Component:** A component where a single point is set to indicate precisely what is required to successfully complete the task.

**Scoped Dimension:** A component where a range is set between two specified points, leaving space for discretion. Within that range, one point is worth more than all other points.

**Tolerance:** A tolerance is a range of variation around a specified point. Within that range all points are of equal worth. (Both the specified components and the limits on the scoped component of a task may [or may not] have tolerances.)

The concept of tolerance around a specified value comes from engineering, but it applies generally to all stated quantities. Even though a manager may specify a dimension of exactly 30 mm in diameter, there will still be a tolerance in practice because the measuring equipment cannot deliver on such exactitude. Any number of bars that are measured as being exactly 30 mm in diameter will be a small amount smaller or larger despite the measuring equipment showing "exactly" 30 mm on its readout.

This variation is tolerated because all the pieces are of equal value, and they satisfy the criteria the manager has set. Care needs to be taken in the setting of tolerances by the task assigner because a tolerance that is set too narrow adds to cost for no benefit and that is set too wide generates waste, thus adding to cost as well.

You can have it good, cheap or fast – pick two.

Within the limits of social, legal and policy constraints as well as context and purpose, task doers must have room to exercise discretion as they create a pathway (exercise discretion) to complete the task. To do this effectively, one of the components of the task must be left open, while the other three are specified. The open component has limits as well but these provide space for the exercise of discretion.

Figure 3.1 provides a basic illustration of this. The dots indicate the result desired by the manager. The vertical lines indicate tolerances – the range in which all outcomes are acceptable. The

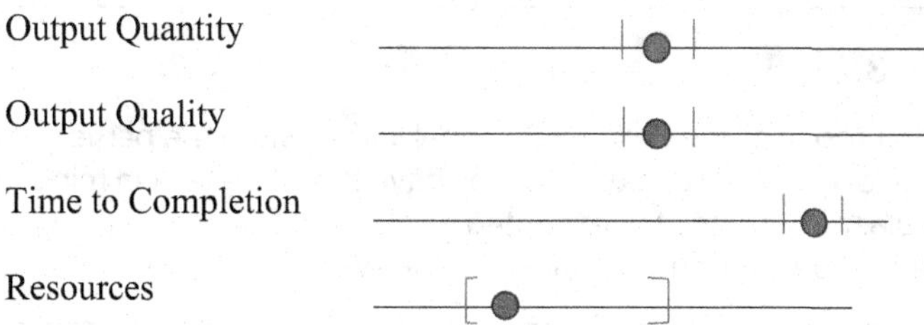


*Figure 3.1* Task Assignment Example

output quantity is 25 metal bars, the quality is 1-inch diameter, anything between 0.98 and 1.02 is acceptable to be completed by Friday. The scoped component is in the bracket with the dot indicating that using fewer resources while achieving the specified components is the best performance, though anywhere within the bracket is acceptable.

If three or even all four components are left open, it impossible to build a system of merit and fair accountability. If the task doer must decide which of the dimensions is most important and thus to be maximised or minimised, it takes time and energy from the actual performance of the task. It creates considerable uncertainty and often worry, which also drains energy. Most importantly, there is real potential for misunderstanding in these circumstances. Should the task doer acting in good faith make the wrong guess as to the manager's priorities, he or she will not willingly accept accountability on the limits nor an assessment of work performance on the scoped component. "If that is what you wanted, why didn't you tell me?"

The ability to exercise discretion to achieve a goal allows and encourages people to use their full capabilities. Managers who allow discretion in creating a pathway to the goal demonstrate their recognition of the humanity of their employees, their respect for their employees' human dignity and their trust in them.

To gain the acceptance of accountability requires an understanding of the conditions that are necessary for such acceptance. No matter what managers may believe, accountability cannot be imposed on people. Accountability is a function of the relationship between a manager and a direct report. This allows for a review where the manager can ask clearly as genuine questions:

- What did you do?
- How did you do it?
- Why did you do it that way?

> **Box 3.2**
>
> The purpose of the CPQ/QRT model is that when the parties (usually two) leave the discussion they have the *same* task in mind and are clear about what is expected.
>
> This allows for a much fairer Task Review.

The Task Formulation, Task Assignment and Review processes provide a methodology and logic for good management practice. As such, they are *guidelines* for managerial *judgement*. It must be emphasised, however, that guidelines can never replace managerial judgement.

The guidelines are not a statement of absolute requirements to be articulated and recorded at every step. As the relationship between a manager and team member develops, clarity in task assignment may be achieved without a complete articulation as provided for in the guidelines. Attempting to articulate everything at all times and under all circumstances becomes mechanistic and unproductive.

## Involving the Team Member in Task Formulation and Assignment

Task Formulation, Assignment and Review are processes to be discussed with the task doer. Even if the manager is clear about the dimensions of a task there should always be an opportunity for a direct report to have input and make comments and suggestions. With more regular and frequent tasks this may not always be needed but the opportunity should still be there.

Involving the direct report in the process allows the manager to gain information necessary for a proper formulation of the assignment. It may also produce a better understanding of the context, purpose and components of the task assignment and gain the commitment of the direct report to achieve the desired task result. It will expose any pre-conceived ideas which are held by either the manager or the team member, and which often inhibit clear communication, leading to errors and waste.

For example, the manager assigns a task with a six-month deadline. The direct report says, “That’s no problem. I can have it for you in a month.” This may well be an indication that the manager and direct report have different ideas about what the task is and what it will take to complete it. Further discussion is necessary to find out what each is thinking and to confirm the nature of the task. In any case managers must use judgement in deciding when and

### Box 3.3

Involving subordinates in task formulation may not always be useful or appropriate. There is not much point if the work is very routine, or the subordinate has experience of this type of task.

In an emergency there may be no time to fully explain the purpose, let alone involve the subordinate in the task formulation process; in this case the subordinate should understand that the task will be assigned clearly but without much discussion.

how to involve team members in task formulation. This judgement is part of the manager's work.

As the complexity of work increases, the team member may play a critical role in helping to clarify the task dimensions and comment on them. The direct report may be a technical expert on the task in question. The manager may be clear on what is needed (the purpose or the output) but does not know how long the task is likely to take or what resources will be required. Discussing with the direct report what you are trying to achieve and getting his/her input is essential.

Such involvement does *not* mean the direct report determines what is to be done. The decision on the output required, the targeted completion time and the resources to be used *must* be made by the manager. Managers may decide to do exactly what the subordinate proposes (this happens frequently with technical experts), but it is still their decision and for which they are accountable.

In practice, the direct report may already clearly understand some or all of these matters, in which case there is no need to discuss them. The point is, however, that the manager must be sure that this is the case, not just assume that it is.

## Summary

By using Context, Purpose, Quantity and Quality of Output, Resources and Time (CPQ/QRT) in assigning tasks, managers can effectively communicate with their team members to ensure they know what to do. Giving them an opportunity to contribute and comment on the task assigned will clarify what is expected, and may offer the opportunity to create a better task assignment. This enables the team member to commit to doing it, while at the same time creating the conditions where they can accept their manager's judgement of their work performance. The other types of task assignment and task feedback and review are presented in Chapter 17.

**Exercise:** You may find it useful to look at the task assignment you wrote at the beginning of this chapter and rewrite it using what you have learned here.

One of the critical issues in task assignment is assessing the capability of your team members' knowledge and capability to carry out task assignments. Most managers are aware of the differing capabilities of their team members. Sometimes the differences are based on their knowledge, technical or social skills or simply their ability to think their way through a problem.

If this introduction to task formulation and assignment causes you to think about the work you are expecting of your team members, the next chapter will provide more insight as we turn to the elements of human capability to do work.

# 4 Human Capability

## Introduction

Working on task assignments reminds us that not every employee who reports to a manager has the same skills or abilities to carry out the tasks that must be completed if the individual and their part of the organisation is to achieve its purpose. Some people know more than others. Some have knowledge in one area but not in another. Some people have more energy and interest in a particular task while others do not. Some need to deal with people and things that are right in front of them – concrete reality rather than some abstract idea. Some have excellent technical skills while others have fine social skills. Some can think their way through a complex problem while others cannot. The difficult question is, how to best match the capabilities and interests of our people with the work and tasks that must be carried out in our organisation?

We have found it remarkable that many organisations lack a shared concept of human capability. They talk of education, experience, training, inter-personal skills and competencies, but they lack an overall, coherent articulation of capability. There may not be agreement about what elements of capability can be influenced or learned or how this might be done, apart from having people attend training courses.

We have encountered a few people who argue that every person can perform any assigned work if they have the interest and training to do so. The data we and others have gathered over many years indicates this is simply not true. You have probably observed this as well. Therefore, we do need to understand human capability, how it may vary from person to person and how it may, or may not, be changed. In this chapter we will explain our concept of human capability and then raise some questions to discuss why we have not incorporated some of the more popular concepts of human capability still used in many organisations. We simply observe that people have different gifts; this doesn't make people better or

DOI: 10.4324/9781003459118-6

worse as people but we do need to recognise that some people have different talents whether learned or intrinsic life qualities.

## Components of Individual Capability

When selecting a person for a role or a task, the following elements are critical. The key to success is to effectively match individuals with their differing capabilities to the complexity required to complete their assigned tasks. When selecting someone for a role (or deciding to whom a particular task should be given), several factors need to be considered:

- Knowledge
- Technical skills
- Social process skills
- Application – energy, drive, determination, desire to do the work of the role
- Mental processing ability (MPA)

The purpose is to identify the attributes an individual needs to bring to the task so he or she can perform it effectively and efficiently. If any one of these elements is not appropriate to the role (or task), the person will have difficulty in carrying out the work of the role (or task). As will be noted below, a deficiency in some elements is easier to remedy than others. Education and experience (which are often used as selection criteria) are means for gaining the appropriate knowledge and skills. The socialisation experience of the individual (of which education is typically a part) contributes to the development of technical and social skills as well as knowledge.

### Knowledge

> Knowledge here consists of two categories. The first comprises knowing part (or all) of an accepted body of knowledge, and the second is knowledge that has been self-generated, often heuristically described as "experience."

Knowing all or part of a body of knowledge is about what we learn in schools and universities and from our own research – learning subjects from an established curriculum. It is concerned with knowledge of currently agreed-upon definitions, theories or facts: for example, calculus, nuclear physics, chemistry or other scientific disciplines. There are bodies of knowledge in other fields such as government, business or the arts which cover facts, history and interpretations of these subjects.

The second type of knowledge has been internalised through experience such as from families, people they have worked with or international travel. It differs from scientific knowledge in that it may not be organised into disciplines or accepted structures. This knowledge tends to be unique to each individual.

Both types of knowledge may be relatively simple and direct. Some knowledge areas will be highly complex with fine discriminations and multiple relationships. In general, experts in a field will have developed a highly complex areas knowledge with a lot of data and inter-relationships based on their drive and interest in their field. Novices, on the other hand, will have less data and fewer relationships, even if over time they too will become experts.

### Skills – Technical and Social

> **Technical skill:** Facility or proficiency in the use of knowledge of a technique. The learned and repeated routines that apply in a specific knowledge area and reduce the complexity of work required to carry out a specific task. The development of technical skills simplifies work.

For example, when one first learns to drive, it takes concentration to keep the right pressure on the gas pedal, to learn to brake smoothly, to stay in the traffic lane, to remember to use the turn signals. Once these techniques are mastered, they can be done without conscious effort allowing the experienced driver to concentrate on road conditions and the movements of other vehicles.

Routines that simplify work are very common in emergency procedures so when the emergency occurs, the people who must handle it can do key parts of their job without conscious effort. Combat drills – taking apart and putting together rifles until this can be done in the dark and under highly stressful conditions – are another example of the simplification of work through the use of learned routines. When people can do these things well, we say they have technical skills.

Other examples of technical skills might include facility in writing, mathematics, public speaking, engineering design, systems analysis, cooking, woodworking, driving a fork-lift, preparing a legal case, playing the piano, etc. Obviously, different roles call for very different technical skills. For many, skills proficiency develops with practice and experience. Some skills may require certain physical attributes with which we are born, for example, piano playing, high-jumping, sharp-shooting, etc. No matter the amount of practice and experience, to do these at the highest level of skill requires certain physical qualities as well as characteristics acquired through drill and practice. The possession of technical skills in a field allows energy and MPA to be devoted to resolving the messy core of a problem.

**Social Process Skill:** The ability to read the signals of human-to-human interaction in social situations, to understand the underlying social processes and to respond in a way that influences subsequent behaviour in a predictable way. In an organisation this results in behaviour that contributes to the purpose of the organisation.

This is not simply the everyday social skill – the ability to be friendly and get along with people socially. It requires an understanding of the shared human values and how they are perceived through the lens of the mythologies of the people you are leading. (See Chapters 9 and 10.) A leadership role requires that you use this understanding to act in a way that influences people to behave more effectively.

Most people learn social process skills early in their lives in families and early interactions with peers as they grow up. We then spend the rest of our lives practising them. This does not suggest that we all have the same, or very similar, social process skills, nor are we aware of any work that suggests a correlation between what we refer to as Mental Processing Ability and social process skills.

**Application:** Kolbe (1991) used the term conation to describe what we are calling application. This describes the energy and drive we bring to our work. It includes the inclination and desire to do the work and achieve the goal as well as the courage to sustain the work even in the face of serious barriers to accomplishment. These characteristics (which may be different under varying circumstances such as stress or hardship) usually bear heavily on the work we are able and willing to do.

While some people appear to be born with more, or less, energy and drive, the energy a person is willing to apply to the performance of tasks is strongly related to the quality of leadership they experience on the job. Clearly, there are also individuals who are prepared to continue to devote significant mental and physical energy to their work even though the leadership they experience is poor, but poor leadership usually saps energy and causes active disengagement from work (Gallup, 2017).

### Mental Processing Ability

The least familiar of these components of human capability is Mental Processing Ability (referred to as MPA). To explain MPA, we begin with Elliott Jaques' definition of Cognitive Processes.

**Cognitive Processes:** "… the mental processes by which a person recognises and takes in information; picks it over; plays with it; analyses it; puts it together; reorganises it; judges and reasons with it; and makes conclusions, plans and decisions, and takes action" (Jaques, 1989:33).

These mental processes are the way individuals organise their thinking when they do work (attempt to turn intention into reality). Thus, our term Mental Processing Ability.

**Mental Processing Ability:** The ability to make order out of the often confusing environments in which humans live out their lives. It is the ability to pattern and construe the world in terms of scale and time. The level of our MPA will determine the amount and complexity of information that we can process in doing so. (This definition draws in part from I. Macdonald, 1984:2, and from Jaques, 1989:33; see his definition of cognitive power.) Not all people have the same ability to generate order (MPA) and therefore the same ability to perform work. Some will be able to resolve more complex problems than others.

The richness and diversity of the mental world that each human creates for themselves is indicative of the complexity of mental processes that the person can apply to make sense out of their experience of the world. Because the environment is always changing, each person must continually make (and re-make) order of that environment. This effort to make order of the universe is, in fact, work – turning intention (to make order) into reality. It is in the use of MPA, a human doing real work, that the patterns of MPAs are revealed.

From your own experience you know that different people are, more or less, able to comprehend a situation, to formulate cause and effect relationships between data that are assembled from their experience of the world, to generate and test hypotheses (about relationships between data) and to predict the outcome of a course of action. All of us have differing abilities to do work. (The specifics of these differences will be discussed in the next chapter.)

Each of us perceives the world in our own way. Some people will see the world as it presents itself in front of them; they are most comfortable with what they can directly see and even touch. They like direct links between the action they take and the result they get. Their solution will deal with what is immediately present. Other people will see that the results they want cannot be achieved directly, but only by dealing with the tangible, concrete environment. They recognise that many different systems and outside influences will have to be changed if there is to be a successful outcome. People differ in the way they take in and organise information, how broadly they see the inter-relationships of what is going on and how much they can encompass in their vision of the world.

These different ways of seeing the world can be divided into distinct groupings. Rather than MPA being seen as a gradual, continuous line along which the whole population is spread, what Jaques originally postulated, based on his research, was a series of types of MPA beginning at I and going up to VIII or IX.[1] Because each approach to the world and problem solving is discrete, someone with Type II MPA will see a problem and its potential solutions in a completely different way from someone with Type IV MPA.

The person with Type II MPA will simply not see the problem with the same range of variables, relationships and consequences.[2] These differing approaches are neither right nor wrong, but their appropriateness depends upon the context and particular task to be accomplished.

## Capability and Selection for Role

It is the interaction of all these elements that makes it possible (or impossible) for individuals to take on specific roles in an organisation. When all the elements are appropriate, we say the individual has the capability to carry out the work of the role.

**Capability:** The entire complex of elements which are required to carry out a role. These include the knowledge, social process and technical skills, application and the MPA appropriate for the level of work required for the role.

When selecting people to carry out specific roles (or tasks), managers are usually aware of the need for appropriate knowledge, experience, skill and the requirement that people behave in ways which are acceptable in the organisation and the role in which they will work. They must also have the drive and desire to do the work (though that may be difficult to gauge in an interview). If an individual has some, but not all, of the necessary requirements for the role, deficiencies in knowledge and skills can be corrected through education, training and/or additional experience.

### Box 4.1

This definition of capability is not used uniformly throughout the literature on stratified systems. Jaques' term, working capacity (1989:33), appears to be closest to our meaning of capability. Others have used the term capability to imply MPA. To avoid the resulting confusion, we have found our two definitions – of MPA and capability – are helpful to managers who need to understand human capability in the selection of people. When used consistently, they enable members of an organisation to develop greater clarity of communication.

Social process skills, however, are not so readily modified. It appears that the early learning and embedding of social process skill renders it relatively difficult to change. Much of its application is in real time, which prevents thinking about the meaning of a facial or body signal and the planning of a response. We simply react.

How many of us have walked away from a social interaction that has not gone altogether to our liking and thought, "if only I hadn't said that" or "why didn't I say that?"

Coaching or counselling may help to change social process behaviour, as can appropriate recognition and reward. In severe instances of behavioural problems, some form of psychotherapy might be appropriate, but we would argue that recommending therapy should not be within the purview of a business relationship.

Individuals who lack application, lack the energy or desire to do a particular kind of work, are unlikely to do it well. Sometimes as people develop a certain level of skill in performing a task, their energy and desire to do so increases. Our experience is that while some people seem to have an inherent drive (or lack of it) most of us can be energised or drained by our context, especially the quality of leadership that we experience. Good leaders have often been surprised that the team that they took over which had a poor reputation does not demonstrate those behaviours when treated well.

Based on our work and the work of others, MPA – the person's ability to order complexity – cannot be changed though its effective use can be. Since greater or lesser complexity is a characteristic of the work required to create a pathway to reach a goal, selecting the person with the appropriate MPA is essential. MPA used to generate a pathway to achieve a goal requires that an individual create an intellectual construct that applies validly to the world in time and space, interprets the situation or problem and then devises a solution to the problem.

Although each pathway to a goal is unique, there are common patterns, which sort the pathways into discrete groups, or levels of work. We discuss these in the following chapter.

### Box 4.2

The concept of an ultimate MPA that differs among different people is at best challenging and at worst can be viewed by some as a basis for some of the ugliest bigotry that has been perpetuated over the centuries. The idea that some people are smarter than others has been perverted to mean they are better than others. This has been used to justify racism, slavery, even genocide.

Nonetheless, misuse of the MPA concept has happened, and still occurs, especially among those who have only partial or superficial knowledge of the theory. We have observed people with high levels of MPA, including those who believe (incorrectly) they have higher levels of MPA, demonstrate their disdain for those they perceive to have a lower level of MPA.

We want to make clear this is not only wrong, but it demeans the humanity and value of individuals of all levels of MPA. Each of us has differing capabilities to solve problems, read social situations, apply technical skills and have the energy and drive to complete tasks. MPA is only one element of the human capability to do work.

Our work rests on the proposition that if people are genuinely treated as of equal value then we are not afraid to recognise differences in capability.

## Summary

Despite the danger of misuse, the concept of MPA has made it possible for us, and others who use the theory, to explain organisational issues we have confronted for which we had no prior explanation. For example, why was this person bored and angry? Why did this manager provide no value to his or her subordinates? Why did these two managers keep getting in each other's way? Why could this person solve difficult problems, but create messes with everyday tasks?

The theory has made possible predictions of human work performance, which could be clearly formulated, tested and verified in many work environments. It has also led to knowledge of how to best structure organisations both for efficient productivity and to meet the human need for engaging and meaningful work, as will be discussed in Chapter 6.

Although each pathway to a goal is unique, there are common patterns, which sort the pathways into discrete groups, or levels of work which we present in Chapter 5.

## Notes

1 One of the authors, Ian Macdonald, working with T. Crouchman found five levels of MPA among people with severe learning difficulties. See *Chart of Initiative and Independence*, 1980. Slough, NFER.
2 See also Jaques, Gibson and Isaac, 1978, for detailed research on a theory of discontinuity.

# Part II

# Organisation Structures and Roles

Here we expand upon Part I, especially Chapter 4, which discusses human capability to do work. It is human capability that appears to be the basis for hierarchical organisational structures over centuries, despite their many flaws. The problems seem to be caused by a lack of understanding of human capabilities, especially their differing Mental Processing Abilities (MPAs).

Chapter 5 explains how differing MPAs among a population create differing levels of work. We have found eight levels of work, and in a properly structured hierarchy, there should be no more than seven levels of management (Level I has no managerial responsibilities). Many smaller organisations may have only one or two levels of management. Only the largest international corporations and some government agencies require Level VIII capability. Other organisations may be led by someone with MPA VIII, and they are likely to prosper in creative ways, even if the organisation could function quite well with lower-level capability in the Chief Executive.

Chapter 6 provides examples of employment structures that function effectively and efficiently with the correct levels of management to achieve their purpose. Chapter 7 looks at organisational roles and their authorities. We note there is high-level work that is carried out by independent contributors who have a few or no subordinates to support their work. There is also a system to preserve the correct levels of work by using specific job titles.

Chapter 8 provides a matrix of productive role relationships which can be used to sort out difficulties that arise between individuals and different units in the organisation.

DOI: 10.4324/9781003459118-7

# 5 Levels of Work Complexity

As shown in Chapter 4, people with differing Mental Processing Abilities (MPAs) create different pathways while working due to the differences in their ability to order complexity. While no two pathways are identical, each level of MPA creates patterns that are similar. The levels of work are simply descriptions of the pathways created by the MPAs of people doing work at differing levels of complexity (turning intention into reality).

**Levels of Work:** The qualitatively different complexity of pathways that must be created to achieve goals when performing work.

The levels of work form a hierarchy of complexity that if used to structure manager/direct report relationships is highly effective. Unfortunately, many organisations do not follow this pattern, put in extra layers of managerial relationships and become muddled and dysfunctional. That is one reason why the word bureaucracy has such a negative connotation.

Despite the way people have attacked and criticised hierarchy, it remains surprisingly robust as demonstrated by its continued usage for at least 2,000 years. Think of the Roman Army and the Mandarin organisation of the Chinese government. If hierarchical systems had failed, they would have been abandoned centuries ago. We do not believe this is mere coincidence; hierarchy reflects the differing MPAs of human beings. We see many of the current fads, criticisms and alternatives as misleading, even vacuous attempts to cash in on the fact that many hierarchies are not nearly as effective as they could be.

The dislike of hierarchy is often because there is a conflation of complexity and authority. If managerial relationships are based on differences in complexity of work then we have found that authority is accepted. The problem comes when there is a differentiation of authority but not complexity. That is, you say you are my "boss" and can assign me work but actually you are not adding any value. The

DOI: 10.4324/9781003459118-8

acceptance of a manager comes from doing work that adds value to my work by addressing the problems that impact on my work.

A hierarchy, when properly structured, can be a highly effective and efficient form of organisation. It is essential, however, to get the levels of hierarchy right. Our experience with a range of organisations has demonstrated the value of levels of work as the principal for building an effective and efficient managerial hierarchy based on complexity of work as we show in Chapter 6.

As one moves up the levels of the hierarchy, the pathways needed to formulate or to accomplish a task will be constructed in less certain conditions relative to tasks at lower levels. In general, as one moves from one level of work to the next, complexity increases in that:

- There are more variables to take into account
- More of the variables are intangible
- There is an increasing interaction of variables
- Results are further into the future
- The links between cause and effect are extended in time, space and logic
- Negative information (what is absent or does not occur) assumes more importance
- The achievement of the objective requires the *simultaneous* ordering of more than one knowledge field

Levels of work have been articulated in a number of different ways by various associates.[1] In this book we use different diagrams to describe the levels of work in order to relate them directly to what people are doing at each level. Each level of work is generated by the thinking processes of individual human beings. These mental processes cannot be observed directly, nor can most people describe their own mental processes. What can be observed is the complexity of pathways individuals create as they carry out their work and the common patterns in formulating the pathways they create. The levels of work are discrete because the problem-solving methodologies created through an individual's MPA are qualitatively different. Using the descriptions which follow can help you judge the level of work required in a particular role.

Each description of a level of work begins with a diagram to help you visualise the work. The little targets indicate the goal of a task at each level of work. If the diagrams are not helpful to you, ignore them and focus on the verbal descriptions. It may also help to think of your observations of work to determine how one or another description might fit that example. Keep in mind, however, that everyone has to do some work that is below their maximum level, including Level I complexity, such as using a printer or emptying a waste basket.

Finally, one warning. None of us can fully grasp our own level of work. When first introduced to these ideas, many managers and students try to analyse themselves. Some worry they may not be as able as they thought. Others develop grandiose visions of their own brilliance. In many ways we are like first-year medical students who are sure they have symptoms of every disease they study. Since we cannot change our MPA (as far as we now know), our advice is not to worry about it. Few of us use all the capability we have. Just do what we all must do, give our work our best effort, develop our knowledge and skills and deal with the world as we find it.

## Level I: Complete Concrete Procedural Tasks Correctly

### Box 5.1

Deals with one task at a time. Takes direct action on immediately available materials, requests for service or information (Figure 5.1).

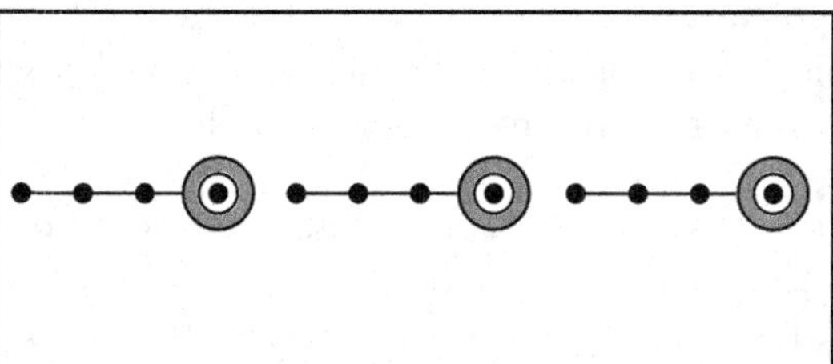

*Figure 5.1* Level I: Hands On

### Maximum Targeted Task Completion Time

- Up to three months.
- Typical task with longest targeted completion time: Minutes, hours, a day or week.

### How MPA Manifests Itself in Work

- Can carry out completely defined procedural tasks correctly. Works through continuous and direct action using known methods and procedures to achieve task output. Uses direct physical contact with the work – information, materials, machines – getting direct physical feedback as the task is performed. Needs specific concrete objectives. Requires clear rules and task steps. When problem cannot be solved, stops until he or she can get help. May need a supervisor to keep work flow moving and to solve problems. Information that is significant at higher levels of work may be missed if it is not pointed out ahead of time.

- Discretion exercised in the choices of sequential steps, large repertoires of which can be built up over time. Can develop new methods by the sensitive use of "touch and feel" adjustments to changing or unexpected conditions. In effect, this is trial and error learning from the environment. Problems solved by:
  - Calling on experience with a similar problem
  - Applying defined troubleshooting procedures previously trained for
  - Trial and error
  - The environment as trainer
  - Asking the supervisor for help with unique problems
- This activity is typically structured by agreed times for starting, finishing and taking breaks. Tasks need to be very clearly defined. Explanation of context and purpose is critical.
- This is the only level of work where it is possible to exactly demonstrate what is required and if the person repeats the demonstration they will succeed: "Watch and Learn."
- Work is not taken home. Work stops at the end of the day or shift and doesn't start until the next day or shift. (This is quite a desirable characteristic of this type of work and makes it attractive for work/life balance.)

### Information Display Preference

- Thermometer-style graph showing progress towards a goal; a run chart on his or her machine or output.

### Examples of Level I Complexity Tasks

- Direct customers to items that are available in the store
- Enrol users in scheduled training classes
- Run through a check list to solve routine user software or hardware problem with their desktop computer
- Operate a machine as directed by one's supervisor
- Fill orders at a fast-food restaurant
- Act as a security guard in a bank
- Create a business report from data provided

### Accountable For

- Working on one task at a time to achieve a specific goal. The goal (output) and the pathway for achieving that goal can be demonstrated by a direct example.
- Following instructions until the task is completed or a problem arises that cannot be resolved by using previously experienced methods of solution, or there is an understood requirement to inform a supervisor or manager.
- Improving methods through practice, on-the-job concrete experience and observation of patterns in the environment. A person operating at this level of work complexity should not be expected to articulate these observations away from the specific environment. Such operators often possess a wealth of knowledge that they have gained from experience, however, and are able to demonstrate how to improve their own work or work processes if given the opportunity.

### *Not* Accountable For

- Thinking up modifications to processes or equipment away from the task.
- Making written reports that analyse work methods.

## Level II: Diagnosing a Particular Situation

### Box 5.2

Identifies significant data from a flow of concrete events and recognises the pattern that fits the data in order to achieve the objective in a particular situation or case (Figure 5.2).

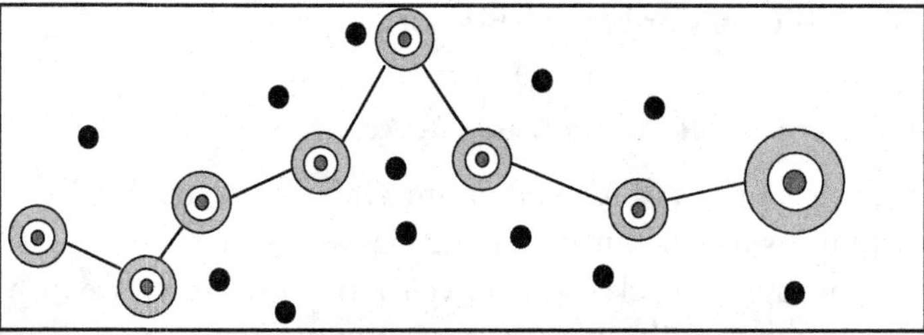

*Figure 5.2* Level II: Diagnosis to Create a Pathway

### Maximum Targeted Task Completion Time

- Up to one year.
- Typical task with longest targeted completion: six to nine months.

### How MPA Manifests Itself in Work

- Diagnoses the situation in a specific case by seeking out indicators of learned patterns (models or systems) to recognise or produce significant data. Patterns are made up of objects and relationships. While creating the pathway, identifies significant data by comparing experience with a known model or system and modifying action on the basis of this data.
- Learns patterns and methods, often through college education, for example, engineering, social work, financial analysis, nursing. Patterns may also be learned through years of experience as when a worker is promoted to become a manager at II.
- Pattern matching: person seeks out data points that he/she compares with stored patterns or systems and looks for a fit. When you have a fit, you arrive at a conclusion that what you are seeing is one of those. Data points can be abstract. Person can search rapidly through a whole repertoire of patterns that are mentally stored to match the existing data. If there is not a good match, the person keeps hunting for more data, keeping in mind a number of choices of patterns.
- Requires the ability to reflect on direct action and to explain how this has affected the chosen methodology. Can create a pathway to achieve an objective, even if the objective cannot be fully specified in advance. Can design a thing they have never seen (engineers).
- Will notice significant information even if it hasn't been pointed out in advance.

### Features of Level II Work

- First level of managerial and professional work (engineer, lawyer, nurse, police officer, teacher, scientist).
- Each situation seen as applying to a unique system of interaction or pattern. Treats each instance as a particular case and analyses it as such. Does not consider categories of cases.
- "Every case is unique." Examples of cases are:

  - My output team (Manager in II role).
  - This family (Social Worker).
  - This computer programme for this doctor's office (Computer Programmer).
  - This gear design for this motor (Engineer).
  - This patient (Nurse).
  - This crime (police officer).

- Diagnoses a situation from information available to determine nature of problem. Collects data perceived to be relevant to the diagnosis to verify it or an alternative diagnosis.
- Works within a given knowledge field (or system). Selects indicators of patterns, alternatives and methods from within a given knowledge field.
- Takes existing known methods and selects the one believed to be most appropriate for a particular situation. Loops back to alternative known systems of interaction if chosen solution does not solve the problem.
- Solves *this* problem (not problems in general). Solves the problem of the client – not concerned how this problem might interact with other problems.
- When data points fit into two or more patterns, e.g., safety, technical or human relations, person using Level II problem solving will deal with each of these separately.
- Problems are solved by:

  - Collecting relevant data.
  - Selecting a solution set.
  - Adjusting the pathway as the situation changes by selection of another solution set.

- When problem cannot be solved, continues to gather data, assuming more data will somehow lead to a solution. Does not like to ask for help from manager, though may ask a peer.

### Information Display Preference

- Bar charts.
- Last week vs. this week.
- My team vs. all teams.

### Examples of Level II Complexity Tasks

#### Managerial

- Manage people carrying out tasks of Level I complexity
- Set up a training schedule that ensures your entire team receives training in the new information modelling procedure within six months and which allows the overall production from your output team to remain steady
- Help a team member solve a non-routine problem by offering a different approach
- Provide a team member with technical direction on documentation standards

#### Direct Output

- Develop a training module to introduce the Performance Review System to Supervisors
- When directing customers, first enquire about their needs, how they will use the product they asked for in order to direct them more effectively
- Develop procedures for chemical analysis of power plant emissions
- Carry out a financial analysis of a business transaction
- Develop case information to assist a family in distress
- Teach a class in an elementary school
- Collect evidence and follow up to solve a series of liquor store robberies
- Design this part for this machine

### Accountable For

- Working on a task by fitting information to a known pattern *and* assessing the significance of the fit at the same time.
- Improving practices by articulating important differences in the way things are done.
- Managing direct, continuous activity so that it is not constantly interrupted by changes in context.

### *Not* Accountable For

- Identifying trends.
- For deciding if this is a significant problem.

- Putting together the judgements made from your own observations and applying them to other situations outside your own experience. For example, a Manager in a role at II is concerned with "my output team" not with output teams in general.

## Level III: Constructs Hypotheses and Projects Trends

### Box 5.3

From a flow of real events discerns a trend from a single knowledge field and conceptualises alternative pathways to achieve an objective, then selects the one judged to be most effective to cope with it (Figure 5.3).

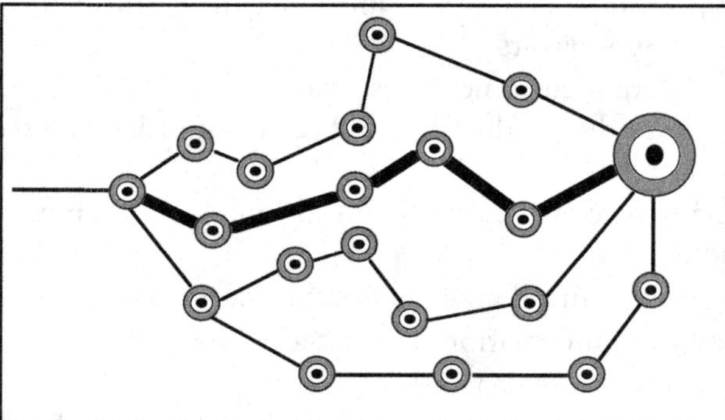

*Figure 5.3* Alternative Pathways, Systems

### Maximum Targeted Task Completion Time

- Up to two years.
- Typical task with longest targeted completion time: 18 months.

### How MPA Manifests Itself in Work

- Can consider the difference between a particular cause and a systemic cause; that is, the system itself is at fault and needs to be improved.
- Projects trends and constructs predictive hypotheses (if-then chains, "If this, then that; if that, then the other, etc."). Using a series of if-then statements, selects the pathway which best links

current activity with future requirements, taking into account such matters as cost, risk, time to completion, urgency of the situation.

- Focuses on various ways given operating goals may be achieved and selects the pathway which is most suitable for local conditions. Improves and refines existing ways of doing things.
- Solves problems by developing and testing hypotheses along branches generated from among currently conceived pathways. Concerned with current observable resources including people and methods and the effects of altering the use of them and the output by modifying the pathway currently in use.
- Takes individual cases developed at II and turns them into general statements, e.g., output teams in general not just one output team; families of a particular type (alcohol problems, new immigrants) rather than a single family; a computer programme for doctors' offices, not just one doctor, prison gangs in general, not just one type of gang.
- Once on a pathway finds it hard to change or deviate because of difficulty coping with negative information, which is seen to cause the destruction of the methodology and not as a positive indicator of a more comprehensive but more complex solution to the problem.

## Features of Level III Work

- Looks for a trend – Are problems of this type developing? What are likely to be the consequences down the road?
- Solves this problem and sees its relation to problems down the track. Will solve this *type* of problem, not just this specific problem. Categorises problems into manageable groups.
- Will ask if it is a significant problem.
- Formulates various means to reach an objective, mentally working through entire pathways to completion, not just considering the next step.
- Generates alternatives. Does not simply take the given alternatives based on a given knowledge field. Evaluates alternative pathways and selects best pathway based on situation today and projected into the future.
- Alternatives perceived as "either/or."
- Relationships are direct and linear.
- Problems are solved by:
    - Generation and test of hypotheses.

    - Choosing alternative branches from among *current inventory* of pathways.
    - Improving current pathways and systems.

- In principle can observe everything in his or her area of responsibility, though, in fact, cannot view everything at the same time.
- Can apply great depth of knowledge in a particular discipline in highly specialised stand-alone roles.
- Strives to conserve resources even when that means the purpose will not be achieved.

### Information Display Preference

- Trendlines.

### Examples of Level III Tasks

#### Managerial

- Manager of Managers at II.
- Manager of professionals at II (engineers, nurses, social workers, computer programmers, laboratory technicians, police officers).
- Can manage a unit of up to 300 people although geographical spread, technology variation and work type all have bearing on the number of people being managed.
- Prepare your unit to change over to new equipment when it arrives about this time next year. It will be similar to the prototype we've been testing. Have all your people and groups prepared for the change. I recognise this may cause a drop in productivity as people are moved about for training. If you see this going beyond 10%, let me know. I will evaluate your performance based on the smoothness and ease of the changeover which should be complete in 18 months,
- Create a system for managing the flow of work in your area of responsibility.

#### Direct Output

- Investigate and analyse a recurring problem in a production system.
- Design, with the help of a small team, a computing application to automate gas meter reading:

- Review changes going into a system/product.
- Analyse growth trends and try to foresee difficulties.
- Estimate future resource consumption.
- Take into account the nine-month lead time for hardware.
- Note system inter-relations and potential technical interactions and user interactions.
- Design test system to take into account these inter-relations and interactions.
- Ensure problems are solved in test systems.
- Ensure [system] is always in position to take advantage of most cost-effective solutions.

- Negotiate a new labour agreement with one union for your business unit (BU).
- Develop a curriculum for grades 1 through 3 in an elementary school.
- Provide medical care to patients as a Nurse Practitioner or as a doctor in private practice.
- Consult with individual client regarding their legal situation (lawyer in small practice).
- Develop a programme for dealing with gang activity in your police division's territory.

### Accountable For

- Trend analysis and correction.
- Generating alternative pathways, deciding which pathway is the best, and putting it into operation.
- Improving existing methods and systems.

### *Not* Accountable For

- Drawing out general principles while operating and deciding where and why this method could be used elsewhere.
- Actively bearing in mind the effect on alternative pathways during the process if the chosen pathway is achieving the goal.
- The construction of task pathways that require the integration of variables from a number of discrete knowledge fields and the positive integration of negative information.
- Recognising the absence of information as significant.

## Level IV: Management of Multiple Pathways

### Box 5.4

Integrates and manages the simultaneous interactions between a number of III pathways by generating patterns in more than one knowledge field simultaneously (Figure 5.4). Linkages between III pathways are "and" links; must do both at the same time.

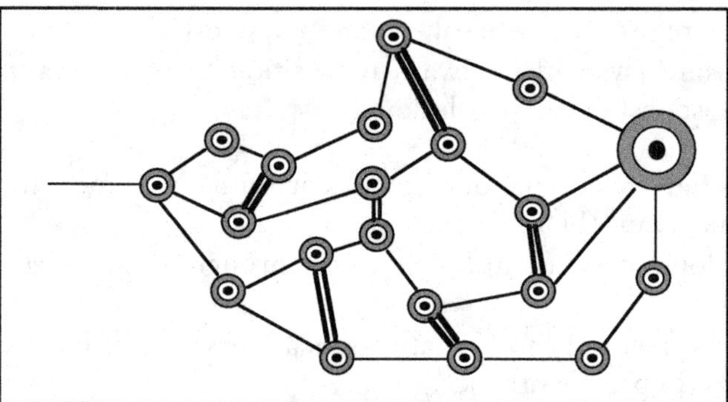

*Figure 5.4* Level IV: Parallel Processing – Integration

### Maximum Targeted Task Completion Time

- Up to five years.
- Typical task with longest targeted completion: 2 1/2 to 3 years.

### How MPA Manifests Itself in Work

- "Parallel processing" – the ability to process large amounts of data quickly and the ability to process a variety of data types simultaneously. Can use theory to understand the abstract linkages between several pathways of Level III complexity in disparate knowledge fields and therefore mesh the Level III activities so they work in concert and achieve the greatest overall effectiveness.
- Develops systems of interaction between variables from disparate knowledge fields.
- Incorporates negative information.
- Alternatives seen as "both/and" rather than either/or. Constructs predictive hypotheses with "and" linkages (if this *and* that, then the other).

- Concerned to develop alternatives to the way things are done now and bring them into being. Analyses events in terms of an abstract general model which may not yet exist, and which may not rely entirely on linear extrapolation from known events.
- Can continuously link III pathways and adjust them in relation to each other, not needing to vary each individually based on its own variables. Is concerned with interacting trends.
- IV is the first level where things may not be as they appear, e.g., although production may be up, the facility may be in trouble and vice versa. It is the first level at which theories have to be applied to develop the abstract "and" linkages between the concrete Level III entities.
- Cannot observe entire area of responsibility, even in principle.
- When none of the existing methods fit, he or she must create something new in order to deal with the problem. Invents new methods.

### Features of Level IV Work

- Looks for what is missing. Gaps in information are significant (negative information – what is not there – is significant).
- Meshes the work and demands of Level III subordinates for best overall performance.
- Generates integrative models.
- When none of the existing methods fit, he or she must create something new in order to deal with the problem. Invents new methods.
- Ensures the pathways of the Level III units are balanced and congruent with overall organisation goals.
- Compares existing methods and processes with potential methods and processes and brings the potential into existence to improve organisational operations. Can imagine the impact on social relationships of a technical change.
- Must consciously sacrifice resources at times in order to achieve priority objectives. This is the first level where people can see the value in sacrificing some elements (resources) of their area of responsibility in order to achieve the overall good of the organisation. (At III, people will try to conserve resources even when this leads to a bad outcome.)
- The language is often of trade-offs and conflicts.
- Can manage by exception.

- Problems are solved by the simultaneous resolution of the "because this then that" hypothesis generation. Must test a process in more than one knowledge field allowing for the interaction of the systems (hypotheses) being generated in each field, i.e., "it might work OK here, but it does not work over in that field so it cannot be a solution to the problem."
- Knowledge fields still look something like trees, but there are links among the branches, and over time there will be links between the trees. One tree might be drawn with dotted lines indicating a hypothetical path that can be compared to an existing path.

## Information Display Preference

- Pie charts that allow comparison of whole units.

## Examples of Level IV Tasks

### Managerial

- Manages a function in a BU such as sales or production.
- As part of a three-year programme to improve quality, a General Manager (IV) agrees to the particular 18-month paths put forward by each of his Unit Managers (III) – in Engineering, Technical Services, Operations, Technical Support, Training and Personnel – as part of this programme. He then adjusts and keeps in balance the rate of progress in each of these Units, adding or withholding resource allocations as necessary, and calling for changes in a pathway when required.
- A corporate survey has shown that what appears to be a commitment to safe working practice by the group leaders is seen by the group members as hypocrisy. They hear a lot of noise but see no real commitment by their leaders.

  Your task is to change the work behaviour of the group so that its members do work safely. Our current lost time incident (LTI) rate is 91, yet a few similarly sized businesses are running at 5 to 10. It may be worth your while to visit a couple of these. I can help with introductions if you wish me to. I suspect you may find there is more to the methods they have used than first meets the eye. The process of change will be a slow one I know, particularly in the first 12 months, but you should be seeing some results in 18–24 months. I am prepared to accept a 2% budget increase in the first two years if this is needed, and I realise there may be some union heat in the early stages. I will use the LTI rate as an indicator of your performance on this task.

- Costs of sales are going through the roof. Examine the system of manufacturer's reps we are using and see if we can't develop a better sales process. Keep in mind we need the reps for some parts of the business, but there may be other selling methods for other parts. The total transition to a new system should be complete in three years, and I don't want to lose any reps if we can help it.
- Lead a police division (often a rank of Captain in large departments).

### Direct Output

- Advise a business client as to the legal repercussions of a sexual harassment lawsuit.
- Develop a science curriculum that is fully integrated with the math curriculum for a school district.
- Examine the balance of the whole computing operating system and, given the direction of the company and its competitive environment, compare alternatives regarding the technology of systems design; assess whole new technologies taking into account your manager's seven-year objectives; and provide him or her with expert advice regarding alternative technical directions for the department.
- A chief geologist explores a newly leased property for signs of rare earth metals which can be mined to meet increasing demand.
- Carry out a line of research to assess the implications of mRNA vaccines in order to develop improved vaccines to replace current vaccines and develop new vaccines for diseases that have no effective vaccine to prevent their occurrence.

### Accountable For

- Creating an abstract model which links apparently independent events in the work, e.g., the work society of the division.
- Producing an explanation that allows for the testing of a general idea, i.e., not limited to an actual specific situation.
- Guiding Managers (III) on different paths so that their work is complementary.
- Continuously generating alternative Level III paths. Keeping in mind the effect on alternative pathways during the process even if a chosen III pathway is achieving its goals.

- Remaining concerned with ends, not becoming wedded to existing means for achieving those ends.
- Leading by using ideas and images.

### *Not* Accountable For

- Synthesising all the pathways to create a whole business entity.
- Reconceptualising a whole business entity.

## Level V: Shaping the Organisation within Its Environment

### Box 5.5

Shaping and managing an organisation within its environment – maintaining the organisation's systems and processes that allow the entity to be self-sustaining in the environment so that the entity continues to be viable in the environment as both entity and environment change over time (Figure 5.5).

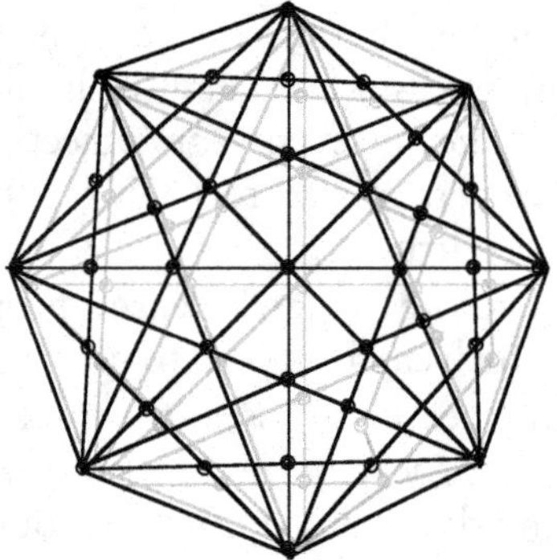

*Figure 5.5* Level V: Whole System in the Environment (Isaac and O'Connor, 1978:95–120)

### Maximum Targeted Task Completion Time

- Up to ten years.
- Typical task with longest targeted completion: Five to seven years.

### How MPA Manifests Itself in Work

- Uses entire theories and not just principles to link multiple knowledge areas or disciplines.
- Interacts with the system's environment to modify it so the entire entity progresses as a unit.
- Manages an entity – which is a unified whole system (organisational entity or area of expertise) by synthesising the relationships of Level IV pathways into one complex model. In the theory, all the sub-parts are explicitly interdependent, and it can be shown how they all affect one another, thus allowing the prediction of second- and third-order effects of change in any one (or more) sub-part(s).
- Combines Level IV entities into a unit (whole P&L business, public agency, NGO or grand theory) in a way that allows it to be managed as a self-sustaining entity. Guides the entity through the conflicts between the entity and its environment modifying the entity to have it prosper in its environment.
- Notices both figure and ground. Will notice a space in the organisation's environment that the entity can fill (a shift in the ground) and will also be able to deal with external demands that require a shift in the entity (the figure).
- Negative information becomes far more important and is used extensively.
- The entity may be a stand-alone business of national scope, a BU of a large corporation, an army division, a charity or a set of social and/or intellectual and artistic constructs which form an accepted whole in the society at any time. The significant issue is that the entity forms a whole and the work at V requires the ability to recognise a mismatch in any field of knowledge which the entity uses as an integral part of its functioning and to resolve this mismatch. The work of V is associated with boundary conditions and the recognition of changes in them. The work at V consists of recognising when and where the entity begins to become out of touch with its environment and modifying the entity internally so the mismatch between the entity and its environment is resolved.

### Features of Level V Work

- Dual perspective: Looks inward to create working systems of the organisational entity; looks outward to ensure adaptation to entity's environment. The systems and processes may be functioning well internally but may require change in spite of this because of a misfit on the boundary.

- Sets and communicates the purpose of the entity.
- Symbolises the entire organisational entity and its purpose – based on changes in external environmental factors, can reconceptualise the purpose.
- Problems are solved by applying theory to control the entire system while considering second- and third-order consequences.
- Complete integration of a set of systems; able to identify indirect and distant linkages.
- Data are both concrete and abstract, observable as well as not observable. Linkages now make clusters of knowledge areas look like a dense network. Impact on one part of the network will potentially have impacts on all other parts of the network, and these remote linkages are understood. Linkages, direct, indirect, remote (changing this data point or relationship will have an impact at a distance in space and/or time).
- Knowledge is dense in areas of interest. An individual with V MPA will not be satisfied with data that do not fit into existing knowledge. Such a person will examine why they do not fit or if they fit into some other area of knowledge.
- Knowledge areas are often collapsed into a single data point, e.g., knowledge about unions, labour board, safety regulators, local government. These collapsed knowledge areas can be expanded at will to deal with a particular issue at hand.
- Relationship can be:
  - Direct: Action affects A.
  - Indirect: Action affects A, and A affects B.
  - Distant: Action affects A, and also affects Q, which is distant in either, or both, time and space.

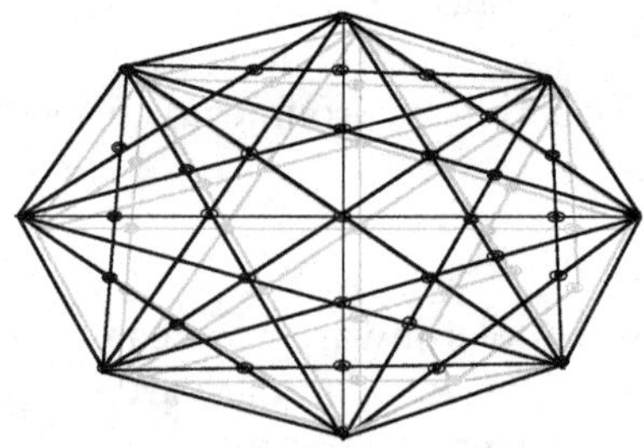

*Figure 5.6* Changing Shape of Business

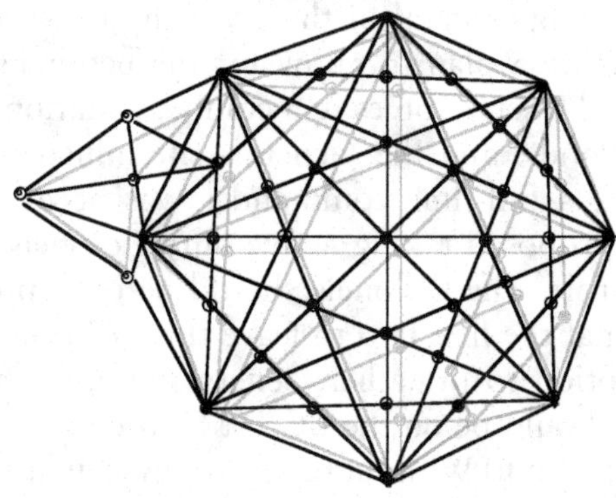

*Figure 5.7* Develop New Space to Grow Organisation

- Changing boundary conditions.
- Internal demands may require changing the shape of the business (Figure 5.6).
- A change in the external environment may open up a space, providing an opportunity for growth (Figure 5.7).

### Information Display Preference

- Uncertain due to insufficient data.
- May prefer to "manage by exception" – see only that information which does not fit within given parameters.

### Examples of Level V Tasks

#### Managerial

- Manage an entire corporate BU integrating product development, product production, product sales, plus service and support functions.
- A technical change is being planned within a production process of the BU. The executive in a role at V should be expected to be able to identify and take into consideration the impact of that technical change on the lives of families whose members are employed by the BU and be able to make a sound judgement about what aspects of that change are the work of the BU and what aspects of the change should be no business of the BU because they fall within the preserve of the family unit to make its own informed decisions about itself.

A Commanding General of the US Army Reserves (AR) was ordered to create a plan to allow for the better integration of active duty and reserve forces in a combat situation. There were 28 AR commands, and the General determined that in order to be effective a full-time commander was necessary for each of them. He proposed taking active duty Colonels and putting them in this role. The Colonels should be of appropriate capability such that the first two to leave this position would leave with a promotion to Brigadier General (BG). (In other words, the Colonels should be on the BG list before their appointment to the AR command.) Without this, the new structure would fail.

The distant relationship the General wanted to affect was the understanding in the officer corps that the AR command was a position from which one got promoted, not a terminal one before retirement. This would ensure the right officers applied for the positions over time.

- The determination of what systems within the BU will be changed as a result of new pollution control legislation. New rules require the development of a new knowledge area – determining where the new knowledge area goes through the business – where relationships within the BU link to data points within the knowledge area. How existing knowledge fields regarding regulators will have to be reconfigured.

### Direct Output

- Create a software architecture to link current and future computing systems and to reduce the time necessary for applications production and maintenance, keeping in mind the current hardware/software configuration as well as future technologies which are being developed worldwide to ensure this networking architecture will be able to accommodate technological advance.
- Design a salary administration system and a performance evaluation system that mesh seamlessly with each other and demonstrate the corporation's commitment to the shared values through the eyes of our managers and workforce.
- Conduct research in entirely new fields. Create general theories.

### Accountable For

- Predicting the effects of change in one aspect of the entity on all other parts.

- Creating a business identity and culture from the constantly shifting events and their consequences using the tools of leadership – behaviour, systems and symbols.
- Setting overall direction of business targets and objectives.
- Working on the general and the particular simultaneously.
- Meeting short-term goals, while simultaneously progressing long-term goals and the entity's long-term viability.
- Understanding the environment's likely impact on the entity and taking action to adapt the entity.

### *Not* Accountable For

- The development of a programme of direct action beyond the entity in order to influence the environment in which it operates (e.g., may be accountable for directly influencing the political, economic and social variables at the national level but is not accountable for the development of the plan of action to do so.)

## Level VI: Shaping the Future

### Box 5.6

**Level VI:** Modifies the environment to allow Level V entities to prosper (Figure 5.8). Shaping the organisation of the future – creating the ethic on a national and international basis that allows entities to function and manages the relationships between entities of a significantly different character.

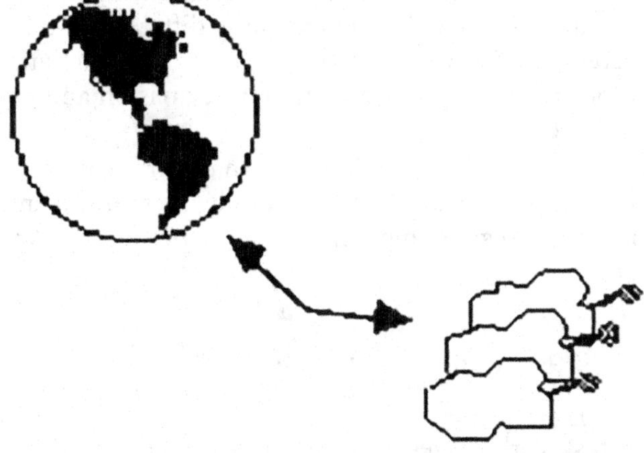

*Figure 5.8* Shaping the Future Globally

### Maximum Targeted Task Completion Time

- Up to 20 years
- Typical task with longest targeted completion: 12–15 years.

### How MPA Manifests Itself in Work

- Gathers information from a myriad of knowledge areas, including emerging knowledge areas, on a global basis. Builds networks of resources to be called on to help solve complex issues.
- Is able to form relationships by understanding what are sometimes very different perspectives and how they might be addressed productively.
- Interprets, interacts with and modifies the political, economic, social, technical and intellectual variables in the environment to stabilise it for whole (Level V) business entities. This requires international networks and an understanding of trends beyond the immediate business of the organisation. Interprets the changes in the environment for business entity leadership. Shapes business entities from the outside.
- Whether in government, business or non-profit organisations, people at this level describe their work as "political." This involves building constructive external relationships with relevant leaders and opinion formers.
- Within the organisation, leadership is demonstrated primarily by symbolism and observable example.
- Must make decisions involving unpredictable and unknowable circumstances.
- Is able to simultaneously manage the relationship between two social organisations with fundamentally different cultures; built on different assumptions and premises, e.g., seniority and meritocracy, business and government, marine division and navy carrier task force.
- Concern for operating within an ethical framework so that the organisations are acceptable in their environment. Goes beyond simple legal compliance to set expectations for ethical behaviour.

### Maximum Targeted Task Completion Time

- Up to 20 years.
- Typical task with longest targeted completion: 12–15 years.

### Features of Level VI Complexity Work

- Leads a group of business entities or a Corps made up of several army divisions.
- Sets conditions within which business entities operate, e.g., "Do not take foreign exchange into account as you make your plans, corporate treasurer will manage that."
- Can create mutually beneficial relationships between groups that may seem adversarial, e.g., a mining company and an environmental NGO.
- Influences social policies through direct engagement with political, social, legislative, technical and economic entities to moderate the environments of the business entities he or she manages.
- Interprets overall corporate strategy to the BU managers to keep unit and corporate direction aligned.
- Because longest tasks may take 15 years to come to fruition, he or she will begin tasks that will be completed by others and will complete tasks begun by a predecessor.
- Long-term goals are set and policies and corporate systems are shaped and audited to achieve them.
- If this work is done well, the businesses experience a stable environment in which to operate that brings confidence to the business and stimulates innovation and growth.
- If this work is not done well, businesses are constantly exposed to unexpected and major problems that are destabilising and distract attention and drain energy from the business (Feltham, 2004).

### Information Display Preference

- Uncertain due to insufficient data.
- May be P&L statements from BUs. Probably prefers to "manage by exception." Graphic display of complex data comparing BUs with each other and with industry benchmarks.

### Examples of Tasks of Level VI Complexity

#### Managerial

- The Deputy Chief of Staff, Personnel (DCSPER) of the US Army, directs the modification of officer training and development to have future officers prepared to function according to the Doctrine projected out for 25 years. It will take a series of DCSPERs about 15 years to complete this task.

- Determine the size and shape of businesses under your leadership and their relationships with investors and other key stakeholders to ensure alignment with the corporation's strategic directions.
- Sell or liquidate declining businesses or bring in new management to foster their growth and success. Provide necessary resources to businesses the organisation wishes to grow.
- Recommend a new business venture in a new market or with new products in an old but growing market.

#### Independent Contributor

- These people may or may not find a place in an employment hierarchy. Often they are independent researchers, writers, consultants, engineers, architects, lawyers or doctors. They will often have national and probably international reputations.

### Level VII: Sustaining a Successful Long-Term Future

#### Box 5.9

Takes into account worldwide trends that will affect the viability of the organisation over a 25–50-year time span (Figure 5.9).

*Figure 5.9* Constructs Alternative Pathways for a Corporation or Army

#### Maximum Targeted Task Completion Time

- Up to 50 years.
- Typical task with longest targeted completion: 25–40 years.

### How MPA Manifests Itself in Work

- Comprehends fundamental forces driving changes in the environment (national and international). This involves global trends that may affect economic, social, political, technological, environmental and intellectual forces far into the future. Develops predictive hypotheses based on that understanding to position the corporation (or government or NGO) to take account of the fundamental forces.
- Takes account of these fundamental forces to construct long-term plans and actions for the organisation's growth and viability. This involves the creation of new Level V organisational entities and the winding down of existing Level V business entities.
- Creates an ethical framework that will allow the organisation to thrive in its social environments. "We have to do what is right." There is a concern for society not just narrow self-interest.

### Features of Work of Level VII Complexity

- Strong ethical dimension. Must create an ethical framework for the entire organisation.
- Construct a series of plausible strategic pathways for the organisation, knowing they will have to be modified as events, problems and opportunities evolve over time, to best align the organisation with the fundamental forces that will drive the environment and therefore the direction of the organisation.
- Where necessary assign tasks to people in Level VI roles to take action to modify or mitigate some of the effects of the fundamental forces to give the organisation more time to develop its strategy. For example, delay the timing of regulations to mitigate global warming to give the organisation time to make the necessary adaptations.
- Develop and promulgate a consistent standard that allows the organisation to operate successfully in many societies, e.g., "we do not take or give bribes." "We treat our workers with dignity and provide decent working conditions in all countries in which we operate."
- Will not see the beginning or the end of most tasks that must be undertaken.
- International networks will include CEOs from comparable organisations, prime ministers and other cabinet officers, legislators, other people of superior accomplishment whether in science, medicine, law, education, foundations, think tanks. Will keep regular and consistent contact with his or her network.
- Will lead major charitable and fund-raising drives for health, environmental, education institutions and other philanthropic causes. May sit on the board of a philanthropic organisation.

### Information Display Preference

- Uncertain due to insufficient data.
- Manages by exception. Graphic display of complex data showing worldwide trends.

### Examples of Tasks of Level VII Complexity

#### Managerial

- Lead a multinational corporation or NGO and ensure its long-term viability by creating an ethical framework that, when followed, will make the organisation acceptable in the societies in which it operates.
- Recognise that global warming is a reality and estimate the likely effects this will have on his or her organisation. Begin taking steps to mitigate these effects or to adapt the organisation to the likely future environment.
- Lead a large army such as the US Army, Europe (four-star general).

  Re-align the BUs, or divisions, of the organisation to take on entirely new products, markets or types of warfare.

#### Direct Output

- Develop the long-term strategy for the continued growth and prosperity of your organisation.
- Create the Training and Doctrine for the US Army.
- Design a health care system for a nation that is scientifically sound, financially stable and politically feasible.

## Higher Levels of Work

As we discuss Levels VIII and IX, we are in an area where we believe we see higher levels of work, but real data is not easily available. We believe people with these types of MPA exist, but we can only give some examples of some individuals who appear to work at these higher levels. We have not met any of the examples cited; we are merely hypothesising based on publicly available material.

### Level VIII

- Maximum targeted completion time at VIII is up to 100 years. People at this level create worldwide institutions that enable fair governance on global issues: conflict or climate change. These people are trying to address the most complex problems on

Earth: conflict, wars, poverty, climate change and the resulting migration of people leaving areas that are no longer habitable.

- One example of someone working at this level might be Robert Schuman. He was born in Luxembourg and became a French statesman who conceived the idea of the European Coal and Steel Community and worked for economic and political unity designed to lead to the establishment of a "United States of Europe." The purpose was to prevent future wars such a World War I and World War II.[2] His work led to the creation of the European Economic Community in 1957, which became the European Union in 1993.
- At this level an individual may create Stratum VII organisations – organisations that can be sustained by a Chief Executive at VII. Alfred Sloan who created General Motors or Bill Gates who created Microsoft might be examples. When multiple Stratum VII organisations must be managed as a group, it is probably only done successfully by someone with at least MPA at Level VIII. Thomas Watson, Jr., might be an example in his development of IBM. Colin Powell, Chairman of the Joint Chiefs of Staff of the US military, may be another example.
- An early example might be the Secretary of War under Theodore Roosevelt, Elihu Root. He and then Army Chief of Staff Leonard Wood set in motion reforms to the US Army that began in 1903 but did not achieve full fruition until 1953, over 50 years later.

### Level IX

- Maximum targeted completion time at IX would be 200 years.
- Creates Stratum VII, and perhaps Stratum VIII organisations, while also creating the social and political context in which they operate. Theodore Vail who created the 20th-century AT&T beginning in 1907 is said to have recognised that telephones would operate most efficiently if they were run as a monopoly. People would not be willing to pay several different phone companies in order to speak with all their various friends and business associates.
- On the other hand, the early 1900s was an era of trust-busting, and Vail realised a monopoly would not be acceptable unless it was regulated by the government. He also recognised that if there was a single federal regulator, one bad decision could put AT&T out of business. Thus, he developed the system of state Public Utilities Commissions. These provided the necessary regulation, but bad decisions in one state would not threaten the business.
- General George Marshall might be another example. In 1942 when it was widely believed World War II might last for a decade or more, and victory was still far from certain, Marshall assigned

a task to one of his subordinates to plan for the defeat and occupation of Japan and Germany. He specifically said he did not want to repeat the mistakes made after World War I that he believed led directly to World War II. He was not only framing the strategy to conduct war on a scale never before seen and selecting the Generals who would carry out that war, he was also planning for the aftermath of war taking into account not only the military but also the social, political and economic contexts that would have to be brought into existence (Neustadt and May, 1986:247–248).

- Konosuke Matshushita, the founder of Panasonic (Yamashita, 1988), may suggest an even higher level of work. In the 1930s he created a 350-year plan for Panasonic. He said, "I will carry out the first 50 years of the plan and those who follow will carry out the rest." The plan was carried forward despite such "*minor*" disruptions as World War II.
- "The mission of an enterprise is to contribute to society." "To succeed in business requires more than just hard work. I must always be aware of my responsibility to society." Each person must believe, "I am doing worthwhile work that benefits the company." The management philosophy means that the individual employee is recognised as a valuable part of the enterprise (Yamashita, 1988:90).
- "A good company is one whose products, policies and employees have earned the respect of its community. A company can survive only by doing work that is valued by society" (Yamashita, 1988:32). This concern for the entire society, in the context of building a business enterprise, may be an indicator of higher MPA.
- Could there be higher levels of work than those we have described? Perhaps; we do not know the limits of the human brain.

## All Levels of Work Are Essential

While we can recognise the extraordinary MPA of certain individuals, and it may be interesting to speculate as to who they might be, most of us work at less exalted levels. This does not mean we have less value as human beings; it simply means we pattern and construe the world differently and that we have differing abilities to carry out work.

Businesses, government agencies and non-profit organisations are all work societies, and if they are to meet their goals and survive, they must have people within their organisations who can work at the levels required to achieve their goals in their respective environments. The quality of work carried out at all levels of the organisation will determine the quality of results obtained. Thus as human beings we should delight in all levels of work. We all have something to contribute to the whole.

## Role and Person

Although work roles have minimum mental processing requirements, individuals who fill those roles may or may not have an ability to match those minimum requirements. There are people in roles with requirements that exceed their MPAs; others are in roles that require less than their full MPAs. The issues that surround the match or lack of match between the capability of the person and the complexity of the work of a role are of vital importance to the organisation, which must set up and operate systems to deal with them. It is also of vital importance to the individual who prospers when the match between person and role is in balance.

As a continuing reminder that the work of a role is a function of the needs of the organisation, and the organisation being an element of a wider society, it has no alternative but to structure work according to its own requirements. The level of work of a role does not tell you much about the MPA of the role incumbent. If the person is successful in a role, it is safe to assume he or she has the required knowledge, skills, application and MPA. Beyond this minimum, the role the person currently fills tells you little about the person's MPA. This is a very good thing because it makes clear we cannot pigeon-hole people based on their current job. Because the question is always open, the intrinsic humanity of the individual must be respected.

### Box 5.10 Appropriate Terminology

The correct usage is to refer to "a person in a Level II (or III, or IV, etc.) role." **Never** say a "Level II person" or a "Level V person." That form of description is both insulting and demonstrates ignorance of the theory.

People have the potential to develop and grow in their capacity to handle higher organisational roles throughout their lifetimes as they grow their knowledge and develop their skills through opportunity and experience. The work a person can accept accountability for at any given time depends not only upon their MPA but also upon the knowledge, skills and drive they have developed by using that MPA.

Early in their careers, persons of higher MPA may be able to solve quite complex problems if they have the knowledge and the access to data to do so. One of the key limiting factors is often the lack of authority to get access to data. This is demonstrated by the opposite situation that occurs in the military during war. In war, casualties or other circumstances require young officers to take over higher levels of command; those with high MPA have again and again demonstrated they can perform superbly. By formally taking over the higher level of command in the armed services, the organisation recognises, and in fact mandates, that they gain the authority and opportunity to have access to necessary information.

Bearing this in mind, it may be that we do not adequately use the high-level talent in our organisations due to traditional rules and ways of doing business. For example, many governments and other organisations have rules that one must be in a role for a certain number of years before promotion can be considered. The underlying reasoning appears sensible since greater experience will usually provide people with more knowledge of patterns that can be used to solve complex problems. Nonetheless, such rules deny individuals of high MPA the rapid development of which they are capable. Provision of opportunity to gain information and test relationships within knowledge areas is arguably essential to rapid development of capability in the early years of employment and in too many organisations this is denied except to a special few who are selected for the "fast track."

From the experience of many managers, those of high MPA can bring that ability to bear on a particular problem, even when they are in lower-level roles. Their manager and manager-once-removed (see Chapter 7) may still judge that such a person may not have the *capability* to take on higher-level organisational roles, but they can contribute to a high-level project team. As will be shown later, roles in organisations that require the continuous use of higher MPAs also require that accountability for decision outcomes be carried for longer spans of time. This capability develops by growing knowledge and developing skills, especially social skills, the lack of which may de-rail more careers than any other factor.

As capability matures (as individuals use their MPA to extend their knowledge and skills) they can carry accountability for higher levels of work. Unlike knowledge or experience that can be enhanced through training and opportunity, at present we do not know of any ways for enhancing a person's MPA in adulthood.

The current theories of brain development suggest there is both a genetic and an environmental component to the development of MPA. Today's brain research suggests that most brain development takes place during pregnancy and the early years of life (thus environmental factors, it is believed, are extremely important). When MPA stabilises, we do not know, though it is tempting to think of it as stabilising around the time of puberty or perhaps around 20 when so many other physical elements achieve maturation.

Essentially, what we are providing is a language to describe differences you can already observe, but may not have had a clear language to articulate. You may have found it difficult to state just what the differences or similarities are, especially when the content of the tasks are quite different. This process is made easier when you have a language to describe the differences in complexity. The levels of work described here provide such a language. These levels of work have been identified in a number of different research studies, and they have been tested in practice in business, governmental and voluntary associations. There are also descriptions of the types of tasks found in organisations, which can be completed by people using the MPAs associated with that level of work complexity.

We also stress that we have talked about a meritocratic, managerial hierarchy based upon a hierarchy of complexity of work. Not all work has to be done in a managerial hierarchy; not all organisations are appropriately managerial hierarchies. Churches, universities and law firms/partnerships, for example, are properly organised in different ways, but all will need to understand the complexity of work to be done and who is able to do it.

**Box 5.11 The Importance of a Person's Worth**

We cannot overemphasise the danger of equating MPA with the worth of a person. A person's worth, in our view, is not calculated just by how "clever" they are, and we must not confuse an organisational hierarchy of work with a hierarchy of worth. People contribute much, much more than intellectual ability to life and society. (For the dangers of misuse, see Freedman, 2016.)

It is these levels of work that make it possible to create more effective organisations where people can have a positive work experience. As we will show in Chapter 6, when the levels of work in an organisation match the differing levels of work complexity found in the human population, organisations are more profitable and better able to serve their customers or clients.

## Notes

1 The original formulation of levels of work was articulated by Elliott Jaques (see his *General Theory of Bureaucracy*, 1976). Our formulations rely heavily on his original work as well as that of Ian Macdonald (1984), Gillian Stamp (1978, 1984) and the contributions of Isaac and O'Connor (1978) and Rowbottom and Billis (1977) plus the unpublished contributions of Larry Ingraham, Lucy Lofting, Carlos Rigby and Roy Feltham.

2 Retrieved June 29, 2023. https://www.britannica.com/topic/European-Community-European-economic-association and https://www.britannica.com/biography/Robert-Schuman

# 6 Organisation Structure

## Introduction

As we discuss organisation structure, it is important to note that *The Work of Management* deals primarily with Employment Hierarchies – their structures, systems and leadership. It is also important to recognise these employment hierarchies do not exist on their own. They are subordinate to the Associations which create them. These two aspects of an organisation are often muddled in current management literature and thinking.[1]

**Association:** "Associations are formed by people coming together for a purpose. The purpose is either agreed tacitly or expressed in a written document" (Brown, 1971:48).

We are all members of associations. If you are a shareholder, you are a member of a business corporation. If you are a worker, you may be a member of a union. You may serve as a volunteer, a member of the Red Cross that is a Non-Governmental Organisation (NGO). In the United States, as a citizen you are a member of several governments – city, county, state and federal. A partnership is a form of association as is a university. Associations may be religious, involved in sport, medical, legal or scientific endeavours.

Larger associations' members elect representatives, usually termed a Board of Directors, to govern the association and set its purpose and policies.

**Employment Hierarchy:** "...that network of employment roles set up by an association of people to carry out work required to achieve the purpose of the association" (Brown, 1971:49).

DOI: 10.4324/9781003459118-9

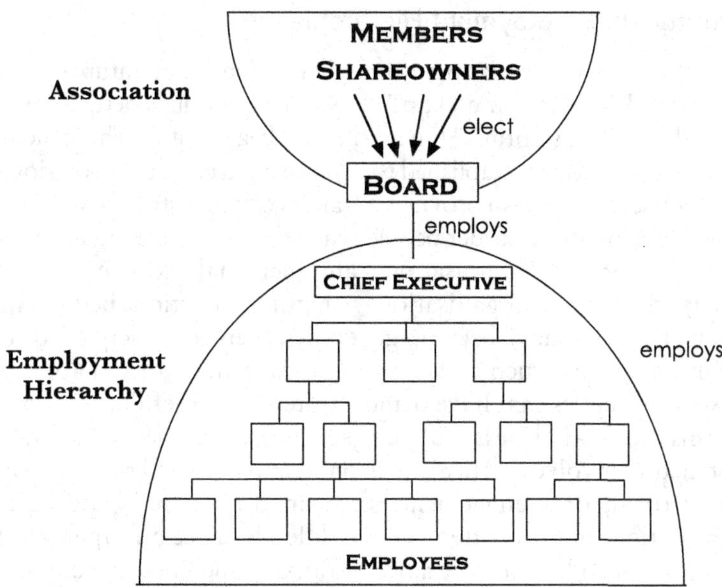


*Figure 6.1* Association and Employment Hierarchy

Employment hierarchies begin when an individual entrepreneur or a governing board is authorised to employ an individual to work to achieve the association's purpose. When the workload becomes too large for one person to handle, this person is authorised to hire additional employees within constraints of the association's objectives, budget, personnel and policies as set by the Board, a legislature or the membership.

Figure 6.1 illustrates generic patterns of member, representative, "governing board" and employee relationships as found in businesses. With some variations there are similar patterns in governments and NGOs.

The failure to make distinctions between these two aspects of organisations leads to endless difficulties and confusion, both theoretical and practical. These two institutional forms differ and the roles of individuals within them differ fundamentally. To be an elected representative of an association is profoundly different from being an employee of that association. Even where terms like "leader" or "accountability" are applied to both roles, the ideas and the lived reality behind these terms are significantly different.

What follows is the most effective structure of an employment hierarchy. This is where the work of managers takes place.

## Structure in Employment Hierarchies

Organisation structure is largely marginalised in the literature of management. "It's boxes on a chart." "It's not how things actually work around here." "It's boring." On all this, we beg to differ. The structure of an organisation is established to achieve a purpose, the provision of goods or services. It also provides a framework to distribute work and provide the necessary order people require in a positive organisation.

The history of organisations and personal experience show clearly that some organisation structures function better than others, but there have been no generally accepted principles for the generation of a structure for an organisation. In this chapter we present principles that have demonstrated their usefulness in many organisations – business, public agencies and non-governmental.

Structure involves vertical, horizontal and diagonal relationships. The vertical, or management, structure forms the spine of the organisation, but this often gets muddled because an organisation of any size also has salary grades or ranks, which become confused with managerial levels. Thus, you have the excess layering found in many large organisations, in other words, a dysfunctional bureaucracy with all its messy, cumbersome, stultifying to employees, slow and inefficient characteristics.

There is a better way which has been tested in many organisations. It has been proven to improve efficiency and effectiveness as well as improve the quality of working life for employees. As discussed in Chapter 5, the differences in Mental Processing Ability (MPA) explains, we believe, the levels of work and why the hierarchical structure has remained so prevalent over centuries even when the actual designs have deep and recognised flaws.

### Box 6.1 The Logic of Hierarchy

(1) Work is the process of turning intention into reality

(2) To do this one must use one's MPA (think) in order to make choices as to what will achieve your purpose and then you must act upon them to bring them into reality

(3) People have different ways of processing information and solving problems

(4) There is a pattern to the differences in the ways human beings process information which are described as Levels of Work

(5) If one wishes to get work accomplished (as required in any organisation), it makes sense to structure the organisation in a way that is in accord with the thinking patterns of the human beings who are asked to do the work

## Levels of Work in People and Organisations

**Organisational Level:** A band across an organisation in which all the roles have a similar distribution of work complexity that replicates the differing MPAs found in the human population.

Thus, we divide the levels of work found in humans into broad levels of work in organisations that replicate the MPAs found in the human population, as illustrated in Figure 6.2.

Each level of work has an upper boundary which reflects the maximum time a person at a particular level can project into the future as necessary to complete a task. These maximum targeted completion times mark the discontinuities between levels. Level I in the organisation describes the complexity of work of MPA 1 and has a maximum targeted completion time of three months. Level II comprises work of Level II complexity with a maximum targeted completion time of one year, and so on up the hierarchy.

Each organisational level requires, respectively, the qualitatively different MPAs found in the human population and requires the creation of pathways of differing complexity. As one moves up the organisational hierarchy, the complexity of these pathways increases. The complexity of the work required of the chief executive officer (CEO) of the organisation establishes the top level of the organisation.

The number of layers of management an organisation requires is determined by the level of work required of the CEO and where the output of the organisation is produced that is sold or delivered to clients or customers. For example, if the CEO must work

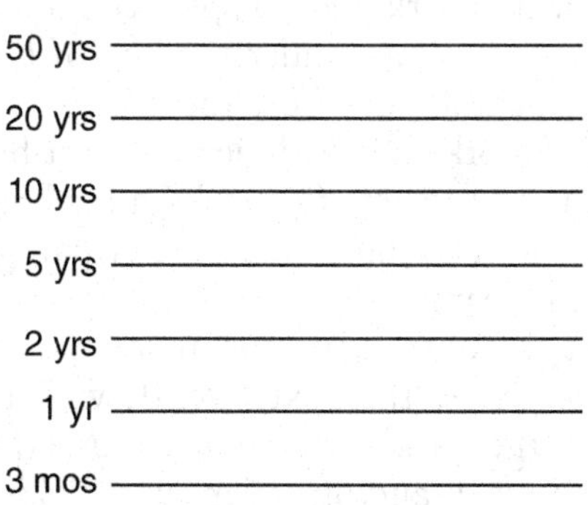

*Figure 6.2* Maximum Time Spans of Organisational Levels

with the fifth level of complexity (Level V) and the products are produced by workers in a traditional factory at Level I, the organisation requires five levels of work. This means there will be four levels of managers, including the CEO. In another organisation, the CEO may work at Level V, but the output of the business is carried out at Level III. In this case there would be a need for three levels of work.

Clearly, not all types of organisations, such as family, tribal businesses or partnerships, can use the structure we have tested and found to work in employment hierarchies; they still need to operate based on the reality of differing levels of work, but not as managerial hierarchies.

The employment hierarchy, whether business, government agency or NGO, is established to have a number of people to do work. The sum total of that work achieves the purpose of the organisation. Therefore, the structure of the organisation should be based on the work people need to do.

A structure with one level for each level of work complexity up to the maximum required to achieve the organisation's purpose has proven to be the most successful over time.

Assigning tasks of a specific work complexity to employees who have the capability to do the work successfully in each role not only gets the work done, it is satisfying for the people doing the work, thus creating a positive organisation.

## Matching Person to Role

To be effective in a role at any specific work level, an individual must be able to exercise discretion in order to turn intention into reality at the required level of complexity. That person must have the capability (knowledge, technical and social skills, application, MPA) to carry out the work and accept accountability for it. Each individual must also have an understanding of the next level up, that is, they must be able to follow the processes involved in the next higher level of work, and critique and contribute to that work but not be able (as yet) to act effectively in the higher role or take accountability for it. This understanding is part of the basis for communication and teamwork.

Similarly, to be effective, a person must also be able to fully articulate and encompass the next level down – have a complete understanding of the processes involved in creating pathways such that they can teach and/or assign work. This does not mean

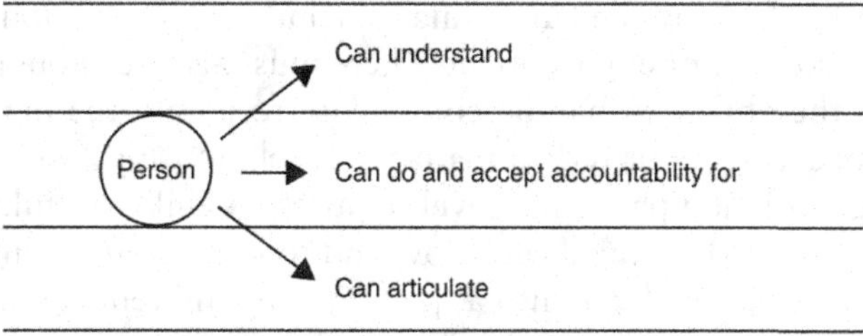


*Figure 6.3* Individual Relationships to Work Levels

managers must have all the technical expertise of their subordinates. It does mean they must be able to articulate the tasks and their context, so that the subordinates can use their expertise effectively to achieve organisational purposes (Figure 6.3).

## Significance of Work Levels for Organisation Design

The work levels form a depth structure for employment hierarchies. They form the vertical skeleton for an effectively functioning organisation. The skeleton is based on two principles:

> Managers are placed one work level above their direct reports (or team members).
> In a single chain of command, there is never more than one manager within a given work level.

The reasons for these principles are rooted in differences in the levels of work found in the human population. For individuals to be perceived as managers by their subordinates, they must be involved in work of significantly different complexity from the subordinate and operate in a longer time span. The combination of higher complexity and longer time span gives managers a larger worldview. This broader horizon, or "big picture," allows them to set the context for their subordinates, and thereby provide a stabilised and understandable setting to allow the subordinates' work to proceed effectively.

The managers' work must be significantly different from that of their subordinates, if they are to add real value by assigning the work to be done by the subordinate including a discussion of the expected context or environment. There must also be enough difference in the ability to handle complexity to justify the manager's authority is consistent with a managerial relationship.

Doing work at a particular level requires an ability to fully *comprehend* the work of the level below and to *transform* the information from the level above into a qualitatively different state, which sets the context for the level below. It is not simply the aggregation and transfer of information, but the transformation of it by seeing how the information shapes the direct report's work and work environment.

Research has shown that people in the hierarchy who are said to be the "real boss" are people who are perceived to do qualitatively different work and to have a range of authorities in relationship to their subordinates. The common elements in this range of authorities are the Veto Selection, Assign Tasks, R3 Recognise, Review and Reward, Initiate Removal from Role (VAR$^3$I) authorities. (See Chapter 7.)

Too much difference between the manager's and subordinate's work also causes difficulties because the subordinate will not be able to understand the manager's perspective. The manager, in turn, becomes impatient with the subordinate's lack of understanding and inability to "keep up." This is true in the vast majority of manager/subordinate relationships, but there is an exception in the case of secretaries and personal assistants where more than one level difference is acceptable (Figure 6.4).

Whether the distance between manager and a direct report is too great or too small, the result is a work environment that is not well ordered. There is a waste of effort and energy because direct reports are frequently unsure about what they are to do and which factors are within or outside their authority. Management must reduce uncertainty and anxiety by taking accountability for the environment within which their team members work.

This can only be accomplished when there is neither more nor less than one work level difference between manager and subordinate. This allows each individual to understand the work above, generate and accept accountability for the work at his or her own level and articulate the work below.

### Value Adding Management

In an organisation where each level of work sets a context for those below, every level of work adds clarity and value, and

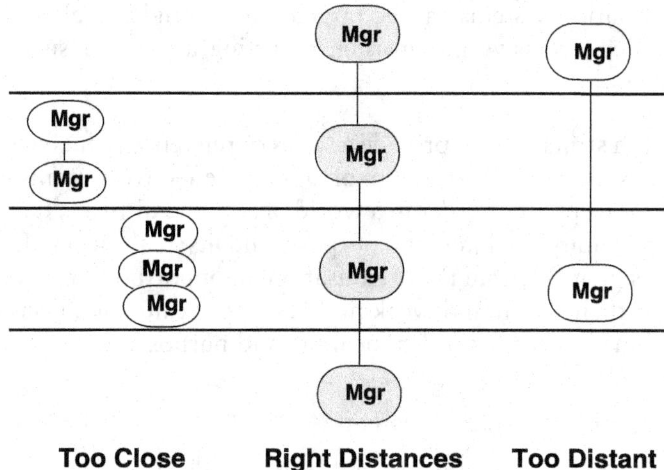


*Figure 6.4* Managerial Distances – Right and Wrong

each role acquires dignity for the contribution it makes to the functioning of the whole. The stabilised environment each level provides to the one below allows direct reports to concentrate on their own accountabilities and authorities in completing their tasks.

A properly structured organisation removes the impediments to effective leadership and management. It provides the necessary, though not sufficient, conditions for an effectively functioning organisation – one where the purposes are clear, the structure supports the purposes and people have the necessary space to exercise discretion in the pattern indicated by the multi-modal distribution of work complexity.

Removing excess managerial layers clears the structure, making possible other benefits as well.

- Priorities can be set because the manager has a larger perspective than his/her team members.
- Team members gain a clearer understanding of what is expected of them.
- Team members are given an opportunity to use their full capabilities in exercising discretion in jobs which are the right size – neither too difficult nor too boring.
- Role relationships can be regularised with no need for by-passing to get adequate direction for work.

- Information systems can be targeted to the right level of work, avoiding excessive monitoring, reporting and other such time wasters.

The depth structure can provide a series of reference points to guide managers in the construction of a more effective organisation. It provides a point of order in a world of seeming disorder. It allows an opportunity to integrate purpose and its realisation. It also provides people within the organisation an opportunity to increase order in their social and working lives – to create conditions that meet human needs for order, meaning and purpose.

### Work Levels and Salary Grades

Work levels are broad spans within which the complexity of the work is essentially similar. Each level has its own pay range which recognises the differences in work complexity in each level. There is no overlap between the pay ranges of each level.

There is also a need for pay bands within each level to distinguish those who are just entering a level of work – performing towards the lower bound of the work level – and those who are performing at the top of the work level. Some organisations use three pay bands within a level, though we have found two overlapping pay bands are sufficient (Figure 6.5).

In many organisations pay bands have become a de facto system of titles and a stand-in for the organisation's management structure. As there are typically more salary bands (or grades) than organisational levels, using salary bands as the de facto organisational hierarchy leads to the excessive layers of management so widely decried as bureaucracy, but rarely fixed.

In the management structure we recommend, the manager-once-removed (see Chapter 7) decides which salary band is appropriate for a particular role, using guidelines set by the organisation. These guidelines are always associated with the size and immediacy of the impact of the decisions required in the normal course of the work of the role. Within that band the manager decides, based on assessment of work performance and hence differential reward, what the actual salary of the individual employee will be.

Advancement can come about in three ways:

(1) Salary Adjustment: change of pay within a salary band.
(2) Upgrade: moving from one salary band to the next.
(3) Promotion: moving from one work level to the next.

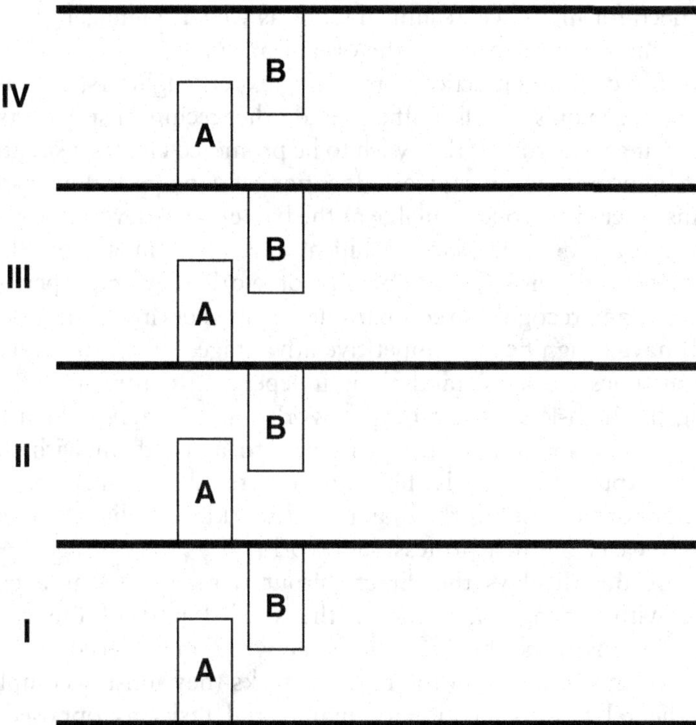


*Figure 6.5* Work Levels and Salary Bands

An adjustment in pay within a salary band is the manager's decision. Upgrading or promotion usually requires a recommendation from the manager and the decision of the manager-once-removed.

When they first hear of the stratified approach to organisation, some employees become concerned about their opportunities for advancement when there are only five levels of work in the entire business unit. The potential for advancement in pay within a salary band, for upgrading to a higher salary band and for promotion to a higher work level, is an important distinction which allows for recognition of superior work performance and growth in capability.

## Managerial and Professional Work

When it is recognised that it is the complexity of the pathway which determines the level of work, it becomes obvious that technical specialists or professionals may do work at the same levels of complexity as that done by managers. In each work level there may be a need for high-level technical work as well as managerial work depending upon the goals of the organisation.

The too common practice of requiring expert engineers, computer scientists, geologists, police officers and other technical specialists to enter managerial roles if they wish to be promoted creates a situation where important technical work does not get done (or is done badly) because there is no one available at the higher work levels to do it.

Organisations that place technical specialists in a work level commensurate with the complexity of work they must perform (with pay and recognition comparable to managers in the same work level) have a significant competitive advantage. Such professionals may at times work as stand-alone independent contributors (ICs) doing the high-level direct output work, or they may have a few (three to five maximum) direct reports to assist them with their direct output. When an IC has subordinates she/he must manage those subordinates, but the managerial workload is light allowing them to carry on their professional work.

Figure 6.6 displays the direct output work shown as a clear circle with managerial work as the shaded part of the circle. This demonstrates the differences between managerial and IC roles which are found in the types of tasks they must accomplish and the relative proportion of managerial tasks as opposed to technical tasks. The difference is not in levels of work because both professional/technical work and managerial work may require the creation of pathways of the same complexity.

To reinforce understanding of this equality of work and to maintain the depth structure of the organisation, it is useful to assign titles to roles that indicate the level of work and whether or not the role is managerial or professional. Such titles should be picked with care since they become drivers of the principal function of the role. The examples shown below provide an example of how titles might be structured, though in different societal and organisational cultures different titles may be chosen.

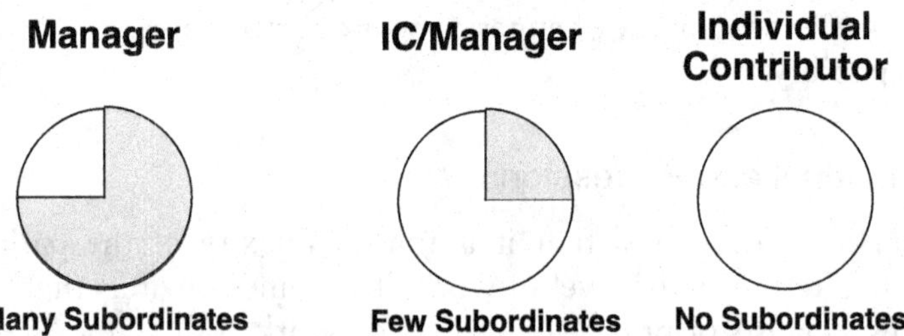


*Figure 6.6* Two Types of Managers and an Individual Contributor

**Note:** There is no room for an *Assistant* General Manager or a *Deputy* Unit Manager. The absence of such titles makes it much more difficult to insert people into hierarchical levels where they do not belong. The use of titles reinforces the stratified structure, making it much more difficult to slip back into the old ways leading to stultifying bureaucracies (Figure 6.7).

| Titles for Level V Business Unit – Examples | | | |
|---|---|---|---|
| **Work Level** | **Organization** | **Manager** | **Professional** |
| V | **Business Unit** | **Vice President** | **Corporate**<br>[Corporate Human Res Cons]<br>[Corporate IS Tech Cons] |
| IV | **Division** | **General Manager** | **Chief**<br>[Chief Applied Technology]<br>[Chief Organization Advisor]<br>[Chief, PC Technology] |
| III | **MRU or Unit** | **Unit Manager** | **Principal**<br>[Prinicipal Personnel Advisor]<br>[Prinidipal Syst. Programmer] |
| II | **Output Team or Service Team** | **Superintendent** | **Specialist**<br>[Operations Sched. Spec.]<br>[Applications Devel. Spec.] |
| I | **Crew** | | **Supervisor***<br>**Operator/Clerk**<br>[Printer Operator]<br>[Library Clerk] |

*** Not a managerial role.**

*Figure 6.7* Titles for Each Level of Work

MRU stands for Mutual Recognition Unit. Any three-level organisation under a single manager is an MRU whatever the level of the work. The term MRU comes from the social and organisational requirement for all people in a three-level unit to be able to recognise one another by name. While it is the manager who properly decides on the recognition and reward of a subordinate, it is the manager-once-removed who decides on upgrade or promotion. Hence the need to know one another. The Output Team may refer to any two-level part of the organisation under a single manager.

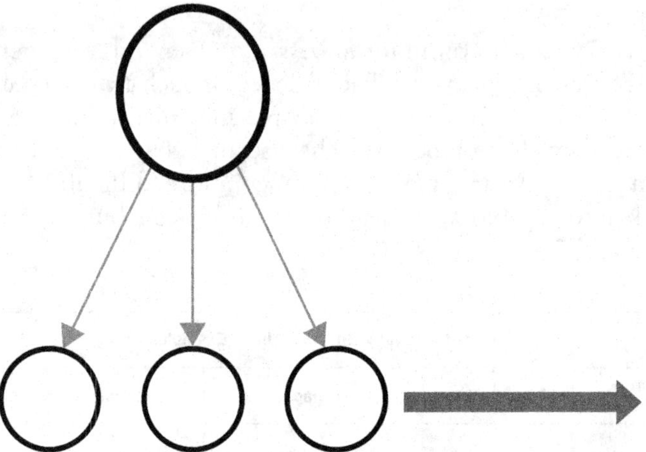

*Figure 6.8* Delegated Direct Output (DDO)

### Three Types of Manager – Direct Report Relationships

In most organisations when they think of a manager, they think of someone who assigns tasks to their direct reports, who then carry out the work of producing the output. Following Jaques (1976:252–257) we call this Delegated Direct Output (DDO) (Figure 6.8). There are, however, other managerial direct report relationships, first articulated by Jaques, that are necessary in most organisations.

This is the most familiar organisational structure where the direct output may be produced by direct reports or further down the hierarchy as in a factory where the output is produced at Level

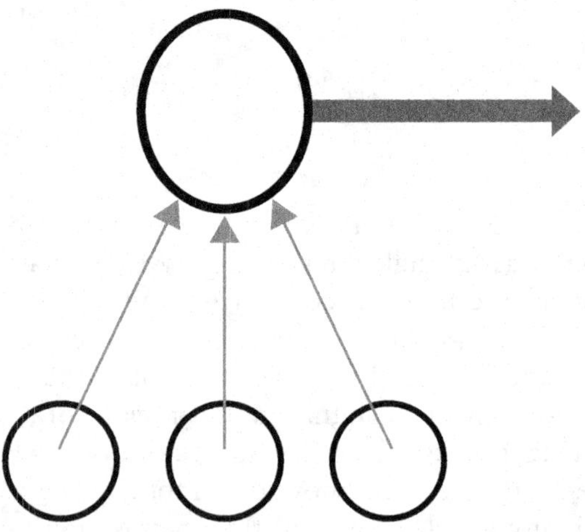

*Figure 6.9* Aided Direct Output (ADO)

I and the manager assigns tasks, provides feedback and review and evaluates the quality of work performance being carried out by direct reports or others further down the hierarchy (Figure 6.9).

This type of management is where the manager produces the output with the assistance of, typically, a few direct reports. It is needed in professional work such as computing application development, architecture, engineering or research where the manager does the major design and development work. The direct reports follow the manager's design and take on tasks that contribute to the manager's output. For example, in architecture, the architect-manager is responsible for the overall design of a building to meet a client's needs. The team members may design the water or electrical system to fit into the overall design as conceived by the lead architect-manager (Figure 6.10).

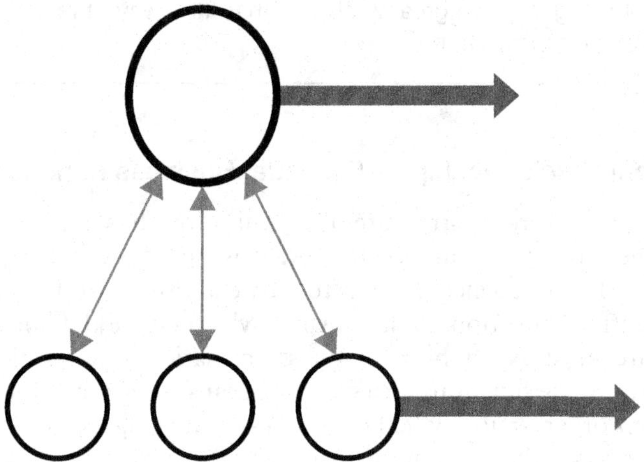

*Figure 6.10* Direct Output Support

This managerial relationship is often found in sales organisations where the sales representatives call on customers, purchasing agents and clients to sell their products or services. A higher-level manager, such as a vice president (VP) of sales, may call on a peer VP in the customer organisation such as a VP of purchasing to reinforce the work of the salesman working at a lower level of the potential buyer.

**Box 6.2 The Importance of Aided Direct Output (ADO) in the Management of Professionals**

Imposing the DDO model in all parts of an organisation can create considerable difficulties. Burke worked with an Information Technology Department in a large organisation, where the presenting problem was that technical people did not know how to manage people effectively. They did too much of the work themselves and did not delegate to their direct reports.

After speaking with a number of managers, they made clear if they did not do the work, their subordinates were not capable of doing it. Higher-level management was always telling them to delegate, not do the work themselves. Introduction of the ADO model made all the difference. At all levels of the organisation they recognised there were two ways to manage within the department. Productivity and employee satisfaction increased and the ADO managers were greatly relieved that their way of managing was the right way after all.

## Horizontal Relationships – Essential Business Functions

Although the vertical structure of organisations has been the most ill-defined and problematic element, it is not the only structural element of consequence if one is to create a positive and successful organisation. Functional relationships which define the horizontal structure must be in place if the organisation is to achieve its purposes. Some functions are essential because they must be carried out if an organisation, whether business, public agency or not-for profit, is to survive and thrive over time.

### Operations Work

This is the core work of the organisation – provide a product or service – which is its purpose, its reason for being.

**Develop** new product/services.

- Research, test, evaluate for purchase, create, adapt new products/services.

**Produce** a product/service to meet customer/client needs. Must be concerned with quality and quantity of output, cost of output, reliability of product/service.

Sell product/service to customers/clients.

- Inform customers/clients about products and their qualities and capabilities.
- Discover customer/client needs for which business might provide products.
- Negotiate agreements to meet customer needs.

Although government agencies typically do not sell products or services, they do need to inform their clients, or customers, of services that are available. They need to develop an understanding of the public's needs in relation to the services they provide. As they learn about unmet needs they must inform their executive and legislative institutions, and recommend budget changes or new legislation.

Not-for-profit agencies have a similar function – informing potential clients, learning of client needs, responding to client questions, informing their product/service development people of the need for new products/services. They must also "sell" their credibility to actual and potential funders.

### Box 6.3 What about the Army?

Years ago Elliott Jaques worked with the US Army on some organisational issues. In using these concepts they could not figure out how "sales" related to their organisation. Finally, they came to realise that the intelligence function was, in fact, a "sales" function – trying to find out what the "customer" did *not* want and when and where they *didn't want it*. Production was then to deliver it in combat. "Our function is to deliver ordinance to an unwilling and combative customer."

The terms from business don't quite fit the military situation, but knowing your enemy – their strengths and weaknesses – is an essential function.

(Jaques in Conversation with Burke)

### Service Work

Service work supports the organisation by keeping the business up and running to enable it to continue to supply product/services and to maintain the work flows and processes which provide product/services. The service function is to ensure the continuity of the organisation – to safeguard the human and physical assets of the business and to handle routine maintenance.

Service work is focused on the internal operations of the Business Unit. Their work is to support the operations work, to remove impediments to efficient performance, to enable the operations to function productively. Operations work cannot go on for long unless there are a variety of services provided to sustain it. Examples of service work follow:

- Employees must be paid.
- Materials and supplies must be purchased.
- Facilities must be cleaned and maintained.
- Corporate financial resources must be accounted for and controlled.
- Contracts and records must be written and kept.
- Computing systems must be purchased and maintained.
- Transportation services.
- Warehousing.
- Laboratory analytical services.

### Improvement Work

Although organisations rarely neglect their customers (since they do not remain in business very long if their customers are dissatisfied), they often neglect the internal improvement of their own productive capacity. Managers typically underestimate the quality and quantity of work required to improve productivity, so crucial improvement roles are frequently understaffed (if they exist at all).

Improving work is concerned with future developments in particular fields of expertise to allow improvement of the business over the longer term. Improving work is high-level intellectual work which is complex and time-consuming. In the long term, an organisation's competitiveness is determined by the quality and quantity of its improving work.

Improving roles provide expert advice to managers and their immediate subordinates as they systematically examine ways in which their performance can be improved. If improving activities are not assigned, the urgent tends to drive out the important. Keeping the business running supersedes the need to make it more productive and better run in the future. To ensure continuing improvement, improving activities should be carried out personally by the people assigned to improvement roles rather than through their directing a team of subordinates. Improving roles typically have few, if any, subordinates.

While less obvious, this work is critical for the future well-being of the organisation. This is the work of analysing the current situation and suggesting improvements. This work requires reflection, analysis and the ability to make proposals. It may include improvements in the design and implementation of systems.

### Improving Roles

- Exist because managers must have ready access to expert advice and to have work performed in the areas of organisation and human resource systems; economic, material and information flows; and technologies.
- Are created to ensure the organisation is using the currently best tools, best methods, best techniques, best processes in its operations.
- Identify, evaluate and implement better ways of doing and supporting the business.
- Improve the work flows and processes which "do" the business and support it.
- Recommend policies and procedures in their area of expertise for implementation by their manager.
- Do project work for their manager. On request may also do project work for their peers.
- Are pro-active – seek out new ideas, get out and about the organisation to identify opportunities for improvement.

#### Box 6.4 Improving Roles Deal with Higher-Level Complexity

- Must be at least one level above work flow or process, technology or human resource systems to make their deployment more effective
- Require disciplined knowledge of processes and their limits

### Improving the Organisation

(Human Assets and their Deployment)

Concerned with improving human resources systems.

Improving task assignment/task reporting systems.

Improving the deployment and development of people.

- Provides expert advice and makes recommendations regarding issues of organisation structure and human resources to manager and peers.
- Develops policy recommendations for manager regarding personnel practices, safety, training programmes, management development.
- Provides expert advice and administrative support to manager for his/her work of assessing the potential of the manager's subordinates-once-removed.
- Develops quality improvement proposals.
- Contributes to manager's business plan regarding deployment of human resources.
- Exchanges information and ideas with other organisation-improving roles in the organisation and with external organisations and professional societies.

### Improving Work Flows and Schedules

(Economic, Material, Information, People)

Must ensure the right things happen at the right time, in the right sequence. Concerned with optimising the balance of business activities – business plans, priorities, resource flows, work scheduling.

- Contributes to a manager's business plan regarding priorities, resource flows and work schedules.
- Provides expert advice and makes recommendations to manager and peers regarding:
  - Business plans.
  - Resource flows.
  - Work schedules.
  - Improving scheduling and priority settings.
  - Optimising the flows of resources – cash, materials, inventory, stock levels.
- Develops policy recommendations for the manager regarding business systems.
- Develops quality and safety improvement proposals.

### Technical Improvement

(Technical Processes and Methods)

Concerned with ensuring that the currently best available methods/technologies are applied to the specific problems/opportunities encountered in selling, developing, producing current or future product/services and in the work of supporting these mainstream functions.

- Provides disciplined knowledge, expert advice and makes recommendations regarding how to make best (most productive) use of existing technical processes to manager and peers.
- Evaluates new technical processes with an emphasis on improving the quality of results, safety and productivity of the organisation.
- Suggests, evaluates and sometimes executes projects or studies to bring about technical improvements in the organisation.
- Develops policy recommendations for his/her manager regarding technical standards for the manager's organisation.
- Provides expert advice on the development and provision of technical training programmes for the Division.
- Develops quality improvement proposals.
- Exchanges information and ideas with other technical improving roles in the organisation and with external organisations and professional societies.

Bringing all this together, a large corporation or public agency might be structured as shown in Figure 6.11. Public agencies have more constraints on their organisation structure since their limits are set by legislatures and the elected executive. They may also use different terms to describe each function, but the basic pattern will be similar if they have developed a stratified structure.

### Box 6.5 As a Practical Matter, All Employees Have Doing, Service and Improving Components to Their Job

Employees are expected to use their resources productively (doing)

Employees are expected to use their resources properly and maintain them in good order (service)

Employees are expected to continually seek to find a better way of using or maintaining the resources (improving)

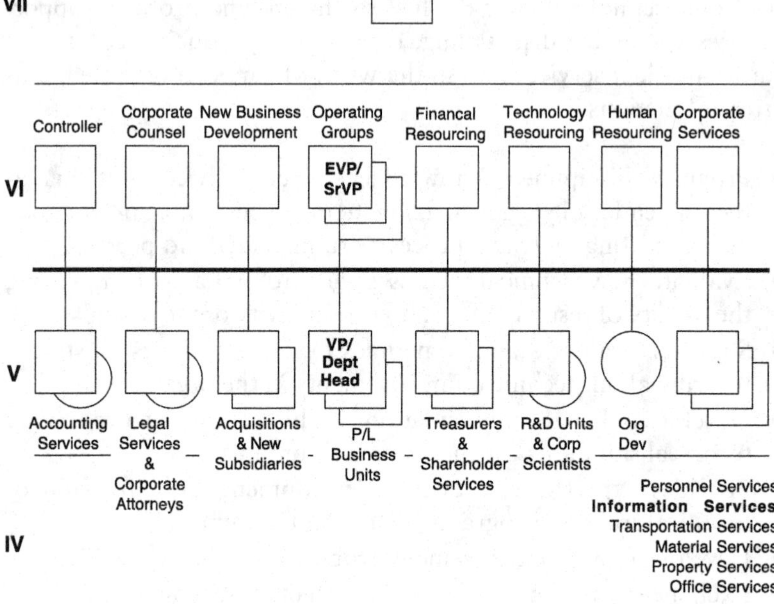


*Figure 6.11* A Stratified Corporate Structure (The Circles Indicate IC Roles, the Squares, Managerial Roles)

## Summary

We have argued that people think differently and approach problem solving in their own unique way. There are, however, patterns to these differences that are described in the Levels of Work. Further, by following these patterns as the vertical structure of the organisation is created, your organisation will work with human nature and not struggle against it. We have also described horizontal relationships – the basic organisational functions which are linked to vertical managerial roles.

In Chapter 7, we extend these ideas examining the use of authority and power in employment hierarchies. We have found these authorities of managers and other vertical roles are necessary if managers are to accept accountability for their own work and the work performance of their direct reports.

## Note

1 Brown, Wilfred (1971) *Organisation*. London: Heinemann. Jaques, Elliott (1976) *A General Theory of Bureaucracy*. London: Heinemann.

# 7 Authority, Power and Vertical Relationships

## Introduction

As the levels of work clarify why a hierarchical organisational structure can be effective and efficient, such a structure requires good leadership from the vertical, managerial roles that form the spine of the organisation. This chapter describes the authorities required for managers at different levels to accept accountability for the work performance of their direct reports.

Before we do that, however, it is essential that we clarify what we mean by authority and power. Systems Leadership is based on the proper use of authority in organisations. It is one of the most important concepts in creating a positive organisation. While we recognise that power is used in organisations and can be effective, more often we have found it hinders and makes it difficult, or impossible, to create positive organisations.

Some of the difficulties and misunderstandings of terms like power and authority reflect their origins from political theorists analysing the power of rulers (usually kings) and the problem of why power was sometimes felt to be legitimate or illegitimate. Their thinking gave rise to two common definitions of power and authority which still influence our thinking.

**Power:** The *ability to act*; capacity for action; sometimes used as the ability to act even when opposed – the ability to impose one's will upon another.

**Authority:** Legal or rightful power; a *right* to command or act; legitimate power; power exercised within legal and moral limits.

In organisations the issues regarding authority and power are concerned with social processes relationships between people. Therefore, we need definitions that deal with the reality of human relations within organisations (see Box 7.1).

Both power and authority, as defined above, can be (and are) used in work hierarchies. Both can be used to achieve an objective but an organisation based on power takes a significant toll on its employees

DOI: 10.4324/9781003459118-10

### Box 7.1 Authority and Power

**Authority**: The exertion of will in the context of the mutual acceptance of agreed limits

**Power**: The exertion of will while breaking one or more limits of authority

In an organisation if A wants B to do something that A wishes, then A is using authority when he or she is:

1) Requiring B to act within the limits of his/her role description
2) Requiring B to act within the limits of role relationships, i.e., that it is clear that A can require B to do something
3) That B is required to act within the existing policies of the organisation
4) That B is required to act within the limits of the law
5) That B is required to act within the ethical framework of the organisation or within custom and practice providing it does not breach 3 or 4 above
6) Further, the context of the relationship assumes that B has freely entered the role, i.e., B has not been coerced or appears to have no other choice. We will explore these elements below

**Power**

If A uses power without authority to influence B to do something, then in bringing that influence to bear, A breaks one or more of the six conditions above, or it is clear that B has unwillingly entered into the role. A has asked B to do something that is:

1) Outside the limits of his/her role description
2) A does not have a role relationship that acknowledges the right to ask for this action
3) Requires B to violate one or more of the existing policies of the organisation
4) Requires B to break the law
5) Requires B to act unethically or outside existing custom and practice

and is detrimental to psychological safety and well-being. These are organisations with stressed employees. Power relationships may often be experienced by one party as being treated like an object. Organisations based on power require a lot of energy to protect one's turf, to gain more turf, to manipulate others to act and to avoid accountability. This drains energy from the productive work of the organisation and causes burnout in some employees.

Power-based systems also alienate a large portion of the workforce. Some studies have indicated that only 15–20% of the American workforce thrive in a work environment dominated by power relationships. The other 80–85% find it debilitating and demoralising to have to deal with *favouritism*, *power games*, *office politics*, unclear accountabilities, blame placing and decisions based on who will gain power rather than their effects on the long-term viability of the enterprise.

The organisations that we propose provide conditions where clear systems of authority and accountability can be created and enforced. Such systems of authority and accountability show respect for human dignity and drive out unauthorised power networks and thus release tremendous energy for productive purposes.

Managers (and other employees) are empowered – more able to act – but they act through authority systems, within limits that are subject to review. Their ability to act derives from a clear grant of authority from the organisation, which holds role incumbents accountable for the proper exercise of that authority. In a positive organisation, people identify with the purpose of the organisation. They advance by demonstrating their capability to do work.

The sources of authority (see Figure 7.1) provide constraints on that authority that go beyond the individual organisation. Some limits – the social customs and practices, the national, state and

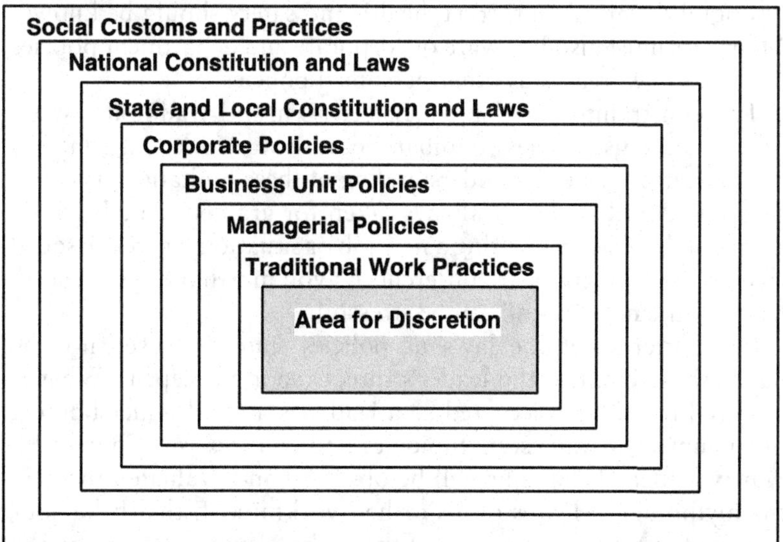


*Figure 7.1* Sources of Authority and Constraints

local laws – apply to all work in a society. In businesses and other employment settings, policies set by the association, its governing board and its managers also apply.

1) Social Customs and Practices.
   These often exist below the level of consciousness, and are accepted as the way we do things in our society. Social process skills mostly apply in this category.
   Traditional Work Practices are a part of accepted social custom and practice in this organisation or in this industry or union.
2) Law – Constitutional, Federal, State, Local.
   These are promulgated by legislatures and administrative agencies of government.
3) Organisation Policies.
   Set by the organisation's charter, its Board and top executives; in the case of government by its authorising legislation and elected or appointed executives.
4) Specified components of a task.
   Its context, purpose, quantity and quality of output, resources and time – set by the manager making a task assignment.

   (See Chapters 2 and 3 for more on work and tasks).

Federal, state and local laws are becoming more complex all the time. Even though the more esoteric details of law may not be familiar to all managers, the basics regarding non-discrimination, wrongful dismissal, anti-trust, health and safety should be known. Managers must also be aware of corporate and department policies in these same areas plus other personnel policies.

The constraints posed by social custom and traditional work practices are usually less familiar. Because we work in a coherent social environment, the understanding of these limitations is rarely articulated and is almost always taken for granted. One becomes aware of them when entering a new job or situation where the social customs and practices are different. As you may have experienced, learning the new "rules" can be stressful.

No matter what the laws or policies state, however, no one has authority unless the leader's direct reports accept it. What is required to be fully accepted as a leader is a good understanding of the universal values, mythologies and cultures (see Chapter 9). A new leader's behaviour will be observed and evaluated through the mythological lenses of his or her workforce. If that behaviour is placed at the negative ends of the scales of universal values, the

### Box 7.2 Royal Courts vs. Positive Organisations

We have observed that organisations that run on power appear to function like a royal court. At court, the only thing that matters is to please the monarch. It is critical to be "in favour" or "to have the ear of the monarch." As is seen in many television dramas, the Wives of Henry the Eighth or Game of Thrones, this promotes in-fighting, cliques and elites that are more concerned with power than with productive results. People advance by manipulating others, starting and spreading rumours that denigrate rivals and withholding knowledge from others. While this can be fascinating to observe, it is hugely wasteful and damaging to many people.

This contrasts with Positive Organisations where people identify with the purpose of the organisation. Capability to do work is paramount and working relationships and authority are explicit and mutually understood. The overall purpose of the organisation and purpose of the roles are more important than status and personal standing.

Our experience is that while the Royal Court produces much more intrigue, gossip and content suitable for television and film, it can be a most destructive place to work. The Positive Organisation is both productive and a healthy place to work. It makes a real contribution to society.

leader is unlikely to gain full acceptance of his or her authority even though the workforce may go through the motions based on the authority of the role.

## Managerial Roles and Their Authorities

Authority always operates within limits. Lawful organisations must act within social customs and practices and follow the laws of the societies in which they operate, as illustrated in Figure 7.1. There is still, and must be, an area for an employee to exercise discretion. While authority is given, its acceptance will depend upon the Social Processes used to enact it.

### Earning Authority

No matter what the laws or policies state, however, no one has authority unless the people the leader is trying to influence accept it. The necessity for a manager's subordinates to accept his or her authority is often not widely acknowledged, except perhaps in the cases of demarcation rules and other restrictive practices found in some industries.

The need for acceptance of authority also may become apparent when a member of a non-dominant group such as a minority or woman becomes a manager in an organisation where only members of the dominant group have been managers. Such people will be very much aware of the need to earn the acceptance of subordinates if they are to exercise the authority of a manager effectively.

Authority without the ability to act effectively is empty. This usually happens when managers are placed in roles that exceed their capability. They may lack the Mental Processing Ability (MPA) to do the job or they may lack other abilities and are therefore unable to influence and exercise their will with their subordinates. This may be seen as weakness or sometimes cowardice. People do not like to work for a manager who is perceived as weak, because such a manager cannot help to advance their careers, nor can such a manager command the respect of others who are necessary to gain better assignments or increase the pay of high-performing subordinates.

In addition, there are times when a good leader must exceed his or her authority in order to achieve a larger purpose for the organisation. This always carries risks, especially if something goes wrong, but it is sometimes necessary. When such power is exercised for what is perceived as a good or right purpose, it is usually applauded and seen as an act of courage. When done for a self-interested purpose, it is viewed at the negative end of the scales of shared values – dishonest, cowardly, unfair, lacking respect for human dignity.

One final point. Subordinates do not have to like a manager's authority for it to be real, nor do they have to dislike it. What they must do is accept it for it to be real and effective.

If your subordinates and your manager – in his/her position of representing the organisation – agree generally upon your authorities and their limits, you have a position of balance and understanding. In some cases it may be necessary to seek to expand such limits, but one must always be aware of the dangers of exceeding them.

## Managerial and Professional Work

> **Definition of Managers:** Persons who are accountable for their own work and the work performance of their direct reports over time.

As noted in the introduction, this defines all managers as leaders of people; they have no choice. Their only choice is whether to be a good or bad leader. Here we will discuss what such leaders require to accept accountability for the work performance of their direct reports. In Chapter 6 we discussed the differing management roles as well as described Independent Contributor (professional) roles. Here we are focused on the authorities of vertical managerial relationships.

### Vertical Authority Relationships

The authorities in all the vertical relationships discussed in this chapter were developed out of an understanding of the minimal authorities required if someone is to accept accountability for their work as a manager. By understanding the four basic authorities of the manager, it becomes easier to follow the variations on this vital relationship that have been developed for the other vertical relationships.

It is important to appreciate that all roles require the exercise of social process skills to an acceptable level of competence. There are no roles without role relationships, but some roles may not require the social process skills of leaders.

## Minimum Authorities of Managers

These authorities are the minimum required by any manager if they are to accept accountability for the work performance of their subordinates (Figure 7.2). The VAR$^3$I authorities are the foundation underlying the definition of the term "manager."

### V: Veto Selection

A manager may veto the selection of a new subordinate. In practice this means the manager of the manager exercising the veto, not anyone else, can force the manager to accept an employee whom they believe, with cause, would be unwilling or unable to contribute positively to the work of the output team.

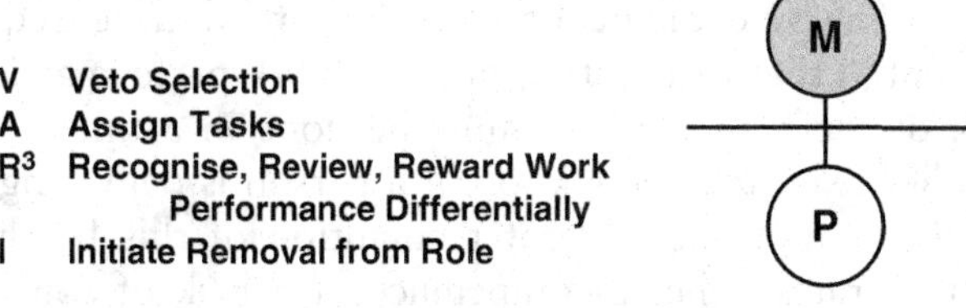


*Figure 7.2* Manager – Direct Report Relationship

It is important to note the difference between the authority to veto and the authority to select. Even when managers are authorised to select a person for a role, that selection is subject to veto by their manager, manager-once-removed, manager-twice-removed, etc. It is also important to note that the veto is an authority and must be exercised within policy limits that include non-discrimination.

Managers who seek to abuse the authority to veto selection to role are rapidly exposed by their managers monitoring the sequence of vetoes and requiring an explanation for a skewed statistical distribution, e.g., a consistent veto of female candidates for a role.

### A: Assign Tasks

The authority to assign tasks to one's subordinates. No one else in the organisation may assign tasks to a manager's subordinates unless they first gain the approval of the subordinate's manager. (See Chapter 17 on the assignment of tasks with an inset trigger where it may appear others are assigning tasks, but in fact the person is responding as his or her manager has authorised.)

### $R^3$: Recognise, Review and Reward Work Performance Differentially

Managers review and recognise overall work performance of direct reports (Persons) in order to improve their work performance and the managers' own work performance. They evaluate individual work performance and, within limits set by organisation policy, recognise and reward subordinates differentially based on the judgement of their work performance. No one in the organisation may differentially reward a manager's subordinates without his/her approval. (See Chapters 19, 20.)

In the application of differential recognition, it is important to realise the strength and necessity of psychological rewards and the importance of social process in their delivery – public recognition, special assignments, etc. The monetary rewards should be a confirmation of the psychological rewards accorded more frequently.

It is essential that recognition of poor work performance is also the work of the manager and must be done in a timely manner. All the other team members know if a person is delivering a poor work performance, and lack of recognition of this by the manager demonstrates either incompetence or a lack of courage. (As one angry employee wrote, "Manager X either has no guts or no brains.") It also degrades the worth of any recognition they receive for good work performance.

### I: Initiate Removal from Role

This authority means a manager may not be required to keep a non-performing member of his/her team after the requirements of organisational policy have been met. The manager will be required to give valid and non-discriminatory reasons for initiating removal from role, and the person to be removed must have been given proper warning and adequate opportunity to improve.

The process is iterative as M+1 may ask M to take specific actions to coach and counsel a person whose performance is not satisfactory. This is done to ensure fairness, and where necessary to build a case for dismissal. When all company policies regarding warnings and help have been given, M+1 cannot force M to keep a subordinate who is not satisfactory.

Once the person is removed from a particular role, M+1 must decide if the person is to be transferred to another role within the organisation (subject to the veto of the manager who must take this person) or is to be removed from the organisation. In some organisations M+1 recommends dismissal to M+2 who decides whether or not to dismiss.

#### Box 7.3 Note

A manager may, in practice, have additional authorities – to spend money; allocate resources; sign contracts; select, subject to the veto of superiors – but the VAR$^3$I authorities are the minimum.

If managers lack the VAR$^3$I authorities, it must be recognised they cannot be fairly held to account for the work performance of subordinates over time. Managers may recognise they may be criticised or disciplined if the work performance of subordinates is inadequate, but efforts to avoid punishment are quite different from the acceptance of accountability. If the realities of corporate policy or industrial practice limit these authorities of the manager, adjustments need to be made to match accountability with the reality of authority limits.

Even though the organisation authorises a person to use the VAR$^3$I authorities, there are still limits on his/her right to veto appointment and initiate removal from role. There are limits on the tasks she/he may assign to his/her subordinates. There are limits on the rewards that may be earned by subordinates. Such limits are inherent in the grant of authority.

The authorities carry with them accountability for their sound exercise. A key element in the judgement of managerial performance is how well these authorities are exercised. Decisions made in the exercise of these authorities are subject to appeal to M+1, as will become clear when we look at the authority of M+1.

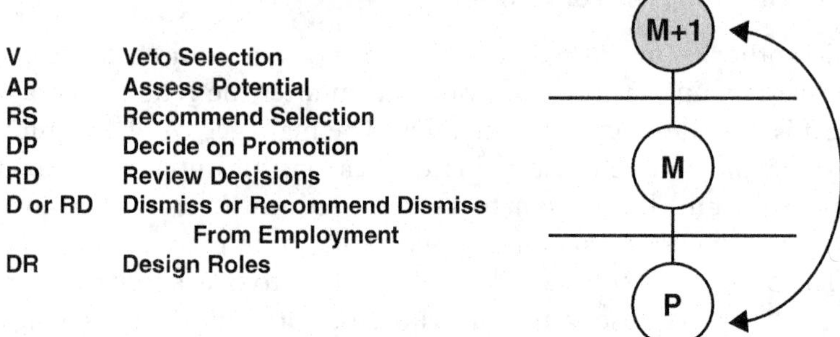


*Figure 7.3* Manager-Once-Removed

## Authorities of the Manager-Once-Removed to Manager's Direct Report

The same constraints apply to the authority held by the manager-once-removed as those applying to the authority of the manager, namely, law of the land, corporate policy, social custom and practices (Figure 7.3). The authorities of the manager-once-removed are:

### V: Veto Selection

Same as for the manager.

### AP: Assess Potential

This involves a judgement about an individual's capabilities to do higher levels of work and their potential for an upgrade or promotion. M will be expected to comment on potential or to recommend an upgrade or promotion, but the authority to decide lies with M+1. This must be the case since only M+1 is positioned to decide if P is ready to work at the level of M, immediately subordinate to M+1.

The individual whose potential is to be assessed must be informed that M+1 has this authority and is accountable for this process. M+1 needs to learn about the person's interests, knowledge, skills, ambitions and the tasks on which the Manager believes P has shown his or her capability at its best. This allows the decision to be made soundly based on data. M+1 needs to discuss the assessment with the individual and learn more about the person's interests and ambitions in light of this assessment. M+1 may indicate possible career paths, education or training opportunities and other steps that might be taken, and their timing, to allow P to undertake self-improvement more effectively. This assessment should indicate when the organisation should be taking steps to provide developmental opportunities to P, taking into account M+1's assessment and P's career aspirations. M+1 must also advise P if he or she is judged not to have any potential for promotion to a higher level. This is often, but by no means always, found to be a liberating judgement.

The process of potential assessment is difficult. It is often the case that an employee who is performing the work of the current role does not demonstrate the capability to perform tasks of a higher work complexity but nonetheless is performing very well in their current role and is keen for promotion. It is not the purpose of the potential assessment to shatter the aspirations of good employees, but no one benefits from the appointment to a role of a person who cannot perform the work of that role. It is also unfair and dishonest to suggest that some form of development activity or course of study will overcome a shortfall in the ability to perform work of higher complexity.

A technique used in some organisations is to assign specific tasks of higher work complexity to such people. The outcome for this work serves to confirm, or disconfirm, the judgement of the M+1, and in the event of a failure serves as a vehicle for the individual to appreciate the basis of the judgement. The proviso with this approach is that the person to whom the tasks are assigned does the work without assistance from others. This includes tasks of higher complexity where the individual needs to bring others into the process and part of the task is leading others.

It is important to recognise the system applied for potential assessment needs to be carefully designed and well controlled. If poorly done, it can be one of an organisation's most damaging systems, for both the organisation and its people.

### RS: Recommend Selection

As part of M+1's work for the improvement of overall performance and the development of their subordinates-once-removed, they also have the authority to recommend selection to the manager of an individual to fill a role as one of M's subordinates. The manager's authority to veto selection still applies. M+1 may recommend an individual based on knowledge of the person's capability, the belief that a particular role or project assignment will be good for the individual's development or any other reason which is within M+1's authority and the limits of law and policy. Managers need to understand the reasons for this authority and accept its validity as part of the process of the development of people for roles at the manager's own level, while knowing the authority to veto can still be exercised.

### DP: Decide on Promotion Or Upgrade

As noted earlier, only M+1 is in a position to decide if an individual is performing at a level that indicates an upgrade is warranted, or the person is ready to work at the level of M+1's direct reports.

### RD: Review Decisions

This is the authority to hear appeals from their managers' subordinates. It is necessary that everyone in the organisation know that the M+1 level has the authority of the organisation to review decisions. Managers must know this and factor it into their approach when making decisions. The subordinate must know this, so neither the subordinate nor the manager feels the subordinate is stabbing the manager in the back by going "over their head."

A practice adopted by several good managers we know, at the end of a discussion resulting in a decision that the direct report may not agree with, is to say, "Now you have the authority to have my manager review this decision and possibly reverse it. You should feel free to ask for a review; 'that is the way we work here.'"

### RD: Recommend Dismissal

The authority to initiate removal from a role will, after appropriate procedures, remove a subordinate from the manager's team, but not from the organisation. The decision to dismiss from the organisation must rest at a higher level to ensure review and fairness when someone's livelihood is to be removed.

Some organisations give M+1 the authority to dismiss; in others this lies with M+2. If it lies with M+2, then M+1 recommends dismissal. (Where the authority to dismiss resides is a policy decision.)

### DR: Design Roles

The authority to design more roles (for more Ps) rests with M+1. (This includes the authority to re-design roles.) There are two main reasons for this. M+1 is in the best position to understand the context of the specific work involved and to judge whether a new role is required to undertake that work. He or she will have a better understanding of the wider business purpose and how the new role helps achieve that purpose. M+1 can ensure consistency of role design and fairness of the work volume for each role across the teams.

### Notes on Sponsorship

The managers-once-removed are also called a Sponsoring Manager to emphasise their work for the development of their subordinates-once-removed. Sponsoring of subordinates-once-removed is a legitimate and vital organisational function. (See Chapter 21.)

While something like sponsorship goes on in many organisations, it is often done only for a favoured few, and is often the vehicle for the use of power. Managers know they are in favour because "their people" get promoted. In some organisations there is continuing gossip about the various power groups as higher-level executives compete to get their people promoted into key positions. This drains productive energy away from the work of the organisation, and it also means that many talented people may never get noticed because they are excluded from the power system.

A system of sponsoring managers reduces these problems and assists in ensuring that everyone in the organisation gets fair consideration from someone who should be able to discern capability due to their position one step above the person's manager. Since an individual is likely to have more than one sponsoring manager over time, the new assessments of potential may change, offering an opportunity to revise judgements as the person develops.

## Authorities of the Supervisor

Although in some organisations the title "supervisor" refers to the first-line Manager in a Level II role, in many industries the Supervisor occupies a lead role in Level I. That is how we are using the term here.

Understanding the authorities of the Supervisor in relation to the Manager in Level II has been a source of contention both in theory and in practice. To clarify, we have represented the Supervisor role in Figure 7.4 including its essential authorities. The Supervisor is not an intervening manager but someone in a leadership role with clear authorities.

- What is most important, as always, is:
- What is the work?
- What is the authority?

> **Box 7.4 Supervisor**
>
> A leadership role in Level I. The leader of a crew within an output team.

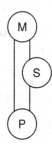

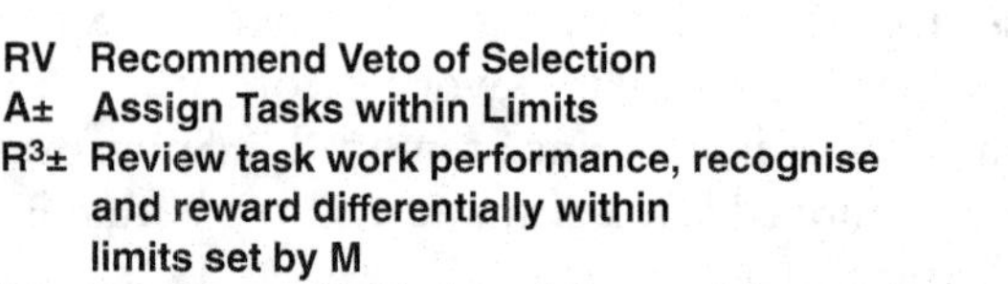


*Figure 7.4* Authorities of the Supervisor

> **Box 7.5 Managers and Supervisors**
>
> The practice of good leadership on the part of managers requires that they make known to the crew where the limits of the supervisor's authority to assign work, and recognise differentially, are. Managers must also make clear that they will not breach these limits without letting the Supervisor know, unless it is an emergency.

In our experience, the term "supervisor" is most often used to describe leadership work at the level of direct output of the organisation where:

- The work cycle spreads across more than one shift per day
- The desired output requires numerous identical roles
- The manager at the level above has too many direct reports to give them day-to-day attention and the feedback they may require
- The work can be ordered into demonstrable procedures in which people can be well trained and that do not require frequent intervention to resolve higher-complexity problems
- The nature of the work is such that a single team performing it will not generate the volume of higher-complexity work required to keep a manager fully occupied in his or her role.

The same constraints on authorities that apply to managers also apply to supervisors. In addition, there are other limits on the authority of supervisor roles, which are determined by their managers in line with organisational policy – for example, a manager may not pass *all* of his or her authority to a supervisor.

**RV:** Recommend the veto of someone being considered for selection to the Manager's Output Team if she/he believes, with cause, that the person would be either unwilling or unable to positively contribute to the work of the Output Team. While a Supervisor has the authority from the organisation to recommend to his Manager that a person not be selected to the Output Team, the decision rests with the Manager.

**A±:** The Supervisor may assign tasks as this is required as part of the work of the role. There are the usual limitations on this imposed by law, corporate policy, social custom, work practices and subordinates' acceptance. In addition, Managers' authority to assign tasks requires that they specify, *at their discretion*, the range (indicated by A±) over which a Supervisor may assign tasks within the Manager's Output Team.

The authority of the Manager allows each of his/her Supervisors to have different limitations on their respective authorities to assign tasks. These limitations may be varied from time to time as the tasks or the experience of the people in the output team change. Tasks outside these limits remain the preserve of the Manager.

**$R^3$±:** Review task performance and recognise differentially within limits set by the Manager. $R^3$± refers to the kinds of performance review and feedback the Supervisor may give to members of his/her Crew and what types of rewards are available to the Supervisor to give to members of the Crew.

It is important to note that the A± and $R^3$± must be kept in balance by the Manager since the subordinates will have no reason for carrying out the assignments of the Supervisor if they lack a commensurate authority to recognise good (and bad) performance.

**RI:** Recommend initiation of removal from role on Supervisor's Crew, where justified, for those people whom the Supervisor has previously given proper help and opportunity to improve and who have not responded. This recommendation may or may not be accepted by the Manager who has the authority to decide on initiation of removal from role.

To better understand the relationship between the Manager, Supervisor and subordinates and their differing authorities to assign work, Figure 7.5 may be helpful.

Each horizontal line represents the total range of authority of the Manager to assign work and reward performance differentially. The vertical lines represent the stop lines, or boundaries, of the

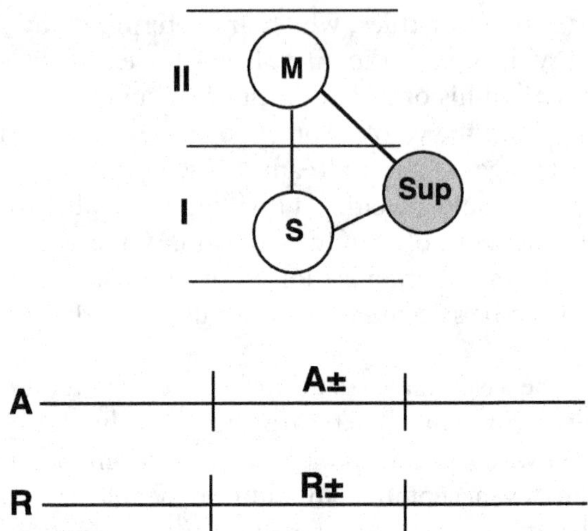


*Figure 7.5* Manager, Supervisor, Direct Report Authorities

range of authorities of the Supervisor to assign work and reward differentially. These boundaries must of necessity always be smaller than the total range of the Manager if the Manager is to maintain their managerial relationship with the subordinates.

It is important for managers at all levels to understand the sensitivity and subtlety of Manager, Supervisor, subordinate relationships.[1] Where the organisation requires Supervisory roles, the success of these relationships is crucial for the effective functioning of the organisation. It is also essential that the differences in authority and accountability be reflected in the systems of Performance Review, Performance Evaluation and Differential Reward.

The Supervisor is held accountable for his/her own work and the work performance over time of his/her subordinates but with important modifications to that accountability when it is compared to the accountability of the Manager because of the different authority limits which apply to each role.

For example, should the performance of the Output Team not be of acceptable standard because of the poor output of one of its members, Supervisors may be held accountable for assigning tasks and recognising differentially on the basis of Performance Review in an attempt to correct the problem. They may be held accountable for recommending removal of the poor performer. Having done that, together with any tasks assigned to them by the Manager in order to achieve the desired improvement in the subordinate's performance, the Supervisor may no longer be held accountable for the poor performance of the team.

**VP** **Veto Selection to Project**
**A±** **Assign Tasks within Limits**
**R3±** **Review, recognise and reward differentially within limits set by Manager(s)**
**RP** **Remove from Project**

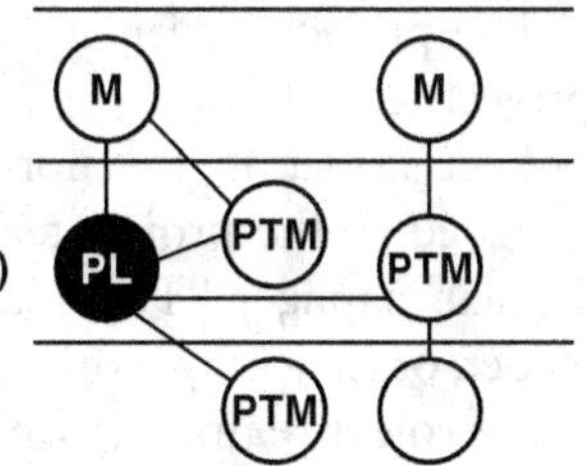


*Figure 7.6* Project Leader Authorities

It is Managers who have the authority to initiate removal from role, and they are held accountable for the poor performance and for the work associated with such removal, not the Supervisor.

This differing accountability, because of differing authority, has important implications for the Manager at Level III of the Manager at II. They need to be very aware of the limitations set by the Manager to the authority of the Supervisor when the work of the Manager is being reviewed.

## Authorities of Project Leaders

A project involves a group of people who are assigned to work on a special task instead of, or in addition to, their normal workload (Figure 7.6). A project is created to give concentrated attention to a task of limited and specific duration that may require interdisciplinary skills and expertise or expertise from various organisational units.

## Project Leader

Such a role may be extremely important for the organisation but is not the same as a manager in that[2]:

i. The project leader, organisationally, may be at the same level as one or more of the project team members (PTMs).
ii. The role usually has a time limit and is not open ended.
iii. The project leader usually does not have the authority to alter salary although his or her input on work performance may be important information to the project member's manager.

The project role may also be part-time. Other roles such as chairing meetings, supervising, leading a specific activity all involve leadership skills, require clear authorities and accountabilities but are not the same as a full managerial role.

The project leader authorities apply in the relationship between a project team leader (PL) and a PTM who is not a subordinate of the project leader in the normal organisation structure but is specially assigned to the project team. PTMs remain the subordinates of their regular manager. PTMs may work in the same work level as the project leader, or they may work one or more levels below the project leader.

A project team may operate on a full- or part-time basis without any need to modify the authority set as shown here. The PTM must be informed of the limitations that apply to the PL's authority.

### VP: Veto Selection to Project Team

The project leader carries the authority to veto the selection of people to the project team.

### A±: Assign Tasks within Agreed-Upon Limits

This authority is similar to that held by the Supervisor, but in this case the additional limits are imposed by the PTMs' managers. The agreed limits apply for the duration of the assignment to the project team though they may be re-negotiated if demands of the work or the work environment require changed limits.

### $R^3$±: Recognise Differentially within Agreed-Upon Limits

Again, the authority to assign work and the authority to recognise differentially must be commensurate. As with the authority to assign tasks, the limits to the authority of the project leader to recognise differentially are set by the PTM's manager(s). The project manager may also have the authority to review performance within the project scope, and he or she may report this review to the team member's manager, which may influence the manager's decision regarding reward.

### RP: Remove from the Project Team

The project leader has the authority to remove a project member from the team. PTMs return to their previous role and organisational unit upon the exercise of this authority by the project leader.

It is essential that the Project Leader have people properly assigned to the project by their managers and that his or her authorities are clear. Too often we have seen people told to lead a project where they must "persuade" others to help them, where team members have to resolve conflicts between their project work and the work

### Box 7.6 Team Defined

A team is a group of people, including a leader, with a common purpose who must interact with each other in order to perform their individual tasks and thus achieve a common purpose.

### Box 7.7 Teamwork Defined

Teamwork is about individuals collaborating for mutual benefit to achieve a purpose, clear about their mutual authority, their work and their relationships with each other and the leader.

assigned by their manager and where the Project Leader has no authority to recognise or reward team members effectively.

We have even been told that giving a person such a project without proper authority is one way to find out if they have a future in management. One of us spoke with a highly talented person who would have made an excellent manager. He was so disgusted with what he had to do on the project, he said he never wanted to be a manager. Without adequate authority and other resources, this person thought he had experienced "management" and he wanted no part of it.

## Team Leadership

A Project Leader is a team leader. Both the terms "team" and "teamwork" have widely used social meanings as do many terms in management. This is not useful if people within the organisation lack a common understanding of these concepts. It is simply not sufficient for leaders to exhort people to remember they are a team or to just work as a team unless there is a deeper and shared understanding as to what this means. Organisations we worked with have found the following definitions helpful.

The key to using these definitions are the phrases "who must interact" and "mutual benefit," which are crucial. They demonstrate the mutual interdependency of the team members. This distinguishes the work of a team from a network where some members of it have no real relationship with some others, and there is no requirement for mutuality even if all the network members do have a common purpose. It also distinguishes the team from a group of people; say, passengers on a plane – all have a common purpose but do not need to interact to achieve it. We emphasise the need to interact and the mutuality. This is the difference between, for example, the members of a shift or project team and the group comprising all the employees of an organisation as a whole.

The use of the word team may cause uncertainty concerning the approach to decision making reflected in phrases like "the team decided," or "the team was against it." These are examples of poor or muddled leadership. Individuals (like a team leader) are paid to make decisions; it is at the core of our understanding of work. It is an essential part of being a professional. This does not mean we do not confer, consult, discuss, suggest or recommend.

Of course, good leaders listen to ideas and suggestions. A good leader will know whether members are comfortable with or even understand a proposed course of action and will not ride roughshod over team members. If the leader does lead using poor social process, then an alternative leader will emerge over time or members will simply find ways to subvert the original leader. Good leadership and teamwork in any organisation is not, however, based on a system of individual veto or majority voting. A leadership role is far more than simply reflecting or representing members' views.

Keep in mind we are discussing an executive/managerial hierarchy with differential pay. There are other types of organisations which are not set up like this. They may be community groups, a legislature, partnerships where there are committees that do vote because the members have equal authority. It is not helpful to run a business as a democracy. In such a case why should one person be paid more than another?

### Team Processes

The team leader must also create and maintain the appropriate social processes in order to achieve the purpose. Team members need to establish constructive and cooperative work relationships with other team members. Below we describe some specific and practical steps to guide how this can be done. Ian Macdonald articulated this into a complementary process outlining the steps and traps that team leaders and members can use (and avoid) to improve their contribution and effectiveness.

### Authority and Teams

The team leadership and membership steps described below should be seen as authorities. Many organisations that have adopted this model require these steps from both leaders and members. They are part of work reviews and performance assessments. This

*Table 7.1* Complementary roles of leaders and team members[a]

| Leader | Member |
|---|---|
| Explain context and purpose | Clarify context and purpose |
| Identify critical issues | Contribute with the "how" |
| Encourage contributions | Listen |
| Make a decision about the plan | Accept decisions concerning which plan |
| Assign tasks | Clarify tasks |
| Monitor progress | Cooperate |
| Coach | Accept coaching |
| Review | Demand review |
| Avoid traps | Avoid traps |

[a]An elaboration of both the steps and traps can be found in Chapter 15 of *Systems Leadership*, 2nd ed., and also on the website www.maconsultancy.com

*Table 7.2* Traps to be avoided by leaders and team members

| Leader | Member |
|---|---|
| Not seeing the members' viewpoint | Keeping quiet |
| Getting over-involved in the action | Not listening |
| Feeling you must have the answer | Getting on with my job – ignoring situation |
| Being the technical expert | Getting on with other people's jobs |
| Ignoring social and scheduling issues | Mentally wandering off |
| Issue fixation | Fragmenting the team |
| Unwilling to stand out in a crowd | "I knew I was right" |
| | Ignoring coaching |
| | Fear of taking over |

demonstrates that, even in an executive hierarchy, authority does not simply flow downwards. Team members have the authority to require the leader to be clear about context, purpose and tasks. They can demand a review. This is a clear and proper flow of authority upwards. Also, team members have authority with regard to each other requiring collaboration, information and feedback (Table 7.1). This approach confounds the simplistic assertion that hierarchy is, by its nature, "authoritarian" or "top down."

The steps are not necessarily a linear process. Depending upon the result of consideration we may go and revisit one or more steps. The critical issues may require a re-evaluation of purpose, and coaching may result in changing tasks and performance monitoring. The important aspect is that all of the steps are covered (Table 7.2).

They are linear in that one cannot logically start anywhere. It is not helpful to assign tasks before clarifying the purpose!

We have found the model can be used to monitor the process in any situation where a team is working together. Whether meetings or as part of their normal tasks people have found this model improves the process. It may seem awkward at first for team members to exercise their authority and raise questions about context and purpose. However, when groups agree explicitly to use this model this authorises the behaviour and the steps can literally be referred to. We see this model functioning well when, for example, a team member reminds the team leader, "Actually, we have not identified the critical issues or addressed them properly." Essentially, it is a very practical tool that can be applied without cost and results in the saving of the most precious resource in organisations, that is, time!

## Summary

Gaining clarity on the difference between authority and power in an organisation illuminates, we believe, the reasoning underlying the authorities of all managers (and others) in the vertical spine of the organisation. The vertical spine of the organisation provides an anchor as other jobs are established to ensure the levels of work are used consistently and accurately. Team leadership and membership can be applied not only to specific projects but anywhere a group of people must interact and work together to achieve a purpose.

In the next chapter we continue to elaborate on ways of clarifying role relationships – vertical, horizontal and diagonal.

## Notes

1 This relationship requires more attention than we can provide here. An article by Stewart, who has been a Supervisor and a Manager of Supervisors and workers early in his career, is available on the Macdonald Consulting website for those who need a more nuanced presentation of these sensitive issues.

2 In some organizations the term Project Manager is used as a management title wherein the managerial authorities are appropriate. In other organizations a Project Manager may work alone without subordinates and thus have neither Managerial nor Project Manager authorities as we describe here. Care in choosing titles along with clear authorities can prevent confusion.

# 8 Improving Role Relationships

## Introduction

"What we have here is a failure of communication." You've probably heard this phrase often. Most of us have, and too often this is accepted as the way it is, and the way it must be – "it's personalities," "it's the bureaucracy," "manager x is impossible," and on and on. All of this may be true, but it does not solve an important problem of how to build better relationships, which are essential if we are to have a positive organisation.

In most organisations, difficulties in role relationships are all too common. Using Systems Leadership and struggling to help people deal with this issue, we have developed a process that has been used successfully in many organisations. It helps to get off on the right foot in a new relationship and to resolve issues that can arise at any time in an individual or group relationship. The system has been proven to work by providing a method for dealing with relationship issues that have sometimes festered for years.

Even using our approach will not solve all your problems. Communications problems have a lot in common with dirty dishes – no matter how often you get them clean, there are always more dirty ones that fill the sink. Thus, failures in communication must be dealt with continuously as they arise.

This chapter presents a way of thinking about role relationships within an employment hierarchy. In addition to the five vertical role relationships, it is important to understand the many horizontal and diagonal role relationships that are essential to the success of a hierarchical organisation. These relationships among peers (horizontal) and associates (diagonal) generate the majority of work-related interactions in any employment hierarchy.

Often these horizontal and diagonal relationships are left to chance or are termed the "informal" organisation. We believe this is the cause of much difficulty in organisations – the "silo" effect, the miscommunications between individuals in different organisational

DOI: 10.4324/9781003459118-11

units, or the unwillingness of some people at a higher level of work to speak with someone at a lower level.

Much is to be gained from clarification of these multiple role relationships. We have found that to be consistently productive it is useful to have a clear understanding of what a role relationship is and the authorities that may productively exist between roles.

In Chapter 7 we defined an authority regime as "a social agreement in which Person A has authority in relation to Person B when Person A is able to have a Person B behave as A directs as long as it is within B's authority." The set of minimum managerial authorities (VAR$^3$I) is an element of an authority regime. The role relationship agreements, which are part of a role description, are another element in an authority regime.

## Role Relationship Agreement

The role relationship agreement is a statement of organisation policy that sets a tone for organisational behaviour. We have found there are six productive modes of interaction in most organisations. These are shown below and demonstrate to everyone in the workforce the value the organisation places on human dignity. They help to open communication channels that are frequently clogged in more traditional organisations, thereby removing another impediment to organisational effectiveness.

The role relationship model provides a process for arriving at a social agreement on the authorities of an individual role incumbent. Its objective is to:

1) Allow an understanding of the interactive processes that constitute a role relationship
2) Provide a language and a process to systematise the management of role relationships in an organisation and to teach people to interact more effectively in their business roles
3) Create a vehicle by which managers may, should they wish, stipulate what is requisite behaviour for the members of an organisation as they go about their work interacting with others. This is not to put people in a straitjacket but to help people (especially people new to a role) understand appropriate behaviour in a given role relationship – to let people new to a role understand what is appropriate behaviour in a given role.

The role relationship matrix was designed with elements specific to a work hierarchy and refers only to the business of the hierarchy. There is no attempt, nor should there be, to categorise and track elements of relationships which do not bear directly upon the work of the organisation. This does not mean that such interactions are not valid or at times necessary. This model, however, focuses on work, and only work, relationships.

### Components of a Role Relationship

Example of a relationship between two individuals, or groups, in the workplace...

**Role Relationship:** the sum of the interactions that take place between the two parties to the relationship.

**Interaction:** may be divided into the information conveyed, the social process used when it is conveyed and its purpose.

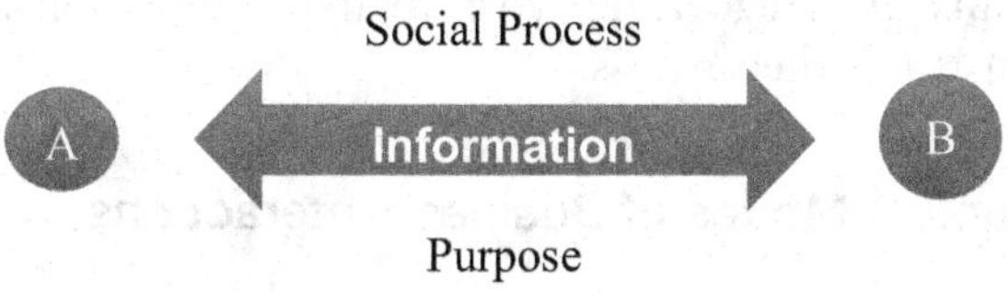


*Figure 8.1* A Productive Interaction

Figure 8.1 Illustrates an interaction between two people, A and B, or two organisational groups.

*Information* is the substance of what is conveyed back and forth between roles A and B.

*Social Process* is the emotional element of the human-to-human transfer of information that takes place in an interaction. A person's way of behaving may be friendly or unfriendly, direct or indirect, humorous or serious, persuasive or sceptical or something else entirely. Information that conveys social process is excluded from the information set within the arrows and is often conveyed by behaviour rather than words, e.g., voice tone or body language, rather than what is said.

*Purpose* is the intent of the interaction itself.

Because role relationships are so varied and so complex, it is difficult to understand them, and the authorities which may be validly exercised within them, without a simple and clear method for categorising what is going on.

**Information** is a very broad category, and it is specific to the particular interaction. Therefore, it will not serve as a simple method for categorising interactions about work.

**Social process** is very important in an interaction, and an understanding of interactive behaviours needs to be developed to improve social interactions. Social process is separate from the work itself and interactive in real time. It is therefore useless as a categorising method for interactions about work.

This is not to suggest that social process is not important; it is, in fact, vital to the sound functioning of a role relationship. It is the social process that is assessed on the values scales through the lens of mythologies of each individual.

A person working in a role relationship with a fellow employee who is perceived to show disrespect for human dignity will not be willingly cooperative. A manager who is perceived to be dishonest and a coward will not have a highly energised and productive team working for him.

**Purpose,** on the other hand, is determined by the work to be done. We have found the set of productive intentions provide a limited number of interaction purposes. Therefore, it provides a useful means of categorising work-related interactions. The next section illustrates the process.

## Six Productive Modes of Business Interactions

The differences between various relationships, whether vertical, horizontal or diagonal, are demonstrated by a difference in the distribution pattern of the purposes of the interactions, not by the use of different purposes. It is good policy to have all modes of interaction valid in all roles. This allows a group of people to agree to behave in a specific and predictable manner under a range of circumstances.

The six productive modes of business interaction are shown below along with simple explanations of their intent.

### Direct/Comply

OPENING MESSAGE: "Do this."
RESPONSE: "I'll do that."

The intent of this interaction is to get someone to do, or not do, something. The authority allows A to get B to do, or not do, something with B recognising that A has such authority. Unfortunately, the terms "direct" and "comply" also carry emotional content regarding social process, which is not intended. In giving a direction, the style may be direct or indirect, in the form of a request, in a statement of need, in a suggestion.

It is also valid to say, "I can't do that," if one does not have the resources or the ability to do what is requested. It is also valid to begin a negotiate/negotiate interaction (see below), e.g., "I can't do that now. I have a rush job going. Would next Friday be all right?" It is not valid to simply refuse.

### Negotiate/Negotiate

OPENING MESSAGE: "We must discuss this and reach an agreement on the *outcome* of the negotiation."
RESPONSE: "I will discuss that with you in order to reach an agreement on the *outcome* of the negotiation."

The intent of this interaction is for the two people involved to gain an agreement on the outcome of the negotiation. It is not necessary to gain agreement on the specifics of the issue at hand for negotiate/negotiate to be a productive interaction. If two people understand they agree that they cannot reach an agreement on the substance of this issue, that too is productive since it makes it clear others must be brought in to resolve the dispute or that the terms of the dispute will have to be changed if agreement on the substance is to be reached.

The authority to negotiate allows A or B to offer alternatives and consider options regarding what is to be done to achieve their individual or collective goals.

### Consider/Consider

OPENING MESSAGE: "What do you think about X?"
RESPONSE: "I'll think about X and get back to you."

The intent of this interaction is to get someone else's opinion or thinking on a particular issue or problem. It can often be confused as a direct comply, so be sure both parties understand the question is real, not an indirect order.

### Teach/Learn

OPENING MESSAGE: "This is how it works."
RESPONSE: "I'll remember that."

The intent of this interaction is to inform or to notify someone. The term "teach" is used to reinforce the idea that the person who is doing the informing has an obligation to be clear, to communicate in a way which is likely to be heard and understood. "Learn" reinforces the idea that the person receiving the information has an obligation to indicate he or she has heard and understood the information and will make an effort to remember it. It also indicates an obligation to enquire if the information being transferred is not understood.

### Learn/Teach

Opening Message: "What happened here?" or "How do I operate this machine?"
Response: "This is what happened." or "This is how you do it."

The intent of this interaction is to ask for information with the reciprocal idea of being obliged to understand and remember the information being given.

### Comply/Direct

Opening Message: "What should I do?"
Response: "Do this."

The intent of this interaction is to find out what you should do. This may occur in a situation where the manager has made an error, and must now ask the subordinate what he or she should do to fix the problem or make amends. It may also occur when a subordinate does not understand what his or her manager wants done.

These interactions can all be shown on a matrix where the productive interactions all fall on the diagonal from top left to bottom right (Figure 8.2).

In addition, there are two other interaction types which occur in organisations but which are not productive. These are "refuse" and "invalid." The intent of refuse is self-explanatory. It is a valid response to say, "I cannot do that; it is not within my authority." It is also valid to say, "I can't do that now," or "I can't do that because I don't have the resources." While these are refusals to do what is requested, they lead to further possibilities – finding the person who has the authority to do what is requested; negotiating when a task can be done; seeking out additional resources.

What is not valid is to simply refuse to participate in an authorised interaction or to carry out a task for which you are authorised and accountable.

An invalid interaction is one in which there is no intent to take constructive action, but which is disguised as a productive mode. For example:

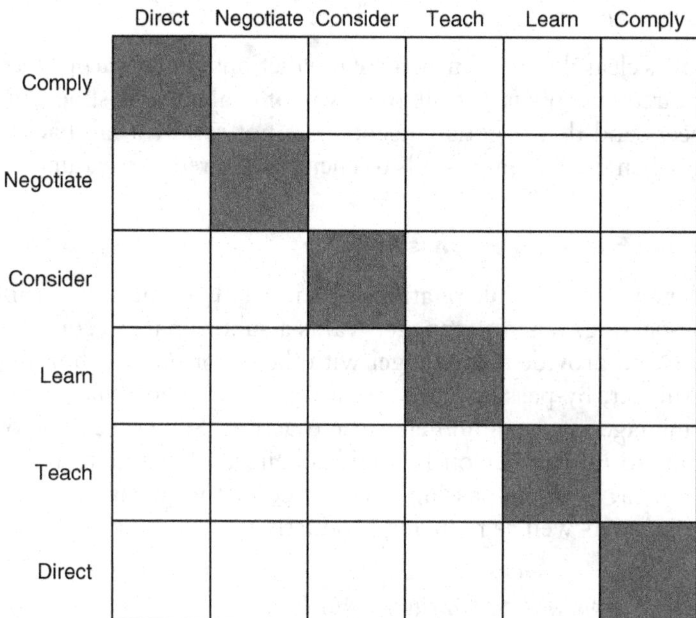


*Figure 8.2* Matrix of Productive Role Relationships

MANAGER: "Get me the report on the Harrison account by tomorrow."

CLERK: "O.K." (with no intention of doing so because from past experience the clerk knows his manager will have a three-martini lunch and won't remember assigning the task)

The ability to break up a role interaction and analyse it using the modes of interaction does <u>not</u> in any way imply that only one mode is used in each interaction. A typical interaction would involve several modes, with the participants shifting easily and without conscious awareness among any or all of the modes of interaction. What begins as a teach/learn may become a learn/teach. These in turn may evolve into a negotiate/negotiate ending in a direct/comply or a comply/direct.

## Usefulness of Role Relationship Model

While at first this model may seem simplistic and rigid (and it can certainly be misused in such a manner), we have found that by understanding the productive modes of interaction, individuals and managers often avoid many of the communication problems which are common in human relationships.

### Enlarges the Inventory of Modes of Interaction

It makes clear there are an array of interactions which are productive, that direct/comply is not the only way of dealing with subordinates or peers and that negotiate/negotiate is not simply a fall-back position when direct/comply fails to elicit the desired behaviour.

### Helps to Eliminate By-passing

Understanding the role relationship model illuminates the problem of by-passing. When a manager wants a subordinate to consider an action and provide the manager with the subordinate's thinking on the subject, by-passing may occur when the subordinate believes the manager wants him/her to take action. Sometimes Person A intends to inform Person B, while B believes A wants to reach an agreement. Such by-passing occurs frequently, causing anger and frustration as well as reducing productivity.

### Provides a Means to Clarify Authorities

Often it is not clear just what authorities individuals have in relation to each other. Can A direct B to do something, in regard to what tasks and under what circumstances? Should A inform (teach) B about problem X or not?

### Provides a Means to Clarify Joint Task Assignments

The model can be used to clarify who is to do what in particular role relationships. Role descriptions can be used to determine where particular individuals have accountabilities for tasks that

**Box 8.1**

Burke has observed this process between a team which had the task of creating a computer application and the client organisation who would use it. They both believed they fully understood what needed to be done, but they were seriously at odds in their understandings. Relationships within and between the groups had gone from bad to worse. Each blamed the others for the problems. The client organisation "knew" what they needed, and the computer people knew that with computing they could build a better system if only the client would listen to them.

The head of the Information Technology department asked Burke to sort out the problem. She arranged for a meeting right after lunch where she began by explaining the model and then suggested to the warring factions they use the model. They initially thought it was a stupid idea, and they were reluctant to even try it. Nonetheless, their managers had told them they were to solve their problems, and Burke was assigned to help them do it.

They did realise there were significant misunderstandings that had led to the impasse that threatened to cause the whole project to fail, and that might affect their continued employment. Reluctantly, they started using the model with a bit of coaching. Then they became absorbed in solving their problems. By the end of the afternoon, they were amazed at how many of their issues could be resolved in a short discussion using this model.

A few weeks later, Burke was passing through their work area, and heard them using the terms in their general conversations. "Is that a consider/consider or a direct/comply?" "This is not a negotiate/negotiate, it's a teach/learn."

Using this, the project had a fine outcome, and the people involved on both sides were proud of their accomplishments.

require interaction with others. These inter-related task types can then become the basis for negotiating role relationships.

**Demonstrates a commitment to the shared values.** The role relationship model makes clear that there are six productive modes of interaction, and organisation policy states that every employee has the authority to use all six productive modes of interaction in their various role relationships within the organisation. Thus, the process demonstrates respect for human dignity, honesty, that both A and B are trustworthy, it is typically perceived as fair, and at times requires considerable courage to fully exchange information.

## Negotiating Role Relationships

The principal Role Relationships which apply in a particular role are best understood by referring to an organisation chart that is attached to each role description (see Chapter 14 and Appendix A for a model role description). The organisation chart provides the title and address of roles within the organisation with which the described role interacts.

The role description should list the other roles with which the role incumbent will have his/her most important interactions. The following should be included in the listing of roles with important interactions that should be negotiated by the role incumbent and each of these role holders:

- Manager.
- Subordinates.
- Peers.
- Associates (subordinates or superiors of a peer – any diagonal relationship). Those outside your immediate organisational unit with whom you will have to interact.

Those outside your immediate organisational unit with whom you will have to interact

A role relationship negotiation involves two people who must interact in the performance of specific tasks. They begin by talking to each other and identifying the tasks from each of their roles that require interaction. From this they negotiate an agreement as to what authorities each requires to accomplish the required tasks. This may involve the authority to request a service (direct/comply), to be informed (teach/learn), or to reach an agreement on when a product will be delivered (teach/learn, learn/teach, negotiate/negotiate).

The discussion alone is usually enough to enable people to generate far more productive role relationships than they have experienced in the past. It is possible to quantify the pattern of purposes of interaction by estimating the percentage of each to be used in relation to each key task. By summing, one can arrive at an overall pattern of interactions, as shown on the following pages. Note the emphasis on *estimating*. The percentages are not meant to be specific or a straitjacket. They give a general idea of how the various purposes are likely to be distributed.

Quantification allows the role incumbents and their managers to analyse their pattern of interaction to see if they are relying too much on one element, such as direct/comply. It also makes clear that in most role relationships consider/consider, teach/learn and learn/teach are the most frequently used purposes of interaction. Direct/comply is used far less than many theories of management imply and that many people believe.

Many who use this model are not too fussed with quantification. It may be useful in the original role relationship discussion, but for the most part it comes into play when the relationship has problems – often too much direct/comply and misunderstandings around teach/learn and learn/teach. The examples suggest some possible productive relationships, but real relationships are up to the judgements of the participants (Figures 8.3–8.5).

## Box 8.2 A Medical Problem

Before this model was developed, the British National Health Service was having problems in the relationships between nurses and doctors. The doctors insisted that they were, and had to be, the managers of the nurses because they gave orders to the nurses on how to treat patients. The nurses said, "no way." The nurses work for the head nurse up to the Director of Nursing. Sorting this out took considerable time. The doctors did not want to provide overall performance reviews for the nurses, nor did the nurses want that, but the docs insisted they had to be the managers of the nurses to get proper care for their patients. The problem was finally solved when they all agreed that doctors could tell the nurses what to do because they had "prescribing" authority. The nurse managers would be recognised as having managerial authorities. They added that nurses had an obligation to inform doctors of their observations of their patients, and the doctors were obligated to listen and "be polite."

The model we have presented here makes solving such problems much easier and without all the *sturm* and *drang*.

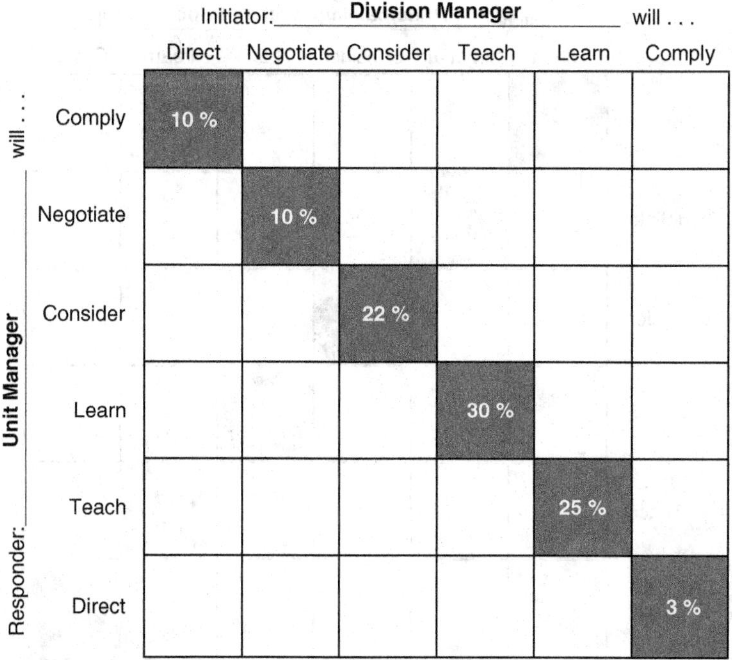


*Figure 8.3* Role Relationships between General Manager IV and Unit Manager III

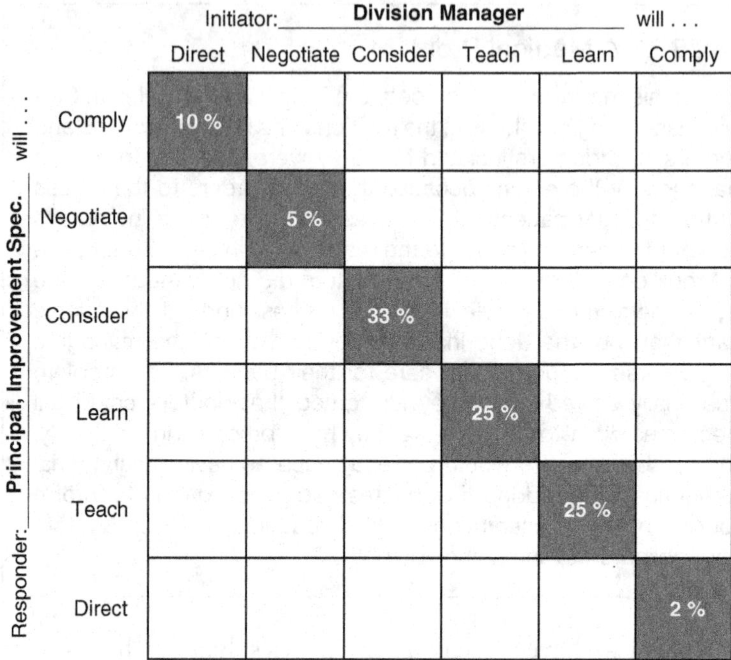


*Figure 8.4* Relationships between General Manager IV and Principal III

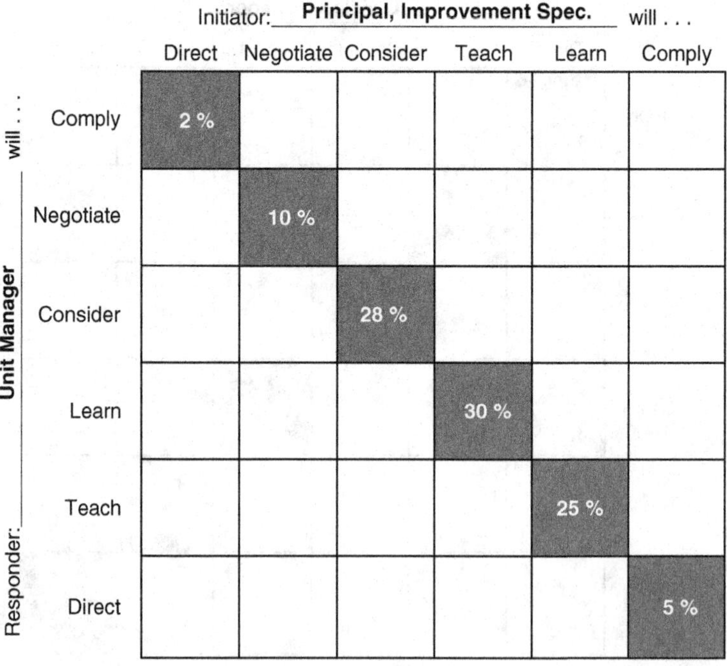


*Figure 8.5* Relationships between Principal Technical Improvement and Unit Manager

## Conclusion

At first glance using such a matrix may appear to be an elaborate and cumbersome procedure, especially for people who have worked together for a long time and know each other well. The experience of people who have used this model indicates, however, that appearances may be deceiving. Users of the model report this process allows rational discussion of their role relationships in a language that is simple, easy to remember and directly related to the work of the organisation.

Because the categories are based on the purpose of the interaction, using them clarifies one of the most common sources of misunderstanding – misinterpretation of purpose (intent).

The model helps clarify existing role relationships and can be used to explain new role relationships. When things are going wrong, it can provide a basis for discussion of the problems. Does A have the authority to direct B in regard to Task Q? Has A been complying with what she/he thought was a direction when B thought she/he was asking for a consider/consider?

The model also provides managers with a method for looking at how their direct reports perceive their role relationships and, when necessary, to approve the pattern that the subordinates have agreed to. It also offers an opportunity, if the manager has some doubts about the pattern, to ask the subordinates to reconsider the pattern, or to direct the subordinates regarding their authorities under certain circumstances or in regard to key task types.

For example, a Principal Technical Advisor may not direct a Unit Manager to use a particular standard. Such direction must come from the General Manager. The Principal Technical Advisor may, however, inform a Unit Manager of the General Manager's policy. Further, the Principal Technical Advisor may be obliged to inform the General Manager if the Unit Manager chooses not to act on the information.

While the authorities of managers have specific minimum requirements, all employees of the organisation should have the authority to use all six productive modes of interaction. Another refutation of the idea that authority flows downward in an employment hierarchy. Too many organisations hire expensive consultants to hear "What you have is a communications problem." With the right organisational structure, the right placement of people in roles and the use of the full range of valid interactions, you can save a lot of money and get the communication channels open and flowing.

# Part III

# The Work of Leadership

Our definition of manager makes clear that all managers are leaders of people (though not all leaders are managers). In this section we focus on the information and methods that have helped many managers to become more effective leaders. The first chapter explains why we believe there is a set of universally shared values which have both positive and negative attributes. For example, there is courage and cowardice, respect and disrespect. We also show why the shared values at the positive end of the scales bind social groups together.

Our understanding of behaviours that represent the positive or negative ends of the scales of shared values are based on our mythologies – stories containing a fundamental truth that inform and explain the myths and link behaviour to the universal shared values. People who share a common mythology form a culture.

The work of leadership is to create or change a culture based on existing mythologies. An understanding of the shared values and the definition of a culture allows the leader to create positive change using behaviour, systems and symbols. A separate chapter provides more information on systems, followed by a chapter on safety, one of the most important set of systems in an organisation.

Finally, we discuss what we have learned about social process in long distance video meetings via Microsoft "Teams" or Zoom Video Communications.

As you will see, these ideas are closely linked and presented in an order to make them as clear as we can at this time. Most people, however, need to read and re-read parts as they start to apply them in their work. It takes time to fully grasp these ideas and understand their importance for leaders in organisations. This effort, we have found, pays off and is the basis for creating a positive organisation.

DOI: 10.4324/9781003459118-12

# 9 The Work of Leadership

## Values, Mythologies and Culture

### Introduction

Leadership is an elusive quality. Whether good or bad, it is easy to recognise, but hard to define. You have probably read articles and books on leadership theory and practice. Many have been dominated by models that stress characteristics or traits of people such as charisma, extroversion, aggression or size (tall is better). Sometimes it is defined by personal competencies – vision, courage, determination, drive or maturity.

Other models have stressed the "situational" approach. It is the characteristics of the situation, whether it is structured or unstructured, whether the leader is in a powerful or weak position, whether the climate for agreement is friendly or hostile, which determine whether or not a leader is effective or ineffective, or how he or she should behave.

Some have said that we "lead people" and "manage things." Leaders are often characterised as visionary, "doing the right things," while managers are characterised as rule-following bureaucrats (in the pejorative sense of that term) who "do things right." Leaders are concerned with effectiveness, managers with efficiency. One gets the sense from these authors that leaders are great, while managers are pedestrian. We believe this dichotomy is both insulting and confusing.

We have found the existing approaches unhelpful. Too often, the concept of leadership is portrayed as almost mystical – the implication is that one is either born a leader or not. Certainly, some people are far more able as leaders than others, and some may be more effective in some situations than others. Unfortunately, many of the current theories of leadership do not give much guidance, whether in selecting leaders or in informing people how to succeed in leadership roles.

As discussed in Chapter 7, we have found managers require a specific set of authorities if they are to accept accountability for the work performance of their direct reports. We have also pointed out that all managers are, and must be, leaders of people if they are to be successful. We have found there are two essential elements in understanding effective leadership:

DOI: 10.4324/9781003459118-13

(1) The capability of the individual.
(2) Understanding the universal shared values and one's own and other's mythologies as discussed in this chapter.

The elements of capability were discussed in Chapter 4. This chapter will focus on the universal shared values which underlie many of our ideas about what constitutes good leadership and poor leadership by a manager. Good leadership is essentially behaviour we value because we see it as exemplifying values we share.

**Box 9.1 The Work of Leadership**

The work of leadership is to create, maintain and improve the culture of a group of people so they achieve objectives and continue to do so *over time*.

Note we emphasise that a leader's success has to be judged "over time." Leadership is not a short-term process. Quick fixes may be effective but do not necessarily last. Leadership is certainly about having people act in a way desired by the leader. But how is it made possible? We have taken away many of the traditional tools: fear, coercion and intimidation. Yet we still want the leader to influence others to behave constructively, productively and creatively, and all of this for the most part willingly. This is not an easy task in any social setting whether at home, in the office, in a religious organisation, a political party or a voluntary organisation.

**Box 9.2 What Makes a Good Leader?**

Good leadership involves effectively directing the behaviour of others without the primary use of force, manipulation or power. Good leadership engenders willing participation.[1]

If leaders are to be effective, they must be skilled in the management of *social processes*. The ability to comprehend a social process and intervene to produce a productive outcome is at the heart of leadership. It is a huge advantage if the leader genuinely respects people and is committed to using social process as the main tool.

If the leader's first and foremost tool of positive leadership is social process, how is this to be used effectively? We have identified work the leader must do to be successful. The leader must be able to answer the following questions to test his or her understanding of social process:

1. How do team members (i.e., those whom the leader is leading) perceive each other?
2. How do they perceive the organisation?
3. How do they perceive the leader?
4. Can the leader predict how they will perceive particular changes, for example, of working practices, organisation, benefits, and so on?

To answer questions 1, 2 and 3, the leader needs to be able to relate the perceptions to the values continua and position them on these continua.

## Values, Mythologies and Culture

To begin, we are all individuals, but we cannot live alone, "No man is an island." We are social animals. Our survival and continuation as a species depends upon maintaining a constructive relationship with others. So upon whom can we depend? Our proposition is that we make such decisions according to a set of values common to all human beings. We use these values to judge behaviour and actually include and exclude members of our social group based upon these judgements. We recognise that in a wide range of organisations and communities, the terms values, beliefs, attitudes and philosophies are often used interchangeably or with a wide overlap in meaning.

Politicians, corporate executives and sociologists often state that values have changed, but they also refer to enduring values or core values. People may explain behaviour by saying this person or group or society has "different values." We even sometimes say that some societies put a different value on human life, as in the phrase, "Life is cheap there." We use the term value[s] to differentiate "us" from "them." Often the purpose of this differentiation is to make a claim of superiority of "our" values over "theirs."

### Box 9.3 Different Values or the Same Values

One of the significant experiences that led to the formulation of the values model was Stewart's experience with employment work groups and community work groups in Western Australia. Developing an understanding of the shared values part of the McKinsey 7-S model was part of his assignment.

The staff (non-unionised) management group and the hourly paid (unionised) workforce were very clear and quite forthright in their assessment that the cause of their fractured and unproductive work relationships was because the other group had very different values from their own.

Stewart had interviewed members of both groups. He also had the personal experience of attending work parties to build a kindergarten and boat club on weekends where the same people who had told him about the shared value disparity in the workplace were demonstrating their ability to work together very constructively and amiably in the local community.

After observing this for some time, he asked quietly how this was possible and was told, "Easy, here we all share the same values." The highly productive effort did demonstrate the importance of shared values but raised the question of how, if shared values were so important, it was possible to change them when you changed your work shirt – there needed to be another explanation.

## Values Explained

It is our argument that universal shared values are the underlying principle that binds human beings to one another. When we examine our evolutionary history, it is obvious that humans would not have survived as a species had they not been able to form and maintain social groups. The other species which co-existed with our earliest ancestors all had sharper teeth, longer claws, were faster, could jump higher and in general physically out-match the earliest humans. Newborn human babies require a social group – a family or clan to support them for several years – or they will die.[2] If this had happened too often, we would have become extinct and our present discussion would not be occurring. To quote Donald (1991), "we are social animals, we have evolved as such and our brains are uniquely developed to process social signals. Our continued survival as a species is dependent upon our ability to build and maintain cohesion in our Social group."

### Central Proposition

We propose that all people, societies and organisations share the same set of universal values. We have articulated these in various publications and articles, and they have been tested in commercial, public and non-governmental organisations (Macdonald, Macdonald and Stewart, 1989). They have been tested in communities and countries around the world, by the authors and their associates, in developed nations and with people still living a semi-tribal existence.

We have identified six values which we believe make up the set of universal shared values which are necessary for the continuing existence of human social groups. Each of these is found on a continuum from positive to negative. Behaviour at the positive end of the continuum strengthens the social group; behaviour at the negative end weakens, and eventually will either destroy the social group or result in the expulsion of those who demonstrate the behaviours assessed negatively.

Most members' behaviours must be at the positive end of the scale in order for them to be accepted and relied upon by others. Without such positive reliable behaviour social groups will fail. Simply predicting behaviour is but the beginning. It is possible to predict that an individual will behave in a cowardly way, but such demonstrated behaviour will inevitably weaken the group when it is under attack, and such behaviour may well lead to the destruction of other members of the group.

Figure 9.1 shows the core values upon which we propose that all societies are based.

The basic propositions are:

(1) If a group of people are to maintain a productive relationship that lasts, then the members of that group must demonstrate behaviour that exemplifies the positive end of the scales of the shared values. Positive values are the defining properties of a cohesive social group.

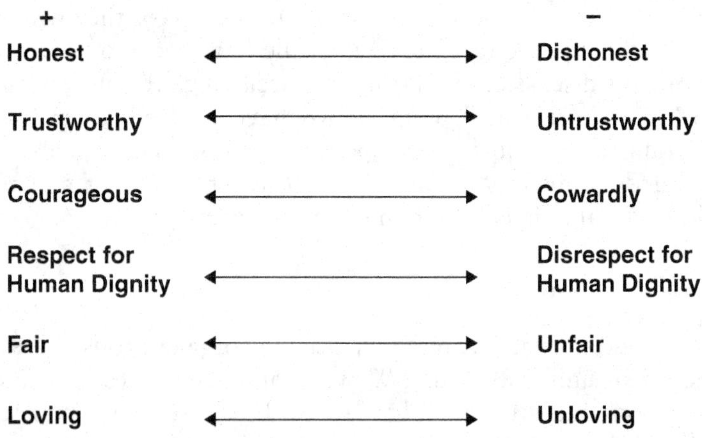


*Figure 9.1* Universal Shared Values

(2) If a member of that group demonstrates behaviour that is judged by the other group members to be at the negative end of the scales of shared values, the person will eventually be excluded (although attempts to change the behaviour may be made prior to exclusion).
(3) If several people exhibit behaviours that are similar but judged by the rest of the group to be at the negative end of the scales of core values, then the group will break into factions or separate groups.

## Why the Six Values?

It is, of course, relevant to ask, why these six? Over the years we have had many debates on this topic, both among ourselves and with others. First, the authors do not posit these as immutable and unquestionable. They are, however, related to two criteria: first if there are other, similar words, are they already covered by the existing six? For example, integrity, which is a similar term, but already covered by honesty and trustworthy. Fairness and justice are very similar, but we prefer fairness because of the possible legalistic implication of the term justice. We can all think of examples of the law being unfair.

The second criterion is that a person's behaviour may be judged to be positive in terms of one value and at the same time be judged negative on another. A manager may admonish a team member publicly for his or her poor work performance. The manager may at the same time be honest, but show lack of respect for human dignity. A soldier may admit fear and run away in the battle. The soldier is again honest, but may be cowardly and not to be trusted in combat. Another person may insist on the exact distribution of resources as authorised, believing they are acting fairly, but at the same time be indifferent to the greater or special needs of some individual or group.

## Myths and Mythologies

Values, per se, cannot be observed and therefore cannot be determined directly. We can and do observe what people say, how they behave, and we rate them on the scales of shared values. We interpret behaviour and draw conclusions about the values that an individual's behaviour demonstrates. Sometimes we have to wait for confirmation that our conclusions are correct, and then we may be left in doubt. In some cases we may disagree with others as to how particular behaviour should be interpreted. In general, however, within a coherent social group, agreement is gained in time, often very quickly.

In essence, values are the ground against which we assess our own worth and the worth of others. We argue that because humans evolved as social animals, all humans use these values as the basis for judging the worth of others as they observe and interpret their behaviour.

The question then arises, what is the connection between the value and the behaviour that enables us to carry out this rating? By what process do we determine that any behaviour should be rated positively or negatively on any one or more of the values? Why do some people interpret the same behaviour quite differently?

The term we have used to explain the linkage between values and our ratings of observed behaviour is mythologies.

**Mythology:** The underlying assumptions and current belief as to what is positively valued behaviour and what behaviour is negatively valued and why it is so. These are the stories that form our beliefs about what is good and bad behaviour.

We call these assumptions, or beliefs, mythologies because they are linked to the shared values. They are a mixture of mythos – stories with emotional content – and logos – rationality. Mythologies, myths in common usage, are stories that contain a fundamental lesson to be learned even if the "facts" are not true. For example, there is the story of Daedalus, the mythical Greek inventor, architect and sculptor, and his son Icarus. Daedalus created wings for Icarus sealed to his body with wax. Daedalus warned his son not to fly too close to the sun, or the wax holding his wings would melt and he would fall into the sea and die. Icarus ignored his father's warning and did fall into what is now called the Icarian Sea and died. Thus, the fundamental truth – the need to show respect for your father and family by listening to and considering advice.

How do we make the linkage? We judge through our "mythological lens." We all effectively wear a pair of mental glasses; we see the world through a lens that refracts what we see onto the scales of shared values. That is, we observe behaviour and our lens directs that behaviour on to the value scales to be seen as fair or unfair, honest or dishonest, loving or unloving, etc. Clearly, this is not a simple bi-polar rating, but the behaviour is placed somewhere

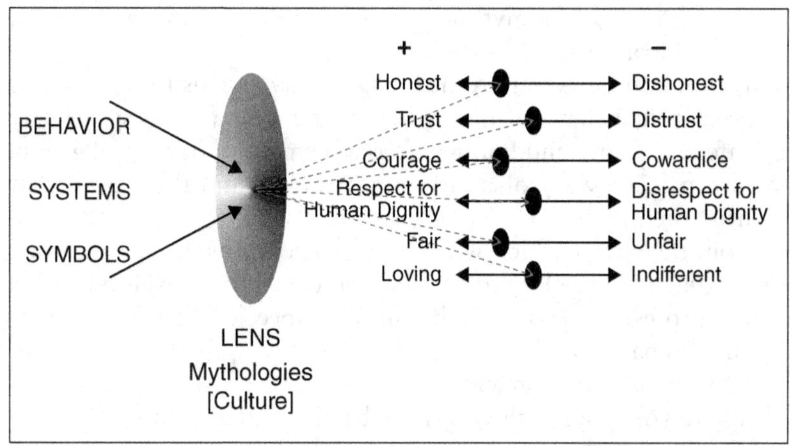


*Figure 9.2* Observations, Mythological Lens and Universal Values

along the continuum of one or more of the core values. If it is not, then it has no value from a social perspective and we are literally disinterested in it in this regard (Figure 9.2).

How is this lens made? Our experience and research is consistent with other psychological research (and common sense) that suggests the lens through which we view the world is generated by our prior experience. It is formed as we are growing up and develops as we develop. We learn, potentially, from every experience: first from our immediate and extended family experiences; from our school, fellow students and teachers; from our community; from the media, from our work mates and bosses.

We also shape our lens from indirect or filtered experience such as television and social media. We learn from literature, film, art and indeed from all of our interactions as we live our lives. Our lens is crafted from a young age and added to as we grow and experience the world.

We learn to recognise patterns. Children can establish patterns quickly; for example, when children swim twice consecutively on Saturday mornings and fail to make the third in a row, there will be a cry of "but we always go swimming on Saturday morning." You can replace "swimming" with almost any activity. For example, a secretary brings cookies to work and leaves them in the coffee room. She does this for two weeks and then stops. Adults will also react and wonder why there aren't any cookies any more.

In time we learn to recognise these patterns in our own behaviour and from that of others, and from these we develop "truths" about people in the world. One characteristic of this process is that the building of a mythology is often self-reinforcing. Take the following example:

In childhood it is important for us to have a lens that allows us to predict the behaviour of our family and close friends so we may be safe and secure and know who is a member of our social group. We learn to be wary of non-group members and the signals that identify them.

From the age at which we are able to comprehend the meaning of language, those close to us and who care for our well-being are seeking to establish our myths through speech and the interpretation of behaviour.

"Do not talk to strangers."

"Share your toys with your little brother – that is fair."

"Don't be mean to your little sister; she loves you and you need to show her you love her."

"You need to tell me if you break a toy, not hide it away in the toy box."

So begins the process of learning the behaviours that are essential for family and then societal coherence. As we grow we have the opportunity to observe and test the validity of these predictive mythologies and to be exposed to many hypotheses about the interpretation of the value of the behaviour of others, including those who raised us.

We use our lens to interpret the world of experience as it rolls by us. Adolescence may bring severe dissonance when we find parents or other significant adults in our lives do not behave as the mythologies they have been teaching us. Observing their behaviour through the lens they have taught us places them on the negative side of the shared value scales. Thus the teenage cry – "hypocrisy." This requires the generation of new myths and the peer group can have a very significant influence in their generation.

### Box 9.4 Creating a Mythology

An employee is transferred to another MRU because of his experience with the new system they are about to install. He meets with his new manager who is enthusiastic about having him join the team. The manager promises they will get together to discuss what needs to be done and get his perspective on how best to do it.

After two weeks, the manager comes in and apologises. There have been some problems and he had to meet with higher-level management to sort things out. It won't happen again, "You go ahead and do your thing, and we can talk next week." However, it not only happens again and again, but the manager also promises to have team meetings, "so we can get the team organised." He also misses these meetings, not always, but often. We now have a clear pattern:

- Manager says they will meet –promises it will happen.
- Manager often, but not always, misses the meeting or is late.
- Manager apologises and says he will make it up (but doesn't).

Manager promises to meet but does not. The employee learns the pattern but, of course, this is not at first an issue. The manager is very busy at work, but over time the manager's behaviour begins to be judged against the values continua and the employee sees him as untrustworthy, disrespectful and maybe dishonest. The employee doesn't like to feel like this and seeks to understand what is going on. He checks with other team members and finds they have similar experiences with the Manager. This reinforces the rating on the values continua and in building a mythology we have constructed a more general proposition that "this manager is untrustworthy and doesn't care about his team members." In summary, the following process has occurred:

- Manager promises to meet and discuss tasks to be completed.
- Series of of similar actions – pattern observed.
- Values continua rating – manager is untrustworthy, disrespectful and dishonest.
- Test with people in a similar situation, other team members – finds commonality.
- Finds team members like himself – build mythology.
- Formulate a general proposition – "Managers (in this organisation) are untrustworthy." Builds a culture.

This mythological development occurs in many settings; it can continue over generations. Stewart has noted that in Australia the relationships between labour and management still reflect the mythologies created when Australia was a prison. There were only two classes of people in the early years – prisoners and guards. The guards could not be trusted, were dishonest, showed no respect for human dignity or love for their charges. From the point of view of the prisoners they were at the negative ends of all the scales of shared values.

Listening to a unionised workforce today, the same perspective of the prisoners pervades their thinking. Managers have too often continued the outlook of the guards, that their workers are bludgers – lazy and unwilling to work, sneaky, not to be trusted, showing no respect for management and in general a poor lot that have to be watched carefully. Bringing the two cultures together in a productive working relationship is a difficult issue for Australian managers.

## Why Mythological?

Over the years some people have found the term mythology confusing, or they would argue it is a misleading term. "This implies our judgments are based on myths and therefore are not true," they have argued. This is, however, a very limited view of mythology. As we said, this term was chosen deliberately after considerable research and experience. Myths are stories that have a fundamental truth embedded in them. Maybe not here, but somewhere. It was chosen because it is a combination of mythos and logos (Campbell, J. with Moyers, B. 1991).

If we take a purely rational or logical view of the world, then we exclude a vast amount of human history (everything from before 3,000 years ago). We also miss out on the essential human need to make sense of the world without the advantage and time it takes to make purely rational and logical decisions. (To use popular fictional characters, we are not all Dr. Spocks or Data from Star Trek.) We are also driven by custom, by feelings and inspired by the stories (myths) told to us by our families, friends and our society (Campbell, J., 2008, 1949).

Children love stories; they demand that their favourite stories be read or told over and over again. In adulthood, the film industry and a large amount of television and entertainment is based on telling stories. (Some of the most popular films, such as the Star Wars series, and books, such as Harry Potter, are based on ancient myths that have been retold for generations.) Even computer games have story lines with heroes and villains. All the major religions are based on books that essentially tell stories about God and people.

All of the above are designed to tell us how good people (heroes) behave, and how bad people (villains) behave, and how most of us muddle along in between (but always with the hero inside ourselves). These stories give us a framework within which we can begin to organise our world and behaviour. Thus, the term mythology combines the story with its essential emotional component with the logos – the logical, rational, scientific element. Thus, our lenses are a combination of the two, neither wholly one nor the other.

This is of particular relevance in organisations when behaviour or opinion is dismissed as "illogical" or "emotional," as if rationality is the only or at least the superior element. Underneath this dismissal is actually an admission of the failure to empathise with the other or to understand how they view the world. As leaders, we ignore other people's mythologies at our peril. Understanding your team members' mythologies enables managers to predict the reactions to decisions or changes that occur in the normal course of business.

To summarise, we all have a unique pair of mental glasses with mythological lenses. (One wonderful quality of such lenses is that we each have a pair which accurately sees the world, while, sadly, everyone else's lenses are slightly, or significantly, distorted.) Nonetheless, while these lenses are unique to the individual, they do have similarities with others and differences with others. We all have experiences both of sharing opinions and of coming into conflict with others with regard to opinions. No one exactly matches our world perfectly, but some have a pretty close match. Others seem to have a totally different (and, usually, therefore "wrong") view of the world. This brings us to the next major concept, culture.

## Culture

Culture is another word that suffers from overuse and underdefinition. We all seem to know what it means, but it is variously defined or, more often, used casually and not defined at all. It variously refers to national or ethnic identity, arts and refinement, organisations, professions, food, language or dress. Certainly, we regard a culture as that which attaches people to each other and at the same time differentiates them from other groups. Here, however, we are more specific.

> **Culture:** A group of people who share mythologies, that is, who judge specific behaviour similarly on the shared values continua.

Mythologies are stories containing a fundamental truth that inform and explain others' behaviours. One way to identify a particular society is to identify the mythologies that are shared by most members of that society. A culture is a group of people who share common mythologies. A nation, an ethnic group, an organisation will all have an identifiable culture (or cultures). People who are from the same culture will have similar interpretations of observed behaviour, while those from different cultures may have quite different interpretations of the same behaviour. This is because a culture is a common set of mythologies, and interpretation of behaviour is based on our mythologies.

Thus, identical behaviour may be interpreted entirely differently in different cultures that share differing mythologies. This becomes

### Box 9.5 A Clash of Cultures

The computing department of a large corporation had employed a number of first- and second-generation Chinese who were very capable as programmers. A problem arose when a manager made a serious mistake which caused an application development to fall weeks behind schedule. The manager was angry because he was sure some of his subordinates had recognised the problem but no one spoke up. In trying to figure out what had gone wrong, one of the authors was asked to speak with all the employees to find out why no one had noticed the problem earlier.

After considerable effort to gain the confidence of the Chinese employees, it turned out several of them had known of the problem, but, in their culture, a subordinate should never tell a manager he is wrong. Pointing out the problem would have embarrassed the manager (he would lose face), shown disrespect, would have made the subordinate appear untrustworthy. Not speaking up was not seen as dishonest, but as polite.

It turned out this problem existed throughout the Department, so the consultant met with a number of teams to introduce the universal values and how our differing mythologies caused us to view the same behaviour quite differently. This opened the minds of both the team members and their managers and encouraged them to share some of their mythologies. It took considerable courage for the Chinese to explain that, in their culture, an important mythology stated one should never correct a manager and why. The Americans found it easier to explain their mythologies that in this country identifying a problem was expected and would be viewed positively. The manager appreciated when people spoke up as it helped the entire team.

Change was not instantaneous, but as one manager said afterward, "Now I understand. I will make sure my team understands we all have a responsibility to correct any mistakes before the problem grows." The Chinese team members said they felt relief because they did not want the manager to lose face, but they knew there was a problem that needed to be corrected and they did not know how to do it. Within a few months, this problem disappeared.

important as our societies become more multi-cultural and we must take into account how others will perceive our behaviour.

In most societies, some cultures are embedded within larger cultures, as organisations are embedded in their societies. The people in any organisation will bring with them mythologies from the larger cultures of which they are part, and over time they will come to share at least some of the mythologies of the organisation where they are work.

The strength of the culture will depend upon:

(1) The extent of shared mythologies – how much overlap among individuals.
(2) The relative importance of these mythologies to cohesion of the group.
(3) The context of the issue/behaviour being judged.

Thus, "culture" in this definition may well cross geographical boundaries, ethnic association, organisational or professional boundaries. While these may be the source of the stories (mythologies) that build a culture, they may also be the source of diversity. Indeed, we would argue that not being precise as to definition may lead to dangerous, even racist assumptions. For example, is there an African-American culture? Do Mexican-Americans share mythologies and to what extent? Do some Chinese-Americans have more in common with people outside this category than inside it, and how do we express that? How are rural Southerners different from urban mid-Westerners?

Many groups of people do have common stories, especially if they have experienced oppression. Mythologies created from oppression are rich in heroes and villains, and they have great strength and depth. It may be a false assumption, however, that later generations will necessarily internalise such mythologies in the same way as their earlier relatives. In fact, history is constantly being rewritten and re-evaluated based on contemporary issues and concerns.

There may be many different cultures within an organisation or ethnic group. It is important to ask the same basic question, "What is similar about the ways in which these people rate behaviour?" We must be careful about assuming there will be significant similarities just because a person is "working class," or "male" or "first generation" or Italian or "in sales" or whatever general and perhaps too convenient label can be stuck to them.

Culture is more subtle than that. Cultures may or may not be long-lasting. Recently "single issue politics" has produced an apparently diverse group of people who join together to resist an urban development, campaign for animal rights or against genetically modified foods and so on. At the other end of the spectrum there is a current anxiety with regard to what is termed globalisation, that international capitalism is creating a dominant culture that rides roughshod over less powerful and localised cultures.

Such concerns were expressed years ago, for example, in *The McDonaldisation of Society*, by George Ritzer (1993). It is interesting to note that Ritzer explains some of the attraction for this process lies in expanding predictability as in McDonald's, Holiday Inn and other similar organisations that are almost identical wherever in the world they are located, including controlled internal climates, furnishings and services.

## Summary

This proposition of universal values is quite radical. We have found that it is very helpful in creating a cohesive workplace because it starts from a proposition that we are essentially the same: all of the values are fundamentally important to all of us. Therefore, we have an opportunity to avoid starting with an "us and them" by being able to ask.... "why do you think that is fair/unfair?" "Why did you think that was a loving/unloving thing to do?"

Macdonald has used this approach in conflict resolution and especially cross-cultural dialogue.

We have stressed the importance of mythologies in creating culture; indeed, we would argue they are essential. We continue to argue for the need for a clear definition, hence the choice and explanation of the term mythology. Essentially we are influenced from birth by not just what we observe but by the way we make sense and categorise these observations. This sense is a combination of the stories we are told and the rational, logical application of reason.

From this we are able to categorise and rate behaviour along the values continua. We are naturally attracted to people who rate behaviour similarly. An entertainment industry is based on this.

TV shows where opinions are sought and commented upon are highly popular and attract like-minded people. Such shows rarely produce any change in view; in fact, they cater to the existing prejudices of their audiences. Their main function appears to be to reinforce views and assumptions and draw even clearer boundaries around cultures.

Cultures do not usually consist of people whose mythologies exactly overlap in every sphere of life and behaviour. Some may come close as in contemplative religious orders. Other cultures may be joined by disparate groups concerned with a single value or small range of issues.

So far we have discussed our definitions of key terms and why we believe these ideas reflect the realities we have found in organisations around the world. The next step is to look more specifically at how these ideas can be used by leaders to create, shape and change cultures in all types of organisations.

## Notes

1 We also recognise that effective leaders can be evil and yet seemingly "successful." Consider the authoritarian rulers such as Hitler and Stalin. They are good at manipulating people, often through arousing their hate of a vulnerable group, Jews, LGBTQ people, immigrants or capitalists. They use force, often violence, to take power. The opposite of our ideas of good leadership.

2 Recent research supports our hypothesis about human evolution. See "Advances in human behaviour came surprisingly early in Stone Age." *Tollefson J. Nature* (2018) Vol. 555, No. 7697, pp. 424–425. doi: 10.1038/d41586-018-03244-y.PMID: 29565410

# 10 The Work of Leadership

## Creating a Culture

### Introduction

We have defined the leadership work which is fundamental to the manager's role as well as the characteristics of a good leader. Part of that work is creating a largely predictable environment where workers can get on with their work without serious disruptions. Although no one can control all elements of the environment of an organisation, or even of a single part of the organisation, managers do make decisions which can improve the working environment whether physical, cultural or social. They must also schedule resources – a key part of leadership.

The physical environment includes such things as safe working conditions, production facilities, office buildings and amenities, transportation and parking, on-site health services among others. The culture of the organisation is also part of the working environment, and creating or changing the culture is a major part of a manager's work. As we have said, the leader's work is to create a single productive culture.

One measure of a positive culture in employment organisations is that all employees willingly work towards the achievement of the purpose of the organisation. In such an organisation improvement and innovation directed towards the achievement of this purpose occur as a matter of course. Creating such a culture builds on clarity of purpose and is achieved through three main leadership tools.

**Box 10.1 The Three Tools of Leadership**

- Behaviour.
- Systems.
- Symbols.

DOI: 10.4324/9781003459118-14

### Behaviour

As a leader, your own behaviour is visible and highly significant. Phrases like "walk the talk" or "practice what you preach" reflect the importance attached to behaviour. Parents are told, "Don't worry if your children don't listen to you; they are watching you all the time." This is also true for leaders in relation to their direct reports.

The consistency of a leader's behaviour will be scrutinised by team members. If the leader emphasises the importance of being on time, but frequently comes in late, this has an impact. Demonstrating the desired behaviour through role modelling makes clear what is valued (and what is not). People really do notice and take heart or are discouraged according to what the leader does.

One thing we warn against is referring to someone's attitude rather than their behaviour. Behaviour can be seen and evaluated; attitude is what someone is thinking and cannot be seen, but only inferred. It cannot be known. Behaviour is what is important. We can see it and it is what leaders must demonstrate in order to change behaviour to improve results and worker satisfaction. In other words, create a positive organisation within their area of authority.

### Systems

> **Box 10.2 System Defined**
>
> A system is a way of organising activities – flows of work, information and resources – to achieve a purpose.

Systems are the major driver of the organisation's behaviour and culture. Systems are to organisations as behaviour is to individual people. Both can be observed, and both are interpreted as visible manifestations of who and what is valued in the organisation. Symbols are also a type of system, but significant enough to deserve separate consideration.

Systems are powerful for two reasons. First, the systems operate all the time, all day, every day, while leaders are not available 24 hours a day, 7 days a week. Second, systems can become embedded and, like habits, they require such a specific repertoire of behaviour that eventually operators may just get used to them and act according to their dictates. "It's the way we do things around here." "Oh, you can't do that; we never do it that way." "We've always done it this way." The major problem is that systems, like all habits, can be good or bad. Even good systems can become outdated and counterproductive.

Systems are supposed to enable and encourage effective working and the achievement of purpose. Anyone who has worked in any organisation knows there are many systems that hinder productive work and make working life less productive and enjoyable than it could be. To have a strong influence on working life, the alignment of systems and behaviour is essential. It is difficult for leaders to counter bad systems and behaviour by others by their own behaviour alone. Leadership dependent on role modelling alone will not last in an organisation of any size beyond that of the leader. Behaviour will revert to what it was unless reinforced by systems.

The impact of systems, in our view, is underestimated both positively and negatively. In many organisations the complexity of work required to design productive systems is also under-rated (see Chapter 11). Systems are one of the key components of the Social domain. Having these organisational arrangements poorly designed and poorly functioning will have a large impact on outcomes and staff well-being as well as the organisation's reputation.

### Symbols

Symbols can be used by all leaders but can be particularly important to Chief Executives whose behaviour is highly symbolic, partly because it is not directly visible to most of the workforce. Their behaviour demonstrates what the organisation values. Same is true when the symbols recognise the work of employees. If symbols are to be seen as positive and helpful, it is essential that the systems and behaviour are aligned, so there are

#### Box 10.3 Symbol Defined

The outward display of a cultural group, e.g., flags, rituals, medals, posters, slogans. A symbol is a physical representation of the values of the organisation. Symbols are interpreted as representing a position that is strongly positive on the values continua by the culture that employs the symbol and strongly negative by members of countercultures.

no contradictions. If they are not aligned, symbols can be counterproductive and can very rapidly and strongly reinforce the negative mythologies that place the behaviour of leaders and the systems of the organisation at the negative ends of the values continua. If lack of trust prevails in the organisation, the workforce can become even more cynical.

### Box 10.4 A Symbol Can Change a Whole Organisation

A large corporation covering a large territory had an annual charitable drive to support various organisations and communities within its territory. Each unit of the organisation had someone representing the charity drive to encourage all employees to participate. This involved not only cash contributions, but volunteer work parties to build a playground or paint a childcare facility. Once a year they would meet at headquarters, some travelling several hundred miles to get there. The only room big enough to hold such a large group was the company cafeteria.

After the meeting broke up, a number of the participants got some food and drinks and sat around discussing with each other how they would approach their work as charity representatives before they hit the road. As it happened, the CEO walked into the cafeteria and saw a couple hundred people chatting and eating, even though it was not a meal or break time. He became furious and ordered steel gates be put on the entrances to the cafeteria and only be opened at certain times for meals and for morning and afternoon breaks.

The workforce did not respond well. They were furious and placed the CEO on the extreme negative ends of the scales of shared values – dishonest, untrustworthy, disrespectful of the dignity of the workforce, unloving and over time lacking the courage to change a highly resented decision. It became widely known that he had not even enquired as to what was going on. He also seemed unaware that the organisation rarely had enough conference rooms available for meeting, so the large cafeteria provided space to meet with enough distance for privacy. In addition, the company operated 24/7, so people on varying shifts counted on the cafeteria being open at odd hours.

When he retired, the new CEO asked his direct reports what should be his first actions as he took over the business. "Take out the damn steel gates." He did this immediately and it moved him to the positive end of the shared values continua. He was off to a good start which lasted for many years.

Certain organisations are much more aware of symbols than others. The military with its uniforms, rank identification and ribbons and medals offers an example. Those medals and ribbons recognise bravery in battle, combat experience and the *raison d'etre* of the armed forces. Churches are steeped in symbolism, whether a simple plain unadorned chapel or a massive cathedral with their gold, colour and rituals.

One of the most significant symbols in organisations are titles. What are you called? Changing titles can be one of the most contentious and difficult tasks to undertake in any organisation and go way beyond rational argument, as to the words being used. Rebranding initiatives are often viewed with scepticism by people within and outside an organisation. Changing the logo can alienate current users and may or may not attract new users.[1]

## Process of Building a Culture

**Dissonance:** Because a culture is made up of a group of people who share common mythologies, there are times a leader must change the prevailing mythologies – to create a new mythology in order that organisational purpose can be achieved. At the highest level of organisations, the most powerful tools to do this are systems and symbols. At lower levels, the primary tool is one's own behaviour (though behaviour is also a tool for chief executives).

Consider the mythologies of Australian labour and management, and how the views of the labour force might be changed. Typical myths would include "Managers will screw employees every chance they get," or, more succinctly, "All managers are bastards." What can managers do through their own behaviour to create a new mythology?

First, the manager must be aware of his or her subordinates' mythologies, how their lenses are constructed; then he or she must behave in ways that contradict the existing mythology. By acting in ways contrary to this myth, a manager can create dissonance, that is, people will experience something they do not expect. The "different" behaviour establishes noise that contradicts the prevailing myth and makes it difficult for people who hold the myth to predict the manager's behaviour, something they must do in order to feel safe. Through new experiences that are contrary to the myth and repetition of the new pattern of behaviour, dissonance accumulates, causing people to generate new hypotheses to explain the behaviour of their manager.

They may discuss different interpretations of the manager's behaviour with others (including spouses who are often influential in offering interpretations which differ from the prevailing myth). This generates a hypothesis that can then be tested against observed behaviour. At first, the new hypothesis may be "Managers will screw employees every chance they get, but watch out. This one doesn't do that; he's a sneaky one trying to make us think he is different and therefore not to be trusted."

**Consistency:** This stage of change is often discouraging, especially for young managers who are trying so hard to be fair, honest, show courage and be respectful of human dignity. Do not, however, give up. Over time new mythologies will take root if the manager's behaviour remains consistent. As with a child, consistency is essential as new hypotheses are being tested. As the manager continues to behave in ways which refute the old myth, the new hypothesis may become, "Managers will screw employees every chance they get, but this one is different. He can be trusted not to do that."

**Persistence:** If you remain consistent, the new hypothesis may be adopted throughout the organisation. "Managers will screw employees every chance they get, but in this company it is different. We can trust them." At the business run by Stewart, members of the workforce volunteered to testify for the company when the unions sued in the labour court claiming they had been voted out because of corporate malfeasance. The company won the case.

Until a new myth is established, even a single instance of behaviour that reinforces the old myth may destroy your efforts at change. Once a new myth is established, occasional deviations will be interpreted as deviations, not as instances of the old myth.

As a manager, any particular situation you confront may cause you to stress one of the shared values over another. Others may not perceive the situation as you do. This too can cause them to interpret your behaviour in a way that is different from your own interpretation. You may believe you are demonstrating the positive value you place on respect for human dignity, while your subordinates may perceive your behaviour as demonstrating their dignity is only important when it is convenient for you, not when the chips are down. Therefore, you are perceived as being dishonest, lacking courage and not to be trusted.

Thus we emphasise the importance of understanding the mythological lenses of your subordinates so that your behaviour will be seen at the positive ends of the scales of core values through their eyes, not simply your own. One of the best ways to learn this is to come up through the ranks, to have experience at the lower levels of organisation and have learned how your friends and peers at those levels see the world. Another way to learn this is to spend time with your employees, get to know them and talk about their views. A third way is used by the military where Sergeant Majors have the role of interpreting the needs and beliefs of the troops to the officers. Whatever the method used, such understanding is essential for effective leadership that is able to change mythologies and organisational cultures.

Macdonald has said that the work of leadership is to turn mythologies into hypotheses, creating questions where there were certainties. Be aware, however, that the attempt to change mythologies carries significant risk. In fact, we do not believe mythologies really change; the old mythologies may recede into the background like silt in a riverbed. They may even be forgotten by some, but they are likely to be present for many years. If behaviour slips to the negative side of the scales of shared values, the old negative mythologies, like silt being stirred up, will be retrieved and will be more powerful than ever, since the newer mythology proved to be false.

Some have suggested to us that knowledge of this model of leadership processes could make it easier for a dishonest manager to fool his subordinates. Any manager who believes he or she could do this should take care. The process is subtle and unforgiving.

The behaviour necessary to delude a subordinate has to be demonstrated in real time with absolute consistency and without flaw. One slip, one contradiction, one false cue instantaneously shifts the values assigned to the behaviour of the manager massively to the negative. The manager who is false is worse off by far as a result of his attempts at deception.

## Applying the Tools of Leadership

Using the tools of leadership, Figure 10.1 summarises the work of the leader.

This is a simple gap analysis describing the desired culture, where you want to go and the existing culture you want to change. How to get there is not often shown in such analyses, but here we provide you with specific tools to help you articulate and then create the desired culture.

### Step 1: Describe the Desired Culture

When applying this model in organisations, we ask people to describe the culture that they want to create in terms of actual

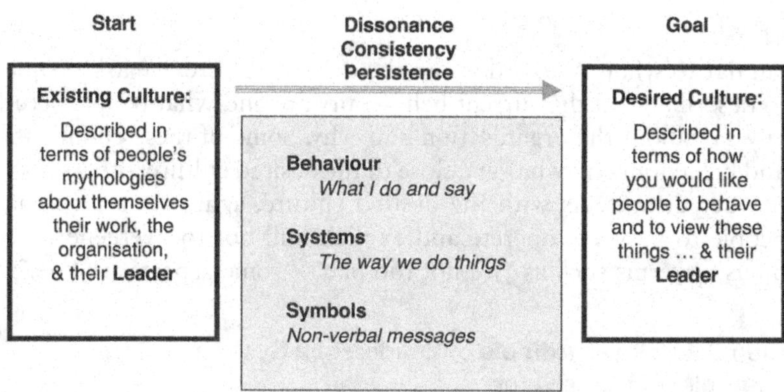


*Figure 10.1* The Tools of Leadership

behaviours. That is, we ask them to describe in concrete terms how they would like people to behave, how they would like people, including customers and other stakeholders, to describe the organisation and what sort of productivity or result they would be expecting.

A simple way of doing this is to ask the question:

> If I was to visit your organisation when it was operating exactly as you would like it to operate what would I actually see? How would I be treated and what would people say about the organisation and its leadership?

We ask people not to use general terms such as "people would be working well together," but to go to the next level of detail such as "when somebody makes a suggestion the leader will acknowledge and listen to that suggestion." "People actually make eye contact with each other and greet each other when walking through the organisation." "There is no litter, offices are tidy, people ask other people if they need help or if they want any help" and so on. These behaviours are observable. Similarly, we ask what would employees say about the organisation and why. For example, in the desired culture we might want people to say that they look forward to coming to work because they feel they are listened to and are given recognition and feel part of the team. They may say, "you've never asked us to do anything unsafe or unethical here and you consulted us about changes."

### Step 2: Describe the Existing Culture

Similar to what we asked about the desired culture, we ask people to describe what the current behaviours are and what people actually say about the organisation and why. Some of these comments and behaviours may be very close to the desired culture; others may be very distant. As with the desired culture, again we are asking people to be very concrete and explicit and not to overgeneralise by using terms such as "it's not too bad," "some aspects are fine."

### Step 3: Look at the Tools of Leadership: Systems, Symbols and Behaviour

We ask the question: "What is helping and what is hindering the creation of the desired culture?" For example, "what current systems are encouraging people to behave as you would like and what are actually making work life more difficult?" Similarly, are there behaviours making the desired culture difficult to achieve, especially the behaviours of leaders. Third, what are the symbols the people are proud of and represent the culture you are trying to build and what symbols are sending messages that are counterproductive? For example, when visiting an organisation, are safety exits and equipment clear and accessible? Are people at reception actually welcoming and helpful? One telling comment about such observations being symbolic is when someone says, "Well, that's typical" (either positively or negatively).

From this analysis we can construct a plan of work to redesign systems and symbols that encourage the desired behaviours in order to create the culture. As we mentioned before, this also requires an understanding of the mythological lenses of various stakeholders. It also requires, as we have said earlier, dissonance, consistency and persistence.

## Summary

The work of leadership is to create a culture. Whether intended or not, we believe that all leaders create a culture. It is just a question as to whether it is the culture they had intended. The concepts presented in Chapter 9 and the tools in this chapter should help the leader in any organisation to better understand the situation they are in and to create a more productive culture and change work behaviour. This is more likely to create a productive and positive organisation where people find their work more satisfying and even fun to work in.

In the next chapter we will discuss various types of systems and the questions that must be answered when creating new systems.

## Note

1 As this book was nearing publication, the change of the Twitter bird logo to a dark X, we would predict, will have significant impact upon existing users, some of whom have already left the site, and others who have been hanging in despite changes and difficulties.

# 11 Systems

## Descriptions and Design

### Introduction

The leadership of any organisation must work to ensure that employees act in such a way that they contribute to the purpose of the organisation while at the same time working within the law and the organisation's policies. Leadership, therefore, is about behaviour and changing behaviour.

As we have shown, a CEO has essentially three means of influencing the behaviour of the people in the organisation – behaviour, systems and symbols. Of these, systems are the major driver of the organisation's behaviour and culture. Systems are to organisations as behaviour is to individuals. Both can be observed, and both are interpreted as visible manifestations of who and what is valued in the organisation.

### Systems of Equalisation and Differentiation

It is useful to distinguish between types of systems and so understand their influence. The first distinction that we make is between equalisation and differentiation:

(1) Systems of equalisation that treat people the same way, whether they are machine operators, supervisors or executives. For example, safety rules are a common system of equalisation. Everyone must wear a hard hat in the construction zone or ear protection in a high-noise area.
(2) Systems of differentiation treat people differently. That is, they make a distinction between people in roles. The most widely used system of differentiation is compensation/pay. In most organisations, some roles are explicitly paid more than others. There may be further differentiation based on individual performance.

The most dramatic impact of change occurs when a change is made in a system that moves it across the boundary from differentiation

DOI: 10.4324/9781003459118-15

to equalisation or from equalisation to differentiation. Think of the discussion which takes place when reserved parking places are taken away and everyone has access to parking on a first come, first served basis – a move from differentiation to equalisation. Or its opposite when reserved parking is created for the top executives of the organisation but no one else.

It is important not to be confused by a system that applies to everyone and then assume it is one of equalisation. Compensation applies to all paid employees. A disciplinary system may apply to all. In fact, all systems that flow from policy should apply across the whole organisation.

The way to understand if a system is one of equalisation or differentiation is to consider its purpose. Is the intention to differentiate or to equalise? For example, we may all be subject to a disciplinary system, but it should only be applied on what we hope is the rare occasion when someone breaches the code or rules, and then not everyone in the organisation is disciplined.

## Equalisation/Differentiation: Good or Bad?

Sometimes, particularly in organisations based in democratic countries, it is easy to slip into the general view that equalisation is good and differentiation bad. This is certainly not the case. While it is very important to reinforce a sense of belonging in the organisation, this involves the proper use of both types of systems. Our basic principle is:

We can all think of a range of systems that could fall into either the equalisation or differentiation category. For example, car parking, clothing/uniforms, health care, cafeterias, facilities, transportation, leisure facilities, cars, office size, hourly rates, etc.

Our argument is that if you are going to differentiate then there should be a clear work-related reason. Thus, if we take sick leave why should some roles have a set number of days and others unlimited? Why should a certain group park within the site boundary and others not? The answer to these questions depends upon

> **Box 11.1**
>
> All Systems of Differentiation should be explained in terms of the work (to be) done. If you are going to differentiate then there should be a clear work-related reason.

whether there is a good work reason. For example, most sites have disabled parking bays near entrances or elevators. We understand the reason for this, and it is widely accepted as fair. Some may question, however, why a manager should have a reserved parking space when sales reps. who must go in and out of the office several times a day do not. If the company carries health insurance for employees, it may be enhanced for some roles where the people in such roles travel to countries where health care is less available or more expensive.

Conversely it is demoralising if systems that are supposed to equalise really differentiate. One of the authors (Macdonald) was running a workshop in a remote Australian mine-site. He asked a group of tradespeople what they saw as the most unfair system in the company. Now these were all members of a union and from a generally very egalitarian culture. The answer came back: "hourly rates are the same." What they meant was that pay for electricians was the same rate no matter how well, hard, poorly or carefully a person worked. Further, they all knew who the good performers were and who were the poor performers, but there was no recognition by the organisation of this fact, especially in pay. This was demoralising to the good performers whose superior contribution seemed to be irrelevant.

Thus, neither systems of equalisation nor systems of differentiation are inherently good or bad. Depending upon the organisation an individual is leading, either a system of equalisation or a system of differentiation may be more appropriate. The key to knowing which is better under what circumstances lies in an understanding of values that are shared by all human beings and the mythologies they use to interpret behaviour or systems. These mythologies determine the values the workforce will believe are demonstrated by the behaviour, systems or symbols.

In our own work in the United States, Australia and Great Britain, we have found that in employment roles, differentiation based on the work of the role is acceptable, even necessary. The principle of differential pay based on different work and differing levels of performance is seen as fair (although the amount may be questioned).

Equalisation is more likely to be perceived as fair in instances that are not directly related to the work. For example, everyone in the plant wears the same uniforms. Other places where equalisation is perceived as fair and differentiation unfair are in health benefits, safety systems, all hands meetings, cafeterias and company services.

**Box 11.2**

Another example comes from General Roderick Macdonald based on his experience as the leader of a British Royal Engineer Commando Regiment. He took over the regiment at a time it was experiencing severe leadership problems. There were a number of elements he had to change, but one in particular illustrates the importance of systems (and symbols).

At the time he took over the regiment, officers were allowed to wear any boot they preferred as long as it was black. The soldiers were required to wear military issue boots only. This was a source of dissatisfaction among the troops. Macdonald was aware of this, so one of his first acts was to allow soldiers the same freedom as the officers. While this may appear trivial, it was widely appreciated by the soldiers who recognised this commanding officer was different. Commandos operate on a basis of greater equality between officers and soldiers, so the change was not disturbing to the officers. The mythologies supported equality as fairness. This was, of course, one of many changes, but its symbolic importance began the overall change process.

Later Macdonald was asked if he would do this in other regiments. He immediately said, "No." For example, in a Guards Regiment (the people we see guarding Buckingham Palace and other prominent places), there is significant differentiation between officers and soldiers as many of the officers come from the aristocracy. The soldiers take considerable pride in having Lord so and so as their leader, so any move towards equalisation would be unacceptable. Here the mythologies support inequality as fairness and showing respect for human dignity.

There is no inherently good or bad choice of equalisation or differentiation. A system should be designed deliberately according to its purpose and the mythologies of the people who must work within it. To be a good leader you must understand your own mythologies and the mythologies of your workforce. When you implement a system you must have a very good idea whether it will be perceived as fair or unfair, honest or dishonest, as demonstrating respect for human dignity or lack of respect.

We have noted that to be a good leader you must behave in ways that are interpreted by your subordinates as being at the positive end of the scales of shared values. More importantly, your systems must demonstrate the positive end of the scales of shared values for those who view it or are part of it. Where a system should be placed depends upon their mythologies.

A system should be designed so the people in the organisation who are genuinely trying to do their best see it at the positive ends of the scales of shared values. People who are taking advantage of the current poor systems might perceive the change negatively. This is fine since they are the people who must either change their behaviour or leave.

## Authorised and Productive?

Another tool that we have developed to analyse systems and their impact on behaviour is one which asks how authorised and productive systems are (Figure 11.1):

| | Productive | Counter-productive |
|---|---|---|
| Authorised | A – Well designed and implemented. | B – Restrictive practices that have been adopted by the organisation. |
| Unauthorised | C – People "cutting corners" or breaking rules in order to get their work done. | D – Alternative leadership based on power e.g. intimidation, racism, sexism, work quotas, etc. |

*Figure 11.1* Systems – Authorised, Unauthorised – Productive, Counter-productive

**A** Good
**B** Area for Change.
**C** Positive opportunities for change or education.
**D** Must be addressed, challenged and done away with.

You will note that we use the term authorised and unauthorised. That is either approved or ratified by the organisation, or not. This distinction reinforces the distinction we made earlier between authority and power. We do not use the distinction between "formal and informal" systems since so-called "informal" systems may not be a matter of choice!

Obviously, we are trying to design and implement systems so that they fit into Box A – authorised by the organisation and productive in the sense that they contribute to achieving the purpose of the organisation, including a positive work environment. We are all familiar, however, with systems that while authorised are actually a hindrance to working effectively (Box B). We often describe such systems as highly bureaucratic or red tape or an annoyance.

They are obstructive and often people will "get around the system" in order to do their job. They cut corners to be more efficient or effective; thus, we get Box C.

Box C behaviours and systems can be very creative and productive, but they can also be dangerous, especially if any safety rules and behaviours are compromised. In public organisations Box C may be seen as the only way to get the job done, but there are dangers of denial of due process, inequities as well as safety issues. Box C may provide ideas for positive change and innovation, but the ideas must be examined carefully to ensure other problems are not being created through the Box C behaviours.

Box D behaviours and systems are not acceptable. Very simply this is behaviour that results in personal gain at the expense of the organisation. It may involve theft, racism, sexism and may be maintained by covert methods of intimidation. Behaviours and systems in Box D must be eradicated. Their existence is evidence of poor and weak leadership. As one worker said, "[the boss] either has no guts or no brains."

Thus, while Box C and D both involve the use of power, they are predicated upon very different motives and intent. It is essential to differentiate between them. A leader who disciplines someone who is well intentioned but who "bent" the rules while turning a blind eye to racism or sexism has effectively destroyed his or her own credibility in the workforce.

### Box 11.3 Working to Rule

Working to rule demonstrates the significance of Box B systems which do not work in practice. Air traffic controllers wanted to demonstrate the problems with their leadership and systems, but not go out on strike. Instead, they "worked to rule." They started following all the requirements of moving planes in airports and between origins and destinations. As a result, the entire air traffic system stalled. It was reported that a normal 2-hour flight from New York to Chicago took 8 hours. The traffic controllers had been making the system work by not following all the rules. This was risky because if there was an accident, the traffic controller could be blamed for not following the rules. A fine "Catch 22."

Something similar happens when police work to rule. They write more tickets and spend time on minor infractions and are late on certain "urgent" calls. The public gets furious and the city council in the United States, more often than not, gives them what they want (but not in the United Kingdom).

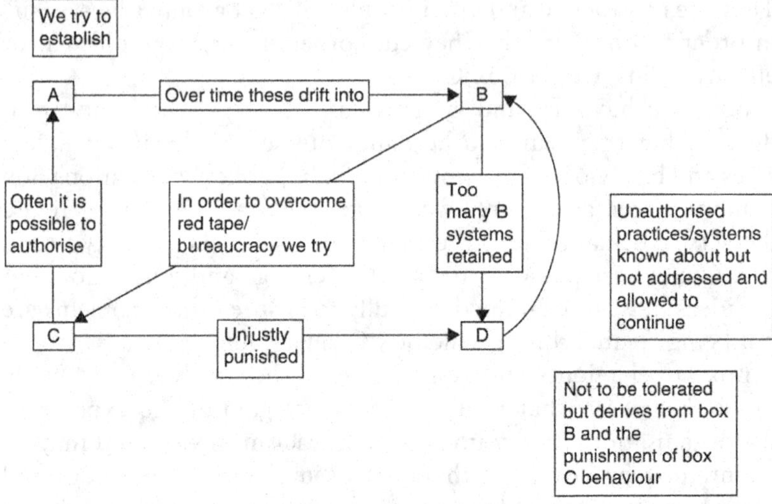


*Figure 11.2* How Systems Can Move from A through D

We have found its application to be one of the most useful of all our models in practice. It is important to see it as a dynamic model with linkages indicating how change may occur (Figure 11.2).

## Systems Design

Systems design is a complex and often difficult process if one wishes to create a positive corporate culture – one that demonstrates the positive end of the scales of shared values. Systems provide a framework within which flows of activity, including the work activity of people, take place. They help to turn the intention of the organisation, as stated in its purpose and policy, into the reality of day-to-day experience. The effectiveness of the organisation depends upon how well those systems are designed and implemented.

Given the importance of systems, it is surprising how many organisations do not properly resource their design and implementation. We believe this is largely for three reasons:

(1) Their significance is underestimated or misjudged.
(2) The difficulty or complexity of the work of design is underestimated and/or assigned poorly.
(3) There is not a simple set of criteria to guide the work of system design and implementation.

As we have tried to make clear, systems as well as behaviour and symbols are significant drivers of behaviour in organisations and have a strong influence upon how people place organisations on the scales of the universal values continua. Their significance should never be underestimated or misjudged.

System design work is of minimum III complexity (see Chapter 5) assuming the system will only apply in one field of knowledge. Such systems are rare. Most systems in organisations have effects on, and are affected by, the three principal domains of organisational activity – technical, commercial and social. This requires a minimum of IV capability which can integrate and manage the interactions from a variety of knowledge fields simultaneously. If the system is organisation-wide, its complexity will be higher depending upon the size of the organisation. Corporate-wide systems of international companies can easily require Level VI complexity work be applied in the design process.

If the complexity of the work of system design is underestimated and the task is assigned at too low a level, the result is likely to be a Box B system, which is inefficient, frustrating to try to use, and likely to lack key elements, particularly regarding social process issues. Instead of enabling process, you are likely to end up with a rigid set of rules that encourage people to find creative ways around the system (Box C) or, worse, promote the development of Box D behaviours.

## Design Criteria: The 20 Questions

These questions were created in response to leaders who wanted a more effective way to design systems. They can be used to both critique and design systems. People can use the questions to understand why systems are not working well, but the real work and gains come when those issues are addressed, and a new design produced. This chapter provides a basis for such work, but if you need greater depth of understanding, our book *Systems Leadership: Creating Positive Organisations* provides more detail.

Many of the readers of this book may be in a university programme or the early years of their career. Therefore, you are unlikely to be an owner or designer of systems, but you will certainly have to work within a variety of systems and as a recipient of their operations you will understand what works, what does not and most importantly why. This understanding will allow you to be an effective critic as well as someone who works on a team that gathers data and contributes to creating a Box A system.

We are aware of the amount of time and resources required to design and implement good systems. Therefore, if there is a problem, it is essential to first ask, is a system needed at all? Often, it is too easy to respond to the problem in an organisation by saying, "it's the system," and then modifying an existing system or bolting on additions to it. How does a proposed system simplify work and eliminate waste? It is essential to ask how this system (or potential system) fits with the organisation's purpose. How will the improved system integrate with what else is happening in the organisation? Is the benefit gained from the system enough to justify the cost, i.e., does the value received ratio exceed the cost invested?

The 20 questions which follow provide a guide to alert you to the key questions which arise as systems are critiqued or designed.

What follows is a brief account of how each question can be used in your organisation.

1) What is the Purpose of the System?

The purpose should be stated in a single sentence without the conjunction "and." This is the most important question because it is pointless asking all the other questions unless you are clear

**Box 11.4 20 Systems Design Questions**

1) What is the purpose of the system?
2) Who is/should be the owner?
3) Who is/should be the custodian/designer?
4) What is the underlying theory?
5) How is it to be measured?
6) Is it a system of equalisation or differentiation?
7) What are the current "benefits" of the poor system? Who gains from its inefficiency?
8) What are the boundaries of the system?
9) What are the linkages with other systems?
10) What structural boundaries does it cross?
11) Is the system one of transfer or transformation?
12) Are authorities and accountabilities consistent with roles?
13) Are there proper controls built into the system?
14) Is there an effective audit process?
15) Has the social process analysis been done?
16) Is there a fully outlined flowchart or flowcharts?
17) Is there a design plan that addresses the critical issues?
18) Is there full systems documentation?
19) What is the implementation plan?
20) What is the final cost of design and implementation?

on purpose. Ultimately the purpose is defined by the owner (see question 2), but it is essential to discuss it with the leadership team and perhaps other stakeholders, including the people who will operate the system.

2) Who is, or should be, the Owner of the System?

The owner of the system is the person in the role that has the authority to change or even remove the system. Too often the system owner either is or is perceived to be a specialist. For example, the head of Human Resources owns the people systems. This dilutes the authorities of leadership to their detriment by handing over authority for a core part of this work of leadership – the design and implementation of systems – to such specialists. They confuse expertise with leadership. System owners should usually be line managers who are appropriately at Level IV or above. All systems will have some variance; limits of the variance must be set by the owner. We have never seen a successful implementation of a system that is perceived to be owned by a Function, such as HR or Purchasing.

3) Who is/should be the Designer/Custodian?

The designer and custodian may be people in different roles or may be the same person in both roles. The designer is the person whose work is to manage the work of system design to the point where a proposal for the complete system can be presented to the owner for authorisation or for more work. This can be complex and time-consuming and can involve specialist knowledge. A small team of three or four members, with a range of knowledge and experience, headed by a highly capable person in at least a Level IV role is an effective way to approach this issue. The team can call on people from all levels, especially users, for comment and advice. The custodian of the system is the person in a role who makes sure the system is operating as it should and collects information concerning its operation. This is where Functions come into their own as advisors and designers.

4) What is the underlying theory?

All systems and processes are essentially methods of changing an input (or inputs) into an output (or outputs). Do you know why these (should) work? Why do you think this system will encourage the behaviour that is intended? Too often systems are designed and implemented in an apparently pragmatic way, or simply because "other organisations do it that way." This is more often the case with Human Resource systems than with technical systems. Consider pay for performance or bonus systems. On what basis are they supposed to encourage more productive or creative behaviour? There is a general misunderstanding that what is most popular at the time is "best practice" when it is just common practice that might be working equally poorly everywhere.

5) How is it to be measured?

The measurement of the effectiveness of the system should be directly related to the purpose. We need to know how or whether the purpose is being achieved. We do not advocate an excess of measures but rather several key measures that can clearly be connected to the purpose. Not all measures have to be quantitative. Qualitative measures are also important and can be quite objective; just ask people: "what do think about this system?"

6) Is the system of differentiation or equalisation?

It is important to decide whether the purpose of the system is intended to apply to all employees or only some. Differentiation is acceptable, even required, for systems related to work. Equalisation is most effective in such systems as safety and health care.

7) What are the current "benefits" of the poor system?

Many poor systems are accepted because they provide benefits for some people. A new system may bring about cost savings and improvements, but some people may gain from the current inefficiency. For example, an overtime system may allow certain employees to earn double time for 4 hours when they are only called out for 30 minutes. These people will not be happy if the system change removes this "benefit." Don't think you will always be praised for bringing in new systems that shed light on or may block unauthorised practices.

8) What are the boundaries of the system?

This question refers to where the system begins and ends. There are no absolute rules for deciding where either the beginning or the end should occur. For example, an organisation may have one system to fill roles in the organisation. This could also be divided in smaller systems such as recruitment, appointment, induction and promotion. Where the boundaries are placed depends upon the needs of the business at any time and is an executive decision (see discussions with owner in Question 2).

9) What are the linkages with other systems?

In designing systems, it is important to be aware of the interaction between systems. Too often, systems are designed and implemented in isolation. It is only after their implementation that we notice they are not compatible with other existing systems.

10) What structural boundaries does the system cross?

Systems that cross structural boundaries, such as between different departments in the organisation, or from one organisation to another, create a potential for conflict and loss of efficiency and effectiveness. This can add complexity and be significantly more difficult to design. If management systems are crossing boundaries, it may indicate a need for a structural review. In general, it is useful to minimise such boundary issues, perhaps by building several smaller systems that can be measured at the boundary.

11) Is the system one of transfer or transformation?

What occurs in the box is either transfer or transformation (Figure 11.3). If it is transfer, the system is intended to deliver C in the same state as A. Transfers are transportation systems like freight or postal deliveries where considerable effort is exerted to make sure what is transferred is not changed or damaged. Some business systems are intentional transformations where C is significantly different from A, such as turning iron ore into steel. Whatever the core activity, transfer or transformation, it is critical in system design to minimise the other as they always add cost.

12) Are authorities and tasks consistent with roles?

This question checks that what employees are asked to do by the system does not contradict or clash with their role in general. Causes of such clashes could be that the system requires more or less discretion regarding budgets and expenditures, or the time allowed for certain actions is too short or too long.

13) Are there proper controls built into the system?

Too often systems are designed and implemented without any forms of control built into them. The controls in the system are designed to make sure it is operating as it was designed to, i.e., within its variance limits; they provide information as to whether or not this is the case. (See question 3 on the work of the custodian.) Sometimes systems with regard to the actions of people

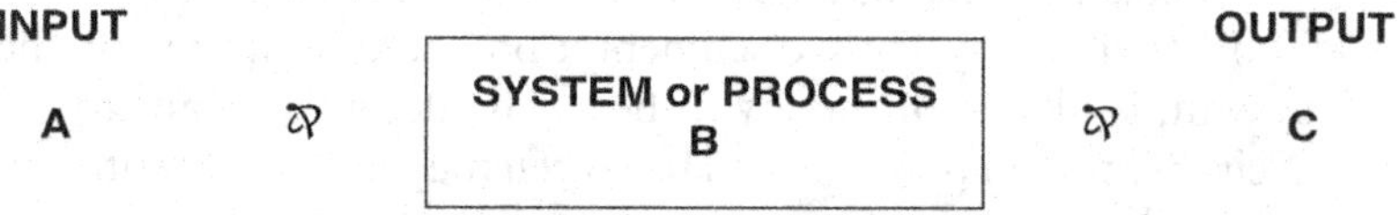


*Figure 11.3* System of Transfer or Transformation

are implemented without knowing whether the system is being implemented as intended. This can be described as reliability.

14) Is there an effective audit process?

Audit is different from control in that it first checks from time to time that the controls are in place, whether or not they are being used and acted on and whether they are still valid indicators of system functioning. The audit then reviews whether the system is achieving its purpose and the best way to achieve that purpose. Auditors are typically independent of system operators but report findings of the audit to the system owner. This can be described as validity.

15) Has the social process analysis been done?

The social process analysis refers to the work that is needed to discover how the current situation is viewed (current mythologies) and the views or mythologies around any proposed changes. This needs to be done with great care as all assumptions need to be checked so that there are no surprises. This question helps in the consideration of how the implementation might be handled (see Chapter 10).

16) Is there a fully outlined flowchart or flowcharts?

Detailed flowcharting specifies the detail, whether it is a flow of materials, money, information, people, work or equipment. There are many methods of flowcharting, many using software. There may be several flowcharts, tracking flows of any items mentioned above.

17) Is there a design plan that addresses the critical issues?

Looking at question 16, it is important that the design team identify and address the critical issues. Critical issues are "what ifs." These are issues if they are not addressed will prevent the achievement of the purpose of the system. For example, what if significant stakeholders hold negative mythologies about the new system? How is this going to be addressed, and how is the context and purpose going to be explained to people? Not everything is a critical issue. There are usually three or four that are most important.

18) Is there full systems documentation?

Systems documentation is the unloved child of systems design. Too often the systems documentation, or description of the system, is absent or patchy at best. The designers want to see their creation in practice, and too often they put documentation off until tomorrow. There is no need to write whole books on each system, but simply consider if someone new was coming into a role, is there a written account that would explain to the person how the system is actually meant to work?

19) What is the implementation plan?

Sometimes systems fail because, even if they are well designed, they are implemented without proper education and training. Training in a new system can be a major undertaking, but it is pointless to introduce a new system half-heartedly. Training and implementation programmes are not just about the technical details but should also be informed by all these questions, especially purpose, gains to be achieved, and social process and behaviour requirements for the new system to be a success. Good systems documentation can inform the implementation and training plan.

20) What is the final cost of design and implementation?

Finally, it is important to revisit the cost. In designing the system, its processes and implementation, critical issues which may arise that must be addressed. It is rare to have an initial cost estimate that is entirely accurate. This last step should estimate more realistically the overall cost and calculate that against the value expected. It may be that the system is regarded as too expensive and is therefore not implemented. This is the opportunity to learn how to cost future system costs and value.

## Summary

This chapter has continued to examine how leaders can use systems to build productive cultures. Recognising there are systems of differentiation based on the work of the role, and systems of equalisation that apply to all employees, systems can be authorised or unauthorised, productive or unproductive.

Leaders who recognise the power of systems make sure they are designed to embody the values and mythologies they wish to put forward to create a productive and positive organisation. The 20 questions can help in systems design.

In the following chapter we will discuss the importance of safety and the systems needed to produce it. It is impossible to have a positive organisation if your employees suffer injuries and even death.

# 12 Safety

## Systems, Behaviour and Symbols

### Introduction

Safety is a key part of developing a positive work culture in every organisation – arguably, the most important people system (McDonald, Ken, 2016). As Stewart said in a speech to the Australian Mines and Metals Association, "It is hard to win the hearts and minds of your workforce if you are killing and maiming them."

To build a safe, positive organisation, however, takes many systems from the technical and social domains of work. In advanced industrial societies, there are legal requirements and penalties for violations to help keep people safe, though enforcement may be problematical. Most important, safety requires leaders at all levels of the organisation to behave in ways that offer consistent, positive reinforcement of safety practices.

We recognise that safety is a large and complex area of study involving many technical fields which are linked to human capabilities and social processes. Safety, in its entirety, cannot be covered in a single chapter, but we can discuss key elements in the social domain. As discussed in Chapter 10, systems, behaviour and symbols can be used to create a culture of safety in the organisation where you work.

The purpose of safety systems and safe behaviours is to allow everyone on the job to go home in as good condition as when they arrived. Therefore, it is necessary to be clear on the work that must be done to achieve that purpose. This chapter will focus on how systems can be applied to manage safety performance covering:

- The types of safety behaviour.
- Individual behaviour versus custom and practice.
- Cultural traits of a safe environment.
- The leadership work required to manage safety.

It is a requirement for every employee to work safely and to remove any unsafe condition or behaviour when they see it, or to report

DOI: 10.4324/9781003459118-16

it to someone who has the authority to do so. It is critical that managers create an environment for their team members where work can be carried on safely and team members are best placed to achieve their task assignments. The Manager's behaviour regarding safety has a highly significant influence on their team members' behaviour. It is and becomes part of the culture.

Is safety a priority? One of the most successful MDs that we worked with, and whose business had a remarkably good safety record, was asked: "is safety your number one priority?" "No," he said, ... "it is an absolute requirement and a condition that sets limits on our behaviour, it is non-negotiable." As such, he was placing safety as part of the limits of a task; it is a boundary condition, not simply a priority. Priorities can change.

Placing people in the right roles at the right level to match their capability is essential. People who are in roles that exceed their capability are more likely to make mistakes that endanger themselves and others. People who are in roles that do not use their capability may become bored, distracted, cut corners or simply become careless.

As employees observe systems and leadership behaviour, they will place it on the scales of shared values for good or ill. Unsafe systems and behaviour are placed at the negative ends of the scales indicating the leadership of the organisation, or specific managers, are not to be trusted; they don't care about their employees. Leaders are seen as dishonest when they say safety is important but they behave in ways that violate safety rules and allow unsafe conditions to persist.

It is behaviour that is observed; when words don't match behaviour, employees know their manager is dishonest. To create a safe and positive organisation, managers at every level must act to demonstrate that safe behaviour is a requirement. We have also shown systems are the drivers of behaviour, especially those of recognition, review and reward. What you recognise and reward is what you get.

## Improving Safety – Work in the Technical Domain

Technical improvements have had a significant positive effect on improving safety whether in mines, factories, traffic, agriculture. Nonetheless, there are still too many accidents and deaths, despite designing machines and systems that take into account human failings, both physical and mental.

We are all aware of the technical improvements in car safety. In the United States 50 years ago, in 1972, there were 56,278 motor vehicle deaths, a rate of 26.9 per 100,000 population. The death rate per 100 million miles driven was 4.43. To compare, in 2021 there were 46,950 motor vehicle deaths, a rate of 14.3 per 100,000 population. The death rate per 100 million miles driven was 1.50.[1]

Improvement is also demonstrated in US data on deaths and injuries at work. Thirty years ago, in 1992, there were 6,217 deaths at work with a death rate of 5.0 per 100,000 workers. In 2021 there were 5,190 deaths with a death rate/100,000 workers of 3.6.[2] There were also 4,260,000 medically consulted injuries.[3]

Despite these and many other improvements, there are still too many deaths at work, 5,190 in 2021 and 2.6 million injuries in the United States. It is also true that some industries and organisations have far better safety records than others. Clearly, some industries have more inherently and therefore potentially dangerous jobs than others. In the United States, Construction, Transportation and Warehousing followed by Agriculture, Forestry, Fishing and Hunting have the highest number of preventable fatal work injuries.[4]

Most organisations have very similar safety systems that include risk assessments, incident investigations, safety procedures, check sheets and so on; i.e., the technical tools are very similar if not identical. There are, however, very different safety results – some very good, some very bad.

Clearly, the technical tools are essential, but what really makes a difference is the way in which people work and the impact of leadership, particularly the way leaders behave. Effective management of safety then involves the technical processes as organised in the safety system as well as the way in which the system is used – the social systems and the resultant behaviour. This is where organisations tend to differ in their approach.

## Damaging Incidents Happen, but Why?

Too often individuals are blamed for incidents that cause damage to humans, organisations or the environment. Nearly 100 years ago, W.H. Heinrich (1931) analysed a significant number of safety incidents. He concluded that nearly 90% of all these were caused by unsafe behaviour, while unsafe conditions accounted for around 10% of the total. It is also noteworthy that these incidences occurred even though organisations had extensive knowledge of how to prevent them, mainly because similar issues had occurred in the past.

Consequently, there is a lot of discussion about behaviour and in the understanding of why work is carried out in an unsafe manner. Some of these discussions are particularly ill informed and, quite naturally, tend to be highly emotional. Unfortunately, safety work based on behaviour tends to get a bad name because it is often associated with a focus on the individual and, quite often, blame rather than accountability.

This is exactly the point that Reason (2008, 1997 1st ed.) makes in his book *Managing the Risks of Organizational Accidents*. Just stating that behaviour matters gives the impression that all at-risk behaviour is of the same psychological origin rather than being due to a number of factors. Human behaviour, though it clearly matters when trying to manage safety, it is what drives that behaviour that is so important in the leadership work as well as the accountability to design, implement or change a system that might induce unsafe work practices.

In general, people know that behaviour matters, but lack an understanding about what drives that behaviour and, more especially, what is to be done about it. By focusing on unsafe behaviour the leaders in an organisation tend to look at the symptom, rather than the cause of the behaviour. In short, unsafe conditions exist because there is a management system that allows them to. More specifically, unsafe behaviour exists because of the systems that drive it. There are reasons that people engage in unsafe behaviour that are often custom and practice (W.H. Heinrich, 1931) driven by management systems such as the way people are rewarded, or the way leaders behave.

As has been demonstrated by Reason (2008, 1997 first ed.) and McDonald, G. (2007), damaging incidents have a number of causes and conditions that must all be present if the incident is to occur. "A condition is not necessarily a cause, but something whose presence is necessary for the cause to have an effect – like oxygen is a necessary condition for a fire, though an ignition source is the direct cause" (Reason, 1997:1). The term "cause" is often interpreted as a single thing that "caused an incident." Geoff McDonald speaks of contributing factors, "defined as any factor that may have contributed to the damage occurring" (quoted in McDonald, K., 2016).

### Box 12.1 Death in a Mine

The three underground coal miners were at the end of their night shift. Transport to the surface was not available because the personnel transport system was broken down. To get to the surface to change and return home, they climbed onto the ore conveyor even though this was forbidden. Unfortunately, one individual fell and was killed.

Were the workers to blame for violating a company rule that it was forbidden that anyone ride the ore conveyor? What were the conditions and contributing factors that led to this tragic incident? What systems, behaviours and symbols contributed to this outcome, and what conditions, if they had not been present, would have prevented it from happening?

The investigation showed that at least once a week the personnel transport system broke down. When this happened, the operators had to walk to the surface; about 800 metres up a steep incline. At the end of the shift the Company Bus took employees to the nearby town where they lived. The bus left 45 minutes after the shift ended to allow employees time to shower and change. If employees missed the bus, they had three options. They could walk, get a taxi (at their own expense) or stay at work. In winter when there is deep snow on the ground, employees are not allowed to walk home, as they could get lost in the snow. They therefore stay at work and miss seeing their families. Because of this it had become common practice to ride the ore conveyor, especially when the personnel transport system failed or was congested.

## Building a Safety Culture – Work in the Social Domain

What were the systems, behaviours and symbols that led to this disaster?

Behaviour: At the end of a night shift, the last thing the miners wanted to do was walk up a steep incline and then choose whether to run for the bus or have a shower and possibly not get home. Very human behaviour.

Leadership ignored or were complicit about riding on the ore conveyor. It was the thing to do. Everyone did it, including the leadership. It was normalised by their behaviour.

Systems: Breakdowns in the personnel transport system happened frequently and fixing it was not a priority. In contrast, when production equipment broke down it was fixed immediately.

The decision to give only 45 minutes to catch the bus put pressure on workers to get to the top quickly.

Most importantly, the mine also had a substantial bonus system that could double an employee's pay on an annual basis if production targets were met. The production was so important because it was set up with a transfer pricing system (to avoid taxes) with a nearby steel works owned by the same company. Thus, if production targets were not met, then neither the mine nor steel works would be profitable.

Symbols: The behaviours of the leadership riding the ore conveyor demonstrated that this unsafe behaviour was authorised. The lack of urgency to repair the personnel transport system could also be considered as a symbol of the concern, or lack thereof, for worker safety.

In sum, the behaviour of riding the ore conveyor had become normalised because of the behaviour of both leadership and workers. No one had been hurt, so even though it was forbidden, "everyone does it."

Whether the systems are about production bonuses, bus timetables or maintenance of equipment, they all have an impact on behaviour. Until they are changed, there won't be much change in the result.

We cannot know the mythologies of the workforce, but even without that, it is clear the culture rewarded production and did not really care about safety. To build a culture of safety requires both technical and social analysis to build systems that drive the safe behaviour desired. Most importantly, it requires the visible and consistent behaviour of leadership, from the floor superintendent to the MD or CEO.

### Box 12.2 Leadership and Safety

Another example of the importance of leadership behaviour demonstrating the importance of safety was from Stewart who put these ideas into practice from the day he started as Managing Director (MD) of Comalco Smelting. The retiring MD took him around to all the smelters (in Tasmania, North Queensland and on South Island, New Zealand). In each one he met with the General Manager and his direct reports (Mutual Recognition Unit (MRU) managers) in a meeting of each smelter's leadership. He asked the question, "what comes first here, safety or production?" "Of course, safety." "Do all of you agree?" "Yes, smelters are dangerous work environments, so safety must be first." Then he would say, "I'm going to visit the workforce here in the smelter, would they agree?" A bit of squirming and discomfort. Then one brave person would say, "Well production is really important, but of course we are concerned with safety as well."

"Wrong. Safety is not negotiable."

Not too long after, there was an opportunity to drive home the point. Stewart was on one of his routine visits to a smelter and was on an "inspection tour" of the pot room (where the aluminium is produced) with the General Manager and Pot Room Superintendent. At one point he noticed a loose lock pin on a transfer crucible and stepped away from the group to kick the crucible. Its lock pin (8″ long and about 1½ inches in diameter with a flange to hold it in place) fell on the floor. Such crucibles carried molten aluminium that was transferred by a forklift crane overhead from the pot room to an open-hearth furnace. If the lock pin came loose while in transit, the crucible could tip and release the molten aluminium at somewhere between 940 and 960 degrees Celsius killing or at least horribly burning anyone below. He did not yell or berate anyone; he just kicked the lock pin across the floor, said nothing and walked back to the group. The shock was palpable.

Everyone there understood the extreme seriousness of the problem. One worker said, "It had to be the bloody MD who saw it." It started the story that he had eyes in the back of his head which is why he saw everything. The story rapidly spread to the other smelters. It was reported a couple of years later to one of the co-authors at a different smelter. The story had grown far beyond the facts into quite a drama – an interesting legend about the MD. Safety clearly came first. The emphasis on safety practices and systems which were being implemented later allowed for many other changes and improvements in the organisation; see Macdonald, Burke and Stewart (2018).

## Improving Safety – The Importance of Law – Accountability in Managing Safety

As with all work, effective task assignment, feedback and holding people to account is essential in managing safety. At higher levels of the organisation, the legal framework can play an important role in ensuring senior leaders are held to account for their work in guaranteeing people are safe in the organisations that they manage. Some organisations are able to do this regardless of the prevailing legal requirements. Some, however, do not.

In the United States there are federal laws and regulations to ensure workplace safety, which is administered by the Occupational Health and Safety Administration (OSHA). There are also state laws that differ from state to state, some quite strict and others less so. The real differences in the United States is that enforcement is spotty and in many places non-existent. Citations are written, but they can be tied up in courts for years.

| | USA | Australia |
|---|---|---|
| Number of Fatalities | 5,190 | 169 |
| Fatality Rate per 100,000 employees | 3.6 | 1.3 |

*Figure 12.1* Industrial Fatalities

In Australia, on the other hand, regulations are seriously enforced. In the case of mine managers, their licence to be a mine manager is removed if there is a death in their facility. A special court will decide if the mine manager was at fault and his licence is then permanently revoked. This is a serious penalty and gives great incentive to keep your mine safe. Figure 12.1 shows the fatalities in all industries in both countries in 2021 together with the fatality rate per 100,000 employees.

It is also noteworthy that the fatality rate in the United States hasn't improved over the last decade, while Australian industries have decreased theirs by 35% in the same timeframe. There are other reasons for this difference, but clearly the notion of accountability, as with all work, is important in managing safety. Awareness and exhortation are not sufficient.

## Types of unsafe behaviour

There are several reasons for unsafe behaviour. There are two broad groups. Either the person(s) involved knew what to do, but intentionally didn't do it (violation), or there was a mistake, lapse of memory or slip (error). Of course, people can intentionally break a "bad" (counterproductive) rule or procedure. This fits Box C of the Systems Matrix and represents an opportunity to improve. It is of utmost importance for leaders to understand these various types and causes for each; otherwise any remedial action is likely to have, at best, no effect or potentially a negative impact.

### Error-Based Safety Behaviour

James Reason (2008, 1997, 1st ed.) is regarded by many to have advanced the thinking about the management of error-based safety behaviour. He also distinguishes between the roles of conscious and subconscious activity.

The subconscious mode is one that is essential for managing those things that we must do automatically, and quite often in parallel, in everyday life. We are generally not aware of the process that generates the action, but are often aware of the result, e.g., breathing and walking.

The conscious mode, however, occupies much less of our brain activity. By comparison with the subconscious, it is typically sequential and laborious. It is the mode used to attend to, and make decisions about, the current environment. It is the type of mental activity that should be helpful in potentially at-risk activities. When other things occupy this thinking mode, it is to the detriment of being attentive, e.g., using a mobile phone while driving. Consequently, many strategies to do with reducing error focus on ensuring that the conscious mind is attentive. Some authors refer to this as mindfulness.

Skill-based errors tend to occur during highly routine tasks when attention is diverted away from the activity. This is especially true when the task has been performed many times before, even though the individual may have the right knowledge and skillset. In fact, the more often the task has been performed, the more mundane it appears, and the more likely errors of this type will be made. This lack of mindfulness is especially a problem when the probability of failure is perceived to be low, but the consequence of that failure is significant.

Errors can occur in planning as well as executing a task. In planning, errors are classified as mistakes, while in execution they are typically the result of slips and lapses due to the lack of mindfulness. They have different causes.

Mistakes can be the result of knowledge and skill deficiencies and can point to competency issues as well as the need for more proactive supervision. Leaders must be visible in the workplace actively helping people carry out their work safely as well as identify any competency needs. Disciplinary action is inappropriate in these cases.

A word of caution, though. Training tends to be an easy default for many safety behaviour issues. It is also likely that similar mistakes are common amongst a group of people, so that the corrective action needs to be applied to everyone.

The type of culture that is required to minimise this lack of attention is one where people have a chronic unease brought about by a preoccupation with failure. Systems must cater for this, not only in a technical way by engineering control systems, but also by appropriate people systems. One such system is an effective use of check sheets as used, for example, by airline pilots. It is known as point and call. In Japan, this system (shisha kanko) has been used on the railways for more than 100 years. Conductors point at critical controls that need checking and then name them out loud. This helps them keep in the moment so nothing gets overlooked. A 1994 study by Japan's Railway Technical Research Institute (Ref Japan Times, October 21, 2008) showed that this simple system reduced error from 2.38 to 0.38 per 100 actions.

The types of systems that can be implemented to prevent these types of errors involve either taking the control of this work from the subconscious to the conscious mind (e.g., point and call) or ensuring that the activities are habitually safe. Options such as workplace design, fail safe systems, good housekeeping, simple line diagrams and labels on equipment, effective use of check sheets, and fatigue management systems are all helpful in this respect.

Other error-based actions (mistakes) are failures of a plan to achieve a desired result. These can be minimised with effective training and competency assurance processes, effective pre-task hazard assessments and pre-start meetings as well as visible leadership practices.

### Safety Violation Behaviour

Intentional failure to apply a rule is a violation. The behavioural drivers of violation differ from those that lead to error, although the outcomes could be the same. Violation tends to be more prevalent in an immature safety culture, especially when carrying out work where the probability of being injured is perceived to be low and the extent of that injury is likely to be minor.

On the other hand, the focus on error reduction is much more relevant in a more mature culture and with work of high injury potential such as flying an airplane or running a chemical plant. In these latter cases corrective actions and controls need to be engineered so that they are error proof.

Very low levels of violation are common in a culture that values operating discipline and effective conduct of operations. Symbols of this are very visible such as good housekeeping, clean smart uniforms, calm and unrushed working, etc.

For organisations that believe that violation is prevalent they tend to adopt programmes that are based on models such as ABC (Antecedent, Behaviour, Consequence; see Figure 12.2) to explain why the unsafe behaviour existed and what to do to prevent such behaviour. Scott Geller (2016/1996) used this model to develop programmes such as BBS (Behavioural Based Safety).

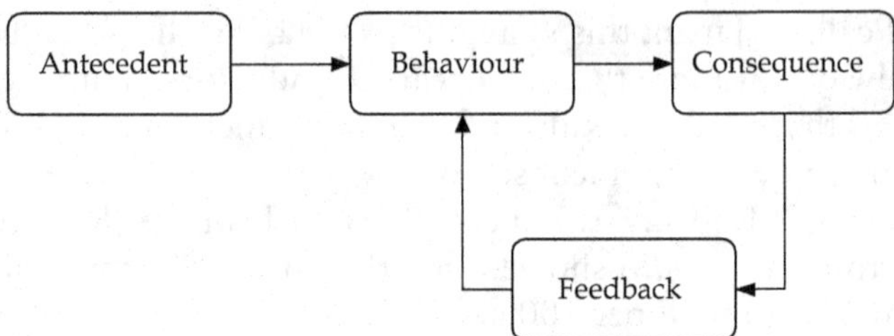


Antecedent - Events that happen before the behaviour
Behaviour - An observable and measurable act
Consequence - Event(s) that occur as a result of the behaviour (positive and negative)
Feedback - Did the consequence positively or negatively reinforce the behaviour?

*Figure 12.2* The ABC Model (after Albert Ellis, 1957)

Source: OSHA and SafeWorks Australia

Albert Ellis (1957) originally developed the ABC model from original work by B.F. Skinner. It highlights a strong link between an individual's perception of consequence (both positive and negative) that will drive behavioural choices. For example, if there is a bonus system for production and an unsafe shortcut has a low injury potential, then the outcome will tend towards unsafe work (i.e., definitely achieving production versus potentially avoiding an injury). This is especially true if others take shortcuts, and it goes unnoticed.

Most of the behavioural safety approaches are based on this model. It is a very helpful model to create an understanding of the drivers of behaviour, particularly those that lead to violation. Other models are typically used, however, for the management of human error.

One further note about the ABC model. Antecedents, consequence and feedback can all be part of the systems that exist in the organisation. The leadership of the organisation are the only ones that can change these systems so that they reduce the likelihood of unsafe work. (See Chapter 11, Systems, on system ownership.)

If organisations are to improve, they need to understand the type of unsafe behaviour and the management systems that drive that behaviour, whether that behaviour is the result of error or violation. Involvement and communicating with the workforce around developing safe work procedures and a process that treats offenders in a fair manner will provide important information. This will help management to predict how that behaviour is likely to change by changing the system. If this understanding doesn't exist, deliberate violations will result in extra training and people that commit an error will be sanctioned. Not only will that not be effective, the workforce will see it as unfair.

It is noteworthy that many of the systems that drive unsafe behaviour are not generally safety systems. Other systems such as the way people are rewarded, the way leaders behave, the way in which check sheets are completed and the way equipment is maintained have a significant impact on safety behaviour.

## Individually Driven Safety Behaviour or Custom and Practice?

The other thing we can learn about safety behaviour (in the language of Edwards Deming) is that it can be "common cause" – the behaviour is custom and practice, or "special cause" – the behaviour is associated with an individual. Whether it is common cause or special cause behaviour, it is almost always rational, albeit not excusable.

In 1995 Neil Johnston (1996), a human factors specialist and an Aer Lingus training captain, proposed the substitution test that supports the concept of common cause. It examines situations where an event has occurred in which unsafe behaviour is clearly implicated; substitute for the person concerned someone coming from the same work area and possessing comparable qualifications and experience. Then ask: "In the light of how the events unfolded and were perceived by those involved in real time, is it likely that this new individual would have behaved any differently?" If the judgement is "probably not," then, as Johnston put it, "apportioning blame has no material role to play, other than to obscure systemic deficiencies and to blame one of the victims".

In safety, the majority of incidents occur as a result of common cause and poor or contradicting organisational systems. As Deming said, "Every system is perfectly designed to get the results it gets." With the safety work it can be said, "The systems are perfectly designed to hurt people at a certain rate."

When many people make the same or unintentional error, it may be due to the way people are trained or there may be a common driver of fatigue such as shift patterns. They may also be associated with the way check sheets and risk assessments are carried out and the way people are prepared for work with effective reminders of the controls required. For these types of errors, the leadership needs to take account of training and competency assessment programmes, shift patterns as well as building better systems including controls and audit.

Where violations with a common cause occur, it is often in an organisation where safety maturity is low and the work being carried out has a low risk profile. Poorly designed bonus, pay and performance review systems as well as leadership behaviour may lead to violations. While the behaviour that is induced is rational, it is never excusable. When there is an incident, leadership must be able to identify the systems that were involved in driving the counterproductive behaviour. Change may require improved systems, which include operators' ideas and positive leadership behaviour.

Special cause problems are those events that are the result of individual behaviour. This behaviour is unlikely to be driven by organisational systems, but rather by systems external to the organisation. This does not mean, however, that systems within the organisation cannot be designed to minimise the impact of externally driven behaviour. Nor does it mean that leaders cannot help by understanding and managing the external issues. For example, if

### Box 12.3 Individual Behaviour or Custom and Practice

Every week the CEO, General Managers and Managers of a copper mine held a meeting to discuss the previous week's performance. Managers took turns to report their department's results. If there were any safety issues, then these were highlighted first. When the Manager of a copper refinery reported, he described a safety incident that had occurred where an operator had stood on the electrolytic cell. The electrodes in this cell were unstable and collapsed. His foot went into the hot, acidic electrolyte and was burnt. The Manager said that it was forbidden to stand on the cells and consequently the operator was disciplined.

After some discussion, the CEO asked the Manager two questions. First, he asked, "Do you think it was the first time the operator had stood on the cells?" The answer was "No," as is almost always the case. People are very unlikely to get injured every time they behave unsafely or break a safety rule. Indeed, this is one of the reasons why they do it.

The second question from the CEO was, "Do you believe that the injured operator was the only person who stood on the cells to do their work?" The Manager thought for a minute and then correctly said, "No." The CEO then commented, "I want to speak to the supervisor who allows custom and practice behaviour and then disciplines someone when this finally results in an injury! I don't believe that is fair. What do you think?"

an individual is fatigued because she or he has an issue at home and doesn't get the appropriate amount of rest, leaders may be able to accommodate this in managing the types of tasks that individuals carry out. Where this is persistent, the individual's work role may have to be changed or the person dismissed.

Where an individual has made a mistake and he or she is the only one who has done that, the error could be one of planning or execution, but in either case, the leadership work is to understand those individual circumstances. This could range from educational needs to assistance away from work.

Intentional breaches of procedure made by an individual are likely to be rare. Most violations are custom and practice. Where an individual consistently violates a safe way of working, dismissal is necessary.

## Summary

Building a safety culture which is effective and perceived by the workforce as positive on the values continua is a challenging but absolutely necessary task. Understanding the mythologies of the workforce before the new systems and leadership behaviour changes are implemented will enable the leadership to predict the likely results of the changes. The potential for success is demonstrated by the organisations which have done it well with excellent safety records.

Too often it is the case that poor safety behaviour can be both rational and commonplace and is driven by poorly designed systems that drive that behaviour. Unless the systems, behaviours and symbols that enhance or enable poor safety behaviour are changed, we can predict that this behaviour will continue. While changes in the technical domain are essential, many of them have already been carried out by companies that care about safety. Getting the social systems right has been less developed in many organisations, but those getting them right have demonstrated real and lasting improvements in safety.

## Notes

1 https://injuryfacts.nsc.org/motor-vehicle/historical-fatality-trends/deaths-and-rates (retrieved 10/4/23).
2 Injuries, Illnesses and Fatalities. https://www.bls.gov/news.release/cfoi.nr0.htm# (retrieved 10/4/23).
3 https://injuryfacts.nsc.org/work/work-overview/work-safety-introduction/ (retrieved 10/4/23).
4 Ibid.

# 13 Social Process at a Distance

## Introduction

In this book we have emphasised the work to be done in the Social Domain. It is concerned with all the ways in which people work together to achieve the purpose of the organisation including the structure and systems. As written, it is assumed, if only implicitly, that people interact primarily in an office or factory. Of course, we were aware that we also communicate via the internet, and by various telecommunications. It is also true that video conferencing has been around for years, though it was primarily used by large corporations, a few universities and government agencies, such as the military.

For most of us, however, working with others at a distance, not just occasionally but as the main method of interaction via Microsoft Teams and Zoom, is a relatively new experience. Covid changed everything as social distancing was mandated and travel was seriously constrained as countries limited or even stopped travel from outside their borders or even between areas within them. The increase and frequency of use of Microsoft Teams and Zoom was exponential and born out of necessity. This has had a lasting effect on the way that we now assume it is possible to work together and for many it has become routine, if not entirely comfortable.

So what have we learned and how do these platforms affect the social process? This chapter draws on the experience from many organisations. It suggests what we have gained and what we have lost by working remotely.

First of all, nothing that has happened in the last few years has fundamentally changed our description of how teams work well together in terms of the Team Leadership and Membership Steps and Traps, as discussed in Chapter 7. Nonetheless, working remotely has a clear impact on the social process. We are still learning how to improve remote meetings, but we now have a better understanding of how we can use these approaches to best effect.

DOI: 10.4324/9781003459118-17

The first part of this chapter looks more at the immediate effects on social process; the second part of the chapter looks more generally at the impact of how and where we work now because of the transformation of the last few years.

## Observations from Participants

1) **It's tiring!**

   Working in this way can be surprisingly tiring. Many people have commented that after an online meeting of, say, an hour, they feel much more tired than they would have done sitting together with people in a meeting room for the same time. Why might this be? Our observation is that working with people on the screen, and particularly when you can't see the whole person, means that we have to work much harder to read the social process and sense subtle changes in mood and engagement. We are not often consciously aware that we are constantly scanning our environment for cues and clues as to how the social process is going. Working remotely, this is just much harder. Certainly, as this way of working suddenly increased we were not used to so much of this type of reading social process.

2) **We need gaps!**

   We have learned, perhaps the hard way, that it is not a good idea to have hourly meetings back-to-back online. A good practice is to have at least 10 minutes between meetings. If possible, a half hour is better for most of us. Interestingly, that is common practice in clinical work and psychotherapy. Both of these practices also require intense social process analysis. It is not a great step to also realise that it is not a good idea, even with the gaps, to have online meeting after meeting all through the day.

3) **What works well?**

   We have found that because of the more intense social process work that needs to be done in such meetings it is easier when we actually know and/or have worked with the people who are now working online together. This is, of course, because it is easier to pick up cues when we know somebody and consequently working with large numbers of people whom we don't know exacerbates the problem.

   Also, this approach works better when we have a clear and obvious purpose and agenda and where there has been preparation done beforehand. So a structured meeting is easier to run rather than the more creative or open-ended discussion and problem-solving meeting, especially with people whom we don't know very well.

4) **Perceived benefits**

It saves money. It saves time. Commuting in cities is costly and cabs add an hour or more to the day's work. Travel between cities and countries is also costly, often uncomfortable and time-consuming. Reducing travel is good for the environment. People working from home save on gas for the commute and the need for "business" clothes. Meetings on the popular systems tend to be more focused with less "wasted" time. (Although some in-person meetings run on too long, the social interaction enhances the team-building process.)

Working from home can be great for some people, for others not so much. Having a quiet place to focus on work is essential. Not everyone can have that when they have children. Some, perhaps most parents, like to have more time and availability for family issues. The organisation may be concerned that they are not getting the person's full attention as they would in an office.

5) **Dealing with technical issues**

For those working at home without competent technical support, it is essential to learn about the technology products and processes. It is not difficult, but as with all technologies which are new to the user, it is important to become familiar with them. Both Zoom and Teams have excellent instructions which are worth reading if you are new to them or if you only use them occasionally. Of course, talking to a techie can usually solve most issues. If you use these almost every day, the process becomes automatic. If you only use it occasionally, it will take a bit longer, but practice will build your confidence.

6) **Should we have hybrids?**

Although it would seem to make sense to have people physically present if they can be and others participating online, most people report this is usually not satisfactory for the online people. It is hard to overcome the natural tendency to engage more fully with the people in the room who are giving and receiving social process cues much more obviously.

The people online can easily feel they are marginalised or an afterthought unless they are specifically presenting some material. Another disruptive element is when some people online are on mute and others have their cameras turned off (supposedly because of bandwidth but maybe for many other reasons).

The team leader or chair of the meeting really needs to have clear protocols with regard to the use of tools such as mute or side chats. Cameras need to be all on or off. Our recommendation is that these should be systems of equalisation. Having people operating in different ways is actually very disruptive to the social process.

7) **Work that is missed**

It is easy to underestimate the importance for social cohesion of interacting with people in ways that are not necessarily only about the task in hand. We need to know about people and how their lives are going. Even very simple interactions about whether and where people have been on holiday, how their family members are, what they've been watching on TV or film and other so-called "small talk" is actually essential for building good working relationships.

It is not just personal information that is passed as people meet before a meeting, but information about the work environment and the work to be accomplished, issues causing difficulty, personality clashes, successes – things that are important to know to understand the broader picture of what is really happening in the organisation, but are rarely voiced in a public setting. Without this knowledge, people may feel they are flying blind, not knowing all the subtleties they would otherwise understand in and around a face-to-face meeting.

We are not work machines; we are curious to know about each other and what is happening in the organisation and its environment. All of this contributes to understanding the deeper context of the work that we are trying to do together. These small interactions, cups of coffee, what has perhaps stereotypically being called the "water cooler chats," are in fact essential parts of the social process that if missed is like running an engine without any oil. Of course, it's not impossible to ask such questions online and, indeed, we would recommend that there is some time put aside for people to say hello or to check in but even so this can tend to seem bit ritualistic or technical rather than easy social communication.

Therefore, like any method that is suddenly introduced or gains rapid popularity we need to understand the best ways to use it. When there is a clear agenda, a simple structure and clear protocols, sharing information with people whom you know, this methodology can be extremely effective and can, in fact, save a great deal of time.

The discipline associated with this can in fact enhance the team leadership and membership steps as they can be used as a structure to make the meetings more productive: has the context been set, have we got a clear purpose what are the critical issues, are tasks assigned clearly? These are just as relevant in online meetings as they are in face-to-face meetings. Working in this way can be tiring and there's no perfect substitute for personal interaction. The possibility of discussions before and after meetings can give rise to innovation and inspiration, and learning from others in a less structured context.

### Some General Observations

The points above are relevant to the conduct of online meetings, where and how they are appropriate and productive. This way of working, however, particularly driven by the pandemic, has had a much deeper impact on our concept of work and where we work. Whereas many small businesses are and have for years been run from people's homes or rooms in their homes, by far the majority of us have, since the industrial revolution, been used to going to work.

This has meant a much clearer separation between where work is primary and where our personal and family lives are primary. Although people may have spent too much time at work, they didn't seem to question whether we should actually be there at all. The requirement to work from home, not just the choice, has inevitably led us to question where and when we should be in the office, at the site or in the factory.

Of course, much work cannot be done at home; working in parks and gardens, working in health services, educating children, to name but a few, but it is quite clearly recognised that it either can't be done or is much less effectively done if we are not together in a physical location. This change requires managers and leaders to think more carefully about who needs to be at work and when. We argue it is not simply a matter of saying you must be in the office two or three days a week or perhaps specifically requiring people to be in on the same days. There are, of course, cost considerations to take into account; do we really need all of this office space, do we need the workplace? Do we need the costs in time and money with daily commuting?

Also, we need to consider whether people are as effective at home or working within a family home where there may be many more distractions and some people may be left feeling that there are no clear boundaries. Others may feel they are potentially working all the time and/or being available to the family all the time. We have been told that some feel neither is being attended to satisfactorily.

We don't have any magical solutions to these questions but rather affirm that these are new questions that need careful consideration and can be considered using the principles in systems leadership. We need to be clear about the purpose of our work; what we mean by teamwork. Who do we need to interact with? What is the effect on the culture of the organisation?

How stories are told will determine how mythologies develop positively or negatively in these different social settings. We can see that the tools of leadership are as relevant as ever if we are to build the culture that we want; what are the systems, symbols and behaviours that are enabling that and what are the systems, symbols and behaviours that are preventing that desired culture. Working remotely is essentially just another system where we have to understand the impact that it has, not simply in the technical domain, but in the social domain and consequently its effect on the social process.

## Summary

While the technical issues that allow us to have meetings at a distance, the social issues are recognised but not entirely solved. Out of necessity, we have created a different kind of system of interaction that is widely available. It creates a social system which is only partially understood, and is not yet entirely comfortable for most of us. This is an opportunity to do more work and to learn more to understand and improve the social processes it requires. Just one more challenge as we work to create positive organisations.

# Part IV

# Essential People Systems

## Introduction

To run a positive, successful organisation, the following chapters describe some essential people systems important for effective leadership. These systems have been used successfully in a number of organisations around the world – business, public and non-governmental. At the end of this section, we have an Appendix which provides some examples and worksheets showing how the ideas have been used. While all the approaches follow a similar pattern, each organisation has made variations based on their own purpose and needs. You are welcome to copy and modify them as you find them useful in your own management practice.

It is crucial that the leader has available good systems to help build a productive work culture. The circle of people systems required is shown in Figure IV.1.

The following chapters outline the essential people systems that should be operating well if the culture is to be positive and effective. We begin with the selection process and the importance of role descriptions in that process. We provide a model role description in the Appendix to illustrate a type that is useful to both the manager and a potential or actual direct report.

Chapter 15 provides an overview of the people systems that all have the purpose of improving the quality of work performance by employees of the organisation. Here we distinguish two definitions of performance, as output that can be measured and how it is distinguished from work performance of an individual which must be judged by the manager. We also differentiate the work of the manager in performance management from the work of M+1 as well as two roles the manager must play (at different times) as the coach/trainer of a direct report and as the "judge" who must assess the direct report's overall work performance with monetary consequences.

DOI: 10.4324/9781003459118-18

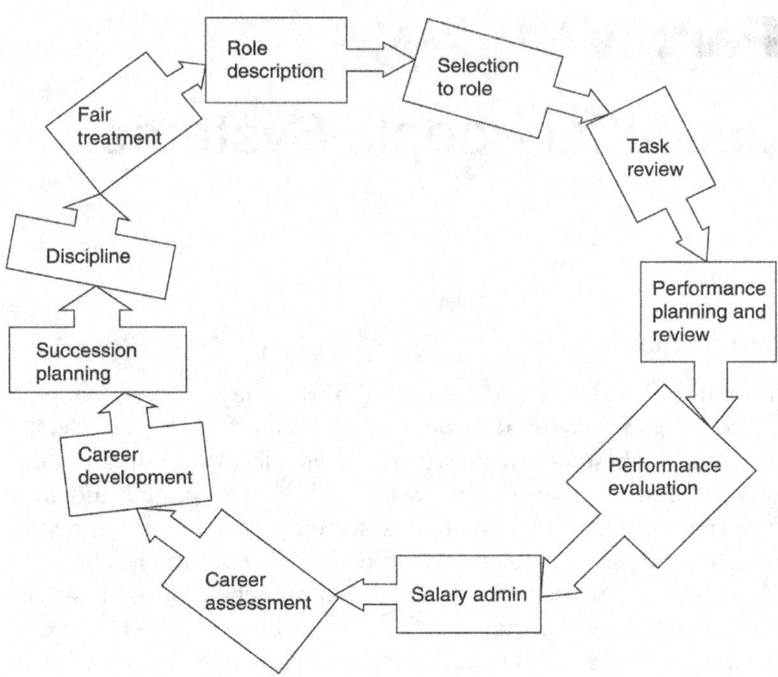


*Figure IV.1* People Systems

In the final chapters we distinguish between career and staff development and the accountability for each process. The last chapter discusses the difficult issue of discipline and the necessity for fair treatment.

# 14 Role Descriptions and Selection

## Introduction

Selection of a person to fill a role is one of the most difficult tasks managers confront. In a well-structured organisation, M+1 will also interview the person, review the potential decision and have a veto, but the M+1 confronts the same demons as the manager. The best executives will tell you that they anguish more over selection decisions than any others, and with good reason.

Wilfred Brown (1971:362) has emphasised that "despite all the efforts deployed on selection [by psychologists, social scientists and others], human judgment in choosing the right person continues to play a central part in the appointment." There is no magic test or formula that will allow the manager to evade his or her ultimate responsibility for the judgement in the decision to select someone for the role.

The quality of the work performance of people the manager selects will have the most profound and long-lasting effect on the manager's success and the success of the enterprise. With the globalisation of trade and services, as the cost of freight, communication and information evens out, as knowledge becomes more widespread, the former competitive advantages of geography, capital, resources, technology and transport are being reduced.

For many organisations, the last remaining field of competitive advantage is people – their capability, their leadership skills, their creativity and initiative. Therefore, the application of, and attention to, selection becomes an increasing source of competitive advantage. Selecting the right (or the wrong) person for a key role can have long-term financial impacts; selection is often a million dollar decision.

The concepts of work, mental processing ability (MPA), capability and the matching of individual capability to the work requirements of the role, as discussed in previous chapters, are all relevant to do the work managers do when they are selecting people for roles, whether it is from within the organisation or external to it.

DOI: 10.4324/9781003459118-19

We recognise, however, there is a lot more to selection than can be included in a single chapter.

The following chapters will discuss career and staff development, assessment of potential and evaluation of work performance. You may wish to consider the use of assessment centres; the role of M+1 assessments of potential; the potential for the use of multiple managers, multiple M+1s, selection committees for certain roles; and the roles of Principal Personnel Advisors and Chiefs, Organisation Effectiveness in the processes.

What follows is a discussion for the individual manager who must select an individual to work on his/her team. Managers who have used these ideas report they were useful, and they have improved their own capability to select people whose work performance has proven to be positive. One manager who used these systems became President of a large corporation in part because he was so good at selecting people for roles.

## Role Description

Organisations need to do work to achieve their purposes. They therefore must organise that work by bundling it into roles. As we said earlier, a role contains a group of tasks. The core work of the role must be focused around a level of work complexity. There will always be some work of differing complexity in a role but it is important to be clear what is at the heart of the work of the role. Therefore, role descriptions should describe the work specifically.

A crucial factor in selecting an individual to fill a role is a clear understanding of the work required in that role. The better the manager understands what is required, the more likely she or he will be able to identify a person who can successfully fill that role. The role descriptions we propose for a stratified organisation are designed to be used by managers and by role incumbents in order to clarify the scope and boundaries of a particular role. These role descriptions take into account the changing nature of work and roles within an organisation.

People bring to a role knowledge, skills, energy and the ability to think. The role description has two parts (see Appendix A). Page 1 is an example of an employment contract. The role description starting on page 2 is one example of the information required in a role description that is useful both to the manager selecting someone for a role and for the potential, and later the actual, role incumbent.

The example is from a mining operation which will not be familiar to most of our readers, but the employment contract and role description format provided is suitable for any type of organisation. The basic content may be presented in a different sequence, and the work to be done may list more or fewer task types, but all elements need to be present if the core work of the role is to be understood by both the manager and the direct report. The basic elements include:

- Date: Every role description should have a date, so when adjustments are made the new date will indicate there has been a change.
- Have a clear purpose statement, that is, a positive description of the role – its distilled essence – in one sentence, without using the word "and." Make sure to be clear if this is primarily a leadership role, a support role or a service role.
- The Role Title should indicate the level in the organisation and the nature of the work to be carried out. Role titles are one of the most significant symbols in an organisation and act as a control to prevent excess organisational layers being added. (See Chapter 6 for the kind of titles we recommend.)
- Role Relationships include the title and name of the role incumbent's Manager and M+1, title(s) of direct reports, titles of key internal relationships and the title(s) of key external relationships, if any.
- Authorities have several elements as shown in the example.
  - May be specific such as an important statement about Safety, Health and Environment which applies to all employees of the organisation.
  - Statement of boundaries of the role – Law, policies, ethical expectations.
  - Managerial authorities – VAR$^3$I or others applicable to the role (titled Human Resources in the example).
  - Structure and systems – What the role incumbent can and cannot do regarding these parts of the organisation.

- Budget/Expenditure of assets – Authorities in role relationships are a resource but there should also be a statement of material resources, for example, a budget, spending limits, equipment, access to information and so on. These limits must be clear to the role incumbent and information provided as to who one should contact in case changes are necessary.

- Task Types – An activity without the specific output, targeted completion time and task resources defined as would happen in a task assignment. A task type always begins with a verb.

  It is not necessary, nor is it desirable, to attempt to list all task types that might be associated with a particular role. Such an exhaustive listing could appear to restrict the perceived discretion of both the role occupant and his or her manager. The purpose of the listing is to clarify the kinds of work most frequently done in this role.

  - General Task Types – These apply to all roles in the organisation.
  - Role Differentiating Task Types – These are the task types specific to the role.

- As specified on the employment contract, the role incumbent should expect tasks to be assigned by his or her manager including Context, Purpose, Quantity and Quality of Output, Time and Resources. The role incumbent should also expect to be called to account for his or her work performance in relation to a specific task, or a collection of tasks assigned to them by responding to the following statements:

  Tell me what you did.
  Tell me how you did it.
  Tell me why you did it that way.

- Provide for performance review. Finally, the role description should be used and useful. It should be used in conjunction with the performance review and reworked by the manager and manager-once-removed (M+1) when it needs changing. The person who should authorise a role description is the M+1 even if the manager and the individual have put a draft together. It is the work of the M+1 to have an overview of the work of the team and to determine how that work is distributed.

## Selection to Role

A current and complete role description becomes the basis for good selection of potential employees. It can also be used to inform a potential role incumbent about the specifics of the role. It is necessary, however, to gather more information than simply knowledge about the role and the person being interviewed.

### Preparation

From the role description it is important to use the capability model to create a specification for the role in terms of:

- MPA
- Knowledge
- Technical skills
- Social skills
- Application

The social process skills needed may be determined by the required role relationships. For example, what are the characteristics of the current team? What sort of customers might the person have to deal with? Are people in other areas, specialists and services easy or difficult to relate to? List other requirements that may be important. For example, is significant travel required?

As you consider the characteristics of your team, their knowledge, skills and application may have a considerable impact on your decisions. What are their strengths and weaknesses? Do you have an adequate mix of technical, organising and social process skills? What are the necessary qualities needed to be part of the team? Do you need more innovation and risk taking or would greater stability improve the team?

You may even want to change some existing roles and therefore need an entirely different kind of role than the one you had previously. You are not just matching an individual to a role in isolation but fitting them into a setting, which may create demands that are not part of an existing role description. Prepare a new role description if that is warranted and have it approved by your manager; make sure the existing one meets your current needs.

### The Selection Process

Do not just rely on interviews. Consider what other methods may be relevant. We have found that giving the person an actual problem to solve or an in-basket exercise, for example, may be helpful. A team problem-solving exercise or case study can also reveal useful information about social process. We are not very impressed with psychometric tests, especially if they are done separately and provide standard reports not specific to the role. It is too easy to use psychometric tests as substitutes for judgement. If they are used, then be clear about their validity and reliability, exactly what quality or skill is being tested and how this is right for the role. Psychometric tests may have little predictive validity with regard to the actual work of the specific role

Ask yourself, "what does it require to carry out this role effectively?"

- Knowledge Fields – be specific, what knowledge is really needed?
- Skills
  - Technical
  - Social

Again, be specific, what do you need on entry?

- Application.
- MPA, a necessary requirement.
- Education (provides knowledge/skills).
- Experience (provides knowledge/skills/develops judgement).
- What made the last person in this role effective (or ineffective).
- Are there any cut-off requirements? (something which, if it is lacking, makes it impossible to do the job).
- Other considerations which may be relevant (these are examples, think of your own requirements).
  - Ethical character.
  - Understanding of corporate politics.
  - Getting on with clients, peers, etc.
  - Appearance (within corporate norms, not a negative).
  - Energy.
  - Willingness to travel.
  - Interests.
  - Licensing requirements.
- What can be developed on the job?

All of these prior considerations place managers in a position to explain the role and its context to an applicant, but, more importantly, equip them to ask probing questions and provide data for evaluation.

**Note:** It is important to clarify the authorities of anyone who is part of the selection process. For example, we have seen people appropriately involved in the process but confused as to whether they have a veto or recommendation or advisory authority.

## Mistakes

We believe it is safe to say that everyone has made mistakes in selection. That is one reason for the "I" authority of the manager. The thing to do is learn from our mistakes. Stewart likes to say that he prefers to make original mistakes not simply repeat the old ones.

As he puts it, "My capacity for originality in error is astounding! Replication is not as rare as I would like either." Think about it. No judgement process is foolproof. It is important to reflect on past errors and successes. We are all susceptible to certain distractions. Stewart is fooled by great technical ability, Burke by people who are articulate and express themselves well and Macdonald by people with excellent social process skills. No one is infallible in this process.

Some typical distractions include:

- Energy and drive (application) – it is easy to be over-impressed and mistakenly see it as compensation for elements of capability.
- Appearance – looking good or not is a classic example. Remember appearances can be deceptive.
- Assumed similarity – the fact that a person has been to a particular college, has a certain qualification or has worked for a particular company can invoke assumptions that are not warranted. One of the authors remembers a particular comment "He must be good. He was in the first eight [rowing]." Think of how many distractions have fooled or are likely to fool you.

  Belonging to the same cultural group (same fraternity at college, same qualification in same discipline, served in the same armed service) can be subtle but strong distractions because it is very easy to assume something about the interviewee based on no data apart from the cultural link.
- References – it is definitely worth checking these directly by talking to referees where possible. We have also learned a great deal from people who have worked for a candidate. Many people are good at managing upwards but treat their team members poorly.

## Monitoring Yourself (Controls and Audit)

When you select an individual, note in writing what you observed that led you to believe the person would be good in this role (see Box 14.2 in Appendix A). In addition to your specific observations, record your interpretations of your observations and your thoughts as to why you picked this individual. Six months or a year later you can compare what was observed and how you interpreted those observations with the reality of the person selected.

If you do this every time you select an individual for a particular role, you will quickly learn your own strengths and weaknesses in the selection process. As we noted earlier, every human being has blind spots when it comes to selection. Some are fooled by a person who has great credentials; others rely too heavily on experience. Some prefer a person who appears very energetic or politically astute. All these characteristics may be useful in some circumstances and may be just what the manager needs. On the other hand, they may also fool a manager into believing the person is capable of something they are not.

You must be aware of the need for the MPA of the person to match or exceed the complexity of the work of the role. A significant cause of failure to perform adequately in a role, but not the only one, is lack of sufficient MPA. Burke has observed that lack of social process skills appears to have derailed more careers than any other factor, even insufficient MPA, which may be harder to identify.

A common trap in selection is to believe that someone who is outstanding at one level of work will be equally good at a higher level. This may be true in many cases, but not all. You know the story of the terrific salesman who became a terrible sales manager, or the outstanding police officer who became a hopeless sergeant.

### Other Ideas that May Help in the Selection Process

Use expert help from your Human Resources staff to:

- Find candidates.
- Help prepare a short list.
- Sit in on interviews to take notes and discuss each candidate with the manager after the interview. Note: The interview is conducted by the manager, although the staff person may also be authorised by the manager to ask questions.

Having someone else sit in on the interview is extremely helpful and highly recommended, but that person must be chosen with care. The team interviewing process requires both interviewers to have the MPA necessary to make judgements about what is being shown in the interview as a result of the answers given to questions.

The advantage of having a second person in the interview stems from the ability for each to ask questions while the other assesses the thinking behind the answer and formulates new questions to test any hypothesis.

In some circumstances having the M+1 sit in as well is advantageous, at least for some part of the interview. Again, however, it must be very clear to the interviewee that the interview is being run by the manager.

In our experience the most difficult part of the process is the assessment of MPA – how *well* does this person think – not *what* they think. The first step is to be looking for it. Although most organisations do not have this criterion identified as a part of their selection interview process, they do have discussions around whether or not the interviewee is smart enough to do the job. Understanding MPA clarifies just exactly what one should be looking for.

In trying to assess MPA, Macdonald recommends a simple process he calls "following the verb." For example, you might ask a person: "what would you do to improve this department?" The person might say, "I would reorganise." Ask: "what do you mean by reorganise?" The person may mean anything from a complete restructure to moving the furniture around. Each time a person uses a verb keep following it to get examples and detailed proposals. Ask, "How would you do that?" or "Why would you do that?"

Of course, MPA is not the only requirement for an individual to be able to perform well in a role, but it is a necessary though not sufficient condition. The other components of capability – knowledge, technical skill, social process skill and application – are all very important, vital in fact, but the difference with these is that most people can learn and change. They can therefore improve over time, though such change may not be easy, or even possible in the case of social process skills or application.

The mythological lens that a prospective candidate brings to the role is rarely discussed, as such, in an interview review; instead, the discussion is about "cultural fit," "attitudes," "beliefs," etc. This is an attempt to assess and predict how the applicant's mythological lens will cause him or her to rate the behaviour of others and his or her own behaviour on the values scales. It is an important element of an interview review.

Given that the manager of the role is conducting the interview, in a stratified organisation he or she should have a MPA at least one level higher than that which is minimally required to perform the work of the role and will be able to ask questions and assess answers that indicate the MPA required.

A highly experienced interviewee will be able to articulate the means of solutions to similar problems he or she has seen before, even though the thinking ability to solve the problem is not originally present. Following the action verbs can help reveal this.

It can be quite revealing for a manager to ask the person how he or she would approach an issue or problem confronting the manager. The person should not be expected to solve the problem of a higher level of work, but can the person contribute to the manager's thinking, adding ideas, asking interesting questions or suggesting possibilities, even if those possibilities are not entirely practical.

## Summary

Selection is always a difficult and time-consuming task, but taking the time to prepare pays great dividends. The key elements are to have a clear understanding of the work of the role to be filled. A complete role description, such has those described here, is essential.

Spend time to consider what knowledge, skills, application and MPA will be required to carry out the work of the role.

Have someone else of equal capability sit in on the interviews.

Finally, to improve your judgement when selecting an individual, write down what you observed that led you to believe the person selected could do the job. Record both your observations and your interpretation of those observations. Six months to a year later, compare what you thought at the time of hiring and how accurate did that turn out. Where were you correct and where did you miss something important.

We have seen managers who did this every time they hired someone become exceptionally good at selection. It's not magic, just consistent recording and comparing prediction to reality.

# 15 Performance Management

## Output Measures vs. Work Performance of Individuals

### Introduction

As with many terms used in the field of leadership and management, Performance Management is often left undefined, and those who discuss it or try to use it have quite different ideas about what it is and what it is not (Behn, 2014). Not only is there lack of agreement about what it is, and what it should be, there are differences regarding how to judge its success or failure. In Systems Leadership we endeavour to clarify our language, so we can all agree on what we are talking about and thus make considerable progress in improving overall organisational performance.

**Performance Management:** The active leadership of managers to improve both performance and work performance.

**Performance:** The achievement of Outputs/Outcomes or measures of the same. The relationship between targeted output and achieved output. Outputs and Outcomes can, and must, be counted or measured.

**Work Performance:** A judgement made by a manager about how effectively and efficiently a direct report has worked in performing an assigned task taking into consideration the actual context in which the task was done.

**Output:** What is produced by an individual, team or organisation that can be counted or measured.

**Outcome:** The effects the output has on citizens, customers or clients, the community or the environment.

**Context:** The situation in which the task assigner predicts the task will be performed, including the background conditions, the relationship of this task to other tasks and any unusual factors to be taken into account. Changes in context may require changes in the task assignment and/or changes in evaluation of work performance.

Our definition of performance as outputs or outcomes that can be measured or counted is the common usage in organisations

DOI: 10.4324/9781003459118-20

and published studies. Exactly what is to be counted or measured depends on the purpose of the organisation and how it intends to use these data. The purpose may be to measure in some way the degree of success and/or failure in business operations to improve the outputs and outcomes. In a public agency if you want to show the public or your political superiors what you have accomplished, simple counting of output or measures of outcomes may be enough. The purpose may be to learn which systems, processes, facilities, resources, etc., need to be changed to improve performance as measured by the outputs or outcomes.

Whatever the purpose, counting or measuring outputs is likely to be more complicated than it first appears. To begin, the metrics used must promote the performance desired. For a public works agency, the number of lane-miles of road repairs produced may be a relevant output. For a police department, the reduction of crime (output) is the purpose, and reducing the fear of crime is the hoped-for outcome. A business may have multiple purposes – profits, increase in share price, superior products, technical leadership, etc. – so metrics supporting each of these areas must be created.

The fundamental purpose of the count or measurement is to improve something; just what is to be improved and why is often more difficult to determine. Do you want to improve the outcomes you have identified? Do you want to improve your systems and processes? Do you want to compare your output/outcomes with another organisation to see how well you are doing against a benchmark? In doing so, be careful to identify the proper benchmark, which can be difficult as apples to apples comparisons may not be easy to identify, and once identified, difficult to get the data.

There may be a need to improve performance within the organisation by making people aware of rate of production (outputs) and how well these outputs are making a difference in the external world (outcomes).

When the purpose is unclear or there are multiple purposes at the same time, gathering the data becomes time-consuming and expensive. Too much data may be gathered such that it overwhelms the staff and much goes unused. Deciding what data is worth gathering for what purpose is not an easy task. It requires higher-level capability and excellent analytic skills. When an organisation gets this right, considerable improvement is possible.

On the other hand, some systems which appear at first glance to be effective and fair turn out to be disasters. It is essential to think through what kind of behaviour are you encouraging and will the measures you have chosen improve that behaviour. Box 15.3 is an example of a system that cannot be distorted, but it can still do considerable damage.

## Box 15.1 Benchmarking Can Be Tricky

One of the authors was working as a consultant to a Division of a larger corporation which had over 70 Customer Service Representatives (CSRs). A respected consulting firm was brought in for a different purpose, but one of the junior members thought the corporation had an excess number of CSRs and asked a comparable corporation, in the same industry, how many CSRs they had – only four. Knowing the work to be carried out, that did not seem possible to us. We knew some people in that company and asked why? It turned out they only had four with that title. The work of CSRs was carried out by roughly the same number of people with a different job title. Moral of the story: dig deeper, don't assume job titles, or other "obvious" measures are the ones you need to compare.

## Box 15.2

In the Los Angeles Police Department where data on crime is gathered through the comp-stat system, Edward Pape, a Division Captain, realised that the data was not being used adequately.[1] In fact, it was used in a punitive way at monthly meetings where a Division Captain was placed on the hot seat and questioned about why he or she had or had not dealt with a given issue. What was needed in the Division was actionable data, such that crimes could be prevented or the perpetrators caught. To do this, Pape needed a full-time analyst who was capable not only of analysing the data, but of recognising ways to react to the analysis. He chose a Lieutenant whom he was confident would soon make Captain for this full-time job, as a way of making sure higher capability was applied to the task.

At shift changes the Lieutenant discussed the most recent data and analyses in a 15-minute meeting where they were presented to the incoming shift, and everyone could suggest how to respond to that data. Usually, agreement was reached on the next steps, and, when necessary, the Captain or Lieutenant gave directions as they developed more productive ways of policing the division. The result was a significant drop in crime and clear information for Pape to present at monthly high-level staff and community meetings, thus avoiding much of the abuse. The Division reduced crime so much that a new Chief who did not know or understand what they were doing in his Division started an investigation to find out if the Pape was manipulating the data (he was not) (Pape, 2012).

1 Pape, E. A., Jr. (2012) Intersect Policing: Bringing CompStat to the Field Level to Reduce the Fear and Incidence of Crime. A Dissertation Presented to the Faculty of the USC Sol Price School of Public Policy, University of Southern California, Dec. 2012. Also from Burke's discussions with him as his dissertation advisor.

### Box 15.3

A medium-sized business decided to evaluate their salesmen based on the average sales per month of the entire sales force. The salesmen liked this idea because most salesmen believe they are above average. To be below average for three months in a row meant dismissal. The salesmen quickly learned there was no way to beat the math – half would always be below average no matter what they did. This system was abandoned in less than a year after several good salesmen had chosen to leave the company.

## From Performance as Output to Work Performance

Accepting that Performance Management may be more complicated than it appears, and assuming your organisation has been able to get the right data, with the right analysis, there is a problem that occurs when outputs alone are applied to evaluate the work performance of the people in the organisation. Too often it is believed we can assess the "work performance" of individuals, teams and the entire organisation by using only the numbers and measures. Work performance appraisal appears to be easy; the only question to ask is: "Did you make your numbers?"

This approach fails for many reasons. Although it remains largely unspoken, everyone knows the numbers can be "rigged." Too often employees are given a target value to achieve and there is considerable pressure to reach that target, but what happens when the target value cannot be reached? Wheeler (2000:20) suggests three ways the individual, team or organisation can proceed:

1 Work to improve the system.
2 Distort the system.
3 Distort the data.

### Improve the System

Improving the system can be done at all levels of the organisation, but at the lowest working level, the changes that can be made without higher approval are usually relatively small. Ed Pape chose to improve the system and as a Division Captain was authorised to do so. He also recognised the need for higher-level analysis to use the data effectively based on his dissertation research.

### Distort the System

Distorting the system is much easier; almost anyone can do it, and many have done it. This occurs because the target set for the worker or team is unreachable due to issues beyond their control, or because the count cannot be reached without distortion.

**Box 15.4**

Using output numbers has problems as well. A large county welfare system decided to rate its employees based on the number of cases closed each month. The rate of closures went up dramatically in the first few months, but then they noticed that some closed cases had to be re-opened. There were also problems occurring in the community that could be traced back to unresolved cases lingering without resolution in the welfare system. When this was investigated, the more complex cases were found in the bottom drawers of the social workers' desks. These cases were difficult to resolve and taking the time to deal with them would reduce the number of closed cases and thus the rated performance of the employees. Clearly, there was a need to change the way work performance was evaluated considering the context of the work as well as simply counting output. Setting the wrong target has negative consequences.

**Box 15.5**

The Internal Revenue Service (IRS) had its budget cut for over a decade, while at the same time their auditors' performance was evaluated (at least in part) based on the cases closed and money collected. Based on IRS published data, *ProPublica* (2019) reported that due to reduced resources, the IRS was more likely to audit poor people than rich people or large corporations. These required complex audits that took much more time and higher-level capability which had become scarce due to budget cuts. Auditing people with incomes below $25,000 for Earned Income Tax Credit fraud was easily and quickly done by computer, and the poor people were less likely to resist or complain.

### Distort the Data

Data can also be distorted (or simply faked). You may recall the scandal when there were reports of teachers and principals changing student grades to make their schools look better and to avoid penalties for failing to achieve the student results required. The penalties could be severe, from reduced funding, loss of employment, up to and including closure of "failing" schools. The more severe the penalties, the more likely the cheating if targets cannot be met.

Use of quotas in police work is another common complaint, usually denied by the police department or the city it serves. In California, such quotas violate the State Vehicle Code. The City of Whittier apparently "imposed an unlawful citation and arrest quotas, according to a lawsuit filed by the City to force two insurance companies to pay compensation of a $3 million settlement paid by the City to recompense officers who were retaliated against for refusing to participate in and/or reported the unlawful citation and arrest quotas" (Pasadena Star-News, 2/28/2020). Basing work performance on quotas can be costly.

It has been common for Boards of Directors to evaluate a CEO's work performance based on a single data point such as return on investment (ROI), gross or net profits, sales or increases in same. The CEO's bonus is then based on hitting the number.

#### Box 15.6

Under the old Soviet system all the factories were given quotas to meet based on the five-year plan. Under Stalin, missing one's quota could mean a trip to Siberia or even death for the plant manager. In the case of trucks, real shortages developed even though every factory in the supply chain reported meeting their quotas. A Russian emigré who was familiar with these problems said the answer was obvious. At each stage of production, if the quota could not be met due to lack of needed resources or parts, human resources or simply incompetent management, the factory would still report it had met its quota. At the end of the supply chain, the factory that was to produce the finished trucks reported they had met the quota. Unfortunately, some of the trucks were missing one or more parts. Some were lacking motors, or the motors were not complete. Of course, some trucks were produced to completion, but whether drivable or not, they were all reported to show the quota had been met.

**Box 15.7**

A Board of Directors set a number for the CEO based on increased sales despite the objection of one director familiar with the ideas in this chapter. The company was in an industry subject to changes in key markets which were beyond its control. As a result, the number could not be reached. The CEO then added the sales from January and February of the following year and made it appear the numbers hit the annual target by the time the Board met in April. Some members of the Board were aware of this, but one Director argued and was eventually supported by a Board majority, "He made the number; he gets the bonus." This had a negative effect on the employees of the organisation who knew what had happened. Their distrust of the CEO and disgust with the Board was palpable.

## Work Performance Evaluated in Context

The examples illustrate a larger issue. Output does not, in and of itself, indicate the quality of work performance of an individual, team or organisation. Its use leads to disgust with "Performance Management," which seems (and is) unfair when work performance is based only on the numbers. Reading just the first paragraph in Box 15.8, how would you judge the performance of the CEOs?

**Box 15.8 Results May Not Indicate Work Performance**

Take the case of three CEOs of large businesses, each with a profitability target of 12%. The results were 8% profit, 17% profit and 8% loss. CEO 1 missed the target, CEO 2 far exceeded the target, and CEO 3 appears to have failed miserably based on measured results.

How would you judge each given the context (industry environment) in which they worked?

- The CEO with 8% profit was in an industry where the average profit was –3%.
- The CEO with 17% profit was in an industry where the average profit was 30%.
- The CEO with –8% was in an industry where the market collapsed and 60% the businesses in that industry went bankrupt. Through great effort the business was saved from bankruptcy and prepared for new opportunities for future profits and growth.

In evaluating work performance, *context* must be considered. Sometimes the situation in which the work was carried out is so simple, or the targets so easy, "a donkey could have done that." The targets may be met, but the manager skimped on maintenance such that future results are threatened. At other times targets are missed, but the individual has taken heroic measures to make sure the entire project did not fail.

Setting the right targets is not easy. If they are too easy, they will not improve performance. If they are too hard, people may not even try to reach them, or they will distort the system or the data to give the appearance of having reached them. Getting it right may take some time and experience with a need to adjust over time.

We have defined "Work Performance" as how well a person has done in producing the outputs and/or outcomes, accounting for all relevant circumstances.

Output or outcomes can, and must, be measured.

- Counts or measures are typically different at each level of work.
- Each employee's measures of performance must be relevant to his or her role's purpose and task assignments.
- Measures are essential for control.
  - to compare achieved outputs with targeted objectives.
  - to allow a manager to adjust the task in terms of quantity, quality, resources or time to ensure the purpose is achieved.
  - to let the employee know if there is an issue that needs to be reported to the manager because the existing assignment is not achieving the purpose.
  - to provide employees with feedback about what is going on to answer, "How am I doing?".
  - to provide a clear statement of what is important, what should be monitored.

Work Performance – how well a person has worked to achieve those results *cannot* be measured. It must be *judged* by a manager.

The question is, how well has the person worked to achieve the assigned output or outcome in the situation, both internal to the organisation and to the external environment in which the work was performed. Note that at most levels of organisations, individuals can fairly be held accountable for what they produce, the output, but their work performance must still be judged. At the higher levels, political and policy decisions are more likely to influence the judgements of work performance.

The accountability process is one of employees answering truthfully the following three questions from the manager:

- What did you do?
- How did you do it?
- Why did you do it that way?

Performance as output relates to the first of these questions; work performance to the latter two. The output resulting from the "what" can be measured; the value of the answers to the second and third questions must be judged.

### Work Performance vs. Output Measures and Results

Work Performance Evaluation – a judgement made by the manager of the overall effectiveness of a subordinate taking into account:

- The planned results as measured by various *indicators*.
- The complexity of the context in which the work was performed.
- The person's effectiveness considering that situation.
- How well the person balanced competing long-term and short-term demands.
- How well the person responded to changing conditions.
- How well the person handled relationships with fellow employees.
- And others specific to the organisation and its purpose.

**Note:** Output is important, but it is an *indicator* of work performance, *NOT* by itself, the measure of an individual's work performance.

While there may be many objective measures of output and results, when it comes to the work performance of the individual employee, there is always an exception, which demonstrates the objective measures are incomplete, as was shown in Box 15.8 where profit was the measure of a Chief Executive's performance as leader of a business.

Clearly, a single number is not adequate to judge a CEO's work performance, or any employee's work performance. One of a manager's key tasks is to create, maintain and improve the work performance of a group of people so that they achieve objectives and continue to do so over time. This cannot be measured. There may be measures to use as indicators of the achievement of these tasks – productivity gains, outputs achieved, cost reductions, number of college graduates hired, number of labour disputes, reduction in absenteeism, number of employees successfully promoted, etc. – but none of these taken separately, or together, can determine if the manager has succeeded in that task.

Improvements in employee morale and enthusiasm for doing the work are critical and cannot be measured; they must be judged. Did the manager have an experienced or newly trained workforce? Were resources constrained making work more difficult for the staff? Was there a change in the political climate that hurt staff morale, despite the manager's best efforts? Overall, the manager of managers must *judge* subordinate manager work performance involving both simple and complex tasks.

## To Improve Work Performance

Once it is clear that work performance must be judged, it changes the way performance counts and measures are used in the organisation. Performance Management changes as measures become indicators, not a shortcut to evaluating work performance. Still there may be impediments to judging work performance. An organisation with the correct levels of work as described in Chapter 6 can mitigate these problems.

1) The manager and/or subordinate may be placed at the wrong levels of work. The system of ranks and pay grades within ranks makes it more difficult to determine who is the real manager of any individual. The manager and employee may be too close within the same level of work, making it impossible for the manager to provide a valid judgement of the employee's work performance. A manager must be one full work level above the employee in order for the employee to accept his or her judgement as valid.
2) Task assignment may be done poorly. A task is an assignment to carry out work within limits that include the Context, Purpose, Quantity and Quality of output expected, the Resources available and the Time by which the objective is to be reached (CPQ/QRT). The purpose of this process is to ensure the people assigned to the tasks:

    a) Have a clear understanding of the task they are to do and why they are doing it.
    b) Believe they can commit themselves to doing it.
    c) Are in a position to accept their manager's judgement of the work performance as fair.

3) The context within which the task is to be carried out may change requiring changes in the assignment. More time or resources may be needed; the existing methods are not working as expected; the political situation suddenly becomes more conducive or less so, etc.
4) One or more resources – human, technical, financial – are found to be inadequate. Thus, the purpose may not be achieved without considerable re-thinking.

## Summary

To improve work performance managers at all levels must be engaged on a continuing basis. The following systems are active throughout the year to clarify purpose and to recognise good work performance to make visible the priorities of this organisation. Recognising work performance (good and bad) is essential as are consequences for the same.

- **Inform** people of your expectations.
  [Planning and Task Assignment]

- **Review** their performance and provide coaching or resources to improve it. [Task Feedback, Task Review and Work Performance Review]

- **Recognise** work performance – good or bad and do it close to the time when the work was done.
  [Task Feedback and Task Review]

- **Evaluate** work performance and adjust compensation and other rewards to reinforce recognition with monetary reward.
  [Work Performance Evaluation and Salary Administration]
  All these processes will be elaborated upon in the following chapters.

Performance Management can and has helped businesses, public agencies and NGOs improve their outputs and outcomes when the proper measures and/or counts are made which focus on the purpose of the organisation. Too much data confuses and ultimately will not be used. Even if the correct counts/measures are used, lack of analysis at the right level of work means various employees will interpret and use the data in ways that may or may not be effective, or the lack of understanding means they are not used at all.

Understanding that Work Performance of an individual must be judged in the context in which the work is performed will make acceptance of the feedback and evaluation more likely. The systems of Work Performance Evaluation we present in Chapter 19 have been used in a number of organisations with considerable success. Both managers and subordinates have stated the system is fair, even when their own Work Performance Evaluation was less than satisfactory.

We recognise that not all these ideas can be implemented quickly in all organisations, especially public agencies, but understanding the difference between Performance as Output and Work Performance can give an organisation a head-start to improving employee morale and productivity. Avoiding mistakes is a beginning, then more improvement can follow.

# 16 Performance Management – Overcoming the "Muddle"

## Introduction

As traditionally practised, there have been many terms used to describe the processes which managers use to evaluate a direct report's output and work performance and to inform the task doer of that evaluation. The confusion of language reflects an underlying conceptual confusion (Figure 16.1).

For both managers and team members the processes have caused considerable anguish, fear, anger and disgust. Managers often say the task of evaluating a team member is the worst part of their job. Team members often find performance appraisal at best irrelevant and at worst demeaning and unfair. Many existing systems are perceived to be on the negative end of all the shared values – unfair, dishonest, untrustworthy, disrespecting human dignity, unloving and demonstrating their managers are cowards. There seem to be two primary causes of this situation.

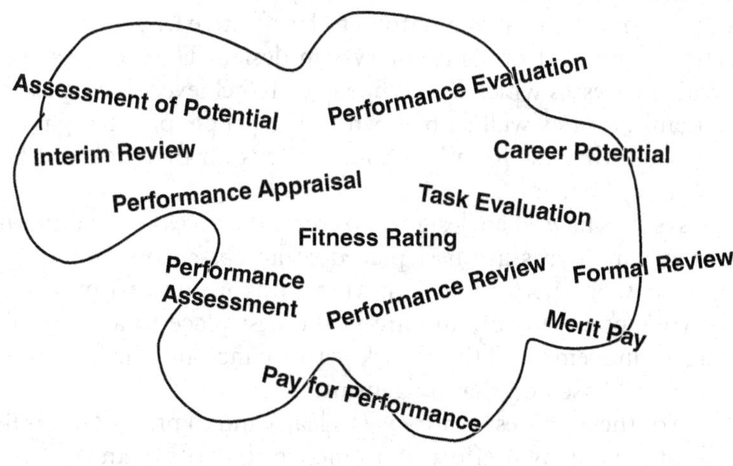


*Figure 16.1* Performance Appraisal Muddle

DOI: 10.4324/9781003459118-21

(1) The muddling of work which is best carried out by individuals in different roles.
(2) The muddling of activities which are fundamentally different in their purposes and which, when put together, require the manager to be both coach/trainer and judge simultaneously. These are two important and necessary parts of the manager's job, but they are psychologically contradictory when carried out at the same time.

Most performance appraisal systems have three purposes which are not mutually compatible:

(1) Improve the direct report's work performance.
(2) Provide information regarding the employee's potential for promotion.
(3) Set the direct report's salary, bonus and other remuneration within organisational policy.

These three purposes are not compatible when they are carried out at the same time by the same person, the Manager. The second purpose to consider an individual's potential for promotion should be carried out by the M+1 using an entirely different system, which will be discussed in detail in Chapter 21. The first and third purposes are to be performed by the manager, but they must be separated in time if they are to be effective.

As managers, teachers and consultants, we have made a concerted effort to develop a performance management system which does not hinder managers in their efforts to be effective leaders of people because of inherent faults in the system design. The idea has been to create processes which assist managers to achieve the purpose of the organisation as well as be open to the people of the organisation because the systems allow human needs for dignified and fair treatment to be met.

The systems have been designed to create the necessary conditions such that employees are best placed to accept accountability for their own work performance, have an opportunity to maximise their work performance, and are in the best place to accept their manager's judgement of their work performance and the fairness of their reward based on that judgement.

None of these processes are easy to learn and to practise skilfully. It will take your own effort and practice to carry them out well. When they can do this, most managers feel a real sense of satisfaction at having helped a fellow human being in one of the most important aspects of anyone's life – his or her work.

## The Manager as Coach and the Manager as Judge (See Figure 16.2)

The job of a Coach is to help team members improve their work performance. This is done in a number of ways – through improving one's own task assignments given to a team member, providing task feedback and task reviews, performance planning and performance reviews, as well as by providing opportunities to learn new skills or systems through training courses or work experiences.

The job of a Judge is to evaluate work performance in the role – passing sentence if you will – since the manager's judgement of the team member's work performance will determine the team member's salary within a salary band and all within the organisation's corporate policies.

**Task Review and Performance Review**

**Manager as Trainer/Coach**

**Process:** Two-Way Discussion

**Purpose:** Improve Work Performance of Both Manager and Subordinate

**Performance Assessment**

**Manager as Judge**

**Process:** Manager Rates Subordinate and informs him or her of that rating

**Purpose:** Assess work performance and apply differential monetary reward

*Figure 16.2* Manager's Two roles as Coach and Judge

These two parts of a manager's job are in fundamental contradiction with each other in a psychological sense. The manager must do both – be a coach and a judge, but the two roles must be carried out at different times. The two-way discussions which are the essence of task assignment, task reviews, performance planning and performance reviews are psychologically incompatible with a judgement of a team member's work performance, which is directly related to what the person is to be paid.

The solution is to carry out task assignments, feedback and review (TA/TR) throughout the year beginning with the Performance Plan at the start of the year. The performance review in the middle of the year is a time for looking at the larger picture as to how well *we* (manager and team member) are doing: are we on track to meet the purpose of the Performance Plan? Are we making progress towards the goals which were set at the beginning of the year? Where are things going well, where is there need for improvement, etc.?

At the end of the year is the time for a work performance evaluation where the manager rates each team member's work performance, and that rating is reviewed by M+1, and in some systems by M+2 and M+3 in order to ensure fairness across the organisation. How this is done is explained in Chapter 19.

## Work Performance Evaluation

Work performance evaluation is often perceived by managers as the most difficult and onerous task in their role as manager. There are many reasons for this feeling; a few of the most common are:

(1) The desire and need for a good productive relationship. Managers are dependent on their team members to carry out tasks which have a direct impact on the quality of the manager's work performance. This dependency creates a need and desire to foster good relationships to ensure the team's work performance is positive.

There is also a problem if the manager confuses judging the work performance with judging the person. Judging the person can damage or endanger a relationship, which is why we place so much emphasis on judging the quality of work performance, *never* the person. It is essential for team members to know where they stand in the eyes of the manager, and if the work performance is to improve over time. It is also essential to ensure the organisation is getting fair value for the salaries it pays. Properly done, a good evaluation of work performance is a healthy element in an honest relationship.

(2) When there is not enough distance between Manager and Team Member, as happens in organisations which have too many layers of management, that is where the manager works at the same level as team members. In this situation, managers are unable to effectively judge the work performance of team members because they don't have a larger perspective to view the work performance or pass judgement on it. When asked about performance evaluation, one manager said, "I'm not about to cut my own throat. These people know more than I do about their work. I want to keep them happy, so why should I criticise what they are doing?"

Typically, team members are not happy as they feel there is no one to judge their work, to let them know how their work fits into the larger picture and to give them feedback on how they were doing. One team member in this situation said, "He's useless. When I need to know something, I go to the manager one up." In a properly structured organisation, based on levels of complexity of work, this is much less likely to occur, though occasional mistakes in promotion may lead to this problem, which will become very visible quickly.

(3) Many existing performance evaluation systems are poorly designed.

a) Too time-consuming to fill out.
b) Asking for objective measures rather than the manager's judgement, disguising what is actually subjective as based on objective standards.
c) Requiring verbal explanations which are subject to arguments with the team member and second-guessing by the M+1.
d) Too often the system demands the two processes of coach and judge be performed at the same time, creating all the psychological problems we have described.
e) These factors cause managers to fudge their thinking and their statements which is known to both managers and team members. This dishonesty puts the relationship at much greater risk than any honest evaluation of work performance, which is so feared.

f) If the evaluation will have an impact on an individual's career, there is a tendency to soften a negative evaluation for fear of doing long-term damage to the person's career or to escalate a positive evaluation to ensure future potential for advancement.

(4) Managers must confront their own inadequacies.

a) Were task assignments clear?
b) Did I give task feedback and conduct task reviews?
c) Did I let the person know I was unhappy with certain aspects of their behaviour?
d) Too often the answer is "no." Thus, evaluating the work performance when feedback and review have been inadequate seems very unfair to the manager, who knows the team member is likely to feel the same way. "If that was what you wanted, why didn't you say so?"

(5) Fear of being different from other managers. Am I too hard on my people or too soft compared to other managers? Here the issue is equity, and few of the most widely used systems have a means to make clear and equitable standards which are visible and therefore correctable.

(6) There is always the fear of a legal challenge where the words on an evaluation may come back to haunt the managers. Too often inadequate employees are given "acceptable" performance evaluations, and when/if it becomes necessary to dismiss them, those performance reviews can be used against the organisation that did not provide honest evaluations.

This can lead to bland, innocuous statements which are less likely to be used in court, but which, in turn, have little or no impact on individual work performance – for better or for worse. Everyone knows Performance Evaluation is an exercise we must go through, a lot of sound and fury signifying nothing.

## Summary

The work performance evaluation and salary administration system we describe in Chapters 19 and 20 have been designed to avoid these problems. It may not solve all your problems, but the organisations which have used it have found it to be more effective than the other systems they have used. As one manager put it,

"The system we had last year pissed off me and my entire team. This system is better; at least it won't piss me off." The system turned out to be well accepted by his team as well.

The next chapters provide information on the suite of systems that we have found work well for both managers and team members. We put Task Assignment in Chapter 3, in order to give you something you could use immediately to improve your communication with your team members. We mentioned that you should look at Chapter 17 on Task Feedback and Review. To complete the process, Performance Planning and Review and Performance Evaluation and Salary Administration then follow.

# 17 Task Assignment, Feedback and Review

## Introduction

In Chapter 3 we presented the basic structure of an effective task assignment using CPQ/QRT. It may be helpful to go back to review that chapter before looking at the types of tasks you might want to assign as presented here in more depth. Task feedback and task review are essential processes to improve work performance in both manager and direct reports and are presented in this chapter. Here we also point out some of the complexities which can arise in the process of task assignment.

There are different types of tasks other than a direct assignment. There may be confusion regarding time which can be a deadline set to complete the task and a resource as in the amount of time available to complete the task. There may also be confusion between the "how" of a task which is where the task doer exercises discretion to complete an assigned task and assigning a task which requires the task doer to figure out how a particular system or practice might be created or improved. In this chapter we are focused on clarifying these differing aspects of task assignment.

## Types of Tasks

Although the examples provided in Chapter 3 assumed the manager will make a specific task assignment to a specific employee, not all tasks are so assigned. There are many variations in the process, and direct assignment may not be the one most frequently used.

### Direct Assignment

The manager assigns the task directly to the task doer.

> Give me the standard monthly budget report by the end of next week.
>
> (This assumes the person knows what the budget report is and the quality standards that apply and the context of the task.

DOI: 10.4324/9781003459118-22

It also assumes the person has the information, staffing and budget resources to do the task.)

### Task with Inset Trigger

The manager assigns the task to the subordinate with the statement that when a "trigger" event occurs, the person should carry out the task. These are the most common type of tasks.

> "Sam, Jane and Ali are authorized to request equipment for their units. When an order comes in from one of them, and it is for items coded for their section's use, make sure it is processed within 48 hours, though 24 hours would be preferable. If this cannot be done due to other commitments, let them know and inform me. The processing of such orders should average no more than 2 errors per month and you should not have to use any staff over-time." If it is for an item not coded for their use, refer it to me.

Many assumptions about expected activity in the work setting remain implicit in the mind of the manager and are only noted when a team member violates an organisational norm. Many of these assumptions are really unspoken tasks and can be stated as tasks with inset triggers, thus clarifying expectations and providing one condition to enable a subordinate to later accept his/her manager's judgement of his/her work performance as fair. By discussing these tasks, managers are more likely to take into account the full range of tasks the employee is carrying out. Too often the tasks with inset triggers are not recognised, leading to problems in task review, performance review and evaluation.

Here is an example of an implicit task, which may be overlooked when performance is reviewed:

> Discuss and resolve with your peers any human relations problems affecting your work. If you cannot resolve it to your satisfaction, refer it to me.

This task is triggered anytime team members encounter a problem in their relationships with other team members. It is therefore valid at the time of performance review to note whether or not this task was carried out effectively as problems arose in the conduct of other tasks.

Most of the work done in service industries involving interaction with customers falls into the classification of tasks with inset triggers. Organisations that appreciate the need for excellent customer satisfaction ratings and the maintenance of them over time put a lot of time, money and effort into training their staff in the performance of tasks with inset triggers. Staff are taught specific triggers for a particular work response and the behaviours required to be demonstrated to the customer during the performance of the task. They are also taught the limits of their own authority and the means of referring a customer with a request or questions they cannot satisfy to someone in the organisation who can do so.

### Sequential Tasks

The manager assigns a short-term task as prelude to a much longer-term task. This may be used to ensure a Team Member understands what is to be done. It may also be used when the manager will have to formulate the larger task based on information the Team Member gathers as to achievable goals, required resources, alternative solutions to a problem.

> We need to develop a new security system for the central office complex which takes into account the total number of facilities and the increasing levels of threat. I want the new system ready for use within 18 months, though it may take as much as two years to be fully operational.
>
> I'd like a report in three months on what might be feasible in this time frame, what the costs are likely to be, whether or not we can purchase such a system from a vendor, whether a vendor's system could be purchased but would require modification, or whether we are better off doing it ourselves. You should also consider if there are some better systems that might take longer to create or some stop-gap solutions we can implement immediately. Come back to me with a proposal as to what we should do. When we agree on what is to be done, I will ask you to lead the project.

### Multiple Tasks

This occurs when several tasks are created in the context of what appears to be a single task. It is important to clarify your priorities as manager if the subordinate discovers that not all the tasks are feasible within your given limits.

> The security environment around our headquarters building is deteriorating. We are getting more physical threats, and

cyberthreats are increasing. We have employed a consulting firm with expertise in dealing with the issues. I want you to put together a small team to work with them in order for all of you to gain an understanding of how these issues can be dealt with effectively. Joe, Harry and Gail have been told you will be calling on them to negotiate for the temporary assignment of one or more of their staff to the project. I want at least two members of the team to be new to security technology and systems, so that they can learn to use them to maintain and improve the systems selected. The analysis needs to be done within six months and all the systems in place within 18 months. At that time, I would like to see your team fully developed with all members trained in security technology and systems, capable of carrying out additional security projects on their own.

(Note the potential for confusion here. If the person cannot get both tasks done, which is more important, the analysis and selection of security technologies and systems or having team members trained to maintain them?)

How could the manager clarify these tasks for the task doer?

### Time – Boundary Condition and Resource

Often there is confusion and difficulty with the idea of time in the task assignment process since it is both a boundary condition – one of the key components of a task assignment – and also quite clearly a resource. Both are measured in the same units – minutes, hours, days, years, but there is a crucial difference when thinking about good management practice. The boundary condition is a deadline (target completion time); the amount of time available prior to the deadline is a resource. Often this resource is expressed in staff-hours available, or over-time hours available, but it is clearly different from a deadline.

### The How – The Task Doers' Job

One of the things we have learned both as managers and as employees is that no one likes to be told how to carry out a task unless the person is new to the role and has no idea how to tackle a new assignment. People who know their job say, "Tell me what to do, but don't tell me how to do it."

The "how" is the creation of a methodology (pathway) to achieve the goal and that must remain within the task doer's area of discretion. There may be some limits on the methodology or pathway which must be created. For example, hiring temporary employees may not be allowed, or purchasing a new computer application may not be allowed. These are simply additional limits on the task, but within those limits the "how" of the task is within the discretionary area of the task doer.

When employees claim they are being micro-managed, more often than not, the manager is telling them not only what to do, but how to do it. That is why we said earlier that the pathway should not be specified in human task assignment. Work for humans is turning intention into reality by exercising their discretion. Correct task assignment for people must concentrate upon the humanity and unique positive qualities of people – their abilities to learn, to create, to innovate.

## The "How" as a Task Assignment

As one moves up an organisational hierarchy (see Chapter 6), the objective of the task may be to articulate and test a methodology (or pathway) that can be used throughout the organisation. Stewart was given such an assignment where the purpose was to develop the methodology by using a part of the organisation as a test bed. He formed an Organisational Development (OD) team to restructure a large corporate business unit and to develop a methodology for carrying out such work in other business units. While he was doing this, he was to use the experience to develop a theory and practice for the generation of systems within organisations. It was recognised that the first task would take somewhere between three and five years. It was hoped that the second task could be completed within one year, or at most two years.

He was given the authority to hire as many people as he needed based on the work required. Because of the extensive need to interview the workforce and gather data, the initial team had ten members. Under work pressure, that was increased for a time to 14. All came from within the corporation – taking some from the business unit under study and others from other business units. He would have to get the permission of their Managing Directors (MDs) to take someone from their staff, but it was made clear to the MDs that unless there was a very good reason, people were to be released for at least one year to carry out this work.

The cost was estimated to be at least $4,000,000, and if it appeared to be likely to exceed $6,000,000, Stewart should get back to his manager and the CEO of the Corporation to discuss the reasons and perhaps revise what needed to be done.

Although it was not specifically articulated, he understood that his work performance would be judged on the quality of recommendations made in the judgement of his manager and the CEO, and also the quality of the methodology developed. Some of the indicators of performance would be a reduction in industrial action (strikes), productivity gains, reduction in costs. There were a variety of other limits, including that no one would lose their employment as a result of the restructuring. Individuals' jobs might change, and they might be transferred to other sites, but employment within the corporation was guaranteed (at that time).

Stewart began to carry out these tasks, which were partially completed in two years. Another manager then took over the first task to restructure the business which was completed two years later, while Stewart went on to develop and articulate the methodology in another role. As can be seen, there was considerable area for discretion, yet the limits were in some cases quite tight (no one is to lose their job) and in others there were large tolerances (three to five years to complete the task). There would have been no reward for completing the task more quickly if the recommendations were of poor quality. There would have been no reward for spending less than $4 million if, again, the recommendations had not been judged as being effective. The restructure took four years, and approximately $6 million was spent, including all training, and this was considered by the CEO to be money well spent given the results which ensued.

A year after the restructure was completed, this was demonstrated under the pressure of a severe global economic downturn; 25% of the workforce had to be cut. The General Manager who had to organise this unpleasant task stated it would have been impossible without the understandings and structures developed in the OD process.

When the recession passed, the reduced workforce was able to produce more than had ever been produced before. With the implementation of new systems and changed managers to support the structural changes, working conditions and trust in management improved to the extent that a few years after that, the workforce chose to work under staff conditions rather than keeping their unions. This was in an organisation that had had very difficult labour-management relations for decades with more than 300 work stoppages per year in many of the years prior to the changes to structure, systems and key managers.[1]

## Issues in Task Assignment

Before a task can be assigned, managers must not only formulate the task, they must also consider the direct report's capability (see

Chapter 4), knowledge, experience and energy. Is this the right person for this task? If the person lacks the essential capability to complete the task satisfactorily, resources will be wasted, the manager will not meet his/her own accountabilities and the direct report's sense of self-worth may be adversely affected.

Managers must also consider how much of their own input will be required if the task is to be carried out effectively. Some complex tasks may be done by people with less capability if the manager is willing and able to break them into smaller tasks and provide considerable feedback and coaching as they are being carried out. This may be acceptable with someone who is inexperienced and who needs to learn the elements of the role. The need to do this may, however, be an indication of someone who is not able to perform the work of the role. When a person is fully competent in the role, the manager can assign an appropriately complex task knowing the person is fully able to carry it out.

The manager must also consider the team member's workload. In the case of overload, the manager may choose to extend the deadlines of other tasks, provide more resources or change the output required, i.e., change the tasks. Team members should advise the manager at any time they believe a task will not be completed within its limits. Judging workload cannot always be done with precision, so the establishment of this information flow is crucial to both the task doers and the manager.

### Level of Detail in Task Assignments

The question is often raised to what level of detail must tasks be specified and scoped? This is an issue of managerial judgement. With people who are competent in the role, the manager will usually not mention many smaller tasks within a larger overall body of work. Other tasks will be left implicit – in fact, they are tasks with inset triggers that have been well practised previously.

When the manager makes this assumption and the direct report does not know this, tasks will not get done. In this case, until the direct report has a better understanding of all the work of the role, more tasks will have to be specified in detail, rather than left to the discretion of the task doer. As a manager-direct report relationship develops, each will learn the expectations and understandings of the other, and communications will become clearer even as they become less formal.

The Task Review and Performance Review provide opportunities to discuss what is being done and not done and allow for corrections and clarification when things are not as they should be.

It is, however, the work of the manager to regularly provide feedback on task performance in the normal course of activity and not wait for formal reviews to complement or take corrective action.

### The Use of Initiative

Does clear task assignment as we have described here mean direct reports never do anything on their own initiative? Of course not. The intelligent exercise of initiative is essential if any organisation is to thrive over time. It is the direct report's clear understanding of the manager's purpose and objectives and where the direct report fits into that purpose, which allows the direct report to exercise initiative, and, where necessary, to deal with conditions which change unexpectedly in order to achieve the manager's purpose.

Direct reports may also check back with the manager when they have some ideas on other tasks to be done in order to ensure their actions are in agreement with the manager's purpose.

We have found that clear task assignment is liberating, not constraining. Clear limits and boundaries provide external reference points that allow the task doer to assess and control the exercise of discretion based on objective outside standards. When properly formulated and stated, the reference points provide a clear space for the exercise of discretion. Unclear task assignment or the lack of assignments are the real constraints that leave people confused, sap energy and make it less likely initiative can be exercised effectively. There is enough uncertainty and ambiguity in work without adding to it by leaving a person to second-guess what is meant or really wanted.

Again, the processes of Task Feedback and Review and Performance Review provide opportunities to discuss issues where employees fail to take effective initiative or where they decide to carry out tasks the manager does not want carried out.

### Developing Skill in the Task Assignment Process

If you are a manager or a leader of a team, think about the target completion times given to you by your manager, and compare them to the target completion times you give to your team members. Do you practise what you would like to have happen to you?

Compare your most able and least able employees. What is the difference in the target completion times you give to each of them? In a crisis, you may ask the most capable employee to take on a task of short duration, confident that he or she will take into account the long-term implications of the immediate problem. More typically, the more capable employees are allowed to work on their own for longer time spans, while less capable employees are given shorter time spans.

Think about an employee who was given a task of, say, three months. After two weeks you notice that there has not been much progress. You will likely call the employee in, discuss what is, or is not, happening. If you are satisfied the employee can do the job, you let him or her get on with it. If there seems to be a problem, you may decide to break up the task into a series of shorter tasks, so you can monitor progress more closely and be more certain the job will get done. Effectively, you are reducing the complexity of work to be done by the task doer and taking it on yourself to achieve your goal.

Consider under what circumstances you would choose to involve the team member in the task formulation process. Under what circumstances would you not choose to involve them? Would these differ depending upon the team member's capability? What is the impact of circumstances as compared to the characteristics of the person when you decide to involve or not involve the person in the task assignment process?

Practise writing out various types of task assignments – direct, tasks with inset triggers, sequential tasks, "how" tasks. How would you assign a task if you do not know how long it should take to complete it? Or what will be needed as resources? Often quality is the most difficult dimension to specify; "I know it when I see it" is not particularly helpful to the task doer. Perhaps you can show the person an example of good quality work; you may be able to teach your quality standards over time as you give the person feedback on the tasks they have carried out.

As you think through these issues, you will be developing your skills in the discipline of task assignment. As your skills improve, the quality of your own and your direct reports' work performance should also improve.

Some managers find it useful to write out task assignments both to clarify their own thinking and to make sure the task is properly communicated to the task doer. For some managers, written assignments are also useful as a means of keeping track of task progress and to provide input into task and performance reviews.

*The decision to write, or not to write, a task assignment is a managerial judgement.* It should not be made a requirement in all cases because it will then become a mechanistic and non-productive process. As a managerial relationship progresses, each party will develop a clearer understanding of what is expected, and a few words "on the fly" may be all that is necessary to make clear what is to be done and how performance will be judged. In other cases, a manager may decide a written assignment would be a more productive means to communicate his or her intentions, and therefore decide to put it down in that form.

## Summary

The variations of task assignment methodology described in this chapter provide what we hope is a clear statement of what is required to get the best work from employees and to respect their human dignity. Granted the examples in this chapter used very simple tasks with short times to completion in order to make the principles clear. We recognise that at higher levels of the organisation the tasks may be significantly more complex, and the term task (which often implies something small) doesn't even appear to be the correct term. If you can think of a task from a Board to a CEO as being, simply put, "We expect you to grow the business at an average rate of 15% throughout the complete business cycle," then you will see that task assignment can apply at all levels of the organisation.

Obviously, tasks will be assigned very differently at different levels of the organisation. As you move up the organisation, the area for discretion grows, and often the limits have much broader tolerances. Many of the prescribed limits are assumed to be understood (though we still recommend a conversation to make sure there is full agreement even at the highest levels of the organisation).

After the assignments are made and acted upon, it is necessary to provide feedback on how, you, the manager, assess the results and a more formal task review.

## Task Feedback and Task Review

Without these two practices task doers will be uncertain as to how their managers will judge the quality of their work performance and the basis on which that judgement is made. This is necessary if the manager's judgement of performance of the task is to be accepted as fair. We begin with definitions.

**Task Feedback:** Information (good or bad) employees receive on how well they carried out the task. Some of it may come from the natural environment or from customers, peers or the manager who assigned the task.

**Task Review:** A discussion between the manager and the direct report about whether the task has been completed as expected and, if not, why not. Its purpose is to learn lessons from both success and failure in order to improve the work performance of *both* the manager and the direct report in the future. (It is important to note that if a task is not completed as expected it may NOT be because the direct report has *failed. There are many reasons why this may be the case, many beyond the person's control.*)

### Task Feedback

Task feedback is information the employee receives regarding how well they carried out the task. Of all the information associated with the task, this is the information that is most important to the employee. It may come from essentially four sources:

1. Directly in response to his or her activities.
2. From customers within or outside the organisation.
3. From peers at work.
4. The Manager.

The most trustworthy task feedback from the point of view of the task doer comes from the result produced by completing the task. Such feedback is effective because it is undeniable. For example, an electrician given the task of putting in the wires and attachments to light up a room knows as soon as he flips the switch whether the task was completed successfully or not. If the power comes on, he's good; if the power does not come on, he knows something is wrong and the task assigned has not yet been carried out successfully. It is undeniable, no room for debate. Not all tasks can produce such certainty, but task doers who are properly placed in roles usually know whether the result is outstanding, adequate or poor. Employees like to take pride in their work; the manager can validate their assessments.

Customers can be a powerful behavioural change or reinforcement agent. One weakness of such feedback is that it may reflect short-term satisfaction (or dissatisfaction) with task output without an understanding of overall work performance or longer-term consequences. What the customer may appreciate is not what the manager expected. Their perspective may be contrary to the manager's purpose. Nonetheless, customer satisfaction is important to the task doer.

Peers can also give feedback, which the task doer may appreciate. It's good to know your work is respected by your fellow workers. Too often, however, the importance of peer approval occurs in poorly structured organisations where the manager is not at the right level of work to give effective feedback. In addition, the real decision maker regarding an employee's rewards and compensation is someone other than the nominal manager. In this situation, peers provide psychological rewards that reinforce the individual's worth to the group – the sense that the work the individual is doing is of value (or without value). Peers can also provide feedback that is at odds with the manager's purpose.

The feedback from managers is of importance because it can provide a longer-term perspective on work performance as well as significant psychological recognition.

In a properly structured organisation where the managerial authorities are real, people are aware that their manager's view of their performance will have a direct impact on compensation and on whether they may remain in their role over time. This ensures that managerial feedback commands attention. It also increases its importance in relation to other sources of feedback.

Most task doers will consider the source of the feedback and will react accordingly. When the feedback coming from the result of the task doers work, it cannot be refuted. It is either positive or negative. Feedback from customers and peers is always subject to consideration.

The feedback from the manager may be as casual as a big smile along with "nice work." It may be an opportunity to do a more challenging task, or it may be more specific, "The way you handled that customer was as good as it gets."

Managers who never, or rarely, give feedback may leave the task doers with uncertainty, and this can create problems when it's time for work performance evaluation. Feedback from the manager must be used with care, immediately if there is a real problem, occasionally to recognise both positive and negative results.

> **Note:** The most efficient method to reinforce behaviour is regular specific but random feedback – feedback which is positive in the sense that it leaves no room for doubt and does not detract from the dignity of the task doer.

## Task Review

The purpose of a task review is to learn lessons from both success and failure to improve work performance in the future. A task review is a more extended form of task feedback. It is recognised in many organisations as the number one system needed for work performance improvement.

Task review is an informal process carried out on a regular but random basis by a manager as he or she comments (in a few words or at length) on task performance with their direct reports. Here the manager's role as trainer/coach is predominant. The emphasis is on a two-way, not a one-way process.

The employee may also initiate a task review when the employee thinks it is needed to improve their own work performance or the manager's work performance. It is valid and necessary to tell a manager from time to time, "I could do my job better if…." and then say what would help – more information, additional training, clearer task assignment from the manager, more advance notice, etc.

Task review is intended to be an analytic process anchored in the concrete reality of specific tasks – where both the manager and subordinate look back at the task assignment, what was expected and why – how well this was understood. Then they look at the execution of the task – what was done, whether the task doer in fact met the specified components of the task and stayed within the range of the scoped component.

The manager and the task doer might discuss the various limits which applied to the task and whether they might have constrained efficient performance. This can be a useful indicator for the manager to assess changes to existing policy, departmental or corporate, or systems, or perhaps even legislation.

They may discuss other tasks with inset triggers such as maintaining productive working relationships with fellow workers or servicing customers. If the task doer did not breach any limits, then task performance can be judged by how well they did on the scoped component of the task.

Task review is the time to look at whether the task achieved its intended purpose, to analyse the chosen pathway and perhaps discuss other pathways which might have been more effective or efficient. There should be discussion as to whether changes in the environment required changing the task assignment and how a similar task might be assigned and done better in the future.

Where things have not gone as well as they should, this is a chance to enquire as to what went wrong and what might correct the problem in the future. This is where, on a regular basis, the manager and the person talk about their work and where the manager can provide coaching to help the person improve their work. The person may also provide information as to what the manager could do which would help the subordinate to achieve task goals.

Coaching and counselling are the everyday processes of leadership and management and should be anchored in the concrete: what the person did; how they did it; how the task was assigned (clearly or not); and whether the performance was good, poor or failed entirely.

A general statement such as "This is a mess!" or "Great job!" conveys the manager's assessment but does not provide any information to change behaviour in the desired direction. Concrete cases not only provide more information to exemplify the issues and concerns regarding performance, they also make it more difficult to show prejudice on the basis of non-work-related issues. Each task review is a teaching/learning opportunity.

The manager might ask the person, "How do you think you might perform such a task more effectively?" "How will you do it next time?" "What can I do to help you improve your work performance?"

Managers should ask themselves, "How should I assign a task like this to ensure it gets done to my standards of quantity, quality, timeliness and cost?"; "Does this person have the capability to do tasks of this type?"; "The capability to do other types of tasks?"; "The capability to do more than is called for in this role?"

It is of absolute importance that in the task review process the manager focuses on the work and on the task result, *not* on the characteristics of the person. Treating an individual in a derogatory manner denies that person's human dignity. It will make the person angry, and even if it does not show, it will give them good cause to ignore the validity of everything else the manager might say.

Exceptionally good or poor performance should be noted in writing *at the time it occurs* and sent to M+1 as well as be reviewed with the person concerned.

## Summary

There are many types of Task Feedback that let people know how well they are accomplishing their task. Task Review is a more formal process where the manager and the direct report discuss what happened and what can be learned from it to improve future task assignments and the way they are carried out.

This work goes on throughout the Planning cycle – from Performance Planning at the beginning of the year through Performance Review in the middle of the year, to Work Performance Evaluation at the end of the year. Chapter 18 presents one Performance Planning system that has proved successful in a number of organisations. We recognise, however, that each organisation may have its own planning process, and we hope these ideas will help to improve that process.

## Note

1 It should be noted that much of what you are reading in this book originated with the work of Stewart and his OD teams. While the earliest work on organisations, termed Stratified Systems Theory, was developed by Elliott Jaques and Lord Wilfred Brown in the 1940s and 1950s, Systems Leadership was built on their ideas as well as our own experiences as managers, consultants and teachers, but Stewart and his teams were a major factor in the origins of Systems Leadership Theory as we use it today.

# 18 Performance Planning and Review

## Performance Planning

Performance planning is the beginning of the performance management cycle, which includes task assignment, task review, performance review, performance evaluation and salary administration. Task assignment and review were covered in Chapters 3 and 17 to provide a tool that is immediately useful to most managers.

The purpose of performance planning is to make clear what is to be accomplished this year (or in a time frame appropriate to the role – one, two, five, ten or more years). Even for the roles that have longer targeted completion times, most large organisations have an annual plan which sets targets for the year. This process:

- Links the work of each employee to the organisation's annual plan.
- Clarifies what the manager and the team are expected to do and where each direct report fits into the manager's plan.
- Provides clear articulation through task assignments that make clear what constitutes excellent performance:
  - Outputs can be counted or measured.
  - Work performance of the employee must be judged by the manager.

The process begins at the top level of the organisation with the plan's approval by the chief executive and the Board of Directors. This plan is then passed down through each level of the hierarchy to link their plans to the purpose of the overall business plan. Managers get information informing them regarding what is expected from their parts of the organisation. You can think of this process as recurring, cascading and increasingly granular.

To ensure team members understand what their part of the organisation is expected to do, it is useful to discuss the overall organisation's purpose and plan in a team meeting. This enables the team to have a two-way discussion where the manager lays out

DOI: 10.4324/9781003459118-23

his or her perspective on what the situation for the division or unit is likely to be, given what is known about corporate, business unit and department purpose and goals.

This meeting is an opportunity to get the team's input and ideas regarding how best to meet the overall objectives (or in some cases to suggest that what has been proposed may not be feasible at this time or with available resources). It is important to clarify, as far as possible, the work each team member is expected to accomplish and how it fits into the larger team effort. This meeting is then followed by the manager meeting with each individual team member to discuss how their role fits into the plan, their task assignments and their understanding of their own and the unit's purpose.

Task assignment and task review are ongoing throughout the year. Performance planning, performance review and performance evaluation form an annual cycle with performance review required at the mid-point of the cycle. (More frequent performance reviews may be productive if managers or their reports wish to have them, but only one is required.) Performance evaluation is the end of the cycle and is immediately followed by performance planning for the next cycle.

In addition to the essential tasks, which the person must complete in order to meet the manager's requirements, the plan should indicate the resources allocated and the freedom of action available to the person (areas where the person is encouraged to exercise initiative to improve the quality of output). This is also the time to discuss context, purpose, quantity and quality of output, resources and planned time to completion for the significant activity planned.

At the end of the discussion, there should be a statement of what actions are planned by both the manager and the direct report to carry out the plan. These may include any training or on-the-job experiences that are planned for the person as well as special projects assigned by either the manager or the manager-once-removed (M+1) to develop the person's career potential. (See Appendix A for an example.)

We believe any such training must be needs-based, costed and budgeted for. We have seen many organisations wherein promises of development are made and ignored year after year.

## Performance Review

The purpose of a performance review is to improve future work performance by examining how well *both* the manager and the direct report are doing in carrying out their respective elements of the plan and their specific tasks. Performance review is a formal two-way analytic learning process for both manager and team member in order to:

- Review what they planned to do – their purpose and plans – and what they have accomplished to date.
- Review their work performance as individuals and as a team.
- Make specific plans to improve their work effectiveness for the rest of the year (or next year).

Note: In the review process, the manager's role is to act as a coach where needed.

Performance review must be carried out at least once a year, typically about six months into the performance plan. For persons new to a role, a performance review may be helpful given quarterly, in addition to the six-month performance review. We also recommend that it be done again, at the end of the year to inform the next year's performance plan.

Both managers and their direct reports have the authority to decide that a formal performance review is needed at any time during the year due to particular issues or perceived problems. The requested performance review should be done at the earliest possible time given overall work commitments. As with all task and performance reviews in a work environment, the focus must be on the work, not on the person.

Scheduling a performance review is particularly important if someone is performing poorly. Such a discussion may uncover the source of the difficulties and provide a solution that will allow the manager and direct report to devise clear steps that need to be taken to improve performance.

The performance review process involves an analysis of the work and tasks of both manager and team member to assess what has been accomplished over the six months or year, to evaluate the quality of what has been accomplished and to discover better ways of working together to achieve better results.

This is, in effect, a summing up of the task reviews that have taken place at the manager's discretion during the year and provides a longer overview of performance – a look at the forest as opposed to the trees. It is a joint effort designed to reduce defensiveness by involving both manager and team member in an appraisal of what was accomplished and an analysis of what happened. Typical questions would include:

- What have we done? Results?
- How have we done it?

- Have we achieved our purpose?
- How did we do it?
- Where are we in relation to the plan?
- Can we devise better methods for finding out how we are doing? Any measures?
- Where things have gone well, why has this occurred? How can we replicate this in the future?
- Where things have gone badly, what went wrong?
- Was the purpose unclear?
- Did the environment change in ways which were unanticipated when the task was assigned?
- Was there clarity on what was to be done – the manager's standards of quantity, quality, timeliness and cost?
- Can we think of alternative ways of doing this? Might one of these be better?
- Has the manager provided clear task assignments, adequate task feedback and review, appropriate resources – material, staff hours, budget, information, enough time to get the work accomplished?
- Does either person need additional training to perform their current role more effectively?
- Is there evidence of a deeper problem such as Mental Processing Ability (MPA) not matching the work of the role?
- Are there one or more issues that should be discussed as a team?

A Performance Review Guide (see Appendix A) provides a checklist to trigger thinking about important issues, especially key task types which are often left implicit even though they could be assigned as tasks with inset triggers. The Guide also provides space to enter other points which either the manager or team member thinks are important in their roles and work relationship.

As both the manager and the team member use these checklists, they should note specific examples of tasks or incidents which exemplify the point they are trying to make. Anchoring the discussion in the concrete reality of specific tasks is essential if both are to understand the issues of concern. These concrete examples should provide clues as to how they can do better in the future. They may also indicate what was successful as a guide to build on.

## Issues in Performance Review

Recognise that the tasks with inset triggers are not directly assigned. It is easy to overlook these tasks, especially the tasks involving social process, but it is essential that these be discussed in a Performance Review. For example, the assigned task may have been completed on time and within budget, but the entire team is angry about what they perceive as unfair treatment and lack of respect for their dignity. Very few tasks do not have attached tasks which may not have been discussed in task assignment, such as adequate scheduling, social relationships as well as health, safety and environment concerns, but which need to be noticed in a Performance Review.

Performance Review is a good time to review the assumptions about the conditions predicted for the duration of the plan. This may be a time to revisit the assumptions to check if there has been variation from what we believed was the case when we assigned the task. If there has been a change, has it been significant enough that we need to modify the criteria for task or performance reviews?

After the individual reviews are completed, many managers have found it useful to have another team meeting to discuss their overall plans and review what went well and what went badly, and why. Individual performance may either strengthen team performance or sometimes damage it, and this deserves discussion.

At the end of this review both manager and direct report should agree as to what work will be done to carry out the plan in the future. For example, they may agree on steps to be taken by each of them to clarify task assignments. Any other steps agreed to for either party should be noted. This should be written down and signed by the manager and the team member. This Performance Review Record then goes to M+1 to indicate the review has taken place (the system control). It also provides data for M+1s as they consider the career potential of their reports-once-removed.

The Performance Plan and Review provide information relevant to the next step to be taken at the end of the year when the manager acts as a judge to evaluate the work performance of each team member with consequences for wages and salaries.

# 19 Performance Evaluation

## Introduction

In Chapter 16 we gave some of the reasons we have observed that make Performance Evaluation the dreaded task. In this chapter we present a system that has been designed to help overcome those difficulties. In practice, it has had a positive impact on the work performance of both managers and team members.

Managers have reported that the system is simple, easy to use and understand and its mechanics require less managerial time than other systems of which we are aware. Of course, observing work being done, thinking about needed improvements, reflecting on the employees' work performance and making an evaluation is, and should be, a time-consuming job. The system itself does not require additional time to get the wording just right, to anticipate arguments, to ensure there is no misunderstanding. To illustrate the process, try the following exercise.

### Box 19.1

**Exercise:** List the names of your team members in rank order from best to poorest. Then select the poorest performer on the list and rate him or her a 1. Then select the next poorest performer and rate him or her a 2. Using the difference between the respective work performance of these two as a guide, then rate the respective work performance of each other pair of team members on your list. You can't use the same number twice. Then add up all the scores of difference (in the case of the two worst, the difference is one).

What you have at this point is a scale width for ranking the relative work performance of this particular team of subordinates and an ordering method to assist your thinking when it comes to performance evaluation. We have had many managers do this exercise for their own teams in training exercises on performance

DOI: 10.4324/9781003459118-24

evaluation. It is rare for a manager to require more than 15 minutes to do this. Managers said they found it very useful in that at the end of the exercise they were more satisfied and confident in their ability to make judgements for performance evaluation.

Now consider how well you think you did after completing this exercise. Was it difficult? How much confidence do you have in your judgement? Think about this as you read the rest of this chapter. We have found both managers and team members view this system as better than any they have used, or been subject to, in the past.

The system has been tested in several organisations, and to date it has shown no internal contradictions. It is simple, easy to use, easily understood, and in its mechanics requires less managerial time than other systems of which we are aware.

## The Work Performance Evaluation System

**Purpose:** To evaluate the work performance of team members in order to recognise and reward differentially.

This requires managers to make clear what they and the organisation prioritise by what they recognise and reward. They must recognise the differences in the quality of work performance of their team members. It must be done in a way which is fair and perceived to be so by team members and upper management. The intent is to create conditions where all team members can recognise that this organisation is a meritocracy (a place where people advance based on their capability and work performance).

The process is straightforward and makes use of the knowledge and skills managers have and use all the time. This does not, however, make it easy. Nonetheless, managers have the task of making hard decisions, including decisions regarding the relative value of their employees' work to the organisation.

The system provided here allows them to do this in a way which is clear, provides for review to help ensure equity all the way to the top of the organisation, and which asks managers to do what they are paid to do, to exercise their human judgement in this most human of processes.

In developing this system, a concerted effort has been made to develop a process of performance evaluation that does not hinder the manager in his or her effort to be an effective leader of people because of inherent faults in the system design.

Even when individuals do not like the results of their own evaluation, they still tend to say the system is fair. They have also said they are finally getting information which allows them to improve, or perhaps seek employment elsewhere.

The system provides clear recognition, which is undeniable because it is directly linked to pay. The system is designed to allow people to be paid according to their value to the organisation within limits set by the salary structure. Over time, the system also generates trend information that should inform the M+1's assessment of an individual's potential for advancement.

There are no automatic escalators that can send payroll costs through the roof. There is no assumption that an individual must automatically get a pay increase simply for being in a role for another year. This system is designed to allow managers to pay for work performance. It is not a seniority system. The system also allows management to keep overall control of the payroll budget while allowing individual managers to set the relative distribution of pay fairly for their subordinates.

These factors have been demonstrated to be an improvement over many existing systems. The purpose is to design a system which, at a minimum, does not impede good management practice and which supports and fosters good management practice. It is designed to place the organisation on the positive end of the scales of shared values, and to allow managers to place themselves at the positive end of the scales as well. Only their actual behaviour, the work they do carrying out this process, will determine the outcome. The system provides necessary, but not sufficient conditions for good management practice.

There is often a search for an "objective" Holy Grail that seems not to require judgement, only a measure or counting of output or targets. No system can or should avoid judgement as working relationships are human relationships. Only sensitive human thinking is adequate to the difficult task of evaluating work performance in context and with all its subtle nuances. In the end, Performance Evaluation will always require competence; it also requires courage. It is only human to want to be liked, and it is also human to fear that a negative evaluation will damage an important relationship.

The system allows managers to demonstrate their courage, their respect for human dignity, their fairness, honesty, trust and love. It is up to the managers, however, to do it. As demonstrated in the exercise at the beginning of the chapter, there are three basic steps in this process – Rank, Rate and Review.

## Rank

As you demonstrated in the exercise, experienced managers can usually do this within 15 minutes or less, though there may be a bit of uncertainty in the middle. All managers know who are their best and worst team members. Now that it is for real, do you have doubts about the validity of this ranking? Most managers do not. The rapid and sure ability of managers to do such a ranking in order of work performance is well-known and understood.

Nonetheless, some managers resist placing people in rank order. They may have been abused by systems of forced ranking which meant the best organisation units still had to put good team members at the bottom of the order, while poorly performing units were able to place poor performers at the top of the order. In the case of one exceptionally badly designed system where 15% of the people would be rated as best and 15% had to be rated the worst with a higher 35% and a lower 35% in the middle – no exceptions. One manager growled, "What really pisses me off about this system is that HR will have 15% of their people in the top category."

The system we propose is not like that. Ranking is not even a *necessary* step, just a *convenient* way to help managers by starting with a task they do well when given the opportunity to use their subjective judgement. It also allows managers who have several teams with differing tasks to rank them within those logical categories. Whether to rank or not is a managerial decision; it is the next step, rating, that is a necessary requirement.

## Rate

You have already done this in the exercise. It is important that the manager and direct reports understand that the rating is tied directly to the salary structure. It may also be tied to a bonus system or any other remuneration system an organisation wishes to use. Some compensation systems are clearly better than others, but the system of Performance Evaluation can be used with a variety of compensation schemes. The key point is that the rating sets the pay.

As you have probably experienced, there are a number of scales that are widely used in work performance evaluation. The most common may be a 100-point scale which we recommended in the first edition of *Systems Leadership*. We found this scale evoked memories of school grading systems where 70 was a C, 80 a B and below 60 was fail. This scale was biased towards the top end; very few managers were willing to give a score of 50 or below, even when deserved. A 10-point scale is no better as it is often turned into a 100-point scale with decimals, e.g., 7.5 or 6.8.

In designing this system, we found the rating scale should be broad enough to reflect that this is a system of differentiation. In order to be statistically useful (where a statistical analysis of the data will produce a result with a 95% confidence limit) there need to be at least 21 different scores possible. This is not an obviously convenient scale on which to rate work performance, but testing over the years has found it to be the most effective.

Therefore, we now recommend using the statistically valid scale of 21. This may seem odd at first glance, but we have not found any tendency to use a decimal point to widen the scale as they do with 5 or 10. Managers are also prepared to use the full width of the scale, which is evident with managers who have a sizeable team.

In the exercise we recommended you start the rating process with the worst, and next worse employee, but that's not the only way. Many managers have found it helpful to begin by selecting any two people who are closest in work performance and place them on the scale wherever it seems appropriate. Then rate the others in relation to the first two – some may be higher and some lower. When all direct reports are placed on the scale, go back and see if the entire scale makes sense. The order is likely to be correct, relative differences may not seem right or the overall scale may be skewed high or low. This is easily corrected.

These two steps, ranking and rating, complete the process of Performance Evaluation. The Review process exists to ensure equity across Output Teams, MRUs, Divisions and Business Units.

## Review

Managers must make the judgement of a team member's work performance. They have the most complete knowledge of the team member's performance based on the tasks assigned, task results, the context in which tasks were carried out. This crucial task of performance evaluation, however, must be carried out in the larger context of the organisation, where other managers are rating their subordinates' performance as well.

It is essential that the judgements of managers be compared so that individual employees are not penalised because their managers may over-rate or under-rate their team members. This requires a cross-comparison of ratings among managers to ensure that all managers are using comparable scales.

Just as the initial rating is an exercise in managerial judgement, so is the process of cross-comparison which is carried out by the Manager-once-removed (M+1). The mechanics of the process are straightforward. M+1s rank and rate each of their organisational units, just as the manager ranks and rates each individual employee. In addition, M+1s have data on their subordinates-once-removed because of their work to assess their potential. This provides information on the work performance standards being used by their subordinate managers.

To further test the ratings and to educate both the M+1s and their Managers, M+1 calls for a meeting where the ratings of the managers can be discussed, as described in Box 19.2.

## Box 19.2 Cross-Comparison Process

M+1 involves his management team in a strictly confidential meeting where the managers put their ratings up on a white board to be examined by all their peers. Because the work performance of many of the direct reports is known to many or most of the managers, this is an opportunity for open discussion about the quality of work performance of a significant number of those who are being rated, and the number selected by various Managers for "similar" work performance.

This allows each manager to learn from the rating standards of their peers in order to calibrate their own rating scale. The process provides data to M+1 of the work performance standards being applied by their managers. It also provides M+1 with more information on the work performance of his or her manager's direct reports, which is a necessary part of the M+1's assessment of potential.

Because M+1s also have to rank and rate their own direct reports, this discussion informs their ratings of each organisational unit and allows them to compare judgements made by each manager. It enables M+1s to make judgements about the standards being applied by their subordinate managers as part of M+1's own ranking and rating of their work performance.

While such a meeting can be difficult the first time it is done, the learning of both Managers and M+1s has been viewed by participants as very helpful. It reduces the fear many managers have that they are either too easy or too hard on their team members as compared to other managers. The best people in the organisation are usually widely recognised, and seeing their scores also helps managers calibrate the scales they are using. Following the cross-comparison, each manager reviews his or her ratings and submits a final judgement to M+1 who can accept the judgement or intervene and review the list with the individual manager.

This meeting also acts as a control function of the system to ensure it is being used and used correctly. After the evaluations have been accepted and salary outcomes are conveyed by each manager to their direct reports, a confidential questionnaire is sent to all the people who participated in the performance evaluation process as raters and those rated. It asked four questions with a four-point response – Excellent; Good; Poor; Terrible:

- Did you understand the evaluation process?
- Was the evaluation process fair?
- Did you agree with the results?
- How well did your manager explain his or her reasons for the rating you received?

An intervention does *not* mean the M+1 is, or should be, second-guessing the manager. Only the manager has the detailed knowledge of what an employee was asked to do, how he/she did it and the circumstances in which it was done. The results may be known by the M+1, but the work performance is best understood by the manager.

Asking a Manager to re-do the Performance Evaluation indicates M+1 believes the Manager has failed to carry out the task adequately. This requires a Task Review where the outcome may be a discussion of potential ways to improve, or, at the other extreme, it may lead to the initiation of removal from the role for a manager who has demonstrated again an inability to perform the work of the role to an acceptable standard.

After determining that the Managers have carried out their task properly, the primary task of M+1 is to ensure the comparability of scales among the various managers. Do the ratings of the best-performing unit reflect their high performance and the ratings of a poorer-performing unit reflect that performance. The role of M+1 is to judge equity across his/her part of the organisation.

At each level of the organisation, the applicable M+1 will make the judgement regarding comparability of scales and equity across his/her part of the organisation until the CEO makes the final decision as to the comparability of scales across the entire organisation. The CEO is accountable for ensuring equity across the entire business.

Equity does *not* mean the scales should be normed (meaning all Divisions or all MRUs should have roughly the same average rating); it is a crucial part of the system that the scales *not* be normed. Some managers will have an outstanding group of subordinates and will rightly rate their people higher. Other managers may have a poorer performing group and will rate their people lower. The key is to have clear differentiation of the best performers from the worst performers across the business with appropriate salary adjustment based on performance.

## Issues and Questions in Performance Evaluation

### Objectivity

When introduced, the first objection to this system of performance evaluation is that it is not objective. It relies on managerial judgement. As we discussed in Chapter 16, objective measures and results may be good *indicators* of work performance; but they are *not the same* as the work performance. Objective information must be taken into account, based on the manager's judgement. While many would like greater objectivity (for subordinates objective systems are a means of controlling managers who are not trusted), extensive experience and research have not been able to develop objective criteria which are valid.

When making an evaluation of work performance, the manager draws a complex balance among a myriad of factors, a balance which is, of necessity, subjective because the objective systems are far too simplistic to arrive at a sensible final answer. There are subtleties and nuances which are often difficult to articulate, but they can all be captured in a single rating if the manager's judgement is not impaired by a poor evaluation system.

The system of using a 1–21 scale recognises the necessary subjectivity of the process and asks the manager to record his or her judgement so its worth and validity over time may be assessed by M+1. This is key, since words can be fudged while numbers cannot. How does one manager's "commendable" equate to another's "good"? What does "meets expectations" mean when different managers have different expectations?

### Teamwork

One of the major concerns of many employees and their managers is that a system of individual rating may lead to cut-throat competitive behaviour which will destroy effective teamwork. Such cut-throat competition may, of course, become a problem if managers wish to reward such behaviour. On the other hand, capable managers prefer to reward cooperative behaviour which has a positive impact upon the entire Output Team, MRU or Division. In this case, ratings would also be heavily influenced by the behaviour desired.

### Box 19.3 Fake Objectivity

Consider systems that ask the manager to create objective criteria, weight them, rate them and then come up with an overall rating. Selection of criteria, the weights given to each and the ratings are all subjective, but this awkward fact is often overlooked. In addition, most managers confronted with this task come up with the final rating and then fiddle the figures to make everything add up.

Such a process wastes managerial time and creates a fundamental dishonesty, which is recognised, if not discussed, by both managers and subordinates. Furthermore, such schemes often confuse the prescribed limits of a task or role with the exercise of discretion. People are rated for being on time or for working safely, when these are in fact limits which if breached may lead to dismissal; they are not elements of work performance which have to do with the exercise of discretion.

Using this Performance Evaluation method, managers make visible what they really value. Therefore, they must take care to prioritise those things which are productive for the organisation in both the long and the short term, whether this is to be cooperative or competitive or any other behaviour which the manager believes is productive. In other words, this Performance Evaluation system allows managers to heavily reward contributions to the team and teamwork if that is the behaviour they want.

## Role Expectations and Task Assignment

When doing Work Performance Evaluation, the manager must keep in mind the tasks which were assigned and the results which were achieved by the task doer in the context in which the tasks were carried out in practice. The whole aggregate of tasks must be considered. This must be done with a constant awareness of the work which is expected of the role and similar roles across the organisation.

Sometimes a manager will have a less capable team member who cannot carry out the full complexity of their role. As a matter of custom, they may be assigned less complex, though necessary and valid tasks. They may do these very well, but they are not doing the range of work required of the role. Their task performance may be excellent, but they are failing in the work of the role and should get a lower rating that may indicate that without improvement they should be removed from the role.

In other cases, more highly capable but inexperienced team members may be assigned difficult tasks because of their high mental processing ability. Their work performance in carrying out these tasks may not be as high as a more experienced person might accomplish. They may complete the task within the limits agreed at assignment. They should get a good performance rating for taking on a more difficult task that exceeds their experience and knowledge but which the manager was aware would be a stretch for them.

This practice of giving challenging tasks to your most able subordinates is excellent for their development. It is also an excellent type of recognition. Good managers use this, but it needs to be done with care when evaluating work performance – recognising the difficulty of the task.

## Informing Each Team Member of the Manager's Evaluation

When giving team members the manager's evaluation of their work performance, there should be no surprises if the manager has carried on a regular process of Task Review, and if six months earlier, the manager and team member have conducted a formalised Performance Review.

Because there are no "objective" criteria introduced on which to base an argument, the direct report is more likely to ask, "What do I have to do to get a higher rating?" Or "What is the basis for your judgment?" These types of questions offer an opportunity for further discussion, in brief during the work performance evaluation, but an opportunity to set up a meeting in the near future for a longer, more detailed conversation. The manager might suggest, "If you like, we can do another Performance Review to see what we both need to do to improve. We'll use that to update our Performance Plans for the coming year."

While it is sometimes difficult to confront people with your judgement of their work performance, this act demonstrates your courage, honesty, fairness and your trust that the person will respond like an adult. Your respect for the team member's human dignity is shown by your willingness to be honest, even when it is difficult. It also demonstrates love, that you truly care about the person enough to give them honest feedback. Your willingness to help a direct report improve through your role as trainer/coach demonstrates the shared values of fairness, human dignity and love.

### Ratings Creep

There is a concern held by some managers that other managers will rate their people higher to take advantage of the system. They are afraid that over time all the evaluations will become unrealistically high. (The cross-comparison meeting, if held, makes this virtually impossible.)

Even without such a meeting there are several factors which work against this. First, the CEO has the freedom to adjust the overall scales used in the organisation; this allows the CEO to be in a position to prevent subversion of the system. This is part of the system design.

Second, managers who rate everyone high are stating that the performance of their units should be superior to that of other units due to the quality of their workforce. If the performance of the unit is not significantly different from that of other units, and if the people are truly superior, the only conclusion is that they are poorly led. If the people are not truly superior, the manager has failed in his task of performance evaluation leading to differential reward. In either case managers are in trouble when their manager evaluates their performance.

Third, rating everyone high also means the manager has not differentiated between the best and worst performers. This indicates to all that excellence is not valued by this manager. Mediocre and poor performers flock to such managers since their shortcomings will have less impact upon their salaries. Excellent performers are likely to transfer or leave; if they stay, they will be looking for better opportunities. Again, the poor manager is made visible as the quality of results in his or her area deteriorates with the loss of good people and the influx of poor performers.

It is not only a matter of fairness; managers get best results when they clearly differentiate their best from their worst performers. Any manager who is unable or unwilling to distinguish good from poor performance is demonstrably unable to continue to function in a managerial role. At best such a person would have to rank among the poorer performers regarding this particular and vitally important leadership task.

## The Value of Work Performance Evaluation Linked to a Salary Setting System

### For all Employees

- Know where they stand with their manager
- Know better work performance will receive higher monetary reward

- Through proper task assignment, recognition and performance reviews, they get a clear understanding of the expectations for their role. This allows them to perform well with monetary compensation proportionate with work performance

### For Managers

- Allows them to recognise better work performance with higher monetary reward
- Reinforces the Performance Review discussions with salary consequences
- Provides a method to help analyse the human resource capability available to accomplish the work of their organisation and therefore to develop and deploy those resources effectively

### For the Organisation

- The most important information produced with this system are the trendlines in ratings, which show an individual's progress over the years. An upward trendline may be an indicator of higher-level potential. Trend information differs from other types of rating systems where a lower rating may kill someone's career, so even poor performers may get a higher rating than deserved because a manager does not want to damage their careers. With this system, the progression is far more important than any single number
- Recognition of better work performance and its confirmation through monetary reward will attract and retain employees capable of consistently good work performance, which in turn will result in a more positive, and successful organisation

## Summary

This system of work performance evaluation is based on the demonstrated ability of managers to judge and categorise the work of their subordinates. It is a clear and simple process to carry out and uses an intuitive scale common to all. Managers have told us it does not impede or subvert managerial judgement. Those judgements must be made openly so their worth and validity over time may be evaluated by their managers. It provides a method to review rating outcomes for equity across the organisation to provide better comparability of rating and therefore greater fairness.

Most importantly, it is integrated with work performance planning, task assignment, task review and work performance review processes and is also clearly linked to salary setting as described in Chapter 20. It enables managers to use correctly a salary setting system, and it allows the recognition of better work performance with higher monetary reward.

# 20 Salary Administration

## Purpose

To provide equitable differential pay for all employees based on their work performance as rated by their manager.

The objectives of this process are to recognise better work performance with higher monetary reward. It is also to provide undeniable validation that recognises that the differences in work performance are confirmed with differences in monetary reward. Finally, it is intended to provide monetary incentives for improved work performance.

### Salary Setting Process

Once all the Performance Evaluations have been approved by the M+1 up to the level of CEO, salary decisions based on corporate limits to total remuneration expenditure are applied to those ratings using the Salary Administration system. As a final check for anomalies, the actual dollar adjustment for each individual is again reviewed by M+1 and M+2.

When all the salary decisions have been made, managers inform their subordinates individually and confidentially of their rating of work performance in role – the number between 1 and 21 – the range and limits of their salary band, their salary and where in that band they are placed based on their work performance.

### Linking Ratings to Pay

Based on corporate policy and the size of the pool for adjusting salaries, the numeric ratings are translated into salary action. Within the salary band of the role, those with the highest ratings get the highest salaries; those with lower ratings receive lower salaries.

The link between rating and pay may be made in a number of different ways. The Chief Executive must decide how the ratings relate to the salary bands. Some use the whole scale, 1–21, with a matching salary band. One obvious method is to consider the rating

DOI: 10.4324/9781003459118-25

to be a percentage of the salary band. In other words, a rating of 10 would equal 10/21 of the pay band, a rating of 19 would equal 19/21 of the salary band, etc., as shown in Figure 20.1.

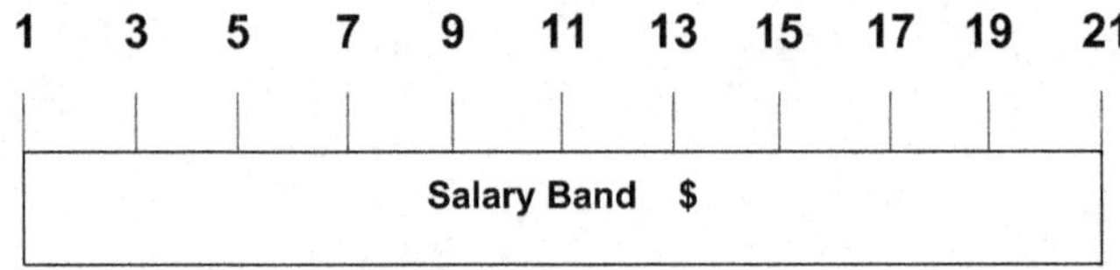


*Figure 20.1* Rating Scale Matches Salary Band

Figure 20.2 illustrates another way the scale can be used. It is based on an organisation which has been using this system for several years. They learned through experience that anyone rated at 7 or below was not qualified to do the work of the role. The salary band started at 8 and ended at 18. Those who scored below 8 would be given an additional review, coaching and if needed training, but if there was no significant improvement by a set time, the manager would initiate removal from role.

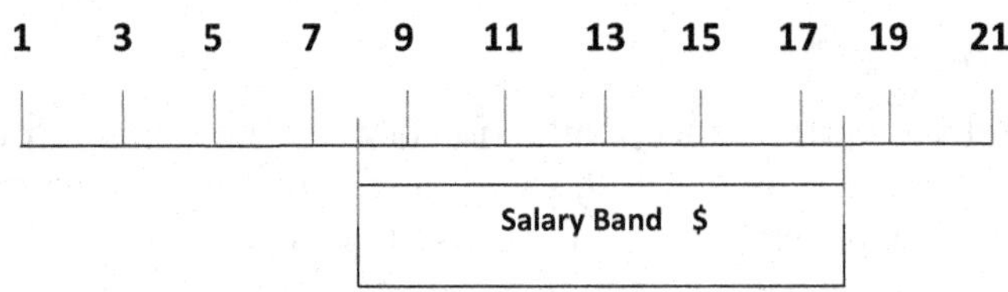


*Figure 20.2* Rating Scale with Smaller Salary Band

Those who scored above 18 would be considered for upgrade or promotion, or perhaps given more challenging work until a higher-level role opened up. If M+1 decided they were the best in their current role, they would be paid at the top of the scale at their current position. This was deemed as fair by both managers and the employees who received this top pay. Their only increase would reflect the organisation's inflation increment (Figure 20.3).

While this illustration has worked well for a particular organisation, each organisation must determine where they should place the low cut-off point. At the high end we recommend that anyone rated above 18 be considered for an upgrade or promotion.

Some would excuse a rating of 7 or below because it could reflect someone who is new to the role, in training or some other valid reason that was temporary. This has a certain appeal, but in practice it has not proven to be necessary. When someone is placed in a new role, the salary is reflected in the existing salary band. A work performance evaluation is done a year later, so the person should be fully able to carry out the work of the role.

This application of the 21-point scale gives space to recognise performance below the requirements of the role, and also to recognise performance above the requirements of the role, while still providing adequate space for differential recognition of work performance.

It is a matter of policy for the organisation to determine the most effective way to link ratings and salary adjustments. It is also a matter of policy for the CEO to set limits below which performance is deemed unsatisfactory or above which current performance calls for an assessment of potential review by the M+1.

This same method can also be used to set bonuses or calculate "at risk" portions of an individual's salary. The ratings can be applied to whatever remuneration structure the corporation wishes to use.

Some may ask, why is it necessary to go through the rating process? Why don't managers just set salaries? The answer is that dollars are much more difficult to use to compare and to check whether the differentials are equitable or not. While using dollars would be difficult for the manager, the comparisons for equity required of the M+1s and higher-level managers become impossible.

In addition, the ratings generate trendlines. Some people move up rapidly, others more slowly; some may have plateaued at the correct level of cost/value for their work, while others may be declining over time. Only a rating can give a genuine trend, since a rating may generate a very different monetary outcome for a person new to role, or as a person is upgraded or promoted or as the salary structure is adjusted to accommodate inflation. The rating remains a consistent measure over time.

The system relies on the total sum available to a manager for salary increase for his or her subordinates, being distributed fairly on the basis of merit. If we assume the system requires that an employee whose work performance rating is the same from year to year be paid a salary equivalent to his or her rating within three years, the annual increment can be calculated based on where the salary is in the band now, and where it needs to be in three years given the same rating score.

Salary increments above the nominal percentage of annual increase, usually an inflation percentage plus a merit component, are funded from those whose work performance ratings generated no merit increase or no merit increase and a lower than normal inflation adjustment. In other words, a salary reduction in real terms.

In most organisations of our experience, it is usually considered equitable for salary reductions to be subject to the same time lag as salary increases.

One organisation had the policy that no one would have their pay reduced, but would be held to zero increases until the salary matched the rating. Where this policy was used, most people were aligned in one or two years, while zero increases for three years brought everyone back to the salary that matched their work performance. Given the discrepancies, with senior people being overpaid and relative newcomers being underpaid, both the chief executive and one of the authors were surprised things levelled out so quickly.

When new employees are hired it can have a significant effect on the salary administration system, as when the organisation's hiring system must set starting salaries high in the band as an enticement for people to join the organisation. This makes the manager's role very difficult when it comes to the application of the salary administration system. It is worth noting that when it is necessary to bring in new people at significantly higher salaries than existing employees, it may be time to look at the whole salary structure which may have fallen behind competition in the market.

### The Normal Distribution of Ratings and Salaries

There is an implicit assumption that if all incumbents in similar or equivalent roles across a country could have their work performance assessed against a common standard, the results would show a normal distribution, such as that shown in Figure 20.3.

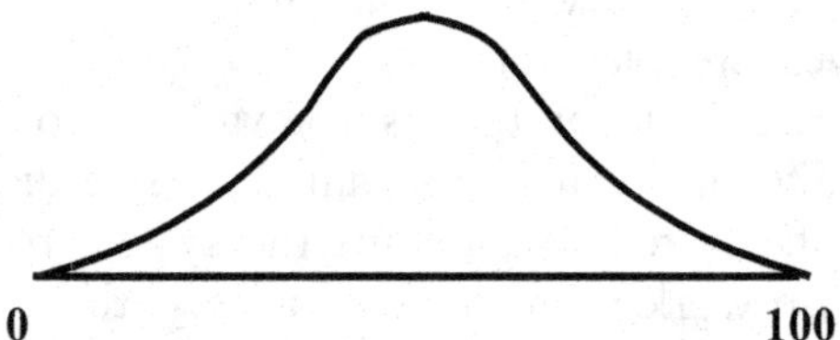


*Figure 20.3* Normal Curve, Total Population

This assumption may or may not be true, but it is important because it may influence the application of monetary reward systems. In fact, most managers do not want a normal distribution of work performance to apply for a population of role incumbents. The goal is to select and lead the employees of the organisation in a way that produces a distribution of performance which is strongly, but validly, skewed to the high end of the scale (Figure 20.4).

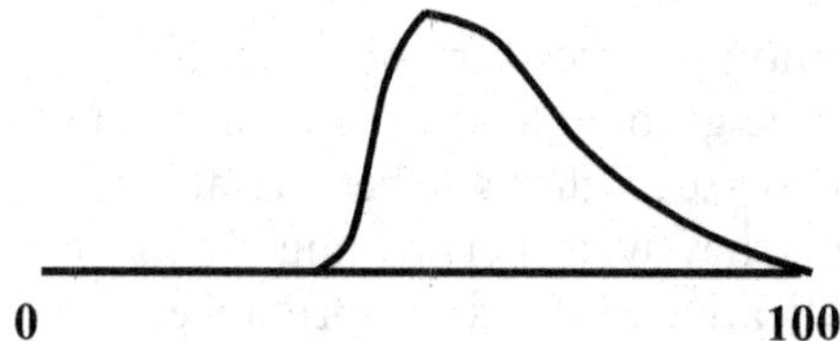


*Figure 20.4* Normal Curve, Lower End Cut-Off

Interestingly, this is the very curve which is observed to develop over time when an effective Performance Evaluation system is in use and managers are performing the work of their role of initiating removal of persistent non-performers.

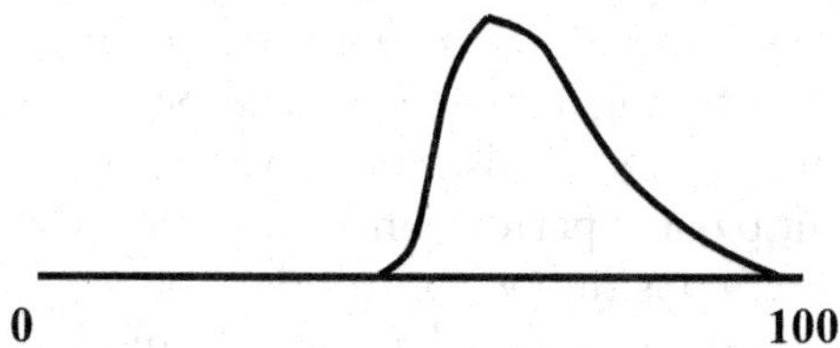


*Figure 20.5* Workforce Over Time When Selected for Performance.

The assumption that in any set of similar roles there will be a normal distribution of work performance delivery leads, in some organisations, to a system that requires the dismissal of a percentage of the workforce from each manager's subordinates in each year.

The proponents of this system argue that it leads to a high-performance workforce, but there is no solid evidence to back this claim. It is a system that punishes good leaders who choose their people well and lead them well. It absolves a poor manager of the work of dealing with substandard work performance, though he or she may be one of those removed if there is any justice in the application of the system that relies on a forced distribution of work performance rankings.

The experience of Stewart is that in a stable workforce with an annual turnover of 12–15%, the average rate of dismissal for poor work performance – breach of limits of the role and breach of policy – was 4%, although this was not uniform across all organisational units year by year.

## Issues and Questions in Salary Administration

### Changing Beliefs and Practices

It has been common practice for non-unionised employees in many organisations to be granted a so-called "merit" increase every year, although that increase might have been relatively small, e.g., 1–2%. People were told they were performing well in their role and any increase was indicative of good performance.

It is a common belief among many employees that consistent good performance will produce an annual "merit" increase in salary and that the award of no merit increase is a "black mark." There is a current belief among managers in general that subordinates will be demotivated unless they are given an annual "merit" increase.

Despite calling it a "merit" increase, the practice of awarding a small annual increase to everyone does not reward the good performers well enough and over-rewards the poorer performers who stay in the role for a long time. In effect, the organisation is creating a pay system based on seniority, not merit. This can be demonstrated by running a simple correlation between time in service and pay. In many organisations, even those which are most vociferous about pay for performance, seniority is still the best predictor of someone's position within a salary band. (This is not to be confused with annual increases because of inflation. This is essentially changing the salary bands, not a comment on performance.)

Using this Performance Evaluation/Salary Administration system, managers are given the opportunity to pay people in accordance with their work performance. Large increases are possible for those who are improving rapidly, while those who are delivering the same standard of work they were doing in the prior year get the same pay (recognising that 50% position within a salary band in one year may lead to a different dollar amount in the next year). The person who stays at the same percentile will get the increase which occurs from the shift in the salary band to take inflation into account.

Even more difficult to accept at first is the idea excellent performers who are at or near the top of the salary band may get no merit increase, receiving band shift only, because they are being appropriately paid for excellent work performance. Such a person may be considered for upgrade or promotion, providing she/he has clearly demonstrated the capability for a higher-level position. If the person continues in the same salary band, however, the highest salary that will be paid is the top of that band.

This may seem at first glance to be unfair, but in almost all organisations, very few are paid at the top of the band. Those who are paid at this level are being paid more than the great majority of people in the society who are doing similar work. This is fair.

### What to Do about Overpayment

When this Performance Evaluation and Salary system is introduced in an organisation, there is frequently an initial shock when it is realised that based on work performance, a number of people are being overpaid and that their salary will be reduced, at least in real terms. In this situation, there are often other people, typically the young bright ones, who are significantly underpaid. Since there is a finite amount of money to distribute, the question arises, should we take money away from those who are being paid too much?

An ancillary question is, should pay swing up and down as people are rated higher or lower in different years? The recommended three-year smoothing markedly reduces this probability, but it is important for a manager to understand the reason for such rating changes.

The question of whether or not to reduce pay is an important policy decision for the organisation to make. In the United States, such salary reductions are rare and are likely to cause considerable consternation. Some organisations do have potential salary reductions though they are usually limited to no more than 2% in any given year. We believe it is probably best to set a floor under the process where zero increase is the minimum change. In real terms this is a salary reduction of the inflation percentage.

In practice, holding someone to a zero increase when salary structures are growing by even 2% or 3% a year moves the person quite rapidly towards the rated level of pay. In Burke's experience virtually all employees are at the correct salary within three years. This proves, at least in the initial stages, to be more acceptable to both managers and employees.

#### Box 20.1 Comments on Pay Reductions

More than one manager has objected to a floor of zero for certain employees. As one said, "This employee has hit rock bottom and continues to dig." Clearly, a case where initiation of removal from role is more appropriate than a reduction in pay. Other comments indicated various levels of dissatisfaction. "He sets low personal standards and then consistently fails to achieve them." "When she opens her mouth, it seems that it is only to change feet." Despite such managerial frustrations, we still recommend a zero increase as the floor.

The system allows for a variety of payment methods and policies. It is up to the organisation to select the set of policies that best meet its needs and the human requirements of its workforce. It is important, however, for the operation of the salary administration system to be explained to all employees subject to it.

### Will the Size of the Salary Pool Prevent Adjusting Salaries as Required by the Ratings?

As shown in Figure 20.6, a salary pool of 4% allows for a wide variation among individuals in terms of the pay increase which may ensue from their Performance Evaluation. Salary pools of 2% have yielded pay adjustments from 0% to 16%. With the use of such a system, everyone becomes aware very rapidly that better work performance does result in significant differentials in pay.

### Controlling Overall Payroll Costs

In all organisations, there is a finite amount of money available for salary increases or bonuses in any given year. This will be based on corporate earnings, fundraising of NGOs or legislative

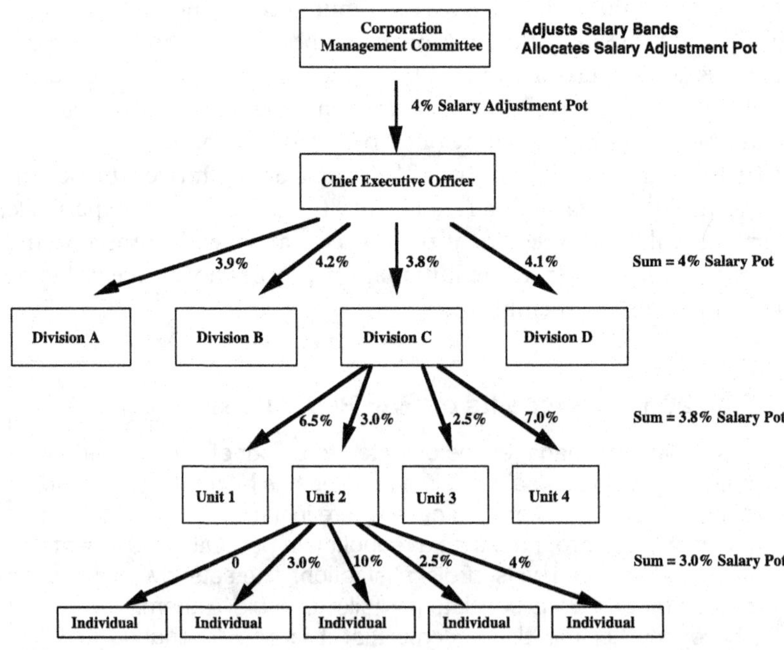


*Figure 20.6* Distribution of Pay Increases

appropriations for government agencies. Consideration of external pay standards applicable to the organisation type and the judgement of the executive committee and the Board regarding what is prudent for the long-term health of the organisation must be carefully thought through. Thus, consideration of the salary pool on an annual basis is a component of the company's annual plan.

The CEO is in a position to adjust the entire company expenditure on salary increments to the available pool – leaving the relative distribution intact.

### Information Produced with the Combined Performance Evaluation and Salary Setting Systems

Perhaps the most important information produced with this system are the trendlines in ratings which indicate an individual's progress in work performance over the years. This may be an indicator of higher-level potential. This information differs from other types of rating systems where a rating below 90% may destroy someone's career. With the system we propose, the progression is far more important than any single number. Even the most promising employee may have poor work performance in a given year, which must be corrected if he or she is to advance. The "shock" of a poor rating makes this very clear.

In organisations where seniority systems have led to significant overpayment of some members of the workforce, this process allows the organisation to calculate the cost of the overpayment. When individuals are held to zero increase, there may still be a discrepancy between what they are paid and the rating given by their manager. All these discrepancies can be added up, by Unit, by Division, by Business Unit. One measure of a manager's effectiveness will be his/her ability to reduce this deficit over time.

Such a system also allows for the calculation of ratings for any particular group along with their salary levels, to find possible systemic types of discrimination. The proportion of the salary pool going to each work level is known, along with the increases or decreases, allowing comparisons to indicate whether one level or another is being advantaged or disadvantaged compared to other levels.

### Summary

All these essential people systems Work Performance Planning, Task Assignment, Task Feedback, Task Review, Work Performance Review, Work Performance Evaluation and Salary Setting are, as managers well know, intensely human processes with great emotional content.

The purpose of the material presented here is to help managers understand these processes more fully and to appreciate the differences in the human interactions which take place in each of them.

When the manager is carrying out the tasks of a trainer/coach, as in the Task Review and Work Performance Review processes, the discussion and its emotional content are quite different from the discussion of Work Performance Evaluation where the manager is a judge, required to make a subjective judgement, albeit with objectively measured indicators, regarding work performance.

The outcome of all these processes working together is to:

- Make clear to the task doer exactly what the manager expects in terms of Context, Purpose, Quantity/Quality of Output, Resources and Time.
- Gain the active commitment of the task doer to doing the task.
- Provide information to both manager and subordinate on how the work is going and how it might be done better in the future
- Allow the task doer to accept accountability for the task and to accept the fairness of the manager's evaluation of his/her work performance.
- Base evaluation of work performance on the exercise of discretion as it plays out in the resultant balancing of all the dimensions of the work of the task.
- Promote an evaluation of work performance that takes into account the aggregate of tasks in the role – including the easily forgotten assigned tasks with inset triggers – and takes into account the changing context in which the tasks played out in practice.
- Promotes a leadership environment in which the best performers receive significant psychological rewards and higher monetary reward. While poorer performers receive psychological rewards directed towards the improvement of performance, receive lesser monetary reward and are put on notice that they need to improve their work performance lest they be removed from role.

Finally, with all payment systems, the questions in the systems design chapter remain highly relevant. It is particularly relevant to ask:

- What is the purpose?
- Is it really a system of differentiation?
- What behaviour do you expect this to drive? Why?

- Do managers and team members understand it?
- Who owns the systems? We have found that an executive, not the HR department should own the people systems.
- Are the controls providing information as to whether or not the system is being operated correctly, that it is working as intended?
- Every three or four years, once the system is stable, conduct an audit of the system in use, whether it is achieving its purpose, and using the control data and any recommendations for change. The audit should be done by a small team of able people chosen for the task.

We have seen many other components of salary given in other forms: cars, allowances, stock options and so on. These perks are most acceptable when they are directly related to the work of a role. We recommend strongly against the use of such systems unrelated to the work of the role as they rapidly create negative mythologies.

Our approach, consistent within Systems Leadership Theory, is to keep systems clear and simple with an unambiguous purpose. One operator at a plant in Australia commented, "I like working here, I have exactly the same contract as the General Manager except for the salary"; he paused and then said, "and I wouldn't want his job for love nor money."

In the next two chapters we show how information developed with these essential people systems can facilitate the career development of the individual and the succession planning of the organisation. The chapter on discipline and fair treatment offers a method to deal with problems that arise in most organisations from time to time, even when they have tested and effective people systems.

# 21 Careers and Staff Development

## Introduction

Although it may not always be obvious, it is important to emphasise that every individual is responsible for his or her own career and its development. In a well-structured organisation, using the systems in this chapter, the Manager and the Manager-once-Removed (M+1) have roles to play in providing opportunities to learn, to improve technical and social skills and to advise an individual about the opportunities within the organisation, but they are not responsible for the person's career. They are responsible for their own work including staff development. When properly carried out, that work offers development and career opportunities for individuals, as part of preparing the organisation to fill higher-level roles and prepare for future growth. Career and staff development are two related processes, but their purposes are different.

## Individual Career Development

When we say every individual is responsible for his or her own career and its development, we are thinking about choices people make like how much education they need and deciding where to take a job. Early in our careers we may discover what we *definitely* do not want to do, look for another job and eventually find work we enjoy if we are lucky. Some people are content to stay in one role for almost all their employment career; others like change and seek career advancement. Even staying in "one role," it is inevitable that the role will change over time, and the person will need to learn new skills and knowledge.

Whatever organisation you choose to work for, whether out of necessity or ambition, your own interests and what you aspire to, your view of your own capability and demonstrated preparedness to do the work is critical in the process of career advancement. Successful completion of assigned tasks makes visible your capabilities as well as your understanding of the organisation's priorities.

DOI: 10.4324/9781003459118-26

Managers can help team members develop in their current role, while their M+1 is to assess their potential and advise them on career opportunities. Understanding the difference between current performance and potential and with whom to discuss this allows the career and staff development processes to succeed or fail.

People who stay in an organisation for a few years are likely to have several Ms and M+1s during that time. Each may be helpful or not, but to advance in an organisation, individuals need to cultivate a whole network of people who can help them, each in his or her own way. Some mentors a person may never meet, but they will read their books and glean some ideas. Others may be teachers or motivational speakers. The key is to remember that all of us need help and support as we advance in our careers. We can also provide help and support to others as we gain knowledge and experience. Both giving and receiving help make us better human beings.

## The Manager's Role in Career and Staff Development

The work of the immediate manager is to act as a *coach* to their direct reports, to help improve their work performance and make progress in their current role by providing opportunities to increase their knowledge, to refine their technical and social process skills and to encourage them to be more effective in doing their current work. *Coaching* is the term to describe helping direct reports improve in their current roles.

Clear task assignment, task and performance reviews as well as work performance evaluation all provide data to the individual and the M+1 about their work performance. The coach will also take notice of teamwork and social process skills which are essential to career advancement.

Managers may assign tasks to a team member at the request of their manager (M+1) who wants to provide a learning experience for someone he or she believes has potential for upgrade or promotion. This is also a way for the M+1 to learn if his or her judgement about the same is correct.

## The Work of M+1 in Career and Staff Development

M+1s are managers of managers and must do the work of direct management in those relationships. They also have the responsibility to find the able people who are the direct reports of those managers. Their job is to find reports-once-removed who have potential for promotion in order to have people who are prepared to take on higher-level roles as they become open to achieve the purpose of the organisation and prepare it for the future.

To do this M+1s must assess who, if any, of their reports-once-removed have the potential to work at a higher work level. They also need to recognise those who need to take on a different role at the same level to improve their contribution and to develop knowledge and skills for potential work at a higher level. Most importantly, it is the work of M+1s to identify the most able employees early in their careers and take steps to foster their development. M+1 is a *mentor* to his or her reports-once-removed.

### Finding and Fostering the Organisation's Human Capability

M+1s are accountable for their work of assessing the potential of *all* their reports-once-removed. This has the effect of opening the capability pool by including people who often go unnoticed in more informal systems.

**Note:** It is important when this system is introduced to consider people at any stage of their career who may have high potential but for a variety of reasons may have been overlooked.

#### Box 21.1 How to Judge Potential

How does the M+1 judge whether a person is ready now or in the near future for promotion? This is done by first being clear about the work of the role into which the person might be promoted, and the capability required to be successful. As has been discussed in the chapters on capability, levels of work and selection to role, certain elements of a role are more amenable to training and improvement than others. One of the most critical issues is Mental Processing Ability (MPA). This is a necessary but not sufficient condition. The M+1 must judge whether the person has the MPA to handle work of the required complexity. Sometimes this is obvious, at other times less so.

We have found that most M+1s, as they come to understand the ideas of MPA, overall capability and levels of work, are fully capable of determining if someone is ready to work for themselves or a peer. After they gain some experience with these assessments, most M+1s can also identify people who might one day work at their own level. In any case, there are always opportunities to test this by assigning tasks that require higher complexity processing to solve. Special assignments, projects and tasks can be given to see if a person can really work at a higher level. Then other elements of capability can be assessed to complement the MPA. We have found that more careers are derailed due to poor social process skills than any other factor.

Finally, the M+1 should not be trying to predict a person's entire career. M+1 should be looking forward only one, two or at most three years. This avoids the negative mythologies associated with labelling and categorising people that can blight not only the work life of the person but also the reputation of the organisation.

On the other hand, there are, admittedly rare, situations where M+1 finds someone who appears to have the potential to go to the top of the organisation. The Division or Corporate head should be told of this and should meet with that person and perhaps take over as mentor if that is judged to be correct.

In the US military, future generals or admirals are often identified early in their careers, typically as Captains in the Army, and given roles where they report to a flag officer for a tour of duty to expose them to their potential future role and for the flag officers to make a judgement about their appropriate career path.

Capability shows itself most clearly over time through work and it is recognised by those in a position to observe it. M+1s have opportunities to observe the work performance of their reports-once-removed and their work products in meetings, by what they produce and in informal conversations. They also have the ratings from the Performance Evaluation system and the comparisons of the units in his or her organisation. Managers and others in the organisation may draw their attention to people who appear to have high potential for promotion.

Special training and job opportunities can be provided to test the judgement of the M+1, by arranging these with the person's manager. This allows possible errors of judgement on the part of the M+1 to be corrected early in a person's career to avoid either too rapid or too slow advancement.

The proper operation of this system provides a series of assessment points through a person's career because in each new role at a higher level, they will have a different M+1, but one that also has the capability to make the required assessment.

The use of the system increases the likelihood that the most able people will have challenges commensurate with capability talents, making them more productive for the organisation over their entire careers. The best people are more likely to stay in the organisation that recognises their capability rather than seeking opportunities elsewhere. This work of the M+1 helps to reduce (and eventually eliminate) the power games of informal mentoring systems.

### The Work of M+1s Is to:

- Get to know their reports-once-removed, not only their current work, but also their interests, ambitions, desired types of work, the challenges they enjoy, how they would like to see their career developing over time and any other information that seems relevant at the time.
- Identify people who are ready for an upgrade to recognise first-class work performance while continuing to do the work of their existing role, and perhaps take on an expanded role at a higher salary grade in the same level of work.
- Identify people who are ready for promotion to the work level of his or her direct reports and to recommend them for selection for such a promotion either within their own team or elsewhere. This practice ensures the organisation can gain full use of its most capable people. The people so identified, in turn, get the opportunity to make full use of the capability.
- Make a judgement of the possible career paths that may be available, based on the individual's abilities and interests.
- Discuss career options on a regular but varying basis depending upon the stage of a person's career. For individuals early in their careers who are judged to have high-level potential and who, therefore, should move rapidly through the organisation, an annual or biennial review might be appropriate until their current M+1 judges their potential has stabilised. A longer review period of three or even five years is appropriate for people who are comfortable at their current level and are judged to have more moderate growth potential.
- Towards the end of a person's career, one assessment of potential may be enough for the person who will not advance further in the organisation and knows it. Conducting assessments of potential too frequently is unnecessary. A good employee who is confident and satisfied that the work of the current role matches his or her capability will not appreciate a discussion that simply repeats what was said two years prior.
- Respond within three months to a request from a subordinate-once-removed to meet and discuss their aspirations, potential career paths and their potential for promotion or upgrade.

In all these discussions, it is essential to make clear that when there is a job opening, the person judged to be best qualified *at that time* will be selected. We have found that many discussions about potential for progression and career advancement end with promises of what might be if certain training is done, and nothing materialises even if the training recommendations are followed. Thus, clarity about how people are selected for a role must be explained carefully.

It is perhaps understandable that managers (in M+1 roles) are reluctant to tell people they will not be promoted because, in their judgement, a person does not have the MPA to work at a level higher than the one they now occupy. From the M+1's perspective, it may appear to be just a little less severe than a death sentence, but from the perspective of the employee, it may be an affirmation of something they already knew. We have known people where this affirmation was a relief, not a disappointment.

On the other hand, the M+1's judgement may clearly be wrong, and once recovered from the initial sense of unfairness, the individual is free to look for opportunities elsewhere in the organisation or in another organisation. They are not kept waiting in false hope, based on implied promises.

## M+1 as Mentor

To be effective doing their work of mentoring, M+1s need to have a clear understanding of the various roles, career patterns and career opportunities that may be available in the organisation. It is helpful if they are aware of future corporate or departmental directions to guide people into new roles that are likely to be needed by the organisation. This knowledge allows them to advise employees about many important aspects of careers in which they may be interested such as:

- The kind of organisation this is – its culture, what behaviour is valued from its employees and why.
- Career patterns, how people advance in this organisation.
- M+1's assessment of the person's career potential.
- What types of roles and tasks the individual might undertake should they become available to gain needed knowledge or skills.
- Education and training programmes the person might find useful.
- Opportunities for special assignments to demonstrate capability.
- Possible timing of various elements of the person's career progression.

With the views of the M+1, the individual can put together, if he or she so desires, a career development plan to fit his or her career aspirations. Discussions with the M+1 should also make clear if certain positions are highly advisable, or essential, if a person is to advance to higher levels of work. For example, in the US Army, few become a major general who have not had experience as a company commander and a battalion commander.

The M+1 is in no position to promise that the person will attain a particular role or a particular level of work in the future as that will depend upon the person's demonstrated work performance, when openings at a particular level or in a particular field come up, and who is available to fill those roles.

In summary, the M+1 is the appropriate person to assess potential, albeit with input and information from a variety of sources. The person being assessed will usually have a realistic view of their own ability if they really understand and have confirmed the nature of the work of their role. Once the assessment is made, career development, if decided upon, can begin with the identification of suitable opportunities for the person to demonstrate their potential.

### Mentors and the Individual

Over time, an individual is likely to have several different M+1s. Each of them may offer slightly different advice. It can also happen that none of them are really giving the person what he or she needs to develop. There is no such thing as one all-knowing, all-caring, wise and experienced individual who will help a person grow and advance his or her career. Each employee must seek information and advice in addition to the ideas of M and M+1 as discussed earlier in this chapter.

#### Box 21.2 Assuring the System Is Working Correctly

To ensure this process is taking place as intended (the control function), one organisation we are familiar with created a system in which all managers in M+1 roles were required to submit to corporate Human Resources the names of those people working in their MRU whom they believed were:

- *Ready now*. Could take an upgrade or promotion now and perform well immediately.
- *Ready within one year*. This is someone who could, within a short time, be ready for a role. He or she only needs some

knowledge or the addition of some technical skills that can be learned quickly.
- *Ready within three years*. This is someone who may need some significant development in knowledge, technical skills or social process skills. They may need to experience a leadership role or a role in a different function such as sales or financial business or systems design to round out their knowledge and technical skills.

The corporate Human Resources department needs to keep copies of all previous potential assessments and return to each M+1 a summary of the previous assessments and the names of those who have not had an assessment. The M+1 is then expected to schedule the missing assessments and have them completed in three months.

An M+1 should not be authorised to promote anyone who is not on the assessment record as being ready for promotion, without the approval of his or her manager. If a person has been on the ready now list for five years without promotion, a reassessment is required.

This system has the advantage of allowing people to decide if they do not want another potential assessment, unless their M+1 believed they had the potential to be promoted.

## Succession Planning

Succession planning is the proper ordering of all the information from potential assessments to create an overall view of the potential human capability in the organisation. The identification and use of its capability pool is necessary if the organisation is to prosper and grow. If the systems of performance management and capability assessment are in place these can form the basis of the succession planning system.

The operation of the system requires the M+2, or higher executive, with all the M+1s and corporate Human Resources advisors to work together to produce a succession plan. They need to consider the present structure of the organisation and the proposed structure, based on the business plan, when determining what roles are needed within a year or two, and what are likely to be needed in the more distant future. Within the organisation, it is desirable for the succession planning exercise to identify three people who have the potential to fill a role.

Identification should use the three categories stated earlier – Ready Now, Ready within one year, Ready within three years. The process does not look at every role in the organisation, but it is usual to plan the succession into Stratum IV roles and above. The planning activity involves an open discussion of who, from the total list of those judged to be capable of working at a higher level, would be able to best perform the work of the role being considered, who would be the next best and who would be able to do the work given another few years' experience.

It is common on the first pass for a small number of people to be chosen for many roles. These are clearly people who have impressed many managers with their capability. A second round of consideration and debate is usually required to introduce a larger succession group. Human Resources provides advice on turnover rate and information about pending retirements as well as any plans for the addition of roles or reduction in numbers.

After the discussion, the M+2 can decide on the final list and the category each is in. A suggested rule is that no name can appear more than twice on the shadow chart. This provides a measure of how well prepared the organisation is for succession. Clearly, fewer names recommended or significant gaps give cause for concern.

Roles that do not have a succession list are noted and relevant managers are required to develop plans to identify potential candidates and the work experience path required to have them ready to step into role. The existence of a name against a role in the succession plan does not mean that the person will be offered the role. The decision is made at the time the role becomes vacant by those authorised to make the decision. Most organisations find they have a shortage of capable people, not an excess.

The context must be considered, however, and having three names in category 1 for every role might indicate an organisation where people are ready to leave. As one leader (M+2) explained to us, "We only have one role at level 5. We recruit highly capable people. The trouble is the best leave if they see their chances diminish."

### Box 21.3 Tracking Succession Data

A large corporation with over 20 businesses and several thousand employees had a well thought out succession plan. They used the system we describe here, but they kept the roles and proposed people to fill them on white boards in a small, locked room where the data could be examined on a regular basis. Making the data available in this format made it immediately visible to those with a need to know the current plan and to update it as required.

We have heard that the CEO would sometimes go in there to think about who was available now and who would likely move up in a few years. When changes were necessary to account for changes in the availability of various people, it was easy to erase one name and fill in with another. The organisation did not always get it right, but their system improved their succession actions considerably.

When considering filling the CEO's role, and the roles of those reporting to the CEO, the Chair of the Board will work with the Board selection committee, if there is one, or the full Board to consider succession to these roles.

The greatest attention must be paid to the CEO's role and the potential to fill it from within the organisation. If the Board's assessment is that the role cannot be filled from within, it is common, depending on the time available, for them to recommend the selection of a suitable person into a role reporting to the CEO. Both the person and the Board will learn whether the person is suited for the CEO role in the near future. When the time comes to find a CEO or other top executive, Boards often seek the advice of outside consultants during this process.

## Summary

While career development is the responsibility of an individual, the systems described here can have a positive effect on employees and the organisation, by identifying people who have the potential for promotion and providing opportunities to develop their knowledge and skills. An organisation which uses these systems is more likely to identify talent and to keep highly capable people in their organisation. They are also more likely to have the right person available when a key role must be filled.

# 22 Discipline and Fair Treatment

## Introduction

Despite the best efforts of managers to build a positive culture and organisation, there will be employees whose quality of work performance is not adequate. There will also be people who violate the limits that bind their work roles. This requires action to correct the work performance, stop the violations or initiate removal from the role.

Throughout this book we have emphasised the importance of human judgement and human relationships. Although we have our own lenses through which we view the world and make judgements about behaviour and work performance, this does not necessarily mean it is biased or idiosyncratic. It is clear, however, that judgement can be flawed, can be prejudiced, can be plain wrong. Human judgement can and should be informed by data and information. We must use evidence. Courts are a good example of the need for evidence, not merely speculation, but there is still a judge and a jury.

If someone has a manager and, in our model, accepts that the manager has the authority to judge work performance, what can be done if the person whose work performance has been judged believes the judgement is wrong? In this chapter we will look at different situations and how they can be addressed before recourse to third parties or the law. We will examine the importance of disciplinary processes and the systems that embody them.

## Issues in Fair Treatment

We have noted that many managers find performance feedback, review and especially work performance evaluation difficult when it is necessary to give bad news, whether that is concerned with work performance or career potential. Nonetheless, most people have been in this situation either as giver or as receiver and can handle this situation.

DOI: 10.4324/9781003459118-27

Avoiding the issue of poor work performance and the disciplinary consequences is perhaps the most costly activity in an organisation. Avoiding difficult issues causes good workers to be alienated. It gives rise to the use of power and generates mythologies that place the leadership at the negative end of the values continua, and hence not a member of the team's cultural group.

In this area, perhaps more than any other, the most important principle is that the systems and processes must be clear and accessible. Task Review and Performance Review should give fair warning if work performance does not meet the requirements of the role. When there are violations of rules or boundaries, managers must ask, "Do people know about and understand the limits of their role?" These limits include:

- Law.
- Policies.
- System Boundaries.
- Code of Conduct.
- Operating Procedures.
- Safety Regulations.
- Limits of a Task.
- Limits of Authority.

It is essential that people are informed and aware of the limits and how they can be disciplined fairly for breaking them. These topics should be part of the induction process and training. All disciplinary systems must clearly articulate the probable consequences of violating the limits. Disciplinary procedure might include:

- Verbal and written warnings.
- Authorised actions such as suspension, stand down or dismissal.
- The exercise of legal rights.

We have found there are two types of problems that are fundamentally different, psychologically.

- Poor performance.
- Breaking limits.

## Poor Performance

It is the work of the manager to gather and synthesise all work performance behaviour into a judgement. It is rarely about breaking limits and more usually about how effectively the person has worked within these limits. Leaders and managers must deal more often with poor performance than with breaking of limits.

Task Review and Performance Review should give fair warning if work performance does not meet the requirements of the role. Coaching, training and other methods may be used to correct the problem, but if poor work performance continues, initiation of removal from the role is necessary. Then the M+1 (or sometimes M+2) will decide if the person might do well in a different role or with a different manager and apply that. If not, then the person should be dismissed from the organisation.

### Breaking Limits

The issue here is whether a law or rule has been broken, for example, safety rules, racial abuse, sexual harassment, drinking at work, fighting, polluting the environment, sleeping on the job, stealing, etc. This is Box D behaviour, that is, unauthorised and counterproductive. This requires an investigation that is more like a legal process.

With a breach of work limits, the initial effort is directed to gathering evidence to determine whether the limit was broken; second, whether the person should reasonably have known of the limit (e.g., wearing a hard hat in that area of a plant) and, third, whether there is any evidence the person acted with intent to breach a limit, or limits.

There must, of course, be due process, which must be open to scrutiny. The consequences are severe, however, if the rule breaking is proven. Unless there are mitigating circumstances, dismissal will be the consequence in most cases. This whole process is similar to a legal process; it is subject potentially to formal legal review if the person chooses to go to court.

### When Assessments Differ

If the person being judged thinks either (a) the overall or (b) a particular judgement is unfair, there must be a process to deal with it that is perceived as fair.

As managerial judgement is at the heart of the managerial hierarchy, the quality of that judgement is one of the most critical issues to address. All the advantages of a meritocratic, managerial authority structure are lost if the judgements made by the managers are unsound. What can we build in to try to ensure they are sound?

Below we outline the system which should operate on a daily basis and, second, the control in that system if there are still problems.

1) The work of a manager as leader involves the management of social process. Therefore, it is part of the role to establish a relationship where decisions can be discussed without appearing to be a direct challenge to authority. Therefore, in the first instance the two people involved should try to resolve their differing assessment of the quality of the judgement evident in a decision. This may mean further explanation or a modification of the judgement or both.
2) If, however, it is not resolved, the next step is to raise the matter with the M+1. Remember it is part of the M+1's work to establish a relationship with reports-once-removed (RoRs) such that these issues can be discussed without any need to go through a formal complaint process. It is also part of the M+1's work to review decisions of direct reports. This may result in a resolution, or it may not.

The first option is to use the normal line of authority. While appeals to the M+1 should not be happening all the time, it should not produce undue concern unless the frequency increases. It can be minimised by good M+1 leadership of direct reports. For this appeal process to work, however, every employee must know that he or she is authorised to use it free of duress.

## Fair Treatment Systems

The person involved in the procedures outlined above may not want or feel able to raise the matter with the manager or even M+1. The matter may be too personal, serious or may demonstrate a fundamental breakdown in trust. This is such a critical area that we recommend all organisations have an internal FTS. We have helped design many such systems and depending on the size and nature of the organisation they may vary in detail. All FTSs, however, have core principles in common.

The system is enabled by the presence of advisors, called fair treatment advisors (FTAs). These people are chosen for their maturity (not necessarily age related), social process skills and reputation for keeping matters confidential. They are trained in the system details and their purpose is to advise on the process. Does the person (complainant) know how the system works? Is it a serious issue? Is it, in fact, a non-work-related issue? They are not, however, advocates for the person complaining.

FTSs are not a substitute for legal complaints. The system should not attempt to replace legal complaints. The FTS is designed to investigate unfair treatment, not illegal treatment. Thus, the FTA may advise only on the existence of a case of sexual harassment, assault, fraud, negligence and so on. This immediately suggests a limit may have been broken. If it is not (at least initially) a legal issue, then the person can initiate the FTS process with the advice but not advocacy of the FTA.

The system requires the appointment of a fair treatment investigator (FTI) to carry out an enquiry. The FTI must be at least the peer, or, more usually, a level above the person against whom the complaint is directed. Thus, if I am complaining about my manager, then a person holding a role at the manager's level or above will investigate. We recommend one level above, but it depends upon the size of organisation.

It must be remembered that this system now operates like a formal internal audit: it is a corporate policy and system owned and authorised by the board and CEO. The FTI has the delegated authority of the CEO. The FTI, who must be trained and advised by the FTA, then has full authority to ask questions of relevant people, look at papers, e-mails, text messages, etc. – the same authority as the internal audit – in order to investigate the complaint and make a recommendation.

The recommendation is then made to the manager of the person who has been accused of unfairness. In larger organisations it is the M+1 of the person unless these people have been a subject of the investigation (and perhaps involved in the complaint), in which case it goes to the manager above. This line manager then decides whether to implement the recommendation. Whatever the decision, it must be communicated to all involved including the FTA.

## Appeal

If the complainant is not satisfied, he or she can then appeal to the CEO (if the complaint is not already at that level). The CEO then reconsiders the evidence, the recommendation and the decision and makes a final judgement.

We have also considered the involvement, during the investigation stage, of an outside party. While not ruling this out absolutely, we recommend against this unless such a person is very knowledgeable about the organisation and is well respected in it, for example, a recently retired executive. The FTS is an internal process and should be recognised as such.

Using the FTS does not prejudice the person from using other avenues, such as an agreed process involving a union or industrial tribunal. If, however, the complainant uses an alternative to the FTS first, then they forfeit their right to use the FTS for the same complaint later or if the outcome is unfavourable.

It should be emphasised that the FTS is not an HR system. Although FTAs may be from the HR stream, it is an executive system.

## Audit and Records

The results of the FTS case histories should be audited by the HR department as *custodians* of the system. The audit does not comment on the nature of the decisions but investigates:

- How many complaints.
- The role of the FTA.
- The acceptability of the decision from the complainant's perspective and, most importantly, the complainant's view of the process.

These audits can provide information about patterns of behaviour, either positive or negative, on the part of managers, complainants or areas of the organisation where there are recurrent issues. This allows leadership to take action to prevent further problems or even lawsuits.

## Summary of FTSs

The FTS is not an alternative to other means of complaint. It is available as a control on managerial judgement, particularly regarding task assignment and work performance review. It is there to demonstrate that a person does not have to rely on third parties to achieve fair treatment.

Some may say it will only support "the bosses." If that is the perception, it already demonstrates low trust and poor leadership. Healthy relationships will still have problems, whether at work, in families or in relationships among friends. We believe it is important to first try and resolve these matters in house. The FTS is a system which is necessary if that is to be possible. It is one of the critical systems for high trust and positive organisations.

## Summary

All the performance management systems discussed in Section "Appeal" of this book work together. They should be integrated and *owned* by line managers not the Human Resources Department.

While the processes need to be well-designed, it is managers and their judgements that link all these systems into a coherent whole, and the managers must be accountable for their successes and failures. There are no quick and easy shortcuts. Although advice from a range of sources can be helpful, it can also be confusing unless authority is clear and the concepts are compatible.

Failure to pay attention to careers and succession means the best people will leave and capability is wasted. The lack of Fair Treatment may have a similar outcome.

The one trap that is most important to avoid is promising a future that cannot be delivered. It is easy at the time to either explicitly or implicitly give a person the impression that either their work performance or their prospects are much brighter than they are. This is often unintended, but dishonesty will cause disillusionment and often anger. It can lead back to power games, destroying the whole purpose of these essential people systems.

In our experience, people are quite realistic about themselves when given accurate information and feedback. They also do not need to have their entire careers mapped out. This may lead to false assumptions such as a false ceiling on promotion, or limitless potential for advancement.

Not everyone performs well; some break limits and this must be dealt with. As with all systems, controls and audits are essential. The FTS is itself a control on managerial judgement. Without it, mythologies will grow that poor judgement rather than poor performance is the real problem and trust will diminish or evaporate.

We hope that many of the people reading this book will be able to use most of the systems we have described for their own and their direct reports' benefit. Even if the place they work is not yet doing all that we recommend, much of the material can be used to improve your own work or the work performance within the area you control. Later, as you move up the hierarchy, you may be able to contribute to the development of, or implementation of, many of the systems to benefit the whole organisation. You will find more detailed information at www.systemsleadership.org.uk.

# Conclusion

## The Benefit of Foresight

This book is primarily concerned with how people come together to achieve a productive purpose. That can only happen when Productive Social Cohesion can be sustained. Our survival as a species has always depended upon our ability to form and sustain social relationships and build organisations. People have deep needs to be creative and to belong. By creating positive organisations, we can fulfil these needs and build a worthwhile society.

We spend so much of our lives in organisations of one sort or another, our lives are seriously impacted by the extent to which such organisations encourage or discourage our creativity. Indeed, our mental health is heavily influenced by our experiences of working in organisations. Positive organisations do not happen by chance. They require real effort to create and sustain. In this book we have discussed social processes in managerial hierarchies as they exist in business, public agencies and non-governmental organisations.

In addition, there are different types of social organisation with different purposes that require different structures and systems if they are to achieve their purpose and support their members and those who interact with them. Our colleagues have produced books on improving schools (Macdonald, Dixon and Tiplady, 2020) and organisational responses to Covid (McGill, Macdonald and others, 2021). We have identified sound general principles of behaviour that are general across organisations. We have endeavoured to outline the work necessary to create such organisations and to give examples of these principles in action.

We have argued that although we expect to approach the Technical and Commercial Domains with rigour, we are often much more cavalier with the Social Domain. It is as if it is all just "common sense" or should just happen. Your experiences should confirm the importance of the Social Domain. It is hard work to create positive organisations. We are often tempted by the magic of the latest best-selling book revealing the few simple secrets to guarantee success.

DOI: 10.4324/9781003459118-28

Understanding the concepts of Systems Leadership, applying them with discipline (not dogma) and creativity, takes effort. Sustaining and modifying them over time requires persistence and consistency. We have observed and admired what good leaders and team members do and tried to distil the essence of productive, value-based relationships.

We do not claim to be totally original. Clearly, we have been influenced by Wilfred Brown and Elliott Jaques in particular, but also by numerous others we have worked with and for. Many are named in the Acknowledgements at the beginning of this book. We have found that creativity is not an individual activity. Ideas and efforts are the products of social relationships, which is why we are sceptical of "gurus" who claim to have all the answers.

We have been influenced by Professor Richard P. Feynman, Nobel Prize winner in Physics from Cal Tech, who said, "The more you know, the more you realize how much you don't know. The less you know, the more you think you know everything. Knowledge is humbling. Ignorance is arrogant."

In the final analysis people are not creative because of a contract, a job title or even pay; we are not primarily externally motivated. We believe people are inherently creative, energetic and positive – just observe small children. We also have a perverse way, however, from childhood of inhibiting, stultifying and depressing that creativity by poor organisational design, inappropriate leadership, lack of capability and the use of power to name but a few.

We have argued that a significant amount of material regarding organisational behaviour is based on fads and fashion. It is often purely descriptive and is not based on sound theory or propositions that can be tested.

When organisations fail, often spectacularly (e.g., banks in 2008), people will claim how this was only understandable with "the benefit of hindsight." We disagree.

By using Systems Leadership to understand how the whole organisation works and interacts with its environment we can make confident predictions of the likely outcomes. We are not impressed by the excuse, "we are experiencing an unprecedented situation." We are more interested in asking, "Was this incident or system predictable?"

Systems Leadership gives you "the benefit of foresight." We can predict what will happen when an unclear structure creates confusion; roles are filled with people unable to do the work; systems are poorly designed and consequently drive counterproductive behaviour and create negative mythologies. We can predict the effects of lack of clarity around work, poor leadership and confusion around teamwork. That is because Systems Leadership is built upon sound theory, tested principles of behaviour and implementation in many businesses, public agencies and NGOs, in many different cultures and countries around the world. We have included case studies in the book but also refer to cases on the related website. In summary, we do not simply say *what* should be done – "build trust," "appoint good leaders," "innovate" or "empower" or "collaborate," "deal with complexity" – but we write about *how* to do that. We simply ask that other approaches be critiqued in the same way.

We have offered the principles and practices in this book to help build social organisations that encourage the creative expression of capability. We have had the privilege of working with people who have tried to do just that and if we, through this book and others we have written, have contributed to that most worthwhile of endeavours – to help build positive organisations and contribute to a just society, then we have turned our intention into reality. As with all work products, it is for you to judge and use, if you find this worth testing, in your work. We hope you will use it to further your own career, improve the place where you work and act for the betterment of our societies.

You have our best wishes. We hope to see you at our website, maconsultancy.com.

# Appendices

- **Recommendations for Effective Role Descriptions**
- **Role Summary for a Mining Supervisor**
- **Potential Role Description for an Executive Director** of a private school prepared for the school's Board of Directors who were considering the need for higher level capability in the school's Principal. This helped them develop a selection process. The final description of the role was edited to cover the most essential accountabilities of the role.
- **Generic Role Description for a Manager at Level III.** Very long as the organization was trying to learn the characteristics of a role and how to articulate them. This version helped them create a shorter but still effective role description.
- **Work of the Role and Selection Preparation**
- **Selection Interview and Review**
- **Performance Planning Guide**
- **Performance Review Guide**

# Recommendations for Effective Role Descriptions

(Based on the experience of a variety of organisations)
Role Descriptions should:

1. Be formulated so they are adaptable to different circumstances, to different requirements and roles.
2. Outline the boundaries of the role. Such boundaries between roles inside the organisation are often poorly understood. One purpose of the role description is to clarify internal boundaries. The required work is contained within the role boundary. Therefore, it is essential to clarify these boundaries if accountability is to be fairly assessed.
3. Give the role incumbent an understanding of what she/he will be expected to do. The role description must be task oriented.
4. Clarify the resources, including authorities, which are available to the role incumbent to perform the work of the role.
5. Provide a basis for understanding and negotiating role relationships that are salient to the work of the role.
6. Integrate with the overall body of work the organisation must carry out to achieve its purpose and objectives.
7. Outline the knowledge base that needs to be developed for the work of the role to be performed to the required standard.
8. Clearly articulate the requirement for the organisation as a whole to operate as a meritocracy based on work.
9. Clearly articulate the expectations of the manager and direct reports that relate to the process of accountability.

# Role Description Components

When used as an educational tool, the complete role description described below can be quite useful. Most organisations have preferred to use shorter versions, but have created a longer version and then cut it back to cover the essentials – the principal function and key task types for a particular role description that is to be used by managers and their subordinates. Examples of role descriptions follow.

1. **Date:** The role description should always carry a date to indicate when it was last revised.
2. **Role Title:** This is the "name" of the role. Select the title with care; it is the organisational indicator of the principal function of a role.
3. **Address:** The position of the role in the organisation. An organisation structure diagram indicating the manager, role incumbent and direct reports is often useful.
4. **Purpose and Principal Function:** Why the role exists and a short description of what the role is about – its distilled essence.

   Managers lead people, schedule resources and perform other tasks assigned by their manager. For example, the principal function of a manager might read:

   > The principal function of [your role] is to lead the people and schedule the use of resources available to your role in order to create conditions within which your subordinates are successful performing the work of their roles.

   Professional/technical contributors provide expert advice and do professional work. Professionals have few or no subordinates. Even when they have a few subordinates, their primary effort is given to their own direct output; managing subordinates is essential, but the managerial workload is light. For example:

   > The principal function of [your role] is to build an understanding of the technologies employed in the unit of which

you are a member, and from that knowledge base provide advice directed towards the improvement, efficiency and effectiveness in the unit's use of those technologies.

5. **Accountability:** Each role or position description needs a very clear statement about acceptance of accountability being a condition of employment and a brief outline of the process.

   "It is a condition of your employment that you accept accountability for the work you do in the performance of tasks properly assigned to you. You should expect that from time to time your manager will call you to account for your work and to provide a response to the following in relation to a specific task, or a collection of tasks, that he or she assigned to you:"

   Tell me what you did.
   Tell me how you did it.
   Tell me why you did it that way.

   You should expect your manager to discuss your responses with you and to advise you of his judgement of their adequacy.

   Should you disagree with your manager's judgement, you have the absolute right to appeal that judgement, in the first instance to your Manager-once-removed (M+1). Your manager is fully aware of this right of appeal and supports its availability.

6. **General Responsibilities and Goals:** It is essential to have a systematic method to break a job up into understandable components aimed at getting work done. Traditional job descriptions have been written in terms of responsibility, e.g., "You are responsible for maintaining a positive climate in your work group." "You are responsible for having your people work safely."

   These statements do not indicate what work is to be done. We have created a language of responsibility-oriented organisations, but people within them are often unclear about what they have to do. Given this, it is not realistic to hold people accountable. For example, what is a "positive climate"? How can it be assessed? People do manage to translate these responsibilities into work, but it is always an "iffy" process. We propose that the use of the term responsibilities be dropped as the true meaning of the word has been corrupted.

7. **Tasks and Task Types:** Written into every role description is a general statement defining tasks and distinguishing them from task types. This is to remind managers of the correct way to set

tasks, and to indicate clearly that task assignment is the work of the manager, not a role description.

A Task is an activity that is defined in terms of context, purpose, output quantity and quality, targeted completion time and resources available for the execution of the task. A role description written in task format becomes obsolete on the completion of the first task.

A task type describes an activity for which the specific context, purpose, output, targeted completion time and task resources are not defined. A task type always begins with a verb.

It is not necessary nor is it desirable to attempt to list all task types that might be associated with a particular role. Such an exhaustive listing could act to restrict the perceived discretion of both the role occupant and his or her manager. The purpose of the listing is to clarify the kinds of work most frequently done in this role.

8. **Categories of Task Types:** The task types in this example may be grouped into eight general categories (you may choose different categories based on the work and situation of your organisation):

Leadership
Safety
Social Process
Work Planning, Scheduling and Organising Work Flows of Material, Money, Information and People
Technical Processes/Work Methods
Environmental Impacts
Training
Equal Employment Opportunity

While all roles may have tasks from each of the categories, managerial roles have many leadership tasks and usually a significant amount of planning and organising work. Professional roles have few tasks requiring the leadership of people and are primarily focused on planning and organising tasks or on technical tasks.

Technical people must have skills in dealing with people but they are not in a leadership role as are managers. Managers, in turn, need to understand the technologies they are managing but they may have subordinates who are more technically expert than themselves.

Human relationships; workflows of materials, information, money and people; and technical processes are elements which are important in every role. It is the balance of tasks that changes from role to role.

The final task type in every role description needs to be as follows: "Perform any other task correctly assigned to you by your manager that you are competent to perform safely." [In some organisations this is put up front.]

9. **Role Resources:** The resources available to a role incumbent include not only physical, human and financial assets but also the authorities which the organisation and the manager provide. Particular role resources can be organised into categories, and the limits applying to them set by corporate policy or the role incumbent's manager must be clearly articulated.

   Some role resources are inherent in a role and do not change as role incumbents change. Others must be agreed between a manager and subordinate to develop a mutual understanding of the resources available in a particular role at a particular time.

   All role resources are, of course, to be exercised within the law and within corporate and departmental policies and guidelines.

   Authorities: Although they are a resource, it is advisable that authorities that are assigned to a role should be separately articulated in order that incumbents can complete their assigned tasks.

   The authorities that define a position of management in a stratified organisation. ($VAR^3I$) or the authorities which define a Supervisor role, Project Leader role and in the case of higher-level managers the M+1 and M+2 authorities.

   The authority to interact with other nominated members of the organisation primarily for information transfer or the provision and receipt of advice.

   The individual approval authorities required to maintain financial and administrative control within the organisation. These require written specification on the Role Resources Agreement.

   Other authorities that may be assigned to an individual from time to time by his or her manager.

   Geography: The physical limits within which the role incumbent is expected to perform his or her work. Most relevant where the organisation has more than one facility.

Assets: The human skills and the items of plant and equipment that are allocated to role incumbents for care and for the performance of their work. The role incumbent is required to sustain the productive capacity of those assets.

Budget: The labour hours, budgeted expenditure and/or consumable materials assigned for the role incumbent's use and allocation in his/her work.

Information: The information assigned/provided for the role incumbent's use in his/her work.

Time Span of the Role: The maximum time a manager might be expected to allow a competent role incumbent to exercise discretion in the execution of his/her longest task. It corresponds to the maximum time span of the work stratum in which the role is placed.

10. **Role Relationships:** What is important in the role description is that the key roles with which a particular role incumbent must interact are shown in an organisation chart that provides their title and address within the organisation.

    **Note:** It is necessary to list the roles with which the role incumbent will have his/her most important interactions. The following should be included in the list of roles with important interactions which must be negotiated by the role incumbent and each of these role holders:

    - Manager.
    - Subordinates.
    - Peers – Persons working at the same work stratum.
    - Associates – Any diagonal relationship. Subordinates or superiors of a peer.
    - Roles outside the Business Unit.

Creating such role descriptions is time-consuming, but we have found the results to be very worthwhile. They improve manager-subordinate understandings of their expected work, and they become the basis for selecting individuals for specific roles.

To begin the process, you might want to start by simply stating the purpose and principal function of each role. This will allow you and your peers to begin to develop a better understanding of the body of work that must be accomplished. Then you can use the examples provided to expand the role descriptions. Even people who have been working together for some time find there are questions about who should do what. You may discover some things that are not being done that need to be done. Other things are being done more than once because the individuals involved do not realise others are carrying out the same, or a very similar, task.

Then go on to examine the task types of Managers as compared to Independent Contributors. Using the examples of role descriptions, go through each category of task types and:

1. Consider why the task type is included in the role description.
2. Indicate if you believe other task types should be added to the category.

3. Indicate which task types are important to the leadership of people.
4. Discuss how one might behave while carrying out leadership task types in order to have that behaviour placed at the positive end of the scales of shared values by those subject to the behaviour and those who observe it.

Statement of Accountabilities. This is a basic list of accountabilities within a role designed to highlight key elements of the role for which the role incumbent will be held accountable. There are task types (see below) that provide specific content for these accountabilities.

The person who occupies the role is accountable for everything inside it and for the flow across the boundary outward. The role description must make clear that the role incumbent will be held accountable for specified activities.

This Statement of Accountabilities always includes a statement that the individual is accountable for using his or her mind; the individual is paid to think and will be held accountable for thinking.

"You are accountable for drawing on the intellectual ability, knowledge, skills and experience which you bring to your job and for exercising reasonable judgement in the execution of your tasks."

The Statement of Accountabilities will differ from organisation to organisation because its purpose is to highlight those task types which the organisation and/or the manager wish to emphasise. When introducing stratified systems, many organisations find it useful to emphasise accountabilities for managerial work in order to improve its effectiveness and productivity. Much of stratified theory is simply the articulation of good management practices, so the emphasis on managerial task types is an obvious progression.

We provide an example of a role description from a real organisation which covers what we state here. It is much shorter because it covers the essentials of the role without all the details described here. We also provide a full-length example, which was used in one organisation, but it was soon recognised that a shorter version would be more useful. We include it to indicate the detail which can be articulated for a specific role. Some managers have found that the "long version" is a good place to start, and then to cut it back to focus on the most important categories and task types.

# Role Summary for a Mining Supervisor

**ROLE SUMMARY**

| DETAILS | | | |
|---|---|---|---|
| ROLE TITLE: | Mining Supervisor | NAME: | |
| DIVISION: | Mining | LOCATION: | |

| RELATIONSHIP | | | |
|---|---|---|---|
| MANAGER ROLE TITLE: | Mining Superintendent | NAME: | |
| M+1 ROLE TITLE: | Mining Project Manager | NAME: | |
| SUPERVISOR OF: | Mine Production Workers | | |
| KEY INTERNAL RELATIONSHIPS: | Specialist SHET Advisor, Maintenance Superintendent, Maintenance Supervisors, Mining Engineer, Mining Surveyor, Site Administration Officer. | | |
| KEY EXTERNAL RELATIONSHIPS: | Client Representatives. | | |

| PURPOSE |
|---|
| To lead the mining crew in the safe and efficient delivery of the project mining requirements such that the crew achieves SHE, quality and production goals. |

| AUTHORITY |
|---|
| **SAFETY, HEALTH & ENVIRONMENT** |
| Every (Insert Employer Name) employee and contractor has the right to stop work or not commence work in situations that may cause harm. Personal action is required to remove or minimise the risk of harm and to immediately bring the risk to the attention of a Supervisor or Manager. |
| **GENERAL** |
| Boundaries to your authority are:<br>• The law (local, state, national);<br>• The policies, systems and procedures of (Insert Employer Name);<br>• The policies, systems and procedures of the client as they apply to the site; and<br>• The ethical expectations of (Insert Employer Name) (as described in procedures in the GMS). |
| **STRUCTURE AND SYSTEMS** |
| (Insert Employer Name) has a disciplined approach to structure and systems in order to create and maintain consistency and efficiency across the organisation. Boundaries to your authority are:<br>• Structure – No authority to add layers of management or change role titles; and |

| |
|---|
| • Systems – Recommend changes to (Insert Employer Name) systems and recommend adoption of a site specific system. |
| **HUMAN RESOURCES** |
| As a Supervisor you have the authority to:<br>• Recommend selection of team members;<br>• Trigger tasks for team members (in accordance with their Role Summary);<br>• Review the work of and recognise team members for their work (within the bounds of HR systems); and<br>• Recommend the removal of a team member from (Insert Employer Name). |

| DETAILS | | | |
|---|---|---|---|
| **ROLE TITLE:** | Mining Supervisor | **NAME:** | |
| **DIVISION:** | Mining | **LOCATION:** | |

| EXPENDITURE |
|---|
| No authority for expenditure or disposal of assets, refer to your Manager for advice. |

| WORK |
|---|
| **PRIMARY ROLE DIFFERENTIATING TASK TYPES** |
| • Lead your mining crew to safely and efficiently deliver the production outcomes required for the project as detailed in the authorised Shift Plan;<br>• Allocate tasks and communicate any other relevant information at pre-start meetings such that team members are clear on the work required;<br>• Conduct toolbox meetings as required by the Project Manager;<br>• Perform shift handovers with the incoming supervisor detailing the status of the work detailed in the Shift Plan (and any authorised variations) and the status of equipment such that the on-coming crew can commence work efficiently;<br>• Work with your Manager to assess the training requirements of your team and recommend to your Manager an appropriate set of skills that should exists within your team;<br>• Plan and schedule the training of operators in accordance with the authorised project Training Plan such that the set of skills authorised by your Manager is achieved;<br>• Provide advice to your Manager on the implementation and application of any plans and schedules that are provided to you;<br>• Monitor and evaluate production performance throughout the shift to identify variance from plan (or indicators of it) and take action where necessary to mitigate adverse variance to plan;<br>• Work with the Maintenance Supervisor to implement any maintenance plans for the shift and agree any deviations to plan with the Maintenance Supervisor, and where appropriate your Manager;<br>• Decide the priority of breakdown maintenance in the event of multiple breakdowns through consultation with Maintenance Supervisor, and where appropriate your Manager;<br>• Monitor and evaluate maintenance related information to identify indicators of impending issues and advise your Manager of your assessment;<br>• Prepare shift reports in accordance with the Production Plan requirements such that they are accurate and timely; |

- Attend and participate in project meetings as required by your Manager;
- Carry out inspections and job observations in accordance with the project SHET Activity Planner;
- Control any SHE incident scene in the production area, unless relieved by your Manager or authorised incident controller (in which case do as directed);
- Collect all necessary incident information, notify all relevant stakeholders as per the (Insert Employer Name) incident notification procedure and return the area to safe operations if authorised to do so;
- Provide technical input into any incident investigation reports as required by your Manager;
- Monitor Fitness For Work of your team members and take action as necessary or authorised; and
- Fulfil the Supervisor obligations as set out in your letter of appointment and in accordance with the project Management Structure, such that (Insert Employer Name) legislative requirements are met.

| DETAILS | | | |
|---|---|---|---|
| ROLE TITLE: | Mining Supervisor | NAME: | |
| DIVISION: | Mining | LOCATION: | |

**GENERAL TASK TYPES OF ALL ROLES**

- Work safely and demonstrate respect for the environment and community in which you work;
- Conduct yourself professionally at all times to assist in building the positive reputation of (Insert Employer Name) as a professional, reputable and ethical organisation;
- Act in a cost effective and efficient manner at all times;
- Provide information stemming from your work to your peers that may be relevant to their work to enhance their work in their roles;
- Advise your Manager of systems that you assess as needing to apply to (Insert Employer Name) work in areas outside your authority;
- Monitor and evaluate the activity of your project for information indicating an impending issue for (Insert Employer Name) and take action within your authority to resolve the issues or refer to your Manager if you believe it lies outside your authority;
- Work only in accordance with your defined authority limits; and
- Perform any other task assigned by your Manager that you are capable of performing safely.

| ACKNOWLEDGEMENT BY EMPLOYEE | | | | | |
|---|---|---|---|---|---|
| NAME: | | SIGNATURE: | | DATE: | |
| ACKNOWLEDGEMENT BY MANAGER | | | | | |
| NAME: | | SIGNATURE: | | DATE: | |
| AUTHORISATION BY M+1 | | | | | |
| NAME: | | SIGNATURE: | | DATE: | |
| VETO BY HR MANAGER | | | | | |
| NAME: | | SIGNATURE: | | DATE: | |

# Potential Role Description for an Executive Director

## Executive Director – Optimal

### Principal Function

To lead the people and organise the resources of the [Name redacted] Technical Institute in order to ensure its educational success and continued viability as a first class college preparatory school enhanced by its technological resources and its ethical character.

### Description of Work

The ideal Executive Director is the person accountable for the integration of all of the functions that must be undertaken by a School to meet the needs of its students, faculty, staff, Board and external environment. He or she should be fully capable of guiding the School through its environment, interacting with that environment to modify the School so it will prosper as a whole unit. It requires the Executive Director to deal with the conflicts caused by the impact of the School on the environment and the modification of the School to meet the demands of that environment. The environment for [this school] includes, but is not limited to, its officers, alumni, parents of students, accrediting institutions, colleges and universities where its students may want to enrol, local governments, grant providing organisations, donors – actual and potential – potential gift givers, industrialists who take an interest in the School.

This requires that the Executive Director be positioned to carry the accountability and commensurate authority for the profit and loss performance of the School as well as its educational development. The Executive Director sets the context in which lower levels in the organisation will undertake their work. This is most effectively done through an annual planning process that, over a five- to seven-year timeframe, sets the strategy, priorities and critical tasks for the organisation as a whole.

The Executive Director must bring the School plan to fruition through the work of other people, and to do this effectively he or she must demonstrate excellent organisational leadership. At this level, the Executive Director cannot interact personally with each and every employee of the School. Nonetheless, he or she must be able to imbue within these employees a willingness to bring their natural initiative and enthusiasm to bear on their work and to collaborate with their leaders and each other in order to move the School in the direction set by the Executive Director. To achieve this, the Executive Director must focus strongly on building a School social climate, or culture, which supports the strategy through fostering employee practices and behaviour that will best achieve the goals of the School.

Work at this level involves the use of theories to create principles that will be used by subordinates in lower-level roles to direct their parts of the School.

The theory involves the creation of a model of a unified whole system of entities into a single (though complex) unit so the unit may be treated as a self-sustaining whole that has to be guided through an environment. In the model (system) all the sub-parts are explicitly interdependent and it can be shown how they all affect one another.

The Executive Director at this level must maintain a dual perspective – looking inward to create working conditions of the organisation, looking outward to ensure adaptation to the School's environment.

At this level it is necessary to work on the general and particular, simultaneously. It is also necessary to take into account second- and third-order consequences of decisions – not just the immediate impact.

Structural change provides one of the levers for modifying and adapting the School to changing environmental demands. Shared values, systems, strategy and staffing are other important components of the change process.

### Key Accountabilities

You are accountable to the Board of Trustees for managing the activities of the school.

You are accountable for working and managing within the policies and procedures of the school's Board of Trustees and within the discretionary limits and standards set by them. Where procedures and limits have not been defined by the Board, you are to define them for the School.

You are accountable for the quality, quantity, timeliness and cost of your work.

You are accountable for assigning tasks to your subordinates and for assigning them correctly.

You are accountable for assessing the work performance of your subordinates and holding them accountable for achieving the standards of quality, quantity, timeliness and cost which you set.

You are accountable for developing a strategic plan to meet the Board's long term (**five to seven years**) goals and its short-term (one year) objectives.

You are accountable for developing, sustaining and improving systems, processes and people of [this school] such that it achieves its objectives and can continue to do so over time.

You are accountable for ensuring School practices and policies that enhance student learning and support faculty and staff in carrying out their work.

You are accountable for providing effective leadership for faculty, students and administrative staff.

You are accountable for supporting development and fund-raising activities of the School.

The *goal* for you and the staff of the School is to create a working environment where the employees of the School are able to work productively to enhance student education.

## Leadership Task Types

Translate/interpret your understanding of Board objectives in order to provide a context for School employees and volunteers.

Set overall direction and priorities of School targets and objectives within limits set by the Board.

Demonstrate the priority you place on the principles of human dignity, fairness, honesty, trust, courage and love in [the school].

Assign tasks to your subordinates providing context, purpose, quality and quantity of output, resources and time to completion.

Review the performance of your subordinates and give them feedback on what you perceive as well done and what needs improvement.

Assess the performance of your subordinates, inform them of your assessment and confirm what you have said with salary adjustments if merited.

Demonstrate genuine care and concern for students and their educational experience.

Develop, sustain and improve [the school] and its people such that the school achieves its objectives and can continue to do so over time.

Communicate effectively, verbally and in writing, with all elements of the School and to outside audiences.

Create a working environment where the people of [the school] are nurtured, respected and treated as fully empowered adults.

Create a working environment where the creativity and abilities of all employees are involved in achieving School goals and are recognised and rewarded based on work performance.

Analyse the structure of the School administration and education staffing and where required change the structure to provide effective outcomes.

Remove impediments to productive working relationships in the School and between the School, the Board and others in the School environment.

Seek continuous improvement in the human relations, business systems and technologies of [the school].

### Education

Ensure processes are developed and implemented to ensure [the school] has high standards of educational quality, consistency and integration.

### Direct the Development of an Integrated Academic and Technology Curriculum to Achieve the Board's Objective of a High-Quality College Preparatory Programme

Ensure that educational systems are in place and that they are being used and are achieving their intended purposes.

Report to the Board on educational trends and achievements in [the school] and at competing private and public schools.

Direct recruitment policies and procedures for increasing the number of high-quality students without regard to ability to pay.

Direct your staff to estimate the cost of providing scholarships for all qualified students who cannot afford tuition.

### Business and Finance

Ensure business practices and systems are documented and institutionalised.

Direct budget preparation and oversee its accuracy for presentation to the Board and its approval by the Board.

Approve expenditures that exceed $-------------.

Seek approval of the Board for expenditures that exceed $------------.

Approve contracts with external vendors.

Direct the development of the business case for various capital expenditures.

Direct the development of a capital plan to fund current and future needs of [the school] (five- to ten-year time frame).

With your financial officer present the budget, capital plans and other financial reports to the Board.

Ensure the physical plant of the School is properly maintained and upgraded as necessary.

Ensure appropriate separation of duties regarding accounts payable and receivable.

### Human Resources

Develop human resource processes and managerial practices, recommend them to the Board for approval and contribute to their implementation throughout [the school].

- Selection.
- Induction.
- Performance management – performance planning, task assignment, task review, performance review, performance evaluation.
- Transfer and removal from role.
- Staff development/workforce management.
- Career development.
- Assessment of potential.
- Recognition and reward.
- Training.

Develop a system for feedback of information on the effectiveness of:

- The current organisation.
- The allocation of work among the elements of the School.
- The allocation of work between roles.

Direct your HR manager to develop standard employment contracts and working conditions for staff and faculty.

Direct your HR manager to monitor employment contracts and working conditions for staff and faculty.

Monitor the school's talent pool and plan for future staffing needs. (Workforce composition, size, skill base, deployment)

Develop policy recommendations for the Board regarding personnel practices, training programmes, employee and management development.

Identify training needs as they are likely to evolve over the next **five to seven** years and recommend actions to meet them.

Identify changes that will be required in the organisation's talent pool if it is to meet future organisational requirements.

Direct your HR manager to develop and implement a method for analysing people costs and their trends.

Direct your HR manager to develop a system for identifying human resource improvement objectives and tasks and for recording progress.

Provide **expert** advice and make recommendations regarding issues of organisation structure and human resources to the Board. Note changes that ought to be made to ensure that the structure of the organisation stays matched to the requirements of a changing workload and its planned future requirements.

Lead organisation development studies to improve the educational people and processes of the school.

Develop system of role descriptions, role relationships, authorities and accountabilities that are available to the Board in order to facilitate continuous improvement throughout the school.

Ensure training and developmental opportunities are made available to all who could benefit from them.

## Technology

Direct an analysis of the computing, communication and network requirements of the school.

Direct the development of a business plan showing costs and value of various network, computing and communications upgrades.

Direct research into the most current educational technologies to improve student learning.

Direct the implementation of current best practices in educational methods and technology.

### Other Tasks

Recommend to the Board policies and strategies to achieve Board objectives.

### Develop Innovative Strategies and Policies in Support of Board Objectives

Ensure Board strategy is implemented.

Direct your subordinates in the implementation of your policies and ensure this is done correctly, on time and within budget.

Develop productive working relationships with the Board and external organisations and individuals who are, or might be, involved with the school.

Facilitate productive working relationships for your subordinates with the Board and relevant external individuals and organisations.

Develop productive working relationships with your education counterparts in other Schools.

Exchange information and ideas with other educational organisations and even other types of businesses involved in education and training – to **scan nation-wide in order to** identify the current best educational practices and bring them into the school.

Inform the Board about the implications – short term and long term – of various educational policies, strategies, actions.

Develop quality improvement proposals.

# Generic Role Description for a Manager at Level III

**Date:**

ROLE DESCRIPTION

Title: Level III MRU Manager
Business Unit:
Division:
Unit:
=================================================

## Principal Function

Your principal function is to lead the people and schedule the resources of the ___________ ____________________ Unit and to create conditions and systems within which your subordinates and your entire unit can be successful in improving the long-term productivity of the ____________________ Business Unit by providing [insert functions of unit].

## Statement of Accountabilities

You are accountable to the Division Manager, [insert title of unit] __________________, for managing the activities of the ______________________ Unit.

You are accountable for working and managing within the policies and procedures of [this company] and the __________________ Business Unit and within the discretionary limits and standards set by your Division Manager. Where procedures and limits have not been defined by your Division Manager, you are to define them for your Unit.

You are accountable for the quality, quantity, timeliness and cost of your work.

You are accountable for assigning tasks to your subordinates and for assigning them correctly.

You are accountable for demonstrating your concern for safety within your unit.

You are accountable for reviewing, recognising and evaluating the work performance of your subordinates and holding them accountable for achieving the standards of quality, quantity, timeliness and cost which you set.

You are accountable for moving about your Unit work area and for establishing mutual recognition throughout your Unit.

You are accountable, in relation to your immediate subordinates, for exercising the four authorities which define a position of management – the authority to:

Veto selection.
Assign tasks.
Review, Recognise and Reward differentially after appraisal of work performance.
Initiate removal from role.

You are accountable in relation to your subordinates-once-removed for exercising the five authorities of the sponsoring manager (M+1):

Veto selection.
Assess potential.
Recommend selection.
Review decisions.
Recommend dismissal.

You are accountable for appraising the potential of your Stratum I employees and where appropriate assigning developmental tasks to your Stratum II supervisors to develop their Stratum I subordinates.

You are accountable for conducting your role relationships with other Southern California Edison (SCE) employees in accordance with your agreed-upon modes of interaction.

You are accountable to your Division manager for managing the subordinates of other managers who have been assigned to work on projects for which you are accountable within the limits of the Project authorities which you have negotiated with the subordinate's manager.

You are accountable to your Division Manager for negotiation of limits for the project authorities as they apply to your subordinates who have been assigned to work on Task Forces for which another manager is accountable.

You are accountable for managing the organisational change process required to implement organisation development in your Unit.

[Insert other accountabilities that are particularly significant in this role or in the overall organisation at this time.]

You are accountable for using the intellectual ability, knowledge, skills and experience that you bring to your job and for exercising logical judgement in the execution of your tasks.

## Industrial Health and Safety

### General Responsibilities

You shall ensure that your Unit achieves its objectives safely.

You shall implement the safety policies of your Division Manager for your Unit directed towards the achievement of your safety goals.

You shall ensure that your unit complies with legislated and corporate requirements relating to industrial health and safety.

The goal for you and the members of your Unit is to eliminate work-related deaths and injuries, damage to equipment and lost production time caused by accidents or violations of safety rules and practices.

### Task Types

[Insert additional safety task types as needed to draw attention to important or unique aspects of the role.]

Comply personally with all safety rules and regulations.

Demonstrate to the members of your Unit the priority you place on industrial health and safety.

Implement your manager's safety policies and procedures for the employees of your Unit.

Educate your subordinates in these safety policies and procedures.

Assign safety tasks to your subordinates.

Demonstrate knowledge of emergency and isolation procedures.

Have your subordinates demonstrate knowledge of isolation and emergency procedures.

Take action to correct unsafe work practices and conditions reported by your subordinates which are outside their accountability.

Review accident investigation recommendations and take appropriate action.

Identify unsafe work practices and conditions and eliminate or report them.

Recommend action on safety issues that have a scope beyond your Unit.

Implement the safety programme for your Unit.

Prepare and implement safety education programmes for your subordinates.

Report safety problems which have become issues in other companies and have implications for the ____________ Business Unit of SCE.

[Insert additional safety task types as needed to draw attention to important or unique aspects of the role.]

## Compliance and Security

### General Responsibilities

You shall ensure that your Unit complies with all statutory requirements related to the security, documentation and reporting of data within the corporation and to regulatory agencies.

You shall implement the security and compliance policies of your Division Manager for your Unit directed towards achievement of your compliance goals.

The goal for you and the members of your Unit is to comply with all legal, regulatory and corporate policies so that it meets all its compliance requirements accurately, completely and on time.

### Task Types

Comply personally with all compliance and security rules and regulations.

Implement your Division Manager's compliance and security policies for the employees of your Unit.

Educate your subordinates in relevant compliance and security policies.

Demonstrate to the members of your Unit the priority which you place on compliance and the proper documentation to demonstrate compliance.

Demonstrate to the members of your Unit the priority which you place on security of data and Company assets and resources.

Assign compliance and security tasks to your subordinates.

Take action to correct work practices and conditions which are not in compliance with laws, regulations, agency directives or SCE policies reported by your subordinates which are outside their accountability.

Take action to correct work practices and conditions that reduce the security of data, company assets or resources reported by your subordinates which are outside their accountability.

Review recommendations from investigations of compliance or security problems and take appropriate action.

Identify work practices and conditions that are not compliant and reduce the security of data, company assets or resources and eliminate or report them.

Recommend action on compliance and security issues which have a scope beyond your Unit.

Implement the compliance programme for your Unit.

Implement the security programme for your Unit.

Prepare and implement compliance and security education programmes for your subordinates.

Report compliance and security problems which have become issues in other companies and have implications for SCE.

[Insert additional security task types as needed to draw attention to important or unique aspects of the role.]

## Human Relations

### General Responsibilities

You shall foster a climate of mutual respect and team identity directed towards productivity improvement in your Unit.

You shall resolve personally, or jointly with your subordinates, human relations problems arising within your Unit.

The goal for you and the members of your Unit is to create a working environment where the employees of your Unit are able to work productively.

### Task Types

Demonstrate the priority you place on the values of human dignity, fairness, honesty, trust, love and courage in your Unit.

Assign human relations tasks to your subordinates.

Develop mutual recognition between yourself and the other members of your Unit.

Drive the programmes of your Division Manager to remove impediments to improved labour productivity in your Unit.

Inform your subordinates of the performance of your Unit, the ________________ Division and the ________________ Business Unit.

Manage the symbolism applicable to your work and the work of your Unit.

Discuss and resolve with your peers any human relations problems affecting your work.

Report any continuing human relations problems affecting your work.

Report human relations issues affecting, or likely to affect, your Unit, the __________ Division or the ______________ Business Unit.

Resolve human relations issues referred to you that are within your authority.

Refer to your Division Manager human relations issues which are outside your authority.

Apply ______________ Business Unit policies and procedures on attendance, discipline and performance.

Identify and report ongoing Company- or Business Unit policy-related issues which have adverse consequences for your Unit.

Hear and decide on appeals by members of your Unit.

Communicate all relevant information to the members of your Unit promptly.

Approve the role relationships to be observed by your subordinates.

Negotiate your own role relationships.

Have your Division Manager approve your negotiated role relationships.

Appraise the potential of your Stratum I subordinates and inform them of your assessment.

Assign training and developmental tasks to your Supervisors to develop their Stratum I subordinates.

Write performance reviews for your subordinates and discuss them along with their input to such reviews.

Assess the work performance of your subordinates and inform them of your assessment.

Reward your subordinates differentially on the basis of your assessment of their work performance.

Assess applicants for positions in your Unit.

Select potential candidates for positions in your Unit (subject to veto by your manager).

Veto the selection of persons whom you believe, with cause, would be either unwilling or unable to contribute positively to the output of your Unit.

Initiate the removal of unsatisfactory subordinates where justified – those people to whom you previously have given the proper help and opportunity to improve and who have not responded.

Assign tasks to your subordinates to implement organisation development changes in your Unit.

Demonstrate the priority you place on clarity of roles and responsibilities in your Unit.
Maintain up-to-date role descriptions for the roles in your Unit.

[Insert additional human relations task types as needed to draw attention to important or unique aspects of the role.]

## Training

### General Responsibilities

You shall ensure that members of your Unit are given the opportunity to learn fully the skills they need to perform well in all aspects of their work.
You shall ensure that members of your Unit are fully trained in the rules, regulations and directives such that their work is compliant and within the bounds of health and safety.
You shall ensure that the members of your Unit have the opportunity to develop their full potential to do work required by the ________________ Business Unit.
You shall take the opportunity to learn fully the skills you need to perform well in all aspects of your work.
You shall ensure that there is a staff succession programme in your Unit.
The goal is for all employees to have the opportunity to develop their full potential to effectively and safely contribute to the work of the ________________ Business Unit.

### Task Types

Formulate an induction procedure for personnel joining your Unit.
Induct new subordinates into your Unit.
Implement your part of the ________________ Business Unit's induction procedure.
Assess the skill deficiencies of your subordinates.
Prepare development plans for your Stratum I subordinates-once-removed.
Assign tasks to correct the skill deficiencies of your subordinates.
Recommend or provide internal or external training courses.
Implement a training programme designed to teach ____________ ____________________.
Recommend to your Division Manager on your own training needs.
Educate your subordinates on the standards of quality, quantity, timeliness and cost to be applied in your Unit.

Assign tasks to train members of your Unit who are potential candidates for positions in your and other Units.

Recommend potential candidates for your role.

Develop these candidates as agreed upon with your Division Manager.

Train the members of your Unit in the priority which you place on quality.

Train your subordinates in the safety and emergency procedures to be used by your Unit.

Train the members of your Unit on the principles and practices needed to implement organisation development in your Unit.

Train your subordinates in ____________________ Business Unit human resources policy and practices.

Maintain a record of your Unit training activity.

Maintain a knowledge of technical developments relevant to the work of your Unit.

Develop and implement a training programme for the members of your Unit.

Train your subordinates in the procedures to be applied at the interfaces of your Unit, the other Units in your Division and other Divisions of the ____________________ Business Unit and other corporate Business Units.

[Insert additional training task types as needed to draw attention to important or unique aspects of the role.]

## Equal Employment Opportunity

### General Responsibilities

You shall ensure that all statutory requirements regarding affirmative action and equal employment opportunity as well as the policies of this Company are followed in the practices of your Unit.

The goal is to provide fair and equal employment opportunity for all persons regardless of age, sex, race, religion or ethnic origin.

### Task Types

Comply personally with all affirmative action and equal employment opportunity rules and regulations.

Demonstrate to the members of your Unit the priority you place on affirmative action and equal employment opportunity.

Assign affirmative action tasks to your subordinates.

Identify problems of sexual harassment in your Unit and eliminate or report them.

Investigate reports of sexual harassment in your Unit, and report on the results of your investigation.

Take action to correct or report problems of sexual harassment reported by your subordinates which are outside their accountability.

[Insert additional equal opportunity task types as needed to draw attention to important or unique aspects of the role.]

## Work Planning and Work Flow

### General Responsibilities

You shall plan and schedule the use of your Unit's resources to efficiently meet your immediate production targets and your targets for organisational change.

You shall balance the allocation of resources within your Unit in response to competing demands, both short and long term.

You shall develop business processes to ensure consistency and accuracy of reporting.

The goal for you and the members of your Unit is to use efficiently the Business Unit's assets and resources so as to sustain and improve the flow of work.

### Task Types

Negotiate with your Division Manager the role resources which will be available to allow you to perform the work of your principal function.

Negotiate with each of your subordinates the role resources that will be available to allow them to perform the work of their principal function.

Assign planning and scheduling tasks to your subordinates.

Allocate tasks to your subordinates.

Plan and schedule the activity of your Unit.

Schedule the activity of your subordinates allowing for the assignment of training tasks.

Manage the vacation schedule of your subordinates.

Report on the activity of your Unit.

Document and report on the compliance activities of your Unit.

Verify the accuracy of your compliance documents and reports.

Prepare the annual budget for your Unit.

Report against your budget.

Verify the accuracy of your cost allocations.
Monitor and adjust the budgeted work flow for your Unit.
Verify the need for the purchase on non-stock items or services.
Prepare the capital plan for your Unit.
Submit capital expenditure applications in accordance with your capital plan.
Identify your staffing requirements and make recommendations for appropriate staffing of your Unit.
Observe and act on the trends in the work and costs of your Unit.
Direct your work flow specialist on the activity in which he or she is to search out more productive methods of working.
Develop with your peers procedures for the transfer of information required to manage efficient production schedules.
Establish the call-out list for your subordinates.

[Insert additional work planning and work flow task types as needed to draw attention to important or unique aspects of the role.]

## Technical Processes/Work Methods

### General Responsibilities

You shall ensure that all the productive assets and facilities assigned to your care are maintained and improved, or their replacement recommended, so that technical obsolescence does not impair the productivity of your Unit.
You shall ensure that all ________________ equipment assigned to your care is operated to the agreed standards of safety, quality, quantity, timeliness and cost.
The goal for you and the members of your Unit is to effectively utilise the productive assets and resources assigned to your care and to devise improved methods of work to enhance the productivity of your Unit.

### Task Types

Assign technical tasks to your subordinates.
Provide technical expertise for your subordinates.
Establish the standards of safety, compliance, quality, quantity, timeliness and cost to be applied in your Unit within the policies set by your Division Manager.
Verify that work is done by the members of your Unit to the agreed standards of safety, compliance, quality, quantity, timeliness and cost.

Verify that work is done by the members of your Unit in accordance with statutory requirements.

Advise other Unit Managers of any problems which may affect the work of their Units.

Report indicators of significant problems with plant, equipment or work processes.

Identify key technical issues to be addressed in forward planning for your Unit.

Direct your subordinates regarding the activities on which they must search out more productive alternatives to current practice.

Prepare recommendations for new or improved systems which affect the work of your Unit.

Develop and implement new or improved systems for your Unit within the limits specified by your Division Manager.

Take action to prevent damage and wastage of Company materials and equipment.

Demonstrate knowledge of contracts relevant to the work of your Unit.

Prepare and negotiate contracts relevant to the work of your Unit.

Verify that work is done by contractors to the agreed standards of safety, compliance, quality, quantity, timeliness and cost.

Negotiate with your Division Manager, peers and subordinates materials, equipment and maintenance technique trials to be conducted by your Unit.

Implement materials, equipment and maintenance technique trials to be conducted by your Unit.

Participate in emergency and scheduled call-outs.

[Insert additional technical processes/work methods task types as needed to draw attention to important or unique aspects of the role.]

## Quality Improvement

### General Responsibilities

You shall ensure that the workers of your Unit constantly and continuously search out and eliminate sources of error and variation in the work processes for which you are accountable.

You shall resolve personally, or jointly with your subordinates, problems affecting the quality of the products and services produced by your Unit.

You shall implement management practices targeted to improve the quality of the products and services you produce.

You shall ensure that the products and services provided by your Unit meet the agreed standards of quality, quantity, timeliness and cost.

The goal for you and the members of your Unit is to eliminate defects and reduce variation in the products and services which your Unit produces and to reduce the need for rework within your own Unit and by your customers.

**Task Types**

Demonstrate to the members of your Unit the priority which you place on quality.

Assign quality improvement tasks to your subordinates.

Establish the standards of quality, quantity, timeliness and cost to be applied in your Unit.

Verify that work is done by the members of your Unit to the agreed standards of quality, quantity, timeliness and cost.

Monitor the level of performance, i.e., quality, achieved by your Unit and take action to increase consistency in performance and reduce instances of error.

Comply personally with all rules and procedures related to quality of Information Services products and services.

Implement your Division Manager's quality policies for the employees of your Unit.

Educate your subordinates in these quality policies.

Take action to correct work practices and conditions that contribute to poor quality which are reported by your subordinates but which are outside their accountability.

Review recommendations resulting from investigations into instances of poor quality and take corrective action.

Identify work practices and conditions that contribute to poor quality and eliminate or report them.

Recommend action on quality issues which have a scope beyond your Unit.

Implement the quality programme for your Unit.

Report quality problems which have become issues in other companies and have implications for the I/S Business Unit of SCE.

[Insert additional quality task types as needed to draw attention to important or unique aspects of the role.]

## Role Relationships

The principal role relationships which apply in your role are best understood while referring to the attached organisation chart.

The people with whom you will have your most important interactions are …

### Manager

The [insert Manager's title] ________________________________ _______ is your manager. He or she assigns your tasks and the authority you will need to perform them. You are accountable to your manager for the quality, quantity, timeliness and cost of the output from your Unit.

You and your manager must negotiate the distribution of your modes of interaction so that the role relationship between you is understood by both of you. A reference role relationship description for your relationship with your manager is attached to aid you in your discussion.

### Subordinates

[Insert titles of subordinates.]

________________________________________

________________________________________

________________________________________

________________________________________

________________________________________

You must assign tasks to your subordinates and the authority they will need to perform those tasks for which you will hold them accountable.

You must discuss with your manager his or her expectations with regard to the distribution of your modes of interaction in your relationships with your subordinates. A reference role relationship description for your relationships with your subordinates is attached to aid you in your discussion.

Peers: (people at the same level of work)

[Insert titles of peers.]

____________________________________

____________________________________

____________________________________

____________________________________

____________________________________

You and your peers within the ___________________ Division are accountable to your division manager for effective two-way interaction so that the tasks for which each of you is held accountable may be completed productively.

You must discuss with your manager his or her expectations with regard to the distribution of your modes of interaction in your relationships with your peers. A reference role relationship description for your relationships with your peers is attached to aid you in your discussion.

When a project requires a continuing interaction with your peer's subordinates, you must negotiate the expected distribution of your modes of interaction for that project with your peer and his or her subordinates.

Associates: (superiors or subordinates of your peers or your manager's peers)

[Insert titles of associates with whom this role will have principal interactions in order to accomplish your work or to help the other person accomplish their work.]

____________________________________

____________________________________

____________________________________

You and your associates are accountable to your respective managers for effective two-way interaction so that the tasks for which each of you is held accountable may be completed productively.

You must discuss with your manager his or her expectations with regard to the distribution of your modes of interaction in your relationships with your associates. A reference role relationship description for your relationships with your associates is attached to aid you in your discussion.

### Outside the Business Unit

[Insert titles of roles from outside the Business Unit with whom this role will have principal interactions in order to accomplish your work or to help the other person accomplish their work.]

________________________________________

________________________________________

________________________________________

You are accountable to your division manager for effective interaction and the sustaining of productive relations with these roles outside the I/S Business Unit.

You must discuss with your manager his or her expectations with regard to the distribution of your modes of interaction in your relationships with people outside the Business Unit. A reference role relationship description for your relationships outside the Business Unit is attached to aid you in your discussion.

### Role Resources

The role resources of your principal function can be divided into the following categories. Your role resources are defined by those categories and the limits imposed upon them by your manager. All role resources are to be exercised within Corporate and Business Unit policies and guidelines. You shall discuss with your manager his or her expectations regarding the role resources assigned to your role in order to develop a mutual understanding regarding the role resources assigned to you.

### Authorities

The authorities which must be assigned to you in order that you can complete your assigned tasks.

[Describe the authorities assigned to this role, e.g., managerial authorities, project authorities, etc.]

The authority to interact with other members of the Business Unit using all six modes of interaction.

The individual approval authorities required to maintain financial and administrative control within the Business Unit. These require written specification.

Other authorities assigned to you from time to time by your manager.

### Geography

The physical limits within which you are required to perform your work.

[Describe the geography associated with this role.]

### Assets

The human skills and the items of plant and equipment which are allocated to you for care and the performance of your work. You are required to sustain the productive capacity of those assets.

[Insert a listing of the principal assets allocated to this role.]

### Budget

The labour hours, budgeted expenditures and/or consumable materials assigned for your use and allocation in your work.

[Describe the budget resources assigned to this role.]

### Information+++

The information which is allocated to you for care and the performance of your work. You are required to sustain the productive capacity of the information under your care.

[Describe the information assigned for care and use in this role.]

### Time Span of the Role

The time allocated to complete the longest assigned task in your role and over which your manager allows you discretion in the execution of that task. Up to two years.

# Work of the Role and Selection Preparation

Probably the single most important factor in selecting an individual to fill a role is a clear understanding of the work required in that role. The better the manager understands what is required, the more likely he or she is to be able to identify a person who can successfully fill that role. Clear articulation of the principal function of the role, its major accountabilities and tasks, its authorities and its role relationships is essential. The listing which follows was created for managers in Stratum III and IV roles to use in the selection process. Nonetheless, it may contain some useful thoughts for higher-level executives involved in a selection process.

## Information about the Role

1. Role Description (Use whatever is available and then discuss the work they do with your direct reports and the work of their subordinates with the direct reports).
2. Specifics about This Role at This Time.

   Given the team which is in place at this time and the work you expect to have to have done over the next three years, what are the skills, characteristics most needed to create an effective work team?

   Human relations skills.

   Technical skills (state specifically).

   Project planning skills.

   Political skills (dealing with other agencies and Congress).

   What specifically will the person be expected to do now and over next one to three years? (if known), e.g., set up and manage an 18-month project, set up a system to better connect intelligence bits and pieces or lead a forensic analysis team?

   What are your expectations for someone in this role?.

   Ability to handle pressure.

   Overtime work.

Attention to detail when examining intelligence.
Good relationship building skills.
Strong managerial/leadership skills.

What are the opportunities provided by this role – professional, career?

What are the obstacles – realistic problems the person can expect to encounter?

What knowledge, experience, skills, conduct are needed to cope with these?

3. What does it require to carry out this role effectively?

Knowledge – be specific, what knowledge is really needed?

Skills – Technical
– Social

Again, be specific, what do you need on entry, what can be developed on the job?

Energy/drive/determination – desire to do this work

Mental Processing Ability – minimum requirement (best if person can think one level above basic work of the role)

Education (provides knowledge/skills)

Experience (provides knowledge/skills/develops drive and determination)

4. Other possible information that could inform you about the role

What made the last person in this role effective (or ineffective)?

Are there any cut-off requirements? (something which, if it is lacking, makes it impossible to do the job)

Other considerations:

Congressional relations

Inter-organisational relations – intelligence community, airport management

Social process skills under pressure

# Selection Interview and Review

## Selection/Evaluation Worksheet

The first four pages of the worksheet are to be used by the manager to prepare for a meeting with the individual to be appointed to the role or to be assessed within the role. Pages 2–4 present specific areas to consider. The space before each item allows the manager to make a mental or actual rating of the person on a 1–21 scale, 21 being best, when the interview takes place. The actual ratings here are less important than the relative distribution.

The words in italics are statements from a real manager thinking about a specific role. Using this approach, the selection was successful, and the person chosen performed very well in the role. The questions in normal type are other suggested questions that managers should think about and perhaps answer to be better prepared for the interview. The specifics are for a role at IV, but the concepts can be adapted for all levels of work.

The last two pages are a summary sheet which includes some reminders of what to look for when selecting a person for a IV role. These two pages should be printed back to back so they can be kept for a period of time. The back page is for the manager to record his/her thoughts about the person selected (or evaluated). Six months or a year later, the manager will know the person selected and at least the early results of the selection. This is where the manager can learn possible weaknesses in his or her selection decision. By knowing the kind of mistakes you are likely to make in selection, you can learn to avoid them. In this learning process, it may be helpful to bring in another person to interview the applicant to get another perspective.

Since good selection of people is such a critical factor in any organisation's success, developing this skill is important for all managers. We have found that managers who use this process become much better at selection.

## Selection/Evaluation Criteria – Stratum IV Managerial Role

Preparation

### Specifics of This Role at This Time

(1) Must help to create the role (creating a role takes higher capability than filling a fully developed existing role). Requires at least the potential to move into next level up.

(2) Personal skills with peers and clients essential.

(3) Leadership of people.

(4) What are the current opportunities provided by this role.

(5) What are the current obstacles – realistic problems the person can expect to encounter (These are good to ask about in the interview. For example, "If you encountered a problem such as ..., how would you propose to handle it?" Look for alternative approaches. The complexity of the answer. The recognition of underlying issues and assumptions. The quality of questions the person asks in order to answer your question. Are these the kinds of questions you would want to hear from a subordinate?).

(6) Projecting out one to three years, what are your expectations of this role? What obstacles might be expected.

(7) Does this person want to do this job? (Fit of person's interests, career ambitions and support of management and corporate direction with this role at this time).

### Questions

_____ **Knowledge** Correctable with enough Mental Processing Ability. Key issue is if this person can learn quickly? Do you have time to allow for education (self-education and courses)?

(1) Technical – environmental rules, regulations and agencies – air, water, land. (Deep knowledge of at least one of these areas, some knowledge of rest)

(2) How to design business systems
(3) Compliance methods and processes
(4) Performance measurement, benchmarking
(5) Managerial leadership processes/procedures)

_____ Skills (Are these claimed skills? How have they been demonstrated? Under what circumstances?)

_____ Technical

(1) Balance technical/business – costs/value (This was something the manager wrote to be sure to focus on this point.)

_____ Social

(1) Leadership of people (capability, integrity, valuing the development of people, valuing management) (Probably a cut-off requirement, must have this to effectively carry out role.)
(2) Work effectively with peers
(3) Work effectively with clients – peers, and their managers and direct reports
(4) Work with Business Units (Bus) managers and employees to inform (educate and influence) their planning in the best interests of the corporation and Environmental, Health and Safety (EH&S) compliance.
(5) Ability to balance corporate and departmental interests

_____ **Application** Desire to do the work of the role, energy and enthusiasm for the work

_____ **Appropriate Mental Processing Ability (type of problem-solving methodology described in levels of work)**

(This is probably a cut-off requirement. Without this, likely to fail. These are notes applicable to a IV role.)

Things to note:

(1) Does this person make use of **negative information** (notice what is not there and see its importance)?
(2) **Timeframe** which seems relevant to them. Do three-year tasks seem reasonable? Can the person act today understanding how to balance current needs and still get to three-year or five-year milestones?

    How do they propose to get from here to there – real ways of proceeding, not just wishful thinking about the future.
(3) Want to do everything demanded or able to talk about priorities, **sacrificing resources** where necessary?
(4) Do they talk about improvement as getting better at what you are now doing (III) or do they compare what is to **what might be** – conceptualise a new way of doing things (IV)?
(5) **What is the character of questions they ask** you, especially in relation to questions 3 and 4 below? Are these questions appropriate? Are they the kinds of questions you want to hear from a subordinate?

## Questions to ask person being interviewed

(1) You have had a chance to read the role description and think about this position. How would you suggest it be implemented?
(2) What do you think needs to be done?
(3) Present a real problem you are confronting, then ask, "how would you suggest I handle this?"

(4) Present a real problem you think the person will confront in the role; ask how they would handle it?

_____ **Opportunity**

Person may not have had an opportunity to demonstrate his/her skills as related to this position. Consider what opportunities the person has had and what he/she has done with them.

## Overall Evaluation

(Rate on a scale of 1–21, 21 being perfect. Look for relative ratings, not absolutes.)

_____ **Appropriate Mental Processing Ability** (type of problem-solving methodology described in levels of work)

(This is probably a cut-off requirement. Without this, all else fails.)

_____ With right knowledge, experience, skills, could probably hold my job one day
_____ Seems fully competent at IV, probably will not go higher
_____ Seems to have some characteristics at IV, not sure
_____ Not yet at IV, perhaps will be ready in a year or two
_____ Can't see this person filling a IV role in the foreseeable future

_____ **Skills** (Are these claimed skills? How have they been demonstrated? Under what circumstances?)
_____ Technical
_____ Commercial
_____ Social

_____ **Knowledge** (Correctable with enough Mental Processing Ability. Key issue: can the person learn quickly? Do you have time to allow for education [self-education and courses]?)

_____ Experience
_____ Application, desire to do the work of the role

Additional Comments: (Strengths/Weaknesses – Pluses/Minuses)

What impact will this person have on my work? What will I have to do to instruct, coach, guide this person?

## After Selection Is Made

Why did I hire this person?

What leads me to believe this person could do the job?

What behaviour, answers, discussion lead me to believe this person could handle IV work?

## One Year Later

Which of my observations of this person were correct?

Which of my observations of this person were erroneous?

What did I observe which caused the errors?

What have I learned from this experience? What would I do differently next time?

# Performance Planning Guide

## Purpose

**The purpose of Performance Planning is to enable both the manager and team member to improve their work performance by making clear the manager's purpose and essential tasks and where the direct report fits into the manager's plan.**

## General Outline

Performance Planning is the beginning of the Performance Management cycle which includes Task Assignment, Task Review, Performance Review and Performance Evaluation. After the Performance Evaluation process a new Performance Plan for the next year must be created. Sometimes it helps to do a second Performance Review which can also inform the new Performance Plan.

Performance Planning is a two-way discussion of the manager's purpose and essential tasks. This is to make clear how the team member fits into the manager's current plan – the major things we intend to accomplish and the resources we have (or anticipate having) to accomplish them. Recognising that the situation in which the work is to be carried out is dynamic, the plan is to provide an overall direction which will be a subject of ongoing discussion and, if necessary, modification. A plan is a guide to action which should allow both the manager and team member to exercise their creativity and judgement in response to changing conditions while still moving in the overall direction set by higher management.

The plan should indicate the essential tasks which the team member must complete in order to meet the manager's requirements, the resources allocated and the freedom of action available to the team member at this time. It should include a statement of what actions are planned by both the manager and the team member to improve their work performance. These should include any training or on-the-job experiences which are planned for the team member.

## Instructions

The Performance Plan should be completed and signed by the manager and team member. A copy should be retained by both as a basis for future discussions, modification and subsequent Performance Review and Performance Evaluation processes.

A copy should also be sent to the Manager-once-Removed. There is space for the M+1 to make notes for his own use in his role as mentor of the Report-once-Removed and to foster the development of R+1's career.

## Performance Plan

*To be completed in consultation with employee*

Name of Employee ______________________________________

Period of Plan: From: ____________ To: ____________________

1. The following essential tasks are to be completed to meet the requirements of the manager's plan.

2. The following resources are allocated to carry out this work effectively.

3. You are encouraged to use your initiative to improve the quality of work. Specifically, you are given freedom to act in the following areas.

4. Actions to be taken to improve the way this team member works and the way we work together. This should include any training agreed to improve work performance and any on-the-job or other experience which would be helpful.

   What the manager would like the employee to do to improve work performance:

What the employee would like the manager to do to support and foster improved work performance:

Training or Job Experiences Recommended:

Our signatures indicate that a Performance Plan has been made and agreed:

Signature:______________________________________ Date:______________

Print or Type Name and Title: ______________________________________

Signature:______________________________________ Date:______________

**Sponsoring Manager's Comments**

Print or Type Name and Title: ______________________________________

Signature:______________________________________ Date:______________

# Performance Review Guide

## Purpose

**The purpose of a performance review is to improve future work performance by examining how well *both* the manager and the team member are doing in carrying out their respective elements of the plan and their specific tasks.**

A performance review is a formal two-way analytic learning process for both manager and team member in order to:

- Review what they planned to do – their purpose and plans – and what they have accomplished to date
- Review their work performance as individuals and as a team
- Make specific plans to improve their work effectiveness for the rest of the year (or next year)

Note: In the review process, the manager's role is to act as a coach where needed.

The performance review process involves an analysis of the work and tasks of both manager and team member to assess what has been accomplished over the six months or year, to evaluate the quality and quantity of what has been accomplished and to discover better ways of working together to achieve better results. Are we on track to achieve the plan or must there be modifications?

This is, in effect, a summing up of the task reviews that have taken place at the manager's discretion during the year and provides a longer overview of performance – a look at the forest as opposed to the trees. It is a joint effort designed to reduce defensiveness by involving both manager and team member in an appraisal of what was accomplished and an analysis of what happened. Typical questions which might be raised are found in Chapter 18.

The Performance Review Guide includes questions that mirror the Performance Planning Guide to trigger thinking about important issues, especially key task types which are often left implicit, though they could be assigned as tasks with inset triggers.

There is also space to enter other points which either the manager or team member think are important in their roles or role relationship.

## Performance Review

Name of Employee ____________________________________

Period of Plan: From: ______________ To: ____________________

1. Given what we had planned, did the conditions change which required modifications of the plan?

2. Of the essential tasks that we planned to be completed by this time, how many have actually been completed? Are we on track to meet the plan?

3. Were the resources allocated to carry out this work adequate to meet the work requirements? Is there a need to add resources, or can some resources be allocated elsewhere?

4. Did you have enough freedom to act to achieve our purposes? Has the team member used their initiative to improve the quality of work performance?

5. Did the agreed training take place? If not, is it scheduled later this year?

6. Given what we have accomplished (or failed to accomplish), what needs to be done by the team member to improve performance?

7. What would the team member like the manager to do to support and foster improved work performance?

8. Other important points either the manager or team member think are important in their work performance, roles and role relationship.

Our signatures indicate that a Performance Review has taken place with both our views:

Signature: ______________________ Date: ____________

Print or Type Name and Title: ______________________

Signature: ______________________ Date: ____________

Print or Type Name and Title: ______________________

<u>Sponsoring Manager's Comments</u>

Signature: ______________________ Date: ____________

Print or Type Name and Title: ______________________

# Glossary

**Accountability:** A component of a work relationship between two people wherein one accepts the requirement to provide an account to the other of the following three questions relating to work.

> What did you do?
> How did you do it?
> Why did you do it that way?

The most common application of the concept of accountability is that which applies as a function of a contract of employment within an organisation and, though, in our experience, this requirement to accept accountability is rarely articulated clearly in the contract, it should be. An effective accountability discussion includes a discussion of the three questions above including how and why the person used particular processes to turn inputs into required outputs.

Accountability is *not* a collective noun for tasks, as in " your accountabilities are ...." Too often this is used in employment, in contracts and in role descriptions, which confuses work and accountability. A role may describe work but we are still to discover if the person is actually held to account for that work.

Accountability as a concept applying within coherent social groups is brought to the fore for society in general by the process of the courts wherein people in the witness box are required to answer, in public, questions as to what, how and why something was, or was not, done and judgement is passed as an outcome of this process.

**Application:** The effort, attention and energy that a person puts into applying the other elements of capability to their work (see Kolbe, 1991).

**Association:** People coming together for a purpose. The purpose is either agreed tacitly or expressed in a written document (Brown, 1971:48).

**Authority:** "The right, given by constitution, law, role description or mutual agreement for one person to require another person to act in a prescribed way (specified in the document or agreement). The likelihood of exercising authority effectively will usually depend upon good Social Process Skills."

The acceptance of the exercise of authority within a work organisation is a function of the contract of employment.

Is it essential that there is a clear understanding of the difference between authority and power (see below) and that authority is not a one-way process. In a correctly functioning organisation, for example, a manager has the authority to assign tasks to a direct report and the direct report has the authority to require a task performance review by the manager.

**Authority and Power:** Person A has authority or power in relation to person B when person A is able to have person B behave as A directs.

If person B does not so behave neither authority nor power applies.

Authority applies within the boundary and constraints of the law, policy and rules of the organisation and those of accepted social custom and practice.

Power breaches one or more of these constraints to authority.

Clarity of understanding of the constraints to authority and its correct distribution to the roles within an organisation is essential for speed of reaction to the unexpected.

Within society at large an acceptance of the exercise of authority is essential to maintain social cohesion; however, there is a sharply attuned recognition within societies of the constraints that apply to that authority and an exercise of power by "appointed authority" is strongly resented.

**Authority (resource):** The ability of a role incumbent to apply resources to a task without reference to another person.

## Capability:

- Knowledge
- Technical skills
- Social process skills
- Mental processing ability
- Application – desire, energy and drive applied to work

**Career Development:** The responsibility for one's own career and its development. (See **Staff Development.**)

**Chaos:** The patterns of complexity and the multiple scales of complexity that are now being studied as part of the general theory of chaos (see Gleick, 1987). This is *not* random disorder. Classical science and much theory of organisation has searched for ordered linear patterns that allow prediction: if this, then that.

Chaos theory studies non-linear patterns where the relationships are not simple and linear, and prediction of the outcomes with any accuracy becomes more and more difficult over time.

Minute differences in initial conditions have profound effects into the future. Most natural systems are chaotic in their functioning.

Chaos theory forces us to confront the fact that no matter how much experience we have and how well we understand the present, the predictions we make about the future will become progressively less accurate as they extend forward in time. Our mental processing ability is the facility to make order of this chaos, to perceive the universe and to "discover" or "create" the patterns (order) which we can then use as we take action.

**Constraints (for a task):** Limitations within which a task must be completed. It is the work of the task assigner to articulate these constraints to the task doer and confirm they are understood.

**Context (of a task):** The situation in which the task assigner predicts the task will be performed, including the background conditions, the relationship of this task to other tasks and any unusual factors to be taken into account. When the task performance is being reviewed the actual context needs to be considered in the review.

**Critical Issue:** Something that if not satisfactorily resolved threatens the achievement of the purpose of the work of an individual, team or organisation. "What if this happens, how will we address it?"

**Culture:** A culture is a group of people who share a common set of mythologies.

The group may be very large or relatively small and the strength of the culture will be determined by the number of mythologies that are common to the group.

It is normal for there to be smaller common interest groups within a large cultural group and these are often referred to as sub-cultures.

The commonality of the mythologies causes all the members of a culture to ascribe the same value assessment to a system, symbol or behaviour that they experience, be that assessment positive or negative.

The process of changing or creating a culture requires the generation of new mythologies that are common to the group.

**Dissonance:** A state of mind generated by the clear failure of a prediction that has been based upon a strongly held belief.

Dissonance can be generated by the behaviour of another person or group, the activity of a system or the appearance of a symbol.

Because we need to be able to predict with reasonable accuracy to be and feel safe, dissonance generates anxiety and the need to formulate an explanation. The generation of dissonance is the first step in the process of formation of new mythologies.

**Domains of Work:** **Technical, Commercial, Social.** Three essential areas of work. No organisation can function unless all these three domains are operating effectively. They are mutually inter-dependent.

**Employment Charter:** A written document to clarify the conditions and mutual behaviours which each member of the organisation is authorised and entitled to expect so that he or she may experience a constructive, productive and safe work environment which encourages people to work to their potential.

**Employment Hierarchy:** The network of employment roles set up by an association of people to carry out work required to achieve the objectives of the association (Brown, 1971:49).

**Fair Treatment System:** A system designed and implemented by the leadership of an organisation that applies to all members of the organisation. The purpose of the system is to provide for a non-biased assessment and judgement on decisions or work place behaviours that are perceived to be unfair by a person who is a member of the organisation.

The fair treatment system functions internally to the organisation and its use is preferred prior to any appeal for judgement from outside the organisation.

**Hierarchy:** An organisation structure wherein the authority available to a role increases upwards through the structure, increasing as work complexity increases.

The authority structure of the organisation is made visible and accessible by means of role titles. In a correctly structured organisation each role has the authority that is necessary to perform the work assigned to the role and this provides the connection between role authority and work.

**Human Decision-Making Model:**

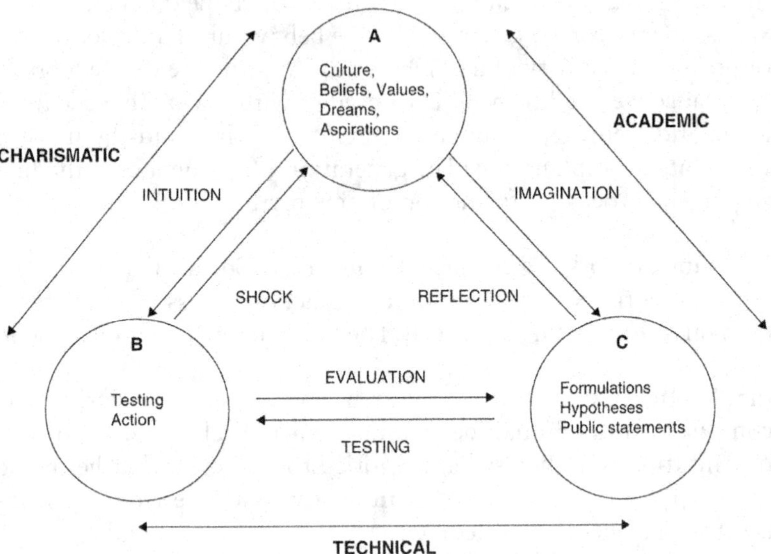


**Influence:** Activity that attempts to have an effect on the behaviour or beliefs of another individual or group.

**Knowledge:** That array of facts and relationships that an individual has available to him or her for the performance of work; it may be part or all of an accepted body of knowledge or knowledge that has been produced as largely self-generated content by the individual.

**Knowledge Field:** The knowledge held by an individual about a specific subject. The knowledge will be gained from a range of sources from personal experience to formal study.

This is the knowledge which a person brings to their work in an endeavour to solve problems that seem to relate to that particular field. Should they appreciate the need to do so, additional knowledge may be sought to resolve a work problem and any knowledge gained then becomes part of that field.

Each person has unique knowledge fields as they are what he or she has built up through life to date about a particular subject. There will be a core of knowledge in each field that is common to most people in a cultural group with similar educational experiences.

**Language – Social and Scientific Meanings**

**Scientific Meaning:** A precisely defined term with deliberately clear boundaries for the purpose of explaining relationships and testing hypotheses: "This is what I mean." An entity or term has a clearly defined meaning by which we can determine whether an entity is "one of those" or not.

**Social Meaning:** A term which is assumed to provide a similarity of understanding for the purpose of social interaction: "You know what I mean?" In our everyday lives we approximate and assume an understanding without concern as to whether we mean precisely the same thing.

**Leader:** A leader is a person who is able to demonstrate the exercise of power or authority, or both, and cause a group of people to act in consort to achieve a purpose.

The objective of a correctly functioning organisation is to have all its leaders clearly identified and exercising authority for the effective and efficient achievement of the purpose of the organisation and where that authority is willingly accepted.

Within an employment hierarchy, all managers are leaders, but not all leaders are managers.

**Leader, Work of:** The work of a leader is to create, maintain and improve the culture of a group of people so that they achieve objectives and continue to do so over time.

**Levels of Work:** The sequence of qualitatively different complexity pathways that need to be created to achieve goals when performing work. Depending upon the inherent complexity of a particular task it will only be completed successfully if that complexity is resolved; hence it will fall into a specific level of work.

**Management:** The work of ordering and sequencing the application of resources to achieve a predetermined purpose. Good management does this effectively and efficiently.

Human capability, in all its aspects, is one of the resources available to a manager that needs to be applied, through a person-to-person interaction, whereas other resources involve person-to-object interactions.

**Manager:** A person who is accountable for his or her own work and the work performance of people reporting to him or her over time. All managers are leaders of people; they have no choice. Their only choice is to be a good or bad leader. The authorities of a Manager are Veto

Selection, Assign Tasks, Recognise, Review and Reward Work Performance Differentially, Initiate Removal from Role.

**Manager-once-Removed (M+1)** The manager of the manager of direct reports. The authorities of M+1 are Veto Selection, Assess Potential, Recommend Selection, Decide on Promotion or Upgrade, Review Decisions, Dismiss, Design Roles.

**Mental Processing Ability (MPA):** The ability of a person to generate order from the chaos by means of thought. The generation of order, which requires the understanding of relationships, is essential if intention is to be turned into reality, i.e., work is to be done. The ability to make order out of the chaotic environment in which humans live out their lives and in which they work. It is the ability to pattern and construe the world in terms of scale and time. The level of our MPA will determine the amount and complexity of information that we can process in doing so. (This definition draws in part from I. Macdonald (1984:2) and also from Jaques [1989:33]).

Not all people have the same ability to generate order (MPA) and hence the same ability to perform work. Some will be able to resolve more complex problems than others. This distribution of MPA in the human population is discontinuous, which leads to differing levels of work complexity or levels of work. There is no evidence that a person's MPA changes in adulthood though the other aspects of capability, and particularly knowledge, are amendable to change over time.

**Meritocracy:** An organisation wherein people are assigned work, rewarded, promoted and titled based upon their capability and work performance to do the work of a role.

**Mutual Recognition Unit (MRU):** A structural unit of an organisation made up of a manager, his or her direct reports, some or all of whom are managers, and their direct reports in turn.

An MRU spans three levels of work structure in the organisation.

The need for mutual recognition stems from the authority of the manager-once-removed (M+1) that applies to the direct reports at the lower level of the MRU.

In relation to these MRU members the M+1 has the authority to veto selection, recommend selection, assess potential, review decisions that relate to them and to either dismiss or recommend dismissal from the organisation. The proper exercise of these authorities requires, as a minimum, that the M+1 and the direct reports know one another's work well enough to allow mutual recognition.

**Mythology:** From Mythos – the story with emotional content – and Logos – the explanatory rationale or meaning of the story.

Mythologies are the stories that inform us about what constitutes good and bad behaviour.

We look at systems, symbols and people's behaviour through the lens of our mythologies and assign what we see to a place on one or more of the scales of human values.

Our mythologies are our beliefs about whether what we see strengthens social cohesion in our group or whether it weakens it.

Mythologies are not changed; new ones need to be constructed. Mythologies may lie dormant for years and can be enlivened by an event in the future.

**Network:** People working towards a common purpose or with common interests where there is no requirement for members of the network to have a work relationship with others, and there is no requirement for mutuality as there is with a team.

**Operations Work:** Work that is directly connected to the output that an organisation has been established to produce.

Operations work will be directed to developing a product to satisfy the perceived needs of customers, producing a product to satisfy the current needs of customers or directed to the selling of those products to customers.

All three aspects of operations work are essential if a business or service organisation is to remain viable over time. (See also Service Work and Support Work.)

**Organisational Level:** A band across an organisation in which all the roles have a similar distribution of work complexity (level of work).

**Organisational Structure:** The arrangement of roles in an organisation that, when correctly done, identifies and matches work complexity and the authority necessary to perform that work so the purpose of the organisation is achieved efficiently and effectively over time.

The structure is the equivalent of the bone structure of the organisation; its form is made visible and accessible by way of its titling system.

**Output:** The observable result of work having been done. It is assessed in terms of quality and quantity.

**Performance (Two Definitions):**

(1) Output/results (or measures of same)
The relationship between targeted output and achieved Output or results can, and must, be measured.

(2) Work Performance: How well a person has done in producing the results (output) taking into consideration all relevant circumstances. How well has the person carried out the work of the role?

Work performance cannot be measured; it must be *judged* by a manager based on how well the person has worked to achieve the assigned output, or result, in the situation in which the work was performed.

**Performance Evaluation:** The judgement of the work performance of a direct report as expressed in the person's rank and rating by the manager.

**Performance Management:** The active leadership of managers to improve both performance and work performance.

**Policy:** A statement that expresses the standards of practice and the criteria required to be demonstrated by the behaviour of people who work for the organisation.

Policy is the formal expressions of the organisation's ethical framework; it is a statement that expresses the intended ethical and operational standards that the organisation seeks to demonstrate through the application of its systems and the behaviour of its people and the symbols it uses.

As stated above, the formal expressions of the organisation's ethical framework lies in the policies of the organisation. Policies are statements of intent.

**Power:** See Authority and Power.

**Process:** The mechanism by which inputs are converted into the specified outputs.

**Project Leader (sometimes titled Project Manager):** A person who leads a group of people who are assigned to work on a special task instead of or in addition to their normal workload. Project leader authorities are **VP** Veto Selection to Project Team; **A±** **Assign** Tasks within Limits; **$R^3$±** Review task work performance, Recognise and Reward differentially within limits set by the Ms of those on the project; **RP** Remove from Project Team.

**Purpose (of a task assignment):** What is to be achieved by accomplishing a task. For an organisation, policy or system, the objective intended by its action in practice. *Why* this is to be accomplished.

**Quantity/Quality (of a task assignment):** The expected output of the task and the standard expected. These are usually treated as a single dimension as one cannot have quantity without quality, nor quality without quantity. Occasionally quantity may be specified, but quality has a preferred point within a range.

**Resources (necessary to complete a task assignment):** Authority, facilities, equipment, money, people, access to information, access to assets, time.

**Responsibility:** Synonymous with accountability but long use in organisations that failed to hold people responsible for their work has led to its general use as a collective noun for tasks, as in "your responsibilities are as follows ..." "the general responsibilities of the role are ...."

**Role Relationship:** The sum of the interactions that take place between the two parties to the relationship. The interactions are divided into the information conveyed, the social process used when it is conveyed and its purpose. There are six productive modes of interaction within the organisation: direct/comply; negotiate/negotiate; consider/consider; teach/learn; learn/teach; comply/direct.

**Salary Administration:** The system whereby Managers' ratings are linked to salary adjustments. Within the salary band of the role, those with the highest ratings get the highest salaries; those with lower ratings receive lower salaries.

**Service Work:** Service work is directed towards the efficient and effective performance of those functions that are essential for the continuing activity of the operations' functions, e.g., accounting and finance, statutory reporting, regulatory compliance, audit, personnel benefits and payroll, etc.

**Social Process:** Person-to-person interaction wherein the behaviour of each has a bearing upon the thoughts, emotions and behaviour of the other.

**Social Process Skills:** Social process skills are those skills that give the ability to observe social behaviour, to comprehend the embedded social information and to respond in a way that influences subsequent behaviour in a predictable way. In an organisation this results in behaviour that contributes to the purpose of the organisation.

**Staff Development:** The provision of opportunities to learn, to improve technical and social skills and to advise an individual about the opportunities within the organisation as carried out by managers as coaches and M+1s as mentors.

**Staff Relationship:** A work relationship wherein a person accepts freely that his or her work performance will be judged on the basis of his or her personal work contribution and recompensed accordingly as opposed to a third-party-determined requirement such as seniority, union-nominated classification or externally determined qualification.

**Strategy:** A military term to do with the disposition and deployment of large military units, such as entire armies, such that the enemy's forces may be defeated.

In business when correctly applied it is a plan for the achievement of the organisation's purpose developed and implemented by the upper levels of the organisation.

**Stratum (plural strata):** In geology and related fields, a stratum is a layer of sedimentary rock or soil with internally consistent characteristics that distinguish it from other layers. In an organisational sense this term refers to layers in organisations that are internally consistent in work complexity (see Organisational Level). This term was first used by Jaques, but we have found it confuses many people. We now prefer Organisational Level.

Stratification on the basis of work complexity is the core of effective organisation structure.

When correctly done it generates a structure that corresponds to the differing capabilities of people to generate order from the chaos and thus perform productive work that is required to achieve the purpose of the organisation.

It makes good sense to structure an organisation in a way that is in accord with the thinking patterns of people.

**Supervisor:** A leadership role in Stratum I, sometimes titled a Crew Leader. A supervisory role does not have the full range of authority that defines a managerial role but is one of the most important leadership roles in an organisation. Authorities are **RV** Recommend Veto of Selection; **A±** Assign Tasks within Limits; **R$^3$±** Review task work performance, Recognise and **Reward** differentially within limits set by **M; RI** Recommend Initiation of Removal from Role.

**Support Work:** Sometimes referred to as *improvement work* is that work which is directed towards the improvement of the systems and processes the organisation employs to perform its operations and service activities.

It is a part of the work of each role incumbent to think of ways to improve upon his or her current work; the support roles develop and test these ideas as well as take a wider perspective and seek to improve the systems and processes that span numerous roles and activities.

**Symbol:** The outward manifestation of a cultural group, e.g., flags, rituals, medals, posters, slogans.

Symbols are interpreted as representing a position that is strongly positive on the values continua by the culture that employs the symbol and strongly negative by members of countercultures.

**System:** A system is a way of organising activities – flows of work, information and resources – to achieve a purpose. Systems drive behaviour.

More specifically, a system is a framework that orders and sequences activity within the organisation to achieve a purpose within a band of variance that is acceptable to the owner of the system.

Systems are the organisational equivalent of behaviour in human interaction. Systems are the means by which organisations put policies into action.

It is the owner of a system who has the authority to change it, hence his or her clear acceptance of the degree of variation generated by the existing system.

**System Audit:** A periodic review of a system by an external party that examines the system in use to determine whether or not it is being used as designed and intended, whether the control data is valid, whether it is being reported, reviewed and acted upon and whether or not the system is achieving the purpose for which it was designed. System audit is performed on behalf of the system owner.

**System Control:** A statistically valid sample of data from the system that allows the system custodian to confirm that the system is operating as it was designed to operate or to institute corrective action should it be required to have the system function as designed.

Note the difference between system control and controls as applied in safety systems. In safe work systems controls are activities that form part of the system itself.

**System Custodian:** The role within the organisation that does the work required to review the control data from a system and to advise the system owner of the state of use of the system and indicators of a system functioning drawn from the control data.

The system custodian may also be the system owner.

**System Owner:** The role within the organisation that authorises the purpose of the system and its design and implementation to achieve that purpose.

Only the system owner has the authority to change the system.

**Systems of Differentiation:** Systems that treat people differently, e.g., remuneration systems based on work performance.

All systems of differentiation should be based on the work (to be) done.

**Systems of Equalisation:** Systems that treat people the same way irrespective of any organisational criteria, e.g., safety systems.

**Systems Leadership:** An internally coherent and integrated theory of organisational behaviour. It is a body of knowledge that helps not only to understand why people behave the way they do, but also and perhaps more importantly to predict the way that people are likely to behave in organisations.

Systems Leadership is essentially about how to create, improve and sustain successful organisations.

**Task:** A statement of intention articulated as an assignment to carry out work within limits that include the context, purpose, quantity and quality of output expected, the resources available and the time by which the objective is to be reached (CPQ/QRT).

**Task Assignment Process:** The clear articulation to the task doer of Context, Purpose, Quantity(CPQ)/Quality of Output, Resources, Time to Completion(QRT).

**Task Feedback:** Information the task doer receives regarding how well he or she carried out the task. This can come from nature, customers, peers or the person's leader.

**Task Review:** An assessment by the task doer's leader of how well the task was performed. Task review provides information that is given to the task doer and comes from the task doer on a regular but random basis. The purpose is for the task doer and the leader to learn from both success and failure so performance may be improved. Note: in a correctly organised work hierarchy a task doer (direct report) has the authority to require a task review and report from his or her leader. Task Review includes all the components of the task: CPQ/QRT.

**Task Type:** An activity without the specific output, targeted completion time and task resources defined as would happen in a task assignment. A task type always begins with a verb. Typically used in role descriptions.

**Team:** A team is a group of people, including a leader, with a common purpose who must interact with each other in order to perform their individual tasks and thus achieve their common purpose.

**Teamwork:** A team member is part of the whole. Teamwork is about individuals collaborating for mutual benefit to achieve a purpose, clear about their mutual authority, their work and their relationships with each other and the leader. It is only by active cooperation, however, that the whole will be greater than the sum of the parts. The work of interaction that needs to be done by each team member to promote efficient and effective team functioning.

**Technical Skills:** Proficiency in the use of knowledge. This includes learned routines that improve the efficiency and effectiveness of work required to complete a task.

**Time (as a resource):** The amount of time available prior to the deadline. This may be expressed as people's work hours available or the sum of hours prior to the deadline.

**Time (in a task assignment):** The targeted completion time is a boundary condition – a deadline indicating by when the task is to be completed.

**Time span:** The targeted completion time of the longest task in a role equals the time span of the role. It is a measure of one property of a work relationship between a manager and his or her direct report.

Time span is the elapsed time to disorder, effectively how long a person of a given capability is able to generate order in the chaos in which he or she is working.

**Universal Values:** A typology of six universal human experiences that rate or judge all behaviours, systems and symbols heuristically. Behaviours, systems and symbols that are demonstrated and rated positively create social cohesion and those that are demonstrated and rated negatively destroy it.

There are six values which are expressed positively: love, trust, fairness, respect for human dignity, honesty, courage.

As a set they are mutually exclusive and comprehensively exhaustive and apply universally in all human societies.

The mythological lens that is used to position a system, symbol or behaviour on the values continua, either positive or negative, which is unique to each person having been developed by their experience of life.

**VAR$^3$I Authorities:** **V**eto Selection, **A**ssign Tasks, **R**ecognise, **R**eview and **R**eward Work Performance Differentially, **I**niate Removal from Role.

**Work:** Turning intention into reality.

**Work Performance:** An assessment made by a leader about how effectively and efficiently a direct report has worked in performing an assigned task taking into consideration the actual context in which the task was done.

# Bibliography


Ackoff, R.L. (1999) *Ackoff's Best: His Classic Writings on Management*. New York: John Wiley & Sons.

Barnard, C. (1938) *The Functions of the Executive*. Cambridge, MA: Harvard University Press.

Barolsky, J. (1994) *A New Vision for the Company: Hamersley Iron Employee Relations and Change Management*. Perth: Hamersley Iron.

Behn, B. (2014) *Performance Leadership Report*, Vol. 12, No. 1, September 2014. http://www.ksg.harvard.edu/TheBehnReport

Bishop, W.S. (1989) *The Exercise of Discretion in the Work of Nursing: Nurses' Perceptions of Their Approach to Work*. D.P.A. Dissertation, University of Southern California, Los Angeles.

Boals, D.M. (1985) *Levels of Work and Responsibility in Public Libraries*. PhD Dissertation, University of Southern California, Los Angeles.

Bolles, E.B. (ed.) (1997) *Galileo's Commandment: An Anthology of Great Science Writing*. New York: W.H. Freeman.

Brown, W. (1960) *Exploration in Management*. London: Heinemann.

Brown, W. (1971) *Organization*. London: Heinemann.

Brown, W. and Jaques, E. (1965) *Glacier Project Papers: Some Essays on Organisation and Management from the Glacier Project Research*. London: Heinemann.

Bureau of Labor Statistics, https://www.bls.gov/iif/

Bureau of Labor Statistics, 'Census of fatal occupational injuries', https://www.bls.gov/news.release/cfoi.nr0.htm#

Burke, C. and Smith, D. (1992) 'Organizing corporate computing: A history of the application of a theory', In *Festschrift for Elliott Jaques*. Arlington, VA: Cason Hall & Co., pp. 119–134.

Burns, T. and Stalker, G.M. (1961, 1966) *The Management of Innovation*. London: Tavistock Publications.

Byrne, J.A. (2005) 'The man who invented management', *Business Week*, 28 November, p. 104.

Campbell, J. (1949, 2008) *The Hero with a Thousand Faces* (The Collected Works of Joseph Campbell). Novato, CA: New World Library.

Campbell, J., with Moyers, B. (1991) *The Power of Myth*. New York: Anchor Publishing.

Carrison, D. and Walsh, R. (1999) *Semper Fi: Business Leadership the Marine Corps Way*. New York: AMACOM.

Chandler, A.D., Jr. (1990) *Scale and Scope*. Cambridge, MA: Belknap Press of Harvard University.

Chorover, S.L. (1979) *From Genesis to Genocide: The Meaning of Human Nature and the Power of Behavior Control*. Cambridge, MA: MIT Press.

Church, M. (1999) 'Organizing simply for complexity: Beyond metaphor towards theory', *Long Range Planning*, Vol. 32, No. 4, pp. 425–440.

Churchman, C.W. (1979) *The Systems Approach and Its Enemies*. New York: Basic Books.

Collins, J. (2001) *From Good to Great*. New York: Harper Collins.

Collins, J. and Porras, J. (1994) *Built to Last*. New York: Harper Collins.

Cross, R., Rebele, R. and Grant, A. (2016) 'Collaborative overload', *Harvard Business Review*, January–February, pp. 74–79.

De Bono, E. (2008) *Six Thinking Hats,* revised Edition. Harmondsworth: Penguin Books.

Deming, W.E. (1982) *Out of the Crisis*. Boston, MA: MIT Press.

Donald, M. (1991) *Origins of the Modern Mind: Three Stages in the Evolution of Culture and Cognition*. Cambridge, MA: Harvard University Press.

Drucker, P. (1954, 1969) *The Practice of Management*. New York: Harper.

Drucker, P. (1999) *Management: Tasks, Responsibilities, Practices*. London: Routledge

Drucker, P. (2001) 'Managing oneself', In *Management Challenges for the 21st Century*. New York: Harper Business, p. 21, 22.

Duhigg, C. (2016a) *Smarter Faster Better: The Secrets of Being Productive in Life and Business*. New York: Random House.

Duhigg, C. (2016b) 'What google learned from its quest to build the perfect team', *New York Times Magazine*, 25 February.

Dunbar, R. (2010) *How Many Friends Does One Person Need?: Dunbar's Number and Other Evolutionary Quirks*. Cambridge, MA: Harvard University Press.

Dunlop, T. (1999a) *Missionaries, Mercenaries and Mechanics*. Macdonald Associates Consultancy, internal paper.

Dunlop, T. (1999b) *Creating a Meritocracy*. Macdonald Associates Paper – unpublished.

Dunlop, T. (2000) *Core Social Process Skills for Leaders*. Macdonald Associates Paper – unpublished.

Ellis, A. (1957) *How to Live with a Neurotic: At Home and at Work*. New York: Crown Publishing.

Emery, F.E. (ed.) (1969) *Systems Thinking*. Harmondsworth: Penguin Books.

Emery, F.E. (ed.) (1981) *Systems Thinking*, Vol. 2. Harmondsworth: Penguin Books.

Emery, F.E. and Trist, E.L. (1960) 'Socio-technical systems', In C.W. Churchman and M. Verhulst (Eds.), *Management Science, Models and Techniques*. New York: Pergamon, pp. 83–97.

Evans, J.S. (1979) *The Management of Human Capacity*. Bradford: MCB Publications.

Freud, S. 1930 (2010) *Civilisation and Its Discontents* (translated and edited by J. Strachey). New York: W.W. Norton & Co.

Freedman, D.H. (2016) 'The war on stupid people', *The Atlantic Magazine*, July/August.

Fuller, B. (1969) *Operating Manual for Spaceship Earth*. New York: Simon & Schuster.

Gallup (2017) *State of the American Workplace*, www.gallup.com/services/182216/state-american-manager-report.aspx.

Geller, E.S. (2016/1996) *The Psychology of Safety Handbook*, 2nd Edition. London: CRC Press, Taylor and Francis Group.

Gelles, David. (2022) *The Man Who Broke Capitalism: How Jack Welch Gutted the Heartland and Crushed the Soul of Corporate America—and How to Undo His Legacy*. New York: Simon and Schuster.

Gerth, H.H. and Mills, C.W. (1946) *From Max Weber: Essays in Sociology* (translated, edited and with an introduction by H.H. Gerth and C. Wright Mills). New York: Oxford University Press.

Gleick, J. (1987) *Chaos: Making a New Science*. Harmondsworth: Penguin Books.

Goldman, L.L. (1999) *Work Strata Selection as a Measurement of Law Enforcement Organizational Leadership*. D.P.A. Dissertation, https://search-proquest-com.libproxy1.usc.edu/ pqdtlocal1006272/docview/304553511/AB4650FF46E149B4PQ/3?accountid=14749.

Goleman, D. (1996) *Emotional Intelligence: And Why It Can Matter More Than IQ*. London: Bloomsbury.

Gould, D.P. (1984) *An Examination of Levels of Work in Academic Library Technical Services Departments Utilizing Stratified Systems Theory*. PhD Dissertation, University of Southern California, Los Angeles.

Gould, S.J. (1996) *The Mismeasure of Man* (revised Edition). New York: W.W. Norton & Co.

Gray, J.L. (ed.) (1976) *The Glacier Project: Concepts and Critiques*. London: Heinemann.

Gulick, L. (1937) *Papers on the Science of Administration* (edited by L. Gulick and L. Urwick). New York: Institute of Public Administration, Columbia University.

Hall, E.T. (1977) *Beyond Culture*. Palantine, IL: AnchorBook Press.

Hammer, M. and Champy, J. (1993) *Reengineering the Corporation: A Manifesto for Business Revolution*. New York: Harper Business.

Hamper, B. (1992) *Rivethead: Tales from the Assembly Line*. New York: Warner Books.

Hargreaves, A. and Fink, D. (2005) *Sustainable Leadership*, 1st Edition. San Francisco, CA: Jossey-Bass.

Harvey, J. (1999) *How Come Every Time I Get Stabbed in the Back, My Fingerprints Are on the Knife?* San Francisco, CA: Jossey-Bass.

Haselton, M.G., Nettle, D. and Andrews, P.W. (2005) 'The evolution of cognitive bias', In D.M. Buss (Ed.), *The Handbook of Evolutionary Psychology*. Hoboken, NJ: John Wiley & Sons Inc., pp. 724–746.

Heinrich, W. H. (1931, 1980) with Dan Peterson and Nestor Roos, 5th Edition. *Industrial Accident Prevention: A Safety Management Approach*. New York: McGraw-Hill.

Intel IT (2016) www.intel.com/content/www/us/en/it-management/intel-it-best-practices/intel-it-annual- performance-report–2015–16-paper.html/ Retrieved March 2017.

Intel IT (2017) www.intel.com/content/www/us/en/it-management/intel-it-best-practices/best-practices- fast-threat-detection-with-big-data-security-business-intelligence-brief.html/ Retrieved March 2017.

IRS Data Book for 2018. Released May 20, 2019. https://www.irs.gov/statistics/soi-tax-stats-irs-data-bookRetrieved17February2020.Table9a 'Examination Coverage…'

Isaac, D.J. and O'Connor, B.M. (1978) 'A discontinuity theory of psychological development', In E. Jaques (Ed.) with R.O. Gibson D.J. and Isaac, *Levels of Abstraction in Logic and Human Action*. London: Heinemann, pp. 95–120.

Jaques, E. (1951) *The Changing Culture of a Factory*. London: Tavistock Publications.

Jaques, E. (1963) *Equitable Pay*. London: Heinemann Educational Books.

Jaques, E. (1964) *Time-Span Handbook*. London: Heinemann Educational Books.

Jaques, E. (1976) *A General Theory of Bureaucracy*. London: Heinemann.

Jaques, E. (1982a) *The Form of Time*. New York: Crane Russak & Co.

Jaques, E. (1982b) *Free Enterprise, Fair Employment*. London: Heinemann.

Jaques, E. (1989) *Requisite Organization*. Falls Church, VA: Cason Hall and Co.

Jaques, E. (1990) 'In Praise of Hierarchy', *Harvard Business Review*, January, pp. 127–133.

Jaques, E. (2002) *Life and Behaviour of Living Organisms: A General Theory*. Westport, CT: Praeger.

Jaques, E. and Cason, K. (1994) *Human Capability*. London: Gower.

Jaques, E. (ed.) with Gibson, R.O. and Isaac, D.J. (1978) *Levels of Abstraction in Logic and Human Action*. London: Heinemann.Kahneman, D. and Tversky, A. (1973) 'On the psychology of prediction', *Psychological Review*, Vol. 80, No. 4, pp. 237–251.

Kiel, Paul. 'IRS: Sorry, but it's just easier and cheaper to audit the poor', *Pro Publica*, October 2, 2019. https://www.propublica.org/article/irs-sorry-but-its-just-easier-and-cheaper-to-audit-the-poor. Retrieved 17 February 2017

Kolbe, K. (1991) *Conative Connection: Acting on Intent*. Boston, MA: Addison Wesley.

Kotter, J. (1999) 'What effective general managers really do', *Harvard Business Review*, March–April, 1999.

Lavoisier, A.-L. (1997) 'Preface to *the elements of chemistry*', In E.B. Bolles (Ed.), *Galileo's Commandment: An Anthology of Great Science Writing*. New York: W.H. Freeman, pp. 379–388.

Lorsch, J.W. and McTague, E. (2016) 'Culture is not the culprit', *Harvard Business Review*, April, pp. 96–105.

Ludeke, T. (1996) *The Line in the Sand: The Long Road to Staff Employment at Comalco*. Melbourne: Wilkinson Books.

Lutz, B. (2013) *Car Guys vs. Bean Counters: The Battle for the Soul of American Business*. New York: Penguin, Portfolio.

Macdonald, B. (2001) *Critical Incidents, Personality and Burn-out in Staff Working in an Intensive Care Unit*. Doctoral Thesis, Department of Clinical Psychology, Cardiff University.

Macdonald, I. (1984) *Stratified Systems Theory: An Outline*. Individual and Organisational Capability Unit, BIOSS, Brunel University.

Macdonald, I. (1988) 'Getting on with the real work', *Journal of the British Institute of Mental Handicap*, Vol. 16, pp. 65–67.

Macdonald, I. (1990) *Identity Development of People with Learning Difficulties through the Recognition of Work*. PhD Dissertation, Brunel University.

Macdonald, I. (1995) *Statement to the Australian Industrial Relations Commission*. Evidence submitted to Commission.Macdonald, I., Burke, C. and Stewart, K. (2018) *Systems Leadership: Creating Positive Organisations*, 2nd Edition. Milton Park, Abingdon, Oxon: Routledge, Taylor & Francis Group.

Macdonald, I., Burke, C. and Stewart, K. (May 2019) 'Social process for project leaders,' *PM World Journal*, Vol. VIII, No. IV, pp. 1–17, www.pmworldjournal.com.

Macdonald, I. and Couchman, T. (1980) *Chart of Initiative and Independence*. Slough: NFER.

Macdonald, I., Dixon, C. and Tiplady, T. (2020) *Improving Schools Using Systems Leadership: Turning Intention into Reality*. Milton Park, Abingdon, Oxon: Routledge.

Macdonald, I. and Grimmond, J. (2000) *Systems and Symbols Audit*. Unpublished paper for Macdonald Consulting.

Macdonald, R. (1991) *Breaking the Frame: The Heart of Leadership*. MA Dissertation, School of Policy, Planning and Development, University of Southern California.

Macdonald, I., Macdonald, R., Stewart, K. (1989). "Leadership: A New Direction", *British Army Review* 93, December.

Marx, K. (1992/1867) *Capital: A Critique of Political Economy*, Volume 1 (Penguin Classics). London: Penguin Publishing.

McDonald, G. (2006) *Better Words, Concepts and Models – Better Safety*. Sunnybank: Geoff McDonald and Associates Pty.

McDonald, G. (2007) *Intermediate Measures for Safety*. Sunnybank: Geoff McDonald and Associates Pty.

McDonald, G. (2016) 'Some thoughts to assist strategic planning', Prepared for the Safety Institute of Australia, 2008, in K. McDonald, Chapter 10, 'Safety Models', unpublished manuscript.

McDonald, K. (2016) 'Safety models,' Unpublished manuscript.

McGill, G., Macdonald, I. et al. (2021) *Organisations and Leadership During COVID-19*. Brisbane: Systems Leadership Development Association.

Micklethwait, J. and Wooldridge, A. (1996) *The Witch Doctors: Making Sense of the Management Gurus*. New York: Times Books.

Micklethwait, J. and Wooldridge, A. (2003) *The Company*. London: Modern Library.

Mintzberg, H. (1979) *The Structuring of Organizations*. Englewood Cliffs, NJ: Prentice-Hall.

Mintzberg, H. (1989) *Mintzberg on Management: Inside Our Strange World of Organizations*. New York: Free Press.

Morgan, G. (1986) *Images of Organization*. Beverly Hills, CA: SAGE Publications.

Mosher, F.C. (1982) *Democracy and the Public Service,* 2nd Edition. New York: Oxford University Press.

Mouzelis, N.P. (1967) *Organization and Bureaucracy: An Analysis of Modern Theories*. London: Routledge.

Mu, D.P. (1993) *Managing Cross-Cultural Interchange: Interpreting Behavior for Mutual Understanding, the Case of China and the United States*. D.P.A. Dissertation, School of Public Administration, University of Southern California.

Mumford, E. and Hendricks, R. (1996) 'Business process re-engineering RIP', *People Management*, Vol. 2, No. 9, pp. 22–26.

Munz, P. (1985) *Our Knowledge of the Growth of Knowledge: Popper or Wittgenstein?* London: Routledge and Kegan Paul.

National Safety Council, https://injuryfacts.nsc.org/work/industry-incidence-rates/work-related-incident-rate-trends/ Retrieved 10 April 2023.

Neustadt, R.E. and May, E.R. (1986) *Thinking in Time: The Uses of History for Decision-Makers*. New York: The Free Press

Obolensky, N. (2014) *Complex Adaptive Leadership: Embracing Paradox and Uncertainty*, 2nd Edition. London: Routledge.

O'Leary, D. and Craig, J. (2007) *System Leadership: Lessons from the Literature*. Nottingham: National College for School Leadership.

Pape, E. A., Jr. (2012) *Intersect Policing: Bringing CompStat to the Field Level to Reduce the Fear and Incidence of Crime*. A Dissertation Presented to the Faculty of the USC Sol Price School of Public Policy, University of Southern California, Dec. C

Pasadena Star-News (2020) *City Sues a Pair of Insurance Firms*, 28 February.

Petzinger, T., Jr. (1997) 'Self-organization will free employees to act Like bosses', *Wall Street Journal*, 3 January, p. B1.

Plsek, P.E. and Wilson, T. (2001) 'Complexity, leadership, and management in Health care organisations', *The British Medical Journal*, Vol. 323, No. 7315, pp. 746–749.

Reason, J. (1997, 2008) *Manaaging the Risks of Organizational Accidents*. Aldershot, Hants: Ashgate Publishing, Ltd.

*Report on Government Services, Commonwealth of Australia* (2016) Australian Government Productivity Commission, www.pc.gov.au/research/ongoing/report-on-government-services/2016.

Ritzer, George. (1993, 2012) *The McDonaldisation of Society: Into the Digital Age.* 7th Edition. Thousand Oaks, CA: Sage Publications, Inc.

Roethlisberger, F. and Dickson, W. (1939) with the assistance and collaboration of H.A. Wright. *Management and the Worker: An Account of a Research Program Conducted by the Western Electric Company, Hawthorne Works, Chicago.* Cambridge, MA: Harvard University Press.

Rowbottom, R. and Billis, D. (1977) 'Stratification of work and organisational design', *Human Relations*, Vol. 30, No. 1, pp. 53–76.

Schein, E. (2016) *Organizational Culture and Leadership*, 5th Edition. New York: Wiley.

Schutz, A. (1972) *The Phenomenology of the Social World.* London: Heinemann Educational Books.

Senge, P.M. (1990) *The Fifth Discipline.* New York: Doubleday/Currency.

Shafritz, J. and Ott, S. (1996) *Classics of Organization Theory.* Fort Worth, TX: Harcourt Brace College Publishers.

Shafritz, J., Ott, S. and Yong Suk Jang (2005) *Classics of Organisational Theory.* Belmont, CA: Thomson/Wadsworth.

Simon, H. (1962) 'The architecture of complexity', *Proceedings of the American Philosophical Society*, Vol. 106, No. 6, pp. 467–482.

Sotham, J. (2016) 'Airline merger wars: The battle for the soul of an airline', *Air & Space Magazine*, March, 2015, www.airspacemag.com/flight-today/airline-merger-wars–180953942/?no-ist/ Retrieved 1 October.

Stamp, G. (1978) 'Assessment of individual capacity', In E. Jaques (Ed.) with R.O. Gibson and D.J. Isaac, *Levels of Abstraction in Logic and Human Action.* London: Heinemann, pp. 251–270.

Stamp, Gillian (1984) 'A Summary of Stratified Systems Theory: An Approach to Understand Human Behaviour in organisations'. *BIOSS Paper*, Rev. March. Uxbridge: Brunel University.

Stewart, K. (1994) 'CRA Pulls the Rug from under Unions', *Business Review Weekly*, 31 January, pp. 34–39.

Taylor, C. (2005) *Walking the Talk: Building a Culture for Success.* London: Random House.

Taylor, F.W. (1911, 1972) *Scientific Management; Comprising Shop Management, The Principles of Scientific Management [and] Testimony before the Special House Committee.* With a foreword by Harlow S. Person. Westport, CT: Greenwood Press.

Technical Research Institute. *Japan Times*, 21 October 2008

Tollefson, J. (2018) 'Advances in human behaviour came surprisingly early in Stone Age.' *Nature*, March 22, Vol. 555, No. 7697, pp. 424–425.

Trist, E. and Bamforth, K.W. (1948) 'Some social and psychological consequences of the longwall method of coal-getting', *Tavistock Institute of Human Relations*, Doc 506.

Trist, E. and Murray, H. (eds.) (1990) *The Social Engagement of Social Science*, Volume 1: *A Tavistock Anthology: The Socio-Psychological Perspective*. Philadelphia: University of Pennsylvania Press.

Trist, E. and Murray, H. (eds.) (1948, 1993) *The Social Engagement of Social Science*, Volume 2: *A Tavistock Anthology: The Socio-Technical Perspective (innovations in Organizations Series*. Philadelphia: University of Pennsylvania Press.

Trist, E. and Murray, H. (eds.) (1997) *The Social Engagement of Social Science*, Volume 3: *A Tavistock Anthology: The Socio-Ecological Perspective*. Philadelphia: University of Pennsylvania Press.

Tversky, A. and Kahneman, D. (1974) 'Judgment under uncertainty: heuristics and biases', *Science*, Vol. 185, pp. 1121–1131.

Van Crevald, M. (1982; 2007) *Fighting Power: German and US Army Performance, 1939–1945*. Westport, CT: Praeger.

Wade, H. (2014) 'Middle managers as innovators', *Management Today*, December.

*Wall Street Journal* (2001) 'Disengaged at work?' 13 March, p. A1.

Way, N. (1994) 'CRA pulls the rug from under unions', *Business Review Weekly*, Fairfax Media Group, 31 January, pp. 34–39.

Weber, M. (1922a) 'Bureaucracy', In J. Shafritz, S. Ott and Yong Suk Jang (eds.) (2016), *Classics of Organisational Theory,* 8th Edition. Boston, MA: Cengage Learning, pp. 78–83.

Wheeler, D.J. (2000) *Understanding Variation: The Key to Managing Chaos*, 2nd Edition. Knoxville, TN: SPC Press.

Whitehurst, J. (2015) *The Open Organization: Igniting Passion and Performance*. Boston, MA: Harvard Business Review Press.

Whyte, D. (2001) *Crossing the Unknown Sea*. New York: Riverhead Books.

Whyte, L.L., Wilson, A.G. and Wilson, D. (eds.) (1969) *Hierarchical Structures*. New York: American Elsevier.

Witzel, M. (2015) *Managing for Success: Spotting Danger Signals – And Fixing Problems before they Happen*. London: Bloomsbury Information.

Woolley, A.W., Chabris, C.F., Pentland, A., Hashmi, N. and Malone, T.W. (2010) 'Evidence for a collective intelligence factor in the performance of human groups', *Science*, Vol. 330, No. 6004, pp. 686–688.

Yamashita, T., English Translator, Baldwin, F. (1988) *The Panasonic Way: From a Chief Executive's Desk*. Tokyo: Rodansha International.

Zimm, A.A. (2003) *Manifestations of Chaos in an Economic Theory of the Organization*. Doctoral Dissertation, School of Policy Planning and Development, University of Southern California.

Zimmerman, E. (2014) Jeffrey Pfeffer: "Do workplace hierarchies still matter?' *Insights by Stanford Business*, Stanford Graduate School of Business, 24 April, www.gsb.stanford.edu/insights/ jeffrey-pfeffer-do-workplace-hierarchies-still-matter.

# Index

Note: **Bold** page numbers refer to tables; *italic* page numbers refer to figures and page numbers followed by "n" denote endnotes.

Printed in the United States
by Baker & Taylor Publisher Services